Series Editors

W. Hansmann
W. T. Hewitt
W. Purgathofer

M. Göbel, J. David,
P. Slavik, J. J. van Wijk (eds.)

Virtual Environments
and Scientific Visualization '96

Proceedings of the Eurographics Workshops
in Monte Carlo, Monaco,
February 19–20, 1996,
and in Prague, Czech Republic,
April 23–25, 1996

Eurographics

SpringerWienNewYork

DI Dr. Martin Göbel
GMD Forschungszentrum, Informationstechnik, Sankt Augustin,
Federal Republic of Germany

Prof. Dr. Jacques David
CEA/DI, CE. Saclay, Gif sur Yvette, France

Dr. Pavel Slavik
Department of Computer Science, Czech Technical University, Prague, Czech Republic

Dr. Jarke J. van Wijk
Netherlands Energy Research Foundation ECN, Energy Engineering,
Petten, The Netherlands

This work is subject to copyright.
All rights are reserved, whether the whole or part of the material is concerned, specifically those of translation, reprinting, re-use of illustrations, broadcasting, reproduction by photocopying machines or similar means, and storage in data banks.

© 1996 Springer-Verlag/Wien
Printed in Austria

Typesetting: Camera ready by authors
Printing: Druckerei Novographic, A-1238 Wien
Binding: Fa. Papyrus, A-1100 Wien

Graphic design: Ecke Bonk

Printed on acid-free and chlorine-free bleached papers

With 169 partly coloured Figures

ISSN 0946-2767
ISBN 3-211-82886-9 Springer-Verlag Wien New York

Preface

The third workshop on Virtual Environments took place on February 19–20 in conjunction with the annual IMAGINA conference in Monte Carlo. The workshop asked for contributions to cover coexistence, communication and collaboration in Virtual Environments. Nineteen contributions were selected by an international programme committee which additionally invited J. Nomura (MEC, Japan) and J. Kent (SGI, US) for talks on applications of virtual environments in Japan and to discuss the VRML relationship to virtual environments.

Revised versions of the workshop presentations are included in this book. The first group of four papers from Austria, the UK, Germany and Sweden discusses VE system design and architecture issues as well as experience with novel programming style for virtual worlds. Mixed reality in a teleconferencing and in a telepresence experiments are reported from Germany and from Sweden.

An algorithm session introduced to several techniques for virtual environments, such as the quick elimination of polytopes from Hongkong, camera based tracking and morphing from Germany. On the second workshop day, human actors and crowd simulation were presented by Swiss and French reseachers.

A further workshop session dealt with modeling aspects in virtual environments. Work based on B-spline modeling (UK) and the impact of concurrent multi-user modeling (France) were demonstrated.

The final paper session of the workshop included papers from various application areas, such as a surgery support system (Japan), the distributed virtual reality lab which is a UK research initiative, applications in geographic information systems (Netherlands), in engineering (Switzerland) and in virtual housing systems (Japan).

Around fourty workshop participants discussed the contributions very heavily during the two days.

As a conclusion, we can say that with its third workshop Eurographics has established the VE workshop as an annual event which serves as a forum for information exchange in VE research in Europe. In all of the 3 workshops, major European VE research labs were presenting and discussing their advance results.

The workshop itself and its preparation was sponsored by ONR – Office of Naval Resarch (US), EDF (France), INA-IMAGINA (France), CEA (France) and GMD (Germany).

The workshop secretary was provided by Tatjana Neiss from IGD Germany. At this place we would like to thank all – the sponsors, the secretary and the local organization. Without their contributions the workshop would not have taken place.

*

The seventh workshop on Visualization in Scientific Computing took place on April 23–25 in Prague (Czech Republic). It was for the first time that an event like this was held in Central and Eastern Europe. One of the workshop's results was the impulse for the promotion of Scientific Visualization in this region. Papers submitted for this workshop were evaluated by an international programme committee.

Besides papers accepted for presentation also two invited lectures were given: G. Nielson (USA): Multiresolution Modelling in Scientific Visualization and V. Hlavac (CZ): Computer Vision and Scientific Visualization. In both lectures new views on some topics in Scientific Visualization were given.

For these proceedings twelve papers were selected. Revised versions of these papers are included in this book. The papers can be divided into four groups: Volume Rendering, User Interfaces in Scientific Visualization, Architecture of Scientific Visualization Systems, and Flow Visualization. The papers in the first group are papers from Italy, Germany, Slovakia, and the Netherlands. The main stress was put on the speeding up of volume rendering algorithms and on their better accuracy. The second group of papers contains papers from Germany dealing with proper use of elements and methods in the field of User Interfaces specific for Scientific Visualization applications. Innovative research from Fraunhofer Institute describes the use of VR techniques in the field of Scientific Visualization. Papers from the Netherlands, Czech Republic and the United Kingdom forms the third group of papers targeted to Architecture of Scientific Visualization Systems. The last group contains results from research in traditional area of Scientific Visualization – Flow Visualization. Improved techniques for this area were presented. All papers presented set up a very good base for discussions in which all 40 workshop participants took part.

Besides the authors we want to thank the Programme Committee that had to evaluate in a short time the papers submitted. The organization of the workshop could not have been manageable without the help of the Department of Computer Science and Engineering at Czech Technical University in Prague and the Czech ACM Chapter. Special thanks should be expressed to Petr Felkel, Jan Vorlicek, Bozena Mannova, Jiri Zara, and Bedrich Benes. Without their help both the Workshop and the book would not have come into life.

Martin Göbel, Jacques David,
Pavel Slavik, Jarke J. van Wijk

Contents

Virtual Environments '96

D. Schmalstieg, M. Gervautz, P. Stieglecker: Optimizing Communication in Distributed Virtual Environments by Specialized Protocols 1

R. J. Hubbold, X. Dongbo, S. Gibson: MAVERIK – The Manchester Virtual Environment Interface Kernel 11

A. del Pino: MPSC – A Model of Distributed Virtual Environments 21

T. Axling, S. Haridi, L. Fahlen: Virtual Reality Programming in Oz 31

C. J. Breiteneder, S. J. Gibbs, C. Arapis: TELEPORT – An Augmented Reality Teleconferencing Environment 41

K. T. Simsarian, J. Karlgren, L. E. Fahlén, I. Bretan, E. Frécon, T. Axling, N. Frost, L. Jonsson: Achieving Virtual Presence with a Semi-Autonomous Robot Through a Multi-Reality and Speech Control Interface 50

K. Chung, W. Wang: Quick Elimination of Non-Interference Polytopes in Virtual Environments 64

P. Wißkirchen, K. Kansy, G. Schmitgen: Intergrating Graphics into Video Image-Based Camera Tracking and Filtering 74

P. Astheimer, C. Knöpfle: 3D-Morphing and its Application to Virtual Reality 85

I.-S. Pandzic, T. K. Capin, N. Magnenat Thalmann, D. Thalmann: Motor Functions in the VLNET Body-Centered Networked Virtual Environment 94

E. Bouvier, P. Guilloteau: Crowd Simulation in Immersive Space Management 104

M. Usoh, M. Slater, T. I. Vassilev: Collaborative Geometrical Modelling in Immersive Virtual Environments 111

P. Torguet, F. Rubio, V. Gaildrat, R. Caubet: Multi-User Interactions in the Context of Concurrent Virtual World Modelling 121

H. Oyama: System Integration of VR-Simulated Surgical Support System 131

M. Slater, M. Usoh, S. Benford, D. Snowdon, C. Brown, T. Rodden, G. Smith, S. Wilbur: Distributed Extensible Virtual Reality Laboratory (DEVRL) 137

H. Jense, K. Donkers: Dynamic Management of Geographic Data in a Virtual Environment 149

J.-F. Balaguer: VRML for LHC Engineering 159

J. Nomura: Virtual Housing System 169

Scientific Visualization '96

Volume Rendering

P. Criscione, C. Montani, R. Scateni, R. Scopigno: DiscMC: An Interactive System for Fast Fitting Isosurfaces on Volume Data 178

F. Weller, R. Mencl: Nearest Neighbour Search for Visualization Using Arbitrary Triangulation 191

M. Šrámek: Fast Ray-Tracing of Rectilinear Volume Data 201

J. Smit, M. Bosma, J. T. van Scheltinga: Metric Volume Rendering 211

User Interfaces and Scientific Visualization

T. Frühauf, F. Dai: Scientific Visualization and Virtual Prototyping in the Product Development Process 223

R.-T. Happe, M. Rumpf: Characterizing Global Features of Simulation Data by Selected Local Icons 234

H. Haase, Ch. Dohrmann: Doing it Right: Psychological Tests to Ensure the Quality of Scientific Visualization 243

Architecture of Scientific Visualization Systems

R. van Liere, J. J. van Wijk: CSE: A Modular Architecture for Computational Steering 257

H. Wright, K. Brodlie, M. Brown: The Dataflow Visualization Pipeline as a Problem Solving Environment 267

D. Hajek, J. Nouza: Unhiding Hidden Markov Models by their Visualization (Application in Speech Processing) 277

Flow Visualization

W. de Leeuw, F. Post, R. W. Vaatstra: Visualization of Turbulent Flow by Spot Noise 286

R. Grosso, M. Schulz, J. Kraheberger, T. Ertl: Flow Visualization for Multiblock Multigrid Simulations 296

Appendix: Colour Figures 309

Optimizing Communication in Distributed Virtual Environments by Specialized Protocols

Dieter Schmalstieg, Michael Gervautz, Peter Stieglecker
Institute of Computer Graphics, Vienna University of Technology
schmalstieg|gervautz|stieglecker@cg.tuwien.ac.at - http://www.cg.tuwien.ac.at/

Abstract. A successful implementation of a distributed virtual environment should be built on a strong network layer. The network as a constrained resource must be used efficiently, and also the structure of communication should allow to select those features that are needed without having to support needlessly complicated protocols. Therefore we designed a set of specialized protocols tailored for dedicated tasks of communication in virtual environments. The combination of these protocols yields the desired communication functions without introducing much overhead. In particular, it is possible for participants with varying degrees of capability to use the virtual environment and to communicate with each other.

1 Introduction

The restrictions that are most hard to overcome in distributed virtual environments are the need for consistency, and constrained network bandwidth. It is because of these restrictions that virtual environments either focus on rich interaction [Carl93, Snow94, Bric94, Brol95] or on large-scale distribution [Mace94], but not both.

Our goal is to develop a distributed virtual environment in which users can participate and contribute content. We favor a client-server based approach, that lets users run client software and connect to servers over a network [Schm95]. Such a scheme will separate the participants from the providers of the VE infrastructure. Users can use the VE with inexpensive desktop machines, and do not have to be responsible for setting up the VE infrastructure. This is important if a large, loosely coupled user community is to be supported. In particular, the simulation of the environment is independent of the presence of users - the VE exists even if no user is currently present. The server provides consistency, concurrency control and persistence, that are otherwise hard to accomplish. Scalability is achieved by localizing the simulation: every server is responsible for a region in the virtual universe, and maintains a loosely coupled connection to its neighbors. Inside the server's region, the influence of objects is also localized to a relatively small area of interest.

Simulation kernel. Our virtual environment consists of actors. An object-oriented hierarchy allows diverse actor types representing different levels of "intelligence". Pure *static actors* serve as "decoration" of the scene (walls, trees etc.) and have no built-in behavior. Such actors can be extended to include key-framed, deterministic animation (e.g. a clock with moving hands). A more sophisticated class of actors exhibits *behavior* that is formulated in an interpreted scripting language. Behaviors are triggered by messages that are exchanged between actors. As messages are exchanged, the simulation progresses. Modifications to the internal state of the actors, in particular their visual representation, are reflected in the virtual environment. The most powerful actor type is controlled by an *external application*.

Multiple levels of participation. The separation of server and clients allows multiple levels of participation, dependent on the type of client that is used:

An *observer* can only explore the VE, but cannot interact with any objects. The client may limit its display to a pure walk-through (only considering static geometry), or also request the dynamic changes of the visual artifacts, that are created by the simulation. Nothing an observer does affects the VE.

A *participant* may introduce his own avatar and use it to fully interact with the simulation, its autonomous agents and other avatars. His actions modify the dynamic state of the VE; they are distributed to other clients and stored persistently in the database.

An *author* may contribute his own content to the virtual environment. He may create and destroy objects, and even more importantly create new types of objects with their own behavior, that can continue to exist as autonomous agents without the user's aid.

This hierarchy of participation is similar to the one found in conventional MUDs (text-based multi-user games) that can in many respect be seen as VEs without a visual component.

To maximize flexibility, we also allow *applications* to function as clients. While most behaviors of objects in the VE can be formulated using our scripting engine, the most interesting behaviors are too complex or computationally demanding for scripts. Therefore an interface is provided to allow external applications to "remote control" objects in the VE. Because the only restriction for an application client is that it complies to the network protocols we use, any application can be made to cooperate with the VE.

Overview of the protocols. The requirements we have for our system are diverse and demanding. A single unified framework for communication that incorporates every form of information exchange into a single protocol is not sufficient. Instead, we define a set of highly specialized protocols that complement each other and can be tailored for the task.

Protocol	Responsible for
Connection management:	login, logout, protocol negotiation, user migration
Avatar control:	navigating the user's representation through the VE
Geometry:	transmitting geometric description of the objects in the VE to the client
Animation:	transmitting changes in the visual database of the VE to the client
Simulation:	exchanging messages concerning the ongoing simulation among actors and between actor and client
Interaction:	letting the user interact with objects in the VE and other users
Authoring:	managing modifications to the structure of the VE, such as object instantiation and deletion, creation of new object types and configuration of external applications

Table 1. Overview and characterization of the protocol framework

This approach allows us to exploit domain-specific properties for efficiency, assign network access to the protocols for an optimal bandwidth usage, and combine protocols as needed by the different levels of participation.

Some protocols (such as the one that builds a network connection to the VE) must obviously be spoken by all types of clients, while others can be used or neglected at the client's disposal. They will, however, determine the client's capabilities. Table 1 gives an overview of the protocols we use and their scope:

2 Connection management protocol

Connection management provides fundamental networking functions on which the distributed environment is built. It handles the login and logout process of users and authentication. It also allows the user to migrate from server to server, in which case the network connection is transiently passed on. Client and server software negotiate the range of protocols used for communication.

3 Avatar control protocol

The avatar control protocol is concerned with the control of the virtual representation of the user. The user may upload his own avatar representation, or else decide to use a default representation. He may also transiently switch to an alternate avatar representation, if the situation or application demands it (e.g. for participating in a game).

The avatar control protocol's task is to determine where the user is and what he can see. The protocol is extremely simple because it only needs to be able to communicate transformation matrices. The avatar control information is sent from the participating client to the server, and then distributed to all relevant clients. High performance regarding this protocol is of extreme importance for high fidelity interaction among a large group of users. We therefore chose to isolate the task in a separate protocol to have room for optimizations, that can be based on proximity [Benf93], visibility [Funk95], dead reckoning [Mace94] or fidelity channels [Sing95].

Other control commands concerning the avatar (object manipulation etc.) are part of a more general protocol, the interaction protocol.

4 Geometry protocol

Detailed models consume a lot of network bandwidth, so usually network transmission is either avoided [Zyda92], or image generation stalls until transmission is complete (such as current VRML browsers do [Hard95]). Our approach differs in trying deliver the model data "just in time" for display.

The overall geometric database held on the server is much larger than the client's area of interest (AOI, comparable to the "aura" [Benf95]). Models contained in the AOI are held in a geometry cache (local memory) for immediate display [Fig. 1]. If an object is no longer in the AOI, it will eventually drop out of the cache. Prefetching of objects that approach the AOI compensates for network delays.

This strategy can still fail if too many and too complex objects are in the user's AOI. We therefore incorporate a level-of-detail (LOD) method: Objects are modeled at multiple resolutions, and the appropriate resolution is selected at runtime based on heuristics [Funk93]. We extend this method to work with our distributed protocol along the lines of [Funk92] by transmitting single LODs instead of objects. This has several advantages: If the object can be represented by a coarse approximation (normally if seen at a distance), only the coarse model has to be transmitted, which saves transmission time and client memory.

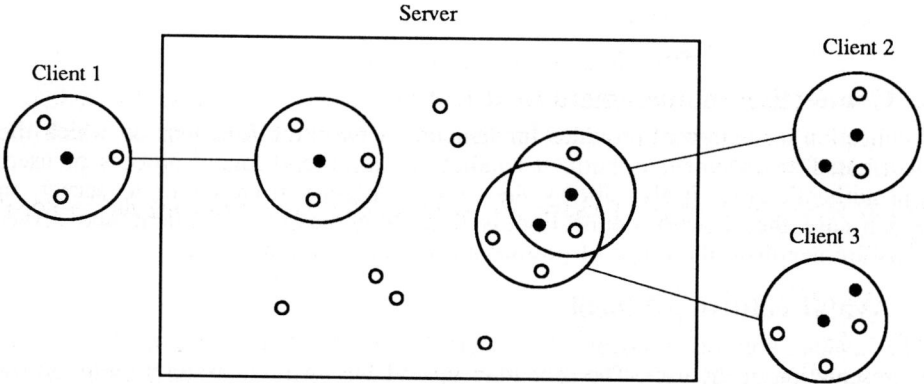

Fig. 1. A server maintains a geometry database of objects (small white circles), and also represents clients (small black circles) and their corresponding AOIs (large circles)

Assuming hierarchically modeled objects, transmission can be incremental (a finer LOD is based on the next coarser LOD), which also saves bandwidth. Finally, if timing constraints cannot be met (i.e. the desired LOD is not delivered in time), a coarser LOD can be used instead, to keep image generation from stalling (at the expense of degraded image fidelity).

Because the client requests the geometry at his disposal, the sophistication of the LOD strategy is up to the client. The server only needs to inform the client about any activity in his AOI. We use the VRML format for our protocol, but are developing a custom compressed variant to reduce the sizes of transmitted models.

5 Animation protocol

The animation protocol communicates dynamic changes in the scene. The nodes of the hierarchical scene graph we use consist of attributes, dependent on the node type. If an attribute is modified, the modification can be encoded by specifying the object ID, name of the attribute, and the new value.

To make the transmission efficient, updates for a particular client are collected and sent at regular intervals. For a particular modified attribute, only the most recent value is sent. Dependencies in the scene graph can be exploited by specifying attributes as functions of one or more parameters. Many attributes can depend on the same parameter, which provides a compact and powerful interface for simulation updates, and also drastically reduces the number of updates that must be transmitted. Parameters can also depend on time, so that self-contained key-framed animations can be constructed. The principle has been known in computer animation for quite a long time [Magn83]. Parameters are built as an extension of SGI's Open Inventor engines [Stra92].

6 Simulation protocol

A uniform mechanism is needed to allow external programs (either clients or external applications) to talk to an actor living on the server. The protocol can automatically be built from the actor's method list. Method invocations with appropriate parameters are used as remote procedure call stubs. We use this protocol for three purposes:

1. to let actors exchange messages within the server,
2. to let external applications or users send control messages to actors, and
3. to let remote-controlled actors pass on all received messages to an external application.

While these three ways of usage are semantically very different, the protocol syntax is identical.

7 Interaction protocol

The interaction protocol addresses several requirements:

- For interaction of actors and humans, the simulation protocol alone is not sufficient. We also need a description of the interaction style.
- We do not want to require everybody to own the same type of I/O hardware (e.g. a position tracker or data glove). Instead, we aim at an abstract workplace characterization such as known from PHIGS [ISO89]. The user interface should be dynamically created from an abstract characterization.
- A client-server system suffers from the lag introduced by the relatively long round-trip an interaction message takes from client to server and back. We want to support local interaction for simple interaction tasks, that do not require the server's simulation capabilities (e.g. positioning in 3-D).

To describe interactions, we use *interaction rules* similar to the dialogue manager presented in [Appi92]. Interaction rules specify how to map input events generated by the user to output, generating feedback both locally (tightly coupled) and globally (distributed via the server). An interaction rule consists of input and output specification:

Input is characterized by the quality of interaction (e.g. positioning, selection, action-trigger), input dimension, input mode (discrete or continuous, absolute or relative), default and range values, importance (priority) and preconditions (to logically link multiple inputs together).

Output is defined by (1) one or more simulation protocol stubs of the simulation protocol to call with the parameters from the input, and (2) direct feedback to the geometry of the actor (replicated at the client, so we use the animation protocol locally). Note that there is no one-to-one mapping between interaction rules and simulation protocol stubs.

With a combination of simulation protocol stubs and interaction rules, we can decouple simple interactions from the server and run them locally with high fidelity, while interaction with the server's simulation is not restricted in any way.

8 Authoring protocol

A virtual environment should allow dynamic modification of all its components. While the modification of existing actors is handled by the simulation protocol, for creation and deletion of actors and actor types we introduce an authoring protocol.

Actors are categorized by type. In our system Python - an object oriented interpreted language - is used to define actor types and to instanciate actors at the server. The authoring protocol allows the creation of a new actor class (actor type), the instanciation of a new actor of a specific type, and the deletion of an actor. New actor types require a description of the actor's geometry (specified in extended VRML), behavior (specified in a scripting language), and user interface (interaction rules). An actor can also be configured to cooperate with an external application that determines the actor's behavior (remote-controlled actor).

All parts of the actor's description can be written using simple text files, that can conveniently be transmitted between sites and edited. The authoring protocol has no time-critical requirements.

9 Tying the protocols together

While the multitude of protocols we use is certainly more complex than a simple uniform protocol, the benefits make it worthwhile:

Efficiency. Every protocol can use specific knowledge from the particular domain to tailor the protocol specifically for the task. This is important because network bandwidth is precious, and must be preserved as far as possible to allow scalability. Measures for efficiency include compact encoding of information, data compression, and the use of multiple low level networking standards (e.g. TCP vs. UPD) as needed by the protocol.

Contention management. Because multiple protocol streams execute concurrently, conflictual situations may arise when multiple communication streams are competing for limited network bandwidth. In particular, if network performance degrades significantly, it is important to prefer those protocols that have tighter timing requirements. A priority mechanism can be used to resolve the problem (for example, transmission of animation has a very tight time window, while authoring is not really time-critical).

Protocol combination. Protocols can be combined as needed by a client [Fig. 2].

An *observer* will only need to support the connection management protocol, avatar control protocol, and geometry protocol. Sending the avatar control protocol allows the observer to navigate the VE. This is sufficient for a simple walkthrough system. Optionally the observer can receive avatar control messages from other avatars, so that its environment is not static, or even the animation protocol for highly detailed animation.

A *participant* subscribes to the same protocols as an observer, plus mandatory support for the animation protocol. The major difference to the observer is that the participant supports the interaction protocol.

An *author* must at least run connection management and the authoring protocol. Usually the author will also run other protocols, so that the user can immediately see the effects of his work.

An application will run connection management and a bi-directional simulation protocol: incoming simulation messages are passed on from the actor to the application for processing, and the reactions of the application are re-inserted into the server's simulation by also using the simulation protocol. An application may also choose to subscribe the geometry and possibly animation protocol (e.g., for collision detection).

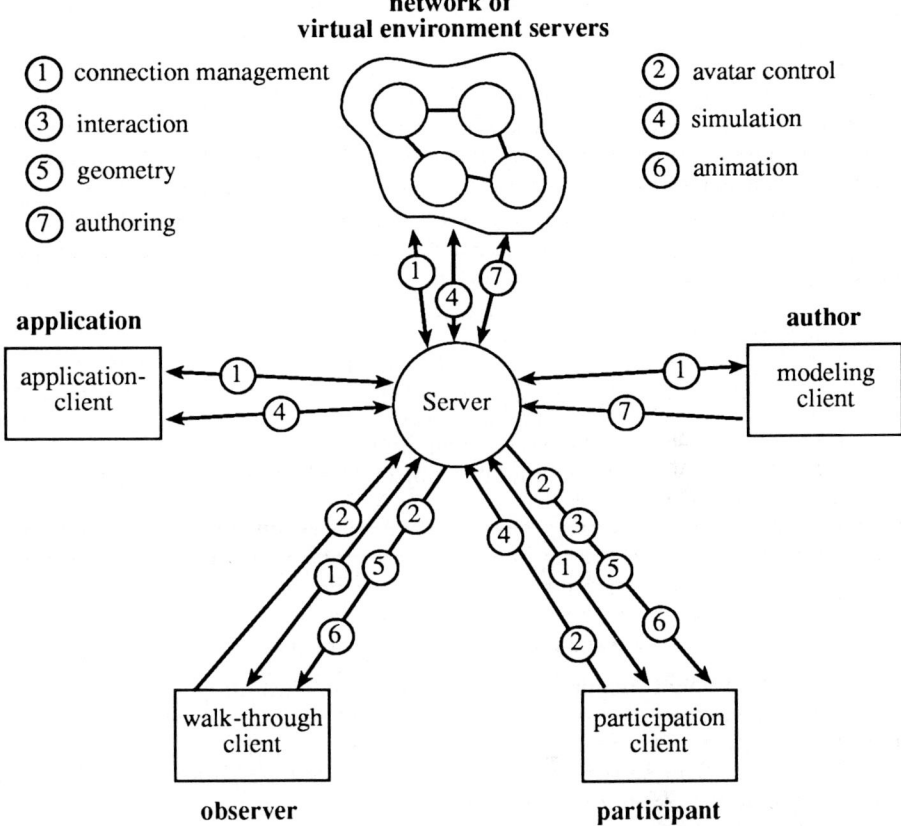

Fig. 2. Different kind of protocols are needed for different kind of clients.

Communication between servers naturally differs from communication between client and server, but basically re-uses the protocols already described. Beside connection management, server-server communication involves actor migration (sending a package containing actor and actor type, mostly the same as the authoring protocol), and the usage of the simulation protocol should actors wish to communicate over server boundaries.

10 Implementation

The possibility to combine protocols allows us to start with a subset of the full architecture, and extend it as needed. We have currently implemented a distributed system supporting communication for what is characterized above as an observer client. Such a systems supports navigation in a large virtual environment composed of static geometry (walkthrough) for multiple users that can also see each other. Of particular interest is the management of geometry data in the very large environment (details can be found in [Schm96]). Client and server software support three protocols: Connection management, avatar control, and geometry management.

Connection management basically allows a client to connect (init_connection) and disconnect (kill_connection) while the environment is running. Upon log-in, the client receives a unique client ID, states his initial position and orientation and the size of his AOI, and uploads the user's geometric description (avatar) to be seen by other users [Table 2] (column labeled „Dir." indicates direction of message - from client to server or vice versa).

Message	Dir.	Parameters
init_connection	c→s	client_id, position, orientation, AOI_data, avatar_data
kill_connection	c→s	client_id

Table 2. Connection management protocol units

Adding avatar control requires two additional protocol units [Table 3]: With update_client_position the client tells the server about its new position after if the user has moved. The server uses update_object_position to inform the client about movement activity in the client's current area of interest. Movement of both animated objects (if the server simulates objects' behavior) and of other users is transmitted to the client.

Message	Dir.	Parameters
update_client_pos	c→s	position, orientation
update_object_pos	s→c	object_id, position, orientation

Table 3. Avatar control protocol units

Geometry management requires communication in two directions: The client decides it needs a particular piece of geometry and issues a request to the server (request_geometry). The unit of transmission is a single level-of-detail of a particular object. The server packages and sends the requested geometry data (transmit_geometry). Additionally, the client must know details about the objects in his AOI, so it can compute its needs and issue requests. This information is continually kept up to date by the server as the environment changes (transmit_object_info). Other necessary information includes: update of the client if an object is deleted (e.g. blown up; kill_object), and update of the server if the client decides to change the size of its AOI (e.g. if running out of memory; update_AOI). Table 4 shows the protocol units.

Message	Dir.	Parameters
request_geometry	c→s	object_id, lod_no
transmit_geometry	s→c	object_id, lod_no, geometry_data
transmit_object_info	s→c	new_object_id, object_info_data
kill_object	s→c	object_id
update_AOI	c→s	AOI_data

Table 4. Geometry management protocol units

Our experiments show that the geometry management as provided by the protocol bring significant savings in the amount of consumed network bandwidth. Not only can a geometry database with well-designed levels of detail yield a net traffic reduction of 2-3 times, but also the peak network load is much lower, since the transmission of single levels of detail instead of complete objects (all levels of detail) tends to distribute the network load much better.

11 Conclusion and future work

We have presented a framework of protocols designed to be used for special communication needs in client-server virtual environments. They address simulation, animation, interaction and VE authoring, and can be combined as needed for multiple levels of participation in the VE. Separating these tasks in different optimized protocols leads to more efficiency in using the given bandwidth of today's computer networks.

Our current implementation allows walkthrough and observation of large multi-user virtual environments by supporting connection management, avatar control and geometry management. Support for the complete communication framework as outlined in this paper is under development. The framework will also allow integration of new protocols, such as support for text or audio based participant communication, that we plan to include in a future project.

References.

[Appi92]   P. Appino, J. Lewis, L. Koved, D. Ling, D. Rabenhorst, C. Codella: An Architecture for Virtual Worlds. Presence, Vol. 1, No. 1, pp. 1-17 (1992)

[Benf93]   S. Benford, L. Fahlen: A spatial model of interaction in large-scale virtual environments. 3rd European Conference on CSCW, pp. 109-124 (1993)

[Bric94]   W. Bricken, G. Coco: The VEOS Project. Presence, Vol. 3, No. 2, pp. 111-129 (1994)

[Brol95]   W. Broll: Interacting in Distributed Collaborative VE. Proc. of VRAIS'95 (1995)

[Carl93]   C. Carlsson, O. Hagsand: DIVE- A platform for multi-user virtual environments. Computers & Graphics, Vol. 17, No. 6, pp. 663-669 (1993)

[Funk92]   T. Funkhouser, C. Sequin, S. Teller: Management of Large Amounts of Data in Interactive Building Walkthroughs. SIGGRAPH Symposium on Interactive 3D Graphics, pp. 11-20 (1992)

[Funk93]   T. Funkhouser, C. Sequin: Adaptive Display Algorithm for Interactive Frame Rates During Visualisation of Complex Virtual Environments. Proceedings of SIGGRAPH'93, pp. 247-254 (1993)

[Funk95]   T. Funkhouser: RING - A Client-Server System for Multi-User Virtual Environments. SIGGRAPH Symposium on Interactive 3D Graphics, pp. 85-92 (1995)

[Hard95]   J. Hardenberg, G. Bell, M. Pesce: VRML: Using 3D to surf the Web. SIGGRAPH'95 Course, No. 12 (1995)

[ISO89]   ISO: Programmer's Hierarchical Interactive Graphics System Functional Description. ISO/IEC 9592: 1 (1989)

[Mace94] M. Macedonia, M. Zyda, D. Pratt, P. Barham, S. Zeswitz: NPSNET: A Network Software Architecture for Large-Scale Virtual Environment. Presence, Vol. 3, No. 4, pp. 265-287 (1994)

[Magn83] N. Magnenat-Thalmann, D. Thalmann: The Use of High-Level 3-D Graphical Types in the Mira Animation System. Computer Graphics and Applications, pp. 9-16 (1983)

[Schm95] D. Schmalstieg, M. Gervautz: Towards a Virtual Environment for Interactive World Building. Proceedings of the GI Workshop on Modeling - Virtual Worlds - Distributed Graphics, Bonn. Also Technical Report TR-186-2-95-08, Vienna University of Technology, Austria (1995). ftp://ftp.cg.tuwien.ac.at/TR/95/TR-186-2-95-08Paper.ps.gz

[Schm96] D. Schmalstieg, M. Gervautz: Demand-driven geometry transmission for Distributed Virtual Environments. To appear in: Proc. of EUROGRAPHICS'96, Poitiers, France, August 1996. Also technical report TR-186-2-96-02, Vienna University of Technology, Austria (1996). ftp://ftp.cg.tuwien.ac.at/TR/96/TR-186-2-96-02Paper.ps.gz

[Sing95] S. Singhal, D. Cheriton: Exploiting Position History for Efficient Remote Rendering in Networked Virtual Reality. Presence, Vol. 4, No. 2, pp. 169-194 (1995)

[Snow94] D. Snowdon, A. West: AVIARY: Design Issues for Future Large-Scale Virtual Environments. Presence, Vol. 3, No. 4, pp. 288-308 (1994)

[Stra92] P. Strauss, R. Carey: An Object Oriented 3D Graphics Toolkit. Proceedings of SIGGRAPH'92, No. 2, pp. 341 (1992)

[Zyda92] M. Zyda, D. Pratt, J. Monahan, K. Wilson: NPSNET: Constructing a 3D Virtual World. SIGGRAPH Symposium on Interactive 3D Graphics, pp. 147 (1992)

MAVERIK

The Manchester Virtual Environment Interface Kernel

Roger J. Hubbold, Xiao Dongbo, Simon Gibson
Advanced Interfaces Group
Department of Computer Science
University of Manchester
Manchester M13 9PL

1 Introduction

MAVERIK is a system under development which is designed to support large-scale industrial and other applications of virtual reality. At the present time it is being used to investigate the development of new CAD interfaces, and for the modelling of buildings with integrated radiosity solutions.

It also serves as a testbed for experiments with new algorithms in areas such as navigation of complex environments, 3D manipulation and construction of models, and performance issues such as culling and level-of-detail techniques, customised for different applications.

In developing MAVERIK we are also investigating architectural issues for VR software systems for large-scale applications.

2 Background

An earlier paper [1] set out a number of important issues for VR system design, some of which were investigated in the AVIARY system [2, 3]. In 1993 we began a collaborative project with CADCentre Ltd in Cambridge, to explore the potential of VR systems for the design of very large-scale process plants – structures such as oil refineries, North Sea oil rigs, chemical plants, and power generation plant. Preliminary results from this work have been reported elsewhere [4]. An early finding was that these models were so complicated that neither AVIARY, nor typical off-the-shelf or public-domain VR systems, would be capable of handling them with anything approaching an acceptable frame rate. This led directly to the design and development of MAVERIK, reported here. This new system provides a vehicle for us to research a wide range of VR issues, including those outlined in the previous paper.

In most VR and related graphics systems, the modus operandi is to import a model into the system, which stores the geometry and other data in a form optimised for the system's own purposes; examples include dvS [5], DIVE [6], AVIARY, BrickNet [7], IRIS Performer [8], Inventor, VRML viewers, Superscape. With these systems it is relatively simple to implement a parser to import data and to produce a walk-through of the resulting model. They also have programming interfaces which permit applications to create and modify objects at run time. Usually, simple manipulations, such as picking up an object and moving it are also supported.

The difficulty with such an approach is to integrate application-specific knowledge in a way which gives the resulting virtual environment a 'realistic' behaviour. For example, consider carrying an object like a ladder through a restricted space such as a doorway. Not only must we have efficient methods for the user to navigate in the virtual environment, but he or she must also be able to manoeuvre the ladder past any obstacles. Performing such tasks efficiently requires customised algorithms which can directly access the data structures associated with the specific application – a CAD database for example. On the other hand, merely using a VR library, such as the MR Toolkit [9], gives insufficient support for a range of common features, such as picking, manipulation, navigation, and collision detection, so that too much work must be performed each time a new application is to be written.

There are systems where this kind of behaviour can be provided, but again the data must usually be imported and restructured into the internal form required by the system itself. An example is the Jack software [10] which provides extensive support for simulation of human activities in virtual environments. Object-oriented systems with suitable class libraries provide a rich environment for rapid prototyping [11]. But for large applications, with a substantial effort already invested, it is not practical to rewrite the code. Here, some middle way must be found to provide a common kernel of VR functions which are easy to interface to existing databases, CAD techniques and simulations. It is this problem that MAVERIK attempts to address.

3 MAVERIK Components

A fundamental feature of MAVERIK is its extensive use of callback functions to customise behaviour. Perhaps the best analogy for this is a window system, such as X, in which the core functions can be adapted for different applications by writing appropriate callbacks. In some ways MAVERIK is like a window system, but manages 3D space rather than a 2D display. In order to avoid writing substantial amounts of new code for each application, MAVERIK supports a library of algorithms and techniques. Where these do not meet requirements, the defaults can be used as a starting point for customised versions.

MAVERIK comprises a number of software components, written in ANSI standard C. Some of these are shown in Figure 1:

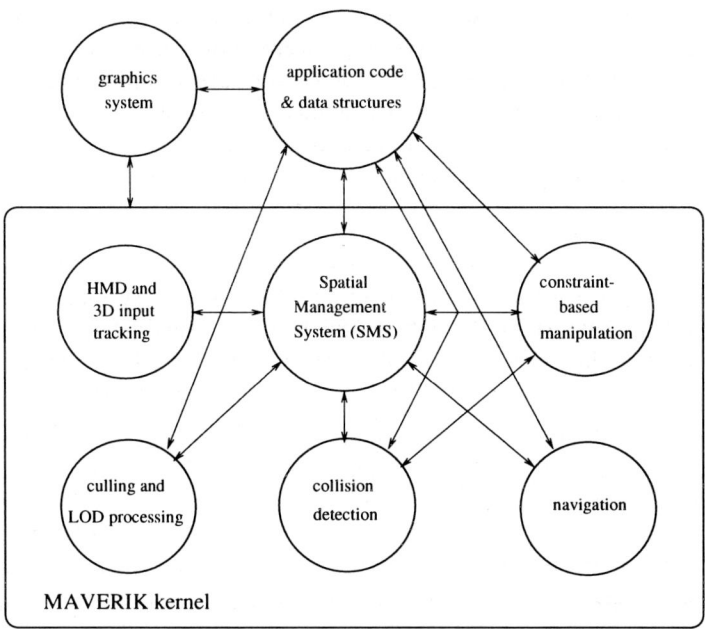

Figure 1: MAVERIK software components

SMS: which stands for spatial management system (data structures and associated algorithms). Spatial management lies at the heart of any VR system. It is required for tasks such as culling and level-of-detail processing, navigation, and collision detection. We have developed several different SMSs, including regular voxel (gridcell) structures [12], hierarchical gridcells (which include the subsets of K-d trees and octrees), and hierarchical bounding volumes. MAVERIK currently supports bounding volumes, hierarchical bounding volumes, gridcells, and hierarchical gridcells.

Culling and level-of-detail processing: we have also developed a number of culling algorithms which depend on the different types of SMS. They are implemented so that the basic culling is performed in an application-independent manner, using callback functions to perform the display of visible primitives. In MAVERIK, LOD processing is the responsibility of these application-dependent display callback functions, but the culling algorithms can provide assistance with this. For example, the hierarchical bounding volume SMS can compute the projected sizes of bounding volumes, and this is then used as one parameter controlling detail. MAVERIK is designed to maintain other LOD parameters, such as rate of movement, and system 'stress'. A separate paper gives details of our experiments and a comparison of the performance of the different SMSs for this purpose [13].

Navigation: is used to move a participant around a VE. Movement may be constrained – for example to prevent walking through walls, to improve ease of control for walking across flat surfaces such as floors, and moving up/down stairs. Navigation also needs to be customisable for different applications. It requires access to model attributes which define, for example, surfaces on which a user may 'walk'. Navigation methods may also vary depending on the task being undertaken. Thus, unconstrained movement may be acceptable when designing and constructing a model, but not suitable when simulating movement of an end-user through a finished design.

Collision detection: is intimately linked with the SMS, which provides a rapid method for narrowing the search space in very complex models. Again, customisation for specific applications is provided via callbacks. CD also interacts with navigation. For example, it may be possible to carry a ladder through a doorway, but only if it is held in a way which enables it to pass through the opening.

Constraint-based manipulation: is responsible for allowing objects to be picked up and manipulated. Again, the SMS plays a central role, but customisation is necessary. It is part of our thesis that VR interfaces are quite difficult to use for construction tasks, unless manipulation and constraint rules are applied. For example, in the case of process plant design, the system must play the role of an intelligent assistant, checking that specific components can be joined, and accurately aligning them. The rules which control this are associated with the particular application and this requires that the VR system be intimately coupled with the component database. It will not generally be easy to support such behaviour in systems which import models and store them in an internal format. Our experience with PHIGS has demonstrated convincingly that maintaining a separate graphics database, while advantageous in many respects, results in a large duplication of code and a lot of housekeeping to keep the application and graphics models in step with each other [14].

Input processing: basic input processing – handling events such as head movement, 3D sensor movement, and spoken input – is managed by MAVERIK. Again, callbacks can be registered (and re-registered to change behaviour) for these different types of input, and for actions such as 3D mouse button clicks. All coordinate data is converted into a single world coordinate system, although multiple modelling coordinate systems are supported. This permits convenient coordinates to be used for object definitions, and provides for some other interesting effects. For example, a user's virtual body may be defined in metres, whilst an application could use light years. The user can then grow or shrink by changing their body size. In the case of process plant design, the user may want to shrink a model, so that it appears as though on a table. Parts can then be assembled and disassembled without reaching over long distances. But the scale relationship between the user and environment may need to be reset to one-to-one to simulate navigation, or real maintenance procedures.

Application code and data structures: provide the necessary functions to customise the behaviour of the other components, via callbacks. An application can elect to use a standard set of callbacks, or to provide its own way of doing things.

Parsing external file formats: generally, we regard the parsing of external file formats as an application-specific function. However, to help in prototyping applications, MAVERIK supports a range of parsers and filters. Currently, we can read file formats associated with the CAD applications, and the Manchester Scene Description Language (MSDL) [15]. Filters allow us to convert between MSDL and other formats such as VRML, Inventor, Radiance, and DXF. Functions are provided for populating the SMS with different types of primitives, and a range of these is already supported (see below).

4 Objects

In general, MAVERIK makes no assumptions about an application's data structures, but relies on the concept of objects within an application. All objects which MAVERIK is required to handle are accessed via generic pointers. Processing is carried out via a generic callback mechanism within the kernel. The actual callback functions are specified by an application – much like the X Window system – although MAVERIK includes a useful set of defaults.

To give a simple example, suppose that we wish to display a model comprising primitives such as polygons, boxes, cylinders, cones, toruses. MAVERIK provides a default set of data structures for storing these, methods for populating the SMS data structures, and for displaying them. It also provides different SMS techniques which link to the application-specific data via pointers. It makes no difference to the MAVERIK kernel whether the data is stored in a tree, a linear list, or some other format, provided that the callbacks registered with the kernel are customised for the selected method. Thus, if an application can be built easily using the default primitive types and functions, then almost no programming is required. On the other hand, if complicated composite objects are needed then appropriate functions for handling these must be written.

MAVERIK objects are divided into classes. A class is defined by an application, together with corresponding methods for kernel operations such as creating and destroying objects, picking objects, and displaying objects of this class. Methods are created by registering the appropriate callback functions.

The system also allows objects to be inserted into different SMSs, and a distinction is drawn between *static* and *dynamic* objects. Parts of the environment which are dynamic will include moving objects (including those being manipulated by a user), and temporary information such as toolkit widgets (menus, cursors etc.). MAVERIK handles these objects differently from static ones, which are assumed to make up the majority of the model. Static objects are inserted into one of the optimised SMSs, such as a hierarchy of bounding volumes. Such structures are essential for large models and provide the key for efficient culling, object selection, collision detection and navigation. An object's status can changed as required between the two states. Typically, objects will be static until they are required to move or change in some way, at which time they become dynamic

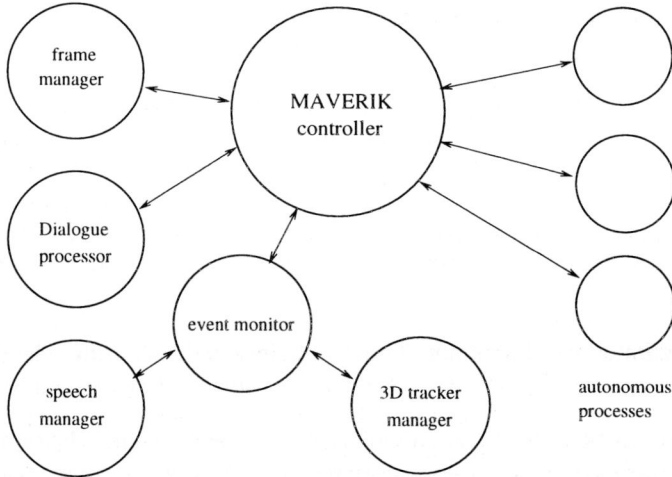

Figure 2: MAVERIK controller

and are temporarily removed from the SMS. Once they stop changing – for example, if a user has picked them up but then puts them down again – they revert to being static and are reinserted into the SMS.

An important tenet of MAVERIK is that it is not possible to design any individual component in a way which will work well for every application. Thus, all graphical display is handled via application-specific functions. This permits extensive optimisation. For example, when displaying a radiosity model, the hierarchy used in the radiosity solution is also used for level-of-detail display.

5 Control Structure

At the time of writing, MAVERIK programs have a simple global loop control structure, akin to the event processing loop of window systems like X. This has permitted us to get a prototype working quickly and to demonstrate its application to different environments. However, the design of MAVERIK includes a threads-based parallel controller which will manage different tasks within the system, using management statistics to control processing whilst meeting any real-time constraints. Pre-emptive thread scheduling is required. Figure 2 shows how the controller manages a series of lightweight processes responsible for head and hand tracking, display frame control, and processing of autonomous objects. Other threads can be associated with the software components mentioned previously. For example, some of our culling algorithms can be parallelised, and in this case multiple threads could be employed. The goal of the threads-based design is to have an implementation which can migrate seamlessly from a uniprocessor workstation to a machine with multiple processors.

6 MAVERIK environment

MAVERIK is being developed on standard workstations, primarily Silicon Graphics machines. Current versions use the GL library, but we plan to migrate to OpenGL to provide portability to other machines. As an aside, it is worth commenting that we prefer to use OpenGL to Inventor, because the latter forces too many decisions upon us about how to structure our data, akin to our previously mentioned experiences with PHIGS. We are experimenting with caching of display code, but in general we use tuned, immediate-mode output.

Our Advanced Interfaces Laboratory houses a Crimson/VGXT with videosplitter, and this is used to drive an Eyegen-3 head-mounted display, a large-screen Sharp stereoscopic projection system, a Roland sound system, and to accept inputs from Division 3D mice (Polhemus-based), and a speech recogniser. This, and other workstations, are connected to a KSR1 parallel machine and a Silicon Graphics Challenge multiprocessor, on which we develop our parallel threads-based algorithms.

7 Applications

7.1 Process plant design

The design of process plants is expensive and multidisciplinary. We are exploring ways in which VR can be used to develop interfaces for interactive model building, and for reviewing designs. MAVERIK can be used with our large-screen stereoscopic projection system, in which mode it can be viewed by several people simultaneously, or with the HMD. Interaction is by means of the 3D mice.

Figure 3 shows two views of a typical model. The upper one shows a more general view, and the lower one a closer position. The raw (binary) data file for this plant contains 5 megabytes of geometric data. This geometry describes high-level primitives, such as pipes, valves, and vessels, each of which require many (10 – 20 polygons to display. With MAVERIK we have been able to build a walk-through of these plants and to experiment with different culling and level-of-detail methods. Changing between a gridcell and hierarchical bounding volume algorithm is transparent to the application, because it merely requires that a different SMS method is selected. The SMS is populated with pointers to data stored in the application's data structures and the culling algorithm automatically calls the application-specific display functions to generate the displayed primitives. The display functions are called only for those primitives within the view volume. The view volume is updated by MAVERIK, but how this is done depends on the selected navigation technique. This will be different if the HMD is used than when using the projection system, as it takes account of the user's head movements as well as movement of the user's 'body' through the environment.

Currently we can achieve an average frame rate of 10 frames per second for the model illustrated here, and 6 fps for a larger model described by 19 megabytes of raw data [13]. Access to the application data structures is essential. We are developing new navigation methods which use application knowledge to constrain movements and provide a natural means for moving through the environment, to climb stairs and ladders and avoid obstacles.

7.2 Interactive radiosity

The second application is the modelling of buildings, and incorporates work on parallel, interactive radiosity solutions [16, 17]. The ability to link application data structures directly into MAVERIK means that the hierarchical data structures used for the radiosity refinement can also be used to display the results, and can be integrated into LOD selection. The radiosity solver runs on a parallel computer and passes data to a walkthrough program implemented with MAVERIK. It employs a cell-to-cell visibility method similar to that proposed by Teller et al [18, 19]. Each cell contains a list of portals through which other cells are potentially visible. Within each cell the objects are clustered into a hierarchy of bounding volumes. Thus, in this application, the culling method is adapted to take account of the cells. But for each cell the same culling methods are used as in the CAD application. Thus a different culling method is registered, but internally it calls the same method used by the CAD application.

The display functions use the results of the radiosity computations directly for display. Because a hierarchical method is employed, the application data is arranged as a quadtree with SMS pointers to individual subtrees. Level-of-detail processing involves descending the quadtrees to an appropriate level and the application-registered display function is optimised for this task.

Figure 4 shows two examples of virtual environments for which a radiosity solution has been computed. The upper one is a view of a corner of our VR laboratory. The lower one shows a close-up of part of a larger model of a garage. We are undertaking a study with the Greater Manchester Police, on the use of VR for crime investigations, and for training. (This garage was the scene of a murder.) Other current projects include modelling an Abbey, and modelling the Silicon Graphics Reality Centre at Theale near Reading, England, in collaboration with SGI.

Acknowledgements

The work described here is part of a broad team effort within the Advanced Interfaces Group. We would particularly like to thank Toby Howard, Alan Murta and Adrian West for their enthusiasm and extensive technical inputs, and our collaborators on the CAD project: CADCentre Ltd, Brown & Root Ltd, and Sharp Laboratories of Europe. The

CAD model depicted in Figure 3 is used courtesy of CADCentre Ltd and E.I. Du Pont et Nemours. Work on the CAD project is supported by the UK's Engineering and Physical Sciences Research Council under grant GR/K99701. Simon Gibson is supported by an EPSRC research studentship, and Xiao Dongbo by the Chinese Government and the British Council.

References

[1] Roger Hubbold, Alan Murta, Adrian West, and Toby Howard. Design Issues for Virtual Reality Systems. In *Virtual Environments '95*, pages 224–236. Springer-Verlag, 1995. ISBN 3-211-82737-4.

[2] A.J. West, T.L.J. Howard, R.J. Hubbold, A.D. Murta, D.N. Snowdon, and D.A. Butler. AVIARY – A Generic Virtual Reality Interface for Real Applications. In R.A. Earnshaw, M.A. Gigante, and H. Jones, editors, *Virtual Reality Systems*, chapter 15, pages 213–236. Academic Press, March 1993.

[3] D.N. Snowdon and A.J. West. AVIARY: Design Issues for Future Large-Scale Virtual Environments. *Presence*, 3(4):288–308, 1994.

[4] R.J. Hubbold and N.P. McPhater. The use of virtual reality for training process plant operatives. In *Proc. CG Expo '94 Conference*, London, November 1994. Computer Graphics Suppliers' Association, Worcester, England.

[5] Charles Grimsdale. dVS – Distributed Virtual environment System. Division Ltd, Bristol, UK, 1991.

[6] Christer Carlsson and Olaf Hagsand. The MultiG Distributed Interactive Virtual Environment. In Lennart E. Fahlen and Kai-Mikael Jää-Aro, editors, *Proceedings of the 5th MultiG Workshop*, Swedish Institute of Computer Science, Box 1263, 164 28 Kista, Sweden, 1993.

[7] G. Singh, L. Serra, W. Png, and H. Ng. Bricknet: A software toolkit for network-based virtual worlds. *Presence*, 3(1):19–34, 1994.

[8] John Rohlf and James Helman. IRIS performer: A high performance multiprocessing toolkit for real-time 3D graphics. In Andrew Glassner, editor, *Proceedings of SIGGRAPH '94 (Orlando, Florida, July 24–29, 1994)*, Computer Graphics Proceedings, Annual Conference Series, pages 381–395. ACM SIGGRAPH, ACM Press, July 1994. ISBN 0-89791-667-0.

[9] C. Shaw and M.Green. The MR toolkit peers package and experiment. In *Proc. IEEE Virtual Reality Annual International Symposium VRAIS '93*, pages 463–469. IEEE Computer Society Press, September 1993.

[10] Norman I. Badler, Cary B. Phillips, and Bonnie Lynn Webber. *Simulating Humans: Computer Graphics Animation and Control*. Oxford University Press, New York, 1993. ISBN 0-19-507359-2.

[11] Robert C. Zeleznik, D. Brookshire Conner, Matthias M. Wloka, Daniel G. Aliaga, Nathan T. Huang, Philip M. Hubbard, Brian Knep, Henry Kaufman, John F. Hughes, and Andries van Dam. An object-oriented framework for the integration of interactive animation techniques. In Thomas W. Sederberg, editor, *Computer Graphics (SIGGRAPH '91 Proceedings)*, volume 25, pages 105–112, July 1991.

[12] M.J. Keates and R.J. Hubbold. Interactive ray tracing on a virtual shared-memory parallel computer. *Computer Graphics Forum*, 14(4), October 1995.

[13] D. Xiao and R.J. Hubbold. Culling techniques for complex scenes. Unpublished.

[14] R.J. Hubbold and W.T. Hewitt. GKS3D and PHIGS – theory and practice. In W.T. Hewitt, M. Grave, and M. Roch, editors, *Advances in Computer Graphics IV*, chapter 3, pages 62–106. Springer-Verlag, 1991.

[15] Neil Gatenby, Martin Preston, and W.T. Hewitt. *The Manchester Scene Description Language (MSDL)*. University of Manchester, Manchester Computing, 1.0 edition, November 1993. Available at http://info.mcc.ac.uk/CGU/MSDL/MSDL-intro.html.

[16] Simon Gibson. Efficient radiosity for complex environments. Master's thesis, University of Manchester Department of Computer Science, September 1995.

[17] S. Gibson and R.J. Hubbold. Efficient hierarchical refinement and clustering for radiosity in complex environments. To appear in Computer Graphics Forum, November 1995.

[18] Seth J. Teller and Pat Hanrahan. Global visibility algorithms for illumination computations. In *Proc. ACM SIGGRAPH '93*, pages 239–246, August 1993.

[19] Seth J. Teller and Carlo H. Sequin. Visibility preprocessing for interactive walk-throughs. In *Proc. ACM SIGGRAPH '91*, pages 61–69, August 1991.

Editors' Note: See Appendix, p. 309 for coloured figure of this paper

MPSC - A Model of Distributed Virtual Environments

Alexander del Pino
delpino@igd.fhg.de
http://www.igd.fhg.de/~delpino
Fraunhofer Institute for Computer Graphics
Wilhelminenstr. 7, D-64283 Darmstadt, Germany
Phone ++ 49-6151-155-162, Fax ++ 49-6151-155-199

Abstract. In terms of the required computing power, virtual environments are an expensive interaction model for human-machine communication, which is one of the reasons for distributing them. In this paper we present the MPSC (Modifier Presenter Sensor Controller) domain decomposition model for distributed virtual environments and its key concepts. The MPSC model establishes a logical concept for the integration of parallel rendering algorithms and parallelized application modules into virtual environments. Beside the aspects of distribution and parallelization, this model serves additionally as a flexible research platform to explore various aspects of distributed virtual environments, including those with multiple users.

1 Introduction

Distributed virtual environments for multiple users are an interesting research field in the computer graphics area, and several realization approaches have already been emerged [1][2][3][4][5]. The main characteristic of multi-user distributed virtual environments is, that *more* than one human user interacts in the virtual environment, and the components of the virtual environment are distributed over several computing nodes, which are connected by a network.

In this paper we present the MPSC (Modifier Presenter Sensor Controller) model as a *functional* domain decomposition model for multi-user distributed virtual environments. The MPSC model establishes a logical concept for the integration of parallel rendering algorithms and parallelized application modules into virtual environments. Beside the aspects of distribution and parallelization, this model serves as a flexible research platform to explore various aspects of distributed virtual environments, including those with multiple users.

We observe two fundamental reasons or driving forces for the distribution of virtual environments. First, with the availability of long distance high bandwidth connections, the term *distributed* is often used, because the participating users in a virtual environment are *geographically* distributed, and therefore the hardware components which are associated with these users, too. Second, the required computing resources for a virtual environment are not only high, but additionally they are *heterogeneous*. In the heterogeneous computing field it is quite well known, that such problems must also be solved within a heterogeneous computing environment [6]. The importance to integrate various maschines like graphics engines and parallel supercomputers as a hardware platform for virtual environments was recently noticed by [1].

A look at the main cycle of an abstract multi-user virtual environment reveals, that there are three fundamental tasks which must be executed for each of the participating users. These three tasks are:

- Rendering the current scene graph as fast as possible.
- Handle the input events, which are generated due to the actions of the human user. The human users interact with virtual objects through input devices[7], which create these input events.
- Modify objects in the scene graph in order to evolve the virtual environment. This requires some care in order to preserve the consistency of the system, i. e. several users should not access the same object in order to modify it at the same time.

The critical components are the scene modification and the rendering, which suggests, that the scene modification and the rendering of a virtual environment can be distributed too. Note, that the term *distributed* is used here in the sense of a *parallelization*, in order to cope with more complex virtual environments. Such a parallelization is needed, because virtual environments are systems with a high degree of interactivity. This means, that at least 10 frames must be rendered per second, or in other words, the main cycle should not take more than approx. 100 milliseconds. This maximum main cycle length is the fundamental limitation for the complexity of the virtual environment. It limits both, the graphical complexity of the scene, and also the complexity of the modification algorithms in the virtual environment. Graphical complexity is usually measured with the number of graphical primitives which can be rendered per second. The complexity of the modification algorithms can be measured e. g. with the number of required floating point operations. If the scene modification and rendering are both performed on a standard graphics workstation, we observe, that the available graphics hardware is not very effectively used. This is, because the graphics pipeline will be idle as soon, as it is not fed with data, which happens immediately during the scene graph modification.

A naive approach to enhance performance is the dedicated use of the graphics workstation for rendering, and the use of another processor for modifying the scene. It is obvious, that the more human users interact in a virtual environment, the more computations must be done. Such an architecture is not scalable and will therefore soon reach its limits. Especially when the scene modification, i. e. simulation, in these virtual environments becomes complex [8], the realtime requirements call for a parallel implementation on a scalable architecture of these simulations, e.g. on a distributed memory architecture. Some recent work towards this direction is e. g. the connection of a CAVE to a CM-5 for the dynamic steering of distributed scientific simulations [9].

A requirement of this approach is, that enough computing nodes are available, so that all needed computations are done in parallel. However, when the computing nodes are directly coupled to the users, the computing nodes must transfer their results to all users, a fact which limits the usability of this approach because of two reasons: First, not every computing node has independent output channels to the hosts, where the scene is presented to the users. Second, each node must be able to handle all user related issues, e. g. the registering or withdrawal of a particular user, which reduces the time, that each node has available for computations. It is therefore necessary, to decouple the users from the modifying nodes with a controller instance, which leads to the MPSC model.

2 The MPSC model

The MPSC model as shown in figure 1, is a functional domain decomposition model of virtual environments into four different domains, i. e. each domain is characterized by the presence of a particular functionality. We call these four domains the *modifier*, *presenter*, *sensor* and *controller* domain. The presenter and the sensor domain together can be thought as a frontend which is associated with the human users, and the controller and modifier domain as the backend of the implementation of a virtual environment.

Conceptually, each domain consists of several independent *nodes* which in turn contain several *components*. The communication of these components requires the services of an appropriate connection network. The separation of the frontend and the backend favours the establishment of a natural *security boundary* and supports the use of this model for the implementation of virtual environments for security sensitive applications. However, the MPSC model proposes a logical decomposition, therefore it is possible to map components from different domains onto several processing nodes of the same parallel maschine.

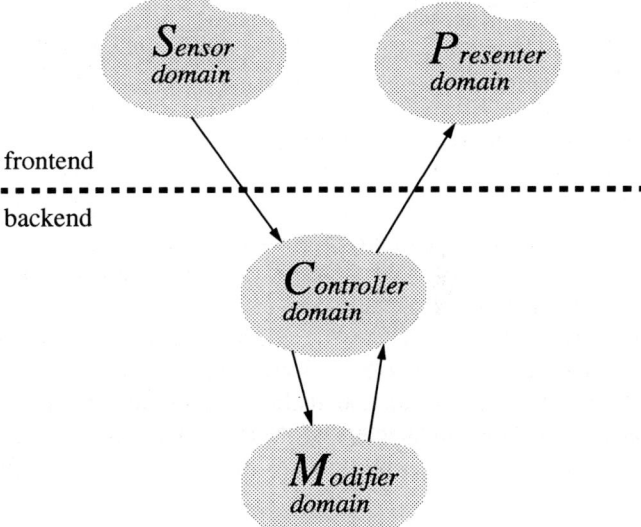

Fig. 1. The MPSC domain decomposition model

Presenter domain. The functionality of the nodes in the presenter domain is to present the virtual environment in a form which can be preceived by humans, in order to provide a feedback to the users about their actions. This includes not only visual rendering, but also auralization as well as haptic feedback [10]. Parallel rendering algorithms are supported by tagging objects for a particular distribution scheme. Another functionality of the presenter domain are not human, but *virtual observers*. A virtual observer is a software object, which *"perceives"* the scene or parts of it.

Sensor domain. The input devices are located in the sensor domain, and the input data sets which are created in the sensor domain are transfered to the controller domain, where they are evaluated. The task of the sensor domain is therefore, to provide input data sets which are associated with a particular user. In analogy to the virtual observers, there exist also *virtual input devices*, which are handled by virtual observers. A virtual observer with a virtual input device can be used, e. g. for collision detection. Every time, when objects of the scene which are observed by a virtual observer collide, the virtual observer notifies the controller domain by using its virtual input device.

Modifier domain. The scene graph, which describes a particular virtual environment is not a static data structure, but a dynamic one, i. e. the scene graph reflects the state of a virtual environment only for a moment. The task of the modifier domain is therefore to provide appropriate objects, which modify the scene graph. Independent modifications can be executed in parallel.

Controller domain. Finally, the task of the controller domain is to connect the nodes in the sensor, presenter and modifier domain, and register dynamic components, e.g. the entering resp. withdrawal of human users into resp. from the virtual environment. The controller domain by itself is not monolithic, but consists of connected objects and components which communicate with each other in order to satisfy the above mentioned requirements. In what follows, we explore some key concepts, which characterize an implementation of a virtual environment under the MPSC model in more detail.

2.1 Dual Scene Graph Traversal
A particular virtual environment is described through a scene graph, consisting of heterogeneous node types. In order to support research in the area of high-level description methods for distributed virtual environments, our strategy is to transfer as much functionality as possible from the system into the scene graph nodes. Especially, the scene desciption language is not static because a particular parser is used, but the nodes have the ability to read themself from a stream resp. write themself into a stream [11]. This enables the designer of a virtual environment to modify the scene description and add new functionality to the system, just by creating new node types, or by deriving new node types from already existing ones.

The semantics of the abstract scene graph node base class is extended, to allow not only the *definition* of objects, but also the *declaration* of dynamically created objects in other domains, which means, that the scene graph consists of definition nodes and declaration nodes. Objects which are derived from a definition node exist, as soon, as such a node is created. But objects, which are derived from a declaration node must first be *linked* with another dynamically registered object in order to be an active node in the scene graph. An implication of this mechanism is the dual scene graph traversal, as shown in the following figure 3. The term *dual scene graph traversal* means that the scene graph is *not only* traversed in the presenter domain in order to render the scene, *but* also in the controller domain, with another functionality. This dual scene graph traversal is done in an asynchroneous manner. This means, that the frequency of the scene modification is another one as the frequency of the presentation, which is essential to preserve the interactivity of a virtual environment. The result of the asynchroneous dual scene graph traversal in the MPSC model is similar to the effect, which is achieved by the decoupled simulation model [5].

Fig. 2. Dual scene graph traversal

The term *dual scene graph traversal* means that the scene graph is *not only* traversed in the presenter domain in order to render the scene, *but* also in the controller domain, with another functionality. Hence, the functionality in the controller domain is directly related to the functionality of the used node types in a particular virtual environment.

When a new user enters an already running virtual environment, only the scene graph nodes, which are relevant to the rendering are transmitted from the controller domain to the host of the new user. The criterion, whether a node is relevant for the rendering depends upon if it is *presentable*. This technique avoids the traversal of nodes, which have no meaningful semantics for a rendering process. Also, the nodes in the presenter domain are updated by the controller domain incrementally, because even with high speed interdomain connections, it is unreasonable to transfer the whole scene graph, only because a few scene graph nodes have changed.

2.2 Parallel Scene Modification

The virtual environment is modified, by modifying the objects of a scene graph. Under the MPSC model, all modifications (e.g. simulations) of the scene graph nodes are done in the modifier domain, which means, that each computing node in the modifier domain contains a number of *modifier* objects, which modify the scene graph nodes. These modifier objects are instances from classes, which are derived from an abstract modifier base class. In order to support research in the field of object behaviour in virtual environments, it is necessary, not to restrict the paradigm, how the behaviour of virtual objects is modeled and implemented. The more human users participate in a virtual environment, the more modification requests must be handled in the modifier domain. This leads to the natural conclusion, that the modifier domain is a first candidate for the implementation on a scalable parallel architecture. No input or output devices are needed in the modifier domain, but a high bandwidth connection to the controller domain is required. The MPSC model does not specify, how the nodes in the modifier domain communicate with each other, therefore it is outside the scope of the MPSC model, whether and how a modifier object implements its task in parallel. When a modifier object is instantiated, it must register itself in the controller domain, because only modifier objects, which are registered in the controller domain, are known. For example in the configuration of figure 3, four computing nodes exist in the modifier domain, and the three modifier objects M_1, M_2 and M_3 are registered and known in the controller domain. The modifier object M_2 uses some supporting objects X_1, X_2 and X_3, which are unknown in the controller domain.

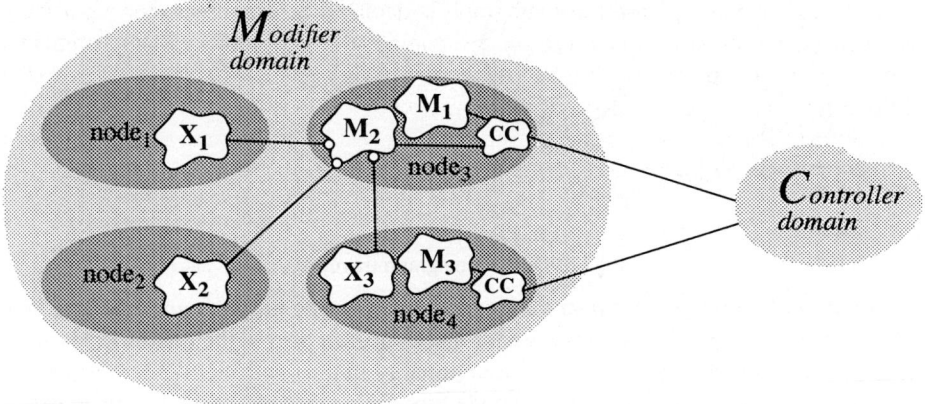

Fig. 3. Modifier objects

Modifier objects are represented in the scene graph through *computation nodes*[1], and each computation node is linked to a proxy of a registered modifier object, because a computation node is also a declaration node. In order to support the portability of a virtual environment under various configurations, it is necessary, that the references to modifier objects through computation nodes in the scene graph are *location transparent*. On the other hand, the modifier objects cannot inquire, which computation node resp. nodes in the scene graph is resp. are linked to their proxys. Therefore it is natural, that the data transfer from the controller to the modifier domain is driven from the controller domain. The communication peer in the modifier domain is not an modifier object, but a kind of a communication control object, which receives the input data, activates the modifier object and transfers the results back to the controller domain. Hence, the data transfer and the message passing is hidden for the modifier objects, and therefore transparent. In this sense, the controller domain can also be seen as an object request broker between the presenter and the modifier domain.

2.3 User Categories
We experience every day, that the behaviour of humans is not uniform, and a key con-

---

1. Note: A *computing* node is a host in the modifier domain, whereas a *computation* node is an object in the scene graph.

cept of the MPSC model is to support *non-symmetric* virtual environments, where the users behave also non-uniform. Non-symmetric virtual environments have been build, e. g. in [12], but at the cost, that this feature dominates the design of the whole system architecture. A mechanism to model this non-uniformity are *user categories*. A human user has therefore not only a name under which he or she is registered, but also belongs to a user category. This allows to model very precise the roles and rights of each user category in a particular virtual environment. For example, a virtual environment could give to a user of the *participant* category more rights than to an user of the *observer* category.

The tool to describe the rights of user categories is the so called *user node*. With the help of an user node, an arbitrary subgraph is declared as a template for a particular user category. Whenever a new user of this category enters the virtual environment, a copy of such a template is activated, by inserting it in the scene graph. The number of children in an user node reflect directly the number of active users in the associated category, and an user node without children means, that at this moment there is no user of the associated category active.

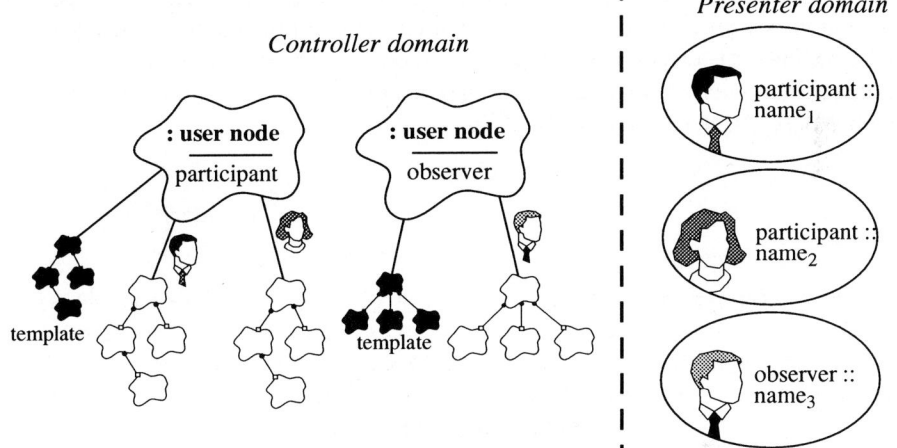

Fig. 4. User categories

3 Requirements for a hardware platform

Because the MPSC model is a functional decomposition model, a heterogeneous hardware platform is favoured for a particular implementation under this model. We already argued in this paper, that it is necessary, to parallelize the modifier domain, by using a scalable architecture, therefore we focus in this section on the controller, presenter and the sensor domain. The controller domain is central to the implementation of an virtual environment under the MPSC model and in order to avoid a bottleneck, the nodes in the controller domain require high bandwidth interdomain connections to the nodes in the modifier, presenter and sensor domain. The huge amount of graphical primitives in the visual representation calls for the use of high-end graphics workstations for the presenter domain, but also parallel architectures with rasterizer hardware can be used for that domain as we will see in the example in the following section.

Compared with the interdomain connection between the controller and the presenter domain, the bandwidth of the connection between the sensor and the controller domain can be much smaller, because the the input data sets are normally small data packages and not high volume data sets.

4 Example

We implemented an application prototype for realtime visualization of particles in a flow field from automotive industry, on the MANNA [13] / VISA [14] architecture, a typical frame from the running system is shown in (see Appendix). It allows an user to place interactively particles in a flow field whose flow is visualized. The system runs at an interactive speed with more than 23 frames per second and can handle up to 5.000 particles. The evaluation of the local velocity of the particles is done in a static flow field on a regular grid with trilinear interpolation and the integration of a particle trace is done by a fourth order Runge-Kutta method [15]. This evaluation in the modifier domain is parallelized over 10 MANNA nodes. In the presenter domain we have a renderer, which is parallelized over 5 MANNA nodes [16]. One MANNA node serves in the controller domain and finally a workstation with a attached spacemouse represents a node in the sensor domain, as shown in figure 5. This configuration of the application prototype under the constraints of the MPSC model was found empirically, there is no support for automatic configuration. A classification of configurations for distributed flow field evaluation can be found in [17].

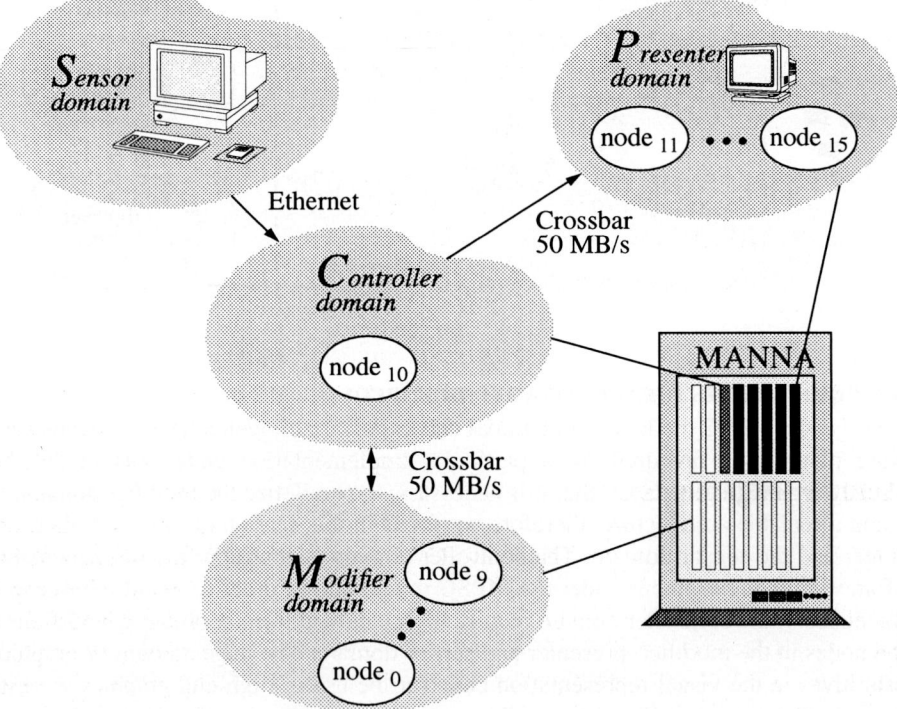

Fig. 5. Functional decomposition of the application prototype

5 Conclusion

In this paper we presented the MPSC domain decomposition model for distributed virtual environments. The illusion of reality in a virtual environment depends much on how real the behaviour of the objects in such an environment is modeled, and how good a human user can interact with this environment. Therefore high compute power and high graphics performance are required. It is very unlikely, that a monolithic architecture can satisfy both requirements and therefore we must look for ways, how to implement virtual environments in a distributed way on heteogeneous machines. To realize virtual environments for multiple human users implicates, that also multiple modifictions are to be executed in parallel, a fact which favours the use of parallel architecures in the modifier domain. Therefore we had the following requirements for a functional domain decomposition model for distributed virtual environments:

- It should split the resources into distinct natural computing domains with clear responsabilities, and thus serve as a guideline for the distribution and parallelization of the functionality of a virtual environment. Both, parallel rendering algorithms and parallelized application modules should be supported.

- It should be applicable for a wide range of heterogeneous hardware plattforms from high-end graphics workstations to parallel shared or distributed memory architectures. The heterogenicity means that we want to use for example the high-end graphics of one machine for a node in the presenter domain and the compute power of another machine for the modifier domain.

- Multiple users, which navigate and interact within the virtual environment, each one with its own view of the world should be supported. Also, research in the area of multi-user virtual environments, where the users are not uniform should be supported.

- The paradigm, how the behaviour of the objects in the virtual environment is described, modeled and implemented, should be not restricted, in order to establish a flexible reseach platform for these fields.

- Finally, it should be open enough, to add incrementally new functionality to the system.

These requirements lead to the MPSC model, and by exploring it, we expect new results and insight in the intrinsics of functional distributed multi-user virtual environments.

Acknowledgements

This work was funded by the German Federal Ministry of Research and Technology (BMBF) under the Grant FKZ 01 IR 409 B3 (Parallel High Performance Computing in Computer Graphics). The data for the flow field evaluation is used by courtesy of the Volkswagen AG. The kindly help of Thomas Frühauf for the flow field evaluation and the helpful comments of the anonymous reviewers are both appreciated. The author would like to thank Prof. Dr.-Ing. Jose L. Encarnação at the Fraunhofer IGD for his support.

References

1. D. N. Snowdon, A. J. West : "*AVIARY: Design Issues for Future Large-Scale Virtual Environments*", MIT Presence, Vol. 3, No. 4, Fall 1994, pp. 288-308
2. C. Carlsson, O. Hagsand : "*DIVE - A Platform for Multi-User Virtual Environments*", Computers & Graphics, Volume 17, No. 6, November/December 1993, pp. 663-669
3. M. R. Macedonia, M. J. Zyda, D. R. Pratt, P. T. Barham, S. Zeswitz : "*NPSNET: A Network Software Architecture for Largs-Scale Virtual Environments*", MIT Presence, Vol. 3, No. 4 , Fall 1994, pp. 265-287
4. C. Greenhalgh, S. Benford : "*MASSIVE: a Distributed Virtual Reality System Incorporating Spatial Trading*", Proceedings of IEEE 15th International Conference on Distributed Computing Systems, Vancouver, Canada, May 30 - June 2, 1995
5. C. Shaw, M. Green, J. Liang, Y. Sun : "*Decoupled Simulation in Virtual Reality with the MR Toolkit*", ACM Transactions on Information Systems, Vol. 11, No. 3, July 1993, pp. 287-317
6. A. A. Khokar, V. K. Prasanna, M. E. Shaaban, C.-L. Wang : "*Heterogeneous Computing: Challenges and Opportunities*", IEEE Computer, Vol. 26, No. 6, June 1993, pp. 18-27
7. W. Felger : "*Innovative Interaktionstechniken in der Visualisierung*", Springer-Verlag Berlin Heidelberg, 1995, (in german)
8. F. Dai, W. Felger, T. Frühauf, M. Göbel, D. Reiners, G. Zachmann : "*Virtual Prototyping Examples for Automotive Industries*", Virtual Reality World '96, Stuttgart, Germany, Feb. 13. - 15. 1996
9. T. M. Roy, C. Cruz-Neira, T. A. DeFanti : "*Cosmic Worm in the CAVE: Steering a High-Performance Computing Application from a Virtual Environment*", MIT Presence, Vol. 4, No. 2, Spring 1995, pp. 121-129
10. G. C. Burdea : "*Research on Portable Force Feedback Masters for Virtual Reality*", Proceedings Virtual Reality World '95 (Stuttgart, 21.-23.2.1995), 1995, pp. 317-324
11. A. del Pino : "*Design and Implementation of Parallel Object-Oriented Virtual Environments with the MPSC model*", Proceedings of the 2nd Parallel and Object-Oriented Methods and Applications Conference, POOMA '96, Santa Fe, New Mexico, February 28 - March 1, 1996
12. J. P. Cater, S. D. Huffmann : "*Use of the Remote Access Virtual Environment Network (RAVEN) for Coordinated IVA-EVA Astronaut Training and Evaluation*", MIT Presence, Vol. 4, No. 2, Spring 1995, pp. 103-109
13. W. K. Giloi : "*From SUPRENUM to MANNA and META - Parallel Computer Development at GMD FIRST*", Proceedings of 1994 Mannheim Supercomputing Seminar, Sauer-Verlag, Munich 1994
14. D. Jackèl : "*Grafik-Computer*", Springer-Verlag Berlin Heidelberg 1992 (in german)
15. T. Frühauf : "*Interactive Visualization of Vector Data in Unstructured Volumes*", Computers & Graphics, Volume 18, No. 1, 1994
16. A. del Pino : "*A Classification Scheme for Rendering Algorithms on Parallel Computers*" in: M. Chen, P. Townsend and J. A. Vince (eds.) : "*High Performance Computing for Computer Graphics and Visualisation*", Springer-Verlag London, 1996, pp. 69-77
17. M. Grave : "*Distributed Visualization in Flow Simulations*", Computers & Graphics, Vol. 17, No. 1, 1993, pp. 9-14

Editors' Note: See Appendix, p. 309 for coloured figures of this paper

Virtual Reality Programming in Oz

Tomas Axling   Seif Haridi   Lennart Fahlen

May 14, 1996

Swedish Institute of Computer Science
PO Box 1263, 164 28 Kista, Sweden, Tel: +46 8 752 15 00
E-mail: `axling@sics.se`
URL: `http://www.sics.se/ axling`

Abstract

To build virtual environments with interesting behavior it is desirable to use a high level language suitable for complex symbolic computations. But languages such as Lisp, Prolog and Smalltalk do not support concurrency, reactivity and real-time control which are vital for Virtual-Reality (VR) applications. However the new concurrent constraint programming paradigm in general, and Oz in particular support these requirements. Oz is designed to support multiple concurrent agents, which makes it well-suited for VR-applications. We have therefore implemented a basic interface between Oz and a toolkit for building distributed VR applications, DIVE. Furthermore we have developed a object layer for supporting agent abstractions. We are using this to build a framework for Agent Oriented Programming (AOP) specialized for defining agents in virtual environments for simulations. The framework is used to develop a system allowing collaborative configuration of virtual battlefields and battle simulations where the computer generated forces are controlled with spoken natural language.

1 introduction

DIVE [Hag96] (Distributed Interactive Virtual Environment) is a tool kit for building distributed VR applications in a heterogeneous network environment. DIVE allows a number of users and applications to share a Virtual Environment (VE) where they can interact and communicate in real-time. This virtual environment is a database of entities: graphical objects (views), and hierarchically organized abstract objects (DIVE objects). The database is actively replicated among all sites participating in a DIVE world. Each replica is controlled by an Application Process (AP) that manages the movement and interrelationship between the objects component parts and responds to interrupts generated by changes in the objects environment.

In order to implement interesting behaviors in a DIVE world, APs become quite complex programs. To handle this complexity it is desirable to use a higher level language. We have therefore implemented a basic interface between Oz [Smo95] and DIVE. Above this have we implemented an object layer (agent abstraction) to further aid in the developing of complex APs. The agents may have a graphical representation in DIVE worlds and a clock with which it can determine its behavior. First, we will give overviews of the DIVE system and the Oz programming language. Then we will describe the interface between them, the object layer, and some examples of usage. Finally we will present the work we are doing on a AOP framework for simulations and an application using it and a discussion of future work.

2   Overview of the DIVE system

DIVE is an experimental platform for the development of virtual environments, user interfaces and applications based on shared 3D synthetic environments. DIVE is especially tuned to multi-user applications, where several networked participants interact over any network supporting IP protocols.

DIVE is based on a peer-to-peer approach with no centralized server, where peers communicate by reliable and non-reliable multicast, based on IP multicast. Conceptually, the shared state can be seen as a memory shared over a network where a set of processes interact by making concurrent accesses and updates to the common memory.

Consistency and concurrency control of common data (entities) is achieved by active replication and reliable multicast protocols. Update messages are sent by multicast so that all nodes perform all updates. To achieve consistency at the individual DIVE entity level, entitys may have locks that should be acquired by the manipulating process. The process that creates a DIVE entity initially acquires the lock.

The peer-to-peer approach without a centralized server means that as long as any peer (AP process) is active within a world, the world along with its entities remains "alive". Since entities are fully replicated (not approximated) at other sites, they are independent of any particular site, and can exist independently of the creator.

DIVE and the Oz interface can be obtained from

http://www.sics.se/dive

3   The Oz Language

Oz is a concurrent constraint programming language designed for applications that require complex symbolic computations, organization as multiple agents, and soft real-time control. It is based on a new computation model for higher order concurrent constraint programming CCP, that provides a uniform foundation for functional programming, constraint and logic programming, and concurrent objects with multiple inheritance. From functional languages Oz inherits full compositionality, and from logic languages Oz inherits logic variables and constraints (including feature and finite domain constraints). Search in Oz is encapsulated and programmable, so it is easy to program e.g. one-solution, best-solution, all-solutions, and branch and bound strategies.

DFKI Oz is an interactive implementation of Oz featuring a programming interface based on GNU Emacs, a concurrent browser, an object-oriented interface to Tcl/Tk, powerful interoperability features (sockets, C, C++), an incremental compiler, a garbage collector, and support for stand-alone applications. Performance is competitive with commercial Prolog and Lisp systems.

Oz and DFKI Oz have been designed and implemented by the Programming Systems Lab of the German Research Center for Artificial Intelligence (DFKI) at Saarbrucken.

DFKI Oz is available for many platforms running Unix/X, including Sparcs and Unix-based PCs. DFKI Oz can be obtained free by anonymous ftp from ps-ftp.dfki.uni-sb.de, or through the WWW from http://ps-www.dfki.uni-sb.de/

4 ODI-DIVE Oz Interface

The basic means to manipulate DIVE worlds from any Oz application is provided by dynamically linking an interface to the DIVE library, and the DIVE library itself. This provides an Oz module called **DIVE**. The DIVE module provides, among others, a set of Oz procedures that give access to the basic DIVE functions as move_object and delete_object.

4.1 The Object Layer

Objects are the primary concurrent structuring concept of Oz. They combine data encapsulation through procedural abstraction with state and mutual exclusion. Objects can be seen as service providing agents. The services of an object are provided through methods and can be requested by sending messages to the object. Objects are created as instances of classes. Classes define methods, attributes and features. The definition of a class may involve inheritance from other classes. Objects and classes are first-class citizens. They are created dynamically. Objects can be spawned as concurrent agents.

The object layer is a hierarchy of Oz classes, with the initial class **DiveObj**. Each **DiveObj** object encapsulates a DIVE entity. The main components of the object layer are:

- The **DiveObj** Class

  DiveObj is a class from which one may create agents that have a graphical representation in DIVE. The graphical representation is determined by a vr-file [AS94] or by an existing DIVE entity. The class has a number of methods with which the coupled DIVE entity can be manipulated.

DiveObj inherits from Time.repeat which can be used to define the real time behavior of agents.

- The CompositeObj Class

  CompositeObj is a class representing composite agent, i.e. CompositeObj is a specialization of DiveObj which have methods for creating and handling subagents.

- The Class Library

  is a library of "useful" specializations of DiveObj and CompositeObj.

- The ObjStore

  ObjStore is an object storing DiveObj objects providing methods for broadcasting messages to all existing DIVE agents or to a selected subset.

4.2 A Small Example

All it takes to make a multi-user football game in DIVE and Oz, some straight forward object oriented programming.

```
class FootBallObj from StreamObj
   attr
      file:ball
   meth init
      <<StreamObj init>>
      <<registerCB(
           collision_signal
           proc{$ E}
              O TId in
              {Dive.getTopmostAncestor E.id TId}
              {Dive.getOrientation TId O}
              {self setOrientation(O)}
              {self roll}
           end
        end
      )>>
   meth roll
      actions<-nil
      <<addActions([
           action(move(pnt(0.0 0.0 3.0)) 100 4)
           action(move(pnt(0.0 0.0 2.0)) 100 4)
           action(move(pnt(0.0 0.0 1.0)) 100 4)])>>
   end
end
```

An object of this class is a concurrent object (agent). All messages coming to a concurrent objects are sequentialized so that only one at the time can change the state. A *FootBallObj* object reacts to a collision by taking the direction of the object which collided with it and setting its own direction to that. Then it will start to move, first quite fast and then slower until it stops.

5 A Simulation Framework

For simulations etc. we are working on a framework for Agent Oriented Programming (AOP) [Sho93]. The term agent is used frequently these days. We use a loose definition of agents: an agent is any process with which other agents can communicate. With an intelligent agent we mean an agent that can to some reasonably complex symbolic reasoning, usually simulating human reasoning. AOP is one way of building intelligent agents. In AOP an agent is an entity whose state is viewed as consisting of mental components such as beliefs, capabilities, choices and commitments. These components are defined in a precise fashion and stand in rough correspondence to their common sense counterparts. The AOP execution model is quite simple. A clock sends time updates at regular intervals to the agents which first reads the current messages, and updates its mental state. Then executes the commitments for the current time, possibly resulting in further belief change.

The basic Oz DIVE interface only support AOP by the addition of a clock to the objects, giving the means for temporalizing their operators, and the inherited features of a language supporting concurrent objects. To further support AOP we are developing a AOP simulation framework which basically consists of

An Agent Class is a class from which AOP agents can be created. The agents are represented as concurrent objects with methods for handling requests, time ticks, and inform messages. An agents state contains attributes and a number of commitment rules which determines its behavior. When an agent receives a tick message it checks its commitment rules and triggers the rules that are fulfilled. A rule that is triggered usually does some computations and changes the state and may invoke some actions. There might also be inform rules, which states what must hold for a new value of an attribute.

A Master Class is a class from which objects that controls a simulation can be created. Such an object works as the clock in in AOP. There are also methods for providing the agents and users with information about the simulation state.

We are using this model for a project involving simulating military entities. The aim is a allow collaborative configuration of virtual battlefields and battle simulations where the computer generated forces are controlled with spoken natural language.

Figure 1: Configuring a battlefield

5.1 Battlefield configuration

Figure 1 is taken from this application in the battlefield configuration phase. Here the Chicken is used to configure a battlefield. This can be used for example by a lower officer located in the field to describe the situation to his commanding officer in the headquarter. The situation may be the actual one or a situation that the lower officer perceives as a good or probable one and wants to show and discuss with his commanding officer. He does this by configuring the battlefield by hatching eggs to military entities. The eggs makes this process simple and fast by presenting only valid alternatives for the military entities. "Dusty", the fish like agent sucking up a tank, has a "cut and paste" functionality which can be useful for rearranging the battlefield. He can suck up things and spit them out at different positions. The commanding officer may, for example, use him to move and regroup the entities to improve the situation.

When the field is configured one can start an interactive simulation.

5.2 Battle Simulation

For the battle simulation application the general AOP classes are specialized to a number of application specific classes. The relationships between these are

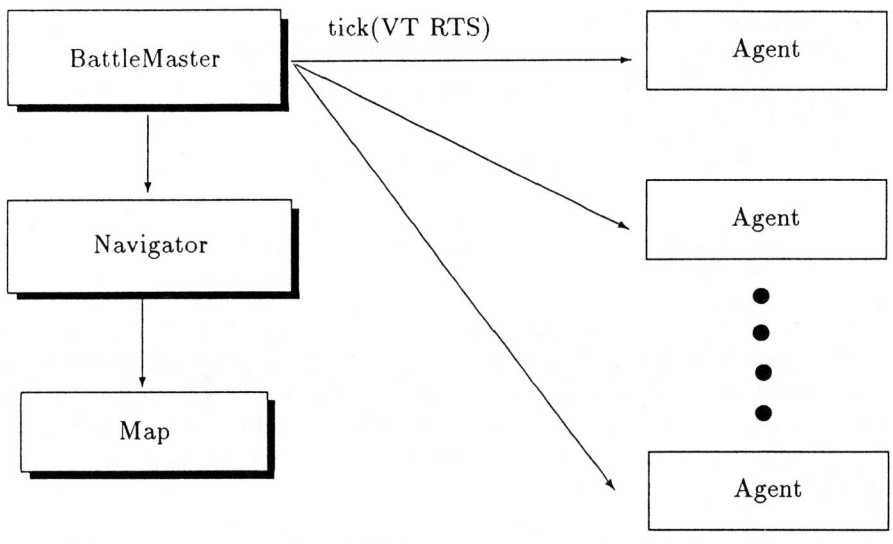

Figure 2: The Simulation Architecture

shown in figure 2 and some them are described below.

BattleAgent Class is a specialization of the *Agent* class with numerous methods for planning movements and actions. The agents state contains attributes like amount of ammunition, current health etc. It also contains a number of commitment rules which are common to all BattleAgents. Orders that are received are converted to commitment rules and actions. The conversion process is responsible to not create inconsistent rules or rules that does not work together. The agents may be organized hierarchically and for that they have methods to handle subordinates. When an BattleAgent receives an order it hence creates a plan for fulfilling it. The plan includes adding commitment rules to itself but also directly issuing orders to its subordinates. It may even directly add commit rules to its subordinates. This violates the idea that the agents should be responsible for their state and should be avoided. When a plan is established the agent will commit to it as long as possible. If the plan becomes impossible to follow the agent discards the plan and tries to create a new.

BattleMaster Class is a specialization of the *Master* class with methods for finding neighbors, enemies etc using the *Map* and the *Navigator*.

TankAgent Class is a specialization of the *BattleAgent* class with commitment rules for simulating a tank such as rules for planning attacks on individual enemy entities, regrouping defending and for retreating. There are also rules for switching between those activities if the situation (state) demands it. There is for example a rule that says that if health is low the agent will switch from attacking to retreating.

CommanderAgent Class is a specialization of the *BattleAgent* class with some high order planning capabilities. For example, an order to take a location involves selecting targets for the subordinates and coordinating their attacks.

To assist the agents in their planning there are some additional modules:

Map is an array of cells with information on speed, protection and terrain type. The *Map* has methods for importing data from common GIS formats. The digital terrain is dynamic, it can be manipulated during the simulation.

Navigator is a module that assists the agents in planning their movements. In order to complete their commitments, the agents need to move around in the terrain. The problem is to find a path which corresponds to their commitments. The *Navigator* has methods for finding paths given a weight function and a goal function. Examples of requests the *navigator* handles is:

- Find a path from position A to B avoiding agents of nationality b.
- Find a path from position A to position within X meters from B with maximum protection.
- Find the fastest path from position A to some position a given distance away.

We have done two different implementations of the *Navigator*. One based on the A-Star algorithm which is a beam search algorithm for the problem of finding the shortest path in a graph. The A-Star algorithm is proven to be the fastest algorithm for this if lower bound of the distance from any node to the goal node can be found. However, the navigator does, as exemplified earlier, a lot more than finding the shortest path. We are not sure how our generalized A-Star algorithm compares to other algorithms for these other problems. We have therefore also implemented a different navigator using agent based planning where a group of agents strives to construct a solution. Each agent, called a tracker, performs a local search, based on adjacent positions on the map. A weighted function of the constraints from the navigation request gives a measure of success for an individual tracker. If the difference between the adjacent positions is small a tracker may split into two which concurrently will explore the paths. Visited positions and the measure of success is communicated to other trackers, which can avoid already visited positions. The search is supervised by a tracker handler which controls the number of active trackers and terminates the search after specific amount of time. The disadvantages with this navigator is that is more complex, harder to analyze and debug and the frequent spawning of new agents introduces some overhead. The advantage is that it is a very general algorithm. It is very easy to define new trackers with different heuristics to solve different path requests. For the types of requests we currently have the A-Star navigator is superior but in the future we may use both.

Strategic Planner is a planning module with knowledge of different attack strategies which will be implemented to assist the *CommanderAgents*. Given the state of a agent and a target it will produce a coarse grain strategy.

5.3 Controlling the Simulation

Clicking on any of the entities involved in the simulation produces an interaction window in which commands can be typed. One can also ask for a control panel with which the entity can be controlled manually. When in manual mode the agent will not try to fulfill its commitments.

We are also working on a speech interface where the commands can be given in continuous spoken natural language. This is done as an extension of the DIVERSE (DIVE Real time Speech Enhancement) [KBFJ95] project at SICS. The speech recognition and text processing is done using commercial tools. A resulting dependency graph is translated to a logical representation, which in turn is inspected for references to entities and objects and matched to the set of conceivable and possible actions.

6 Future Work

Currently distribution and communication is achieved through the DIVE layer. Another possibility is to get distribution at the Oz level. This can be programmed today but a project called PERDIO is on the way to create a fully distributed programming system built on Oz, called Perdio in the following. A single Perdio program will be able to create multiple computations that spread over the network, and computations created by separate Perdio programs will be able to connect transparently. Perdio computations will be able to make use of persistent stores that can hold all data abstractions. It will be possible to access data structures without being aware of whether they are active in primary memory or passive in secondary storage. Hopefully this will have a great impact on distributed programming in general and on distributed simulations in particular.

The project is performed jointly by SICS and DFKI and the results will be successively incorporated in the Oz DIVE interface.

7 Conclusion

With this work we bring the power of a high-level language which supports object-orientation, concurrency, reactivity and real-time control to the development of VR-applications. The agent abstraction is one way of using this power. We showed how this can be used for interactive distributed simulations.

We believe that this is a small but important step towards VEs with interesting behavior.

References

[AS94]   Magnus Andersson and Olov Ståhl. *DIVE — The Distributed Interactive Virtual Environment, DIVE Files Description.* Swedish Institute of Computer Science, February 1994.

[Hag96] Olof Hagsand. DIVE – a platform for multi-user virtual environments. *IEEE Multimedia*, 1996. to appear in Spring '96.

[KBFJ95] Jussi Karlgren, Ivan Bretan, Niklas Frost, and Lars Jonsson. Interaction models, reference, and interactivity for speech interfaces to virtual environments. In *Proceedings of 2nd Eurographics Workshop on Virtual Environments — Realism and Real Time*, Monte Carlo. Darmstadt:Fraunhofer IGD, 1995.

[Sho93] Yoav Shoham. Agent-oriented programming. *Artificial Intelligence*, (60):51–92, 1993.

[Smo95] Gert Smolka. The definition of kernel oz. Technical report, German Research Center for Artificial Intelligence (DFKI), 1995.

TELEPORT - An Augmented Reality Teleconferencing Environment

Christian J. Breiteneder, Simon J. Gibbs and Costas Arapis

Institute for Media Communication,
Department of Visualization and Media Systems Design (VMSD),
GMD – German National Research Center for Information Technology,
D-53754 Sankt Augustin,
GERMANY
{Breiteneder, Gibbs, Arapis}@gmd.de

Abstract. A prototype immersive teleconferencing environment is described that allows small groups of people, although geographically separated, to meet as if face-to-face. The innovative features of the system include the use of wall-sized display surfaces, viewer tracking, subject-background separation by means of computer vision techniques and real-time compositing of live video with synthetic backgrounds. Used in combination, these techniques give the illusion of a virtual meeting area being an extension in space of a real meeting room.

1 Introduction

The use of communication technology to gain visual and audio information from remote locations has been investigated for a long time. Research and development in the field was motivated by saving traveling costs, bridging distances in a short time and connecting several remote locations.

In the mid-sixties the Picturephone was introduced to augment telephony with images for attracting the visual senses. Within ten years it would replace voice telephone, that was the prediction. The euphoria accompanying the release of (traditional) videoconferencing systems in the early seventies led to comparable high expectations and forecasts, that again, were never reached. The factors responsible for the disparity between forecasts and actual acceptance of these systems (see [1] for a detailed discussion) were identified as inadequate needs assessment methodologies and the portrayal of video conferencing as a direct replacement for face-to-face meetings.

The more recent past has seen the advent of desktop videoconferencing motivated partly to overcome disadvantages of the early videoconferencing systems and partly to augment conferencing with groupware services. Desktop videoconferencing systems are certainly advantageous to earlier forms of videoconferencing by offering user-controlled, flexible conferencing services that are continuously available and can be accessed from peoples' offices. The benefit within the context of cooperative work is attained by the integration of shared tools being available on the desktop. However, desktop videoconferencing still suffers from several limitations:

- the windows in which participants are displayed are small allowing, typically, only the presentation of faces,
- there is no spatial coherence between participants at different sites,
- as a consequence, more subtle forms of communication, such as gestures and body language in general, are lost; and to summarize
- the vision of video conferencing as a replacement for face-to-face meetings had be abandoned.

As a consequence projects were started that address the issues of body language, eye contact, gaze awareness and aim at more realistic face-to-face conferences. These systems – sometimes referred to as media spaces – often employ large displays and a sophisticated setup of audio and video equipment (see e.g., [2][4][5]) in order to enable meetings and/or cooperation between remote participants. The conference systems are intended to be superior to desktop conferencing when full body viewing and the accompanying subtleties of body language are an essential element of communication.

The GMD project TELEPORT represents such a system focussing on the realistic representation of conference situations where participants are aware of other participants' reactions, body expressions and gazes. It aims at establishing a natural and "immersive" teleconferencing environment where real and virtual environments are combined without the need for head-mounted displays or similar devices. TELEPORT is not intended to replace face-to-face meetings, but to offer an alternative when such meetings are difficult or impractical, due to lack of time, travelling costs or distances to cover.

The paper is organized as follows. The next section describes related approaches to new types of conferencing that strive for increasing realism. Section 3 overviews the TELEPORT system and focuses on the actual setup, design issues and hardware and software used. Section 4 discusses different usage aspects and planned field trials. The paper concludes with a description of future work.

2 Related Work

The purpose of this section is to survey different approaches of conferencing as a replacement for face-to-face meetings. Shared or common space, eye contact and gaze awareness are the general goals. However, the approaches differ in the means they employ and in the degrees of reality and coherence they enable. Within this context we do not try to give a complete survey, but rather stress diverse directions of work.

VideoWindow [3], a system developed at Bellcore, connects two remote rooms by a wide aspect ratio display (video window). People obtain the perception of looking through the window into an adjacent room.

MAJIC (Multi-Attendant Joint Interface for Collaboration) [5] projects life-size images of conference participants onto a large curved screen. The screen is semitransparent, allowing a camera to be positioned behind the screen and a video beamer projecting the images of participants onto the front. Careful positioning of cameras and participants currently allows one user at each site to have eye contact with other participants.

Panorama [7], a project within the European ACTS program, intends to establish 3D-telepresence amongst conference participants. Autostereoscopic displays will be developed that spatially separate left and right eye view images, in order to avoid wearing glasses. In addition, the display system allows a user to move while observing 3D imagery.

The GreenSpace project [6], funded by the Human Interface Technology Lab and the Fujitsu Research Institute, attempts establishing a "virtual common" for remote collaboration by the use of visual, aural and tactile cues. Currently, faces of participants are scanned and corresponding data sent to connected sites. The heads of participants are positioned in a virtual scene and updated according to head (for viewing) and hand (interaction) movements. The ultimate goal is to construct a meeting space for large groups of people (a hundred and more).

3 The TELEPORT Environment

The TELEPORT environment was designed to overcome disadvantages of desktop videoconferencing and to establish realistic videoconference sessions bringing people together as if face-to-face. The main goals of TELEPORT are

- to demonstrate the use of wall-sized displays integrated in a working or living environment.
- to demonstrate an "immersive" teleconferencing environment without the need for head-mounted displays.
- to develop an image segmentation system capable of extracting foreground objects (participants) from a controlled background while operating at near video rates (10-25 fps).
- to analyze, test and validate user requirements in diverse areas, such as tele-teaching, tele-music and tele-architecture design.

The TELEPORT environment consists of a room where one entire wall is equipped with a display surface serving as a "window" into a *virtual extension* of that room. The geometry, surface characteristics, furniture and lighting of the virtual extension are carefully designed to closely match the real room to which it is attached (see Fig. 1). Conference rooms and their extensions at different sites, however, may have different dimensions and appearance (furniture, wall paper, etc.). Into the virtual extension conference participants may be positioned in order to build a coherent meeting group.

Fig. 1 A sketch of the TELEPORT system.

When a teleconferencing connection is established, a $2\,^1/_2\,D^1$ representation of the remote participant, obtained using video processing, is placed within the local participant's virtual meeting area (Fig. 2). The viewing position of the local participant is tracked, allowing imagery appearing on the wall display to be rendered from the participant's perspective. The combination of viewer tracking, a wall-sized display, and real-time rendering and compositing, gives the illusion of the virtual meeting area being an extension in space of the real room.

---

1. $2\,^1/_2\,D$ representation refers to situations where 2D images can be positioned, scaled and rotated in a 3D space.

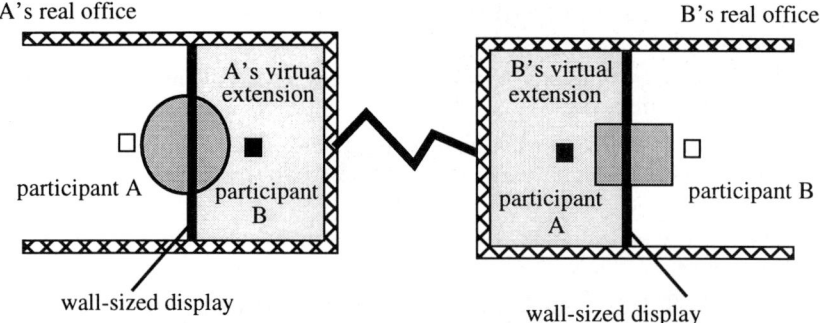

Fig. 2 Two TELEPORT environments connected over the network.

3.1 Display and Display Room

The display utilized in the TELEPORT project has to fullfil at least two requirements: First, it has to produce reasonably bright images even if the room in front of the display is lit. Second, the display should cover an entire wall of the display room.

The display room covers an area of 3m times 3m and a height of 2.25m. It resembles a box of which one surface has been removed to allow people to enter or view the projection from outside. The wall opposite of the missing wall is entirely covered by a display surface. The current setup is an office with a desk, chairs, light sources, speakers and a desktop camera (see Fig. 3 and Fig. 4)

Fig. 3 The rendered room extension with a conference participant.

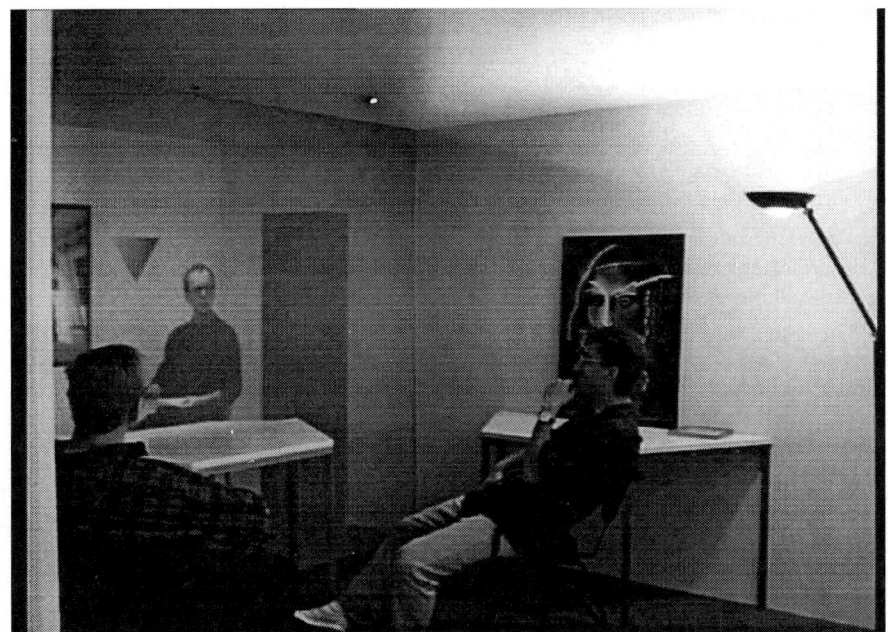

Fig. 4 The TELEPORT system in use.

Behind the display surface a projection area is required to create the necessary distance between projectors and display surface (appr. 5m). Even when using a mirror to cut in half this projection distance, the projection area has almost the size of the display area (office room). However, future display technology will hopefully reduce this additional space.

The environment also allows for stereoscopic rendering and viewing with passive glasses. However, a primary concern is that no special sensors need be attached or worn by participants for videoconferencing. Stereoscopic rendering is employed when the communication aspect of a session is dominated by the requirement to cooperate in a 3D space (see section 4).

3.2 Subject Segmentation

Subject segmentation extracts conference participants from a reference background. Currently the separation is performed by traditional chroma-keying of video, shot in a blue-room. Since it cannot be expected that conference participants have a blue-room at their disposal, we are working on real-time extraction out of a static background. A reference frame R is obtained by averaging a sequence of frames. Foreground objects in a frame F are extracted by computing for each pixel p the difference of RGB values between F and R. If the difference exceeds a given threshold then p is classified as foreground otherwise p is classified as background.

Even though similar procedures have been proposed for identifying foreground objects from outdoor video streams, the solutions are tuned for satisfying different set of requirements and take into account different environmental conditions. In our case environmental conditions remain stable.The requirements which should be satisfied from the implementation of the segmentation procedure are:

- Process frames in real time. Rates less than 10 frames/sec becomes noticeable to the user.
- Process frames with small delay. Delays greater than 250 msec becomes disturbing for the users.
- Once the reference scene is chosen, it should be possible to separate foreground from background without making any further assumptions on background or foreground object properties.
- The segmented images should be of good quality. More precisely, the number of pixels that could be incorrectly classified either as foreground or background should be small enough so as not to be noticeable to the user.

The actual implementation of the segmentation procedure runs on an SGI Onyx machine with four R4400 processors running at 150 Mhz and two graphics pipelines. An SGI Sirius board is used for digitizing the frames got from the camera. The size of frames is 720 x 576 pixels. Each frame is first reduced along its horizontal and vertical dimension according to reduction parameters entered by the user. Then each of the four processors processes different regions of the frame. More precisely, each processor computes the difference between the current frame and the reference frame, tries to detect shadowed regions for classifying them as background rather than as foreground, and finally applies a noise elimination function. The resulting frame is finally expanded to its original dimensions.

Choosing a reduction factor of 4 along the vertical and horizontal dimensions we obtain a processing rate of approximately 8.33 frames/sec and a delay of 120 msec. Fig. 5 shows the original frame (the reference frame is the same as that of Fig. 5 but without a person).

Fig. 5 Frame to be segmented.

Fig. 6 shows the frame prior to the noise elimination step at the left and the frame resulting from the segmentation procedure at the right. We expect that a small upgrade of the hardware configuration described will allow us to satisfy our initial requirements.

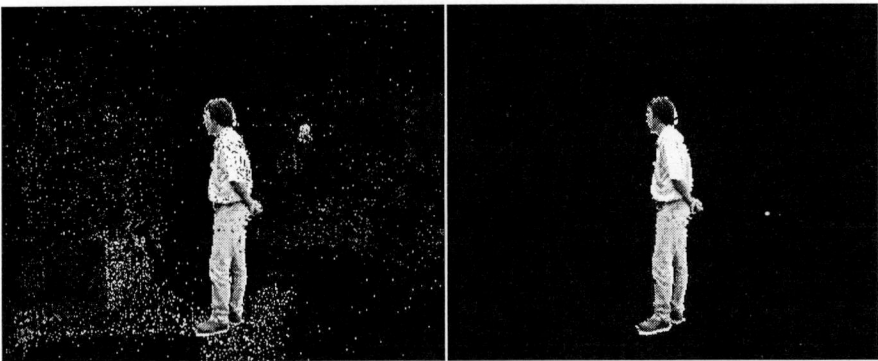

Fig. 6 Frame prior to noise elimination (left) and frame after the completion of segmentation (right).

3.3 Viewpoint Tracking

In order to achieve the correct perspective continuation of the rendered room the viewer's head (and approximately the viewer's eyes) have to be tracked. Ultrasonic and electromagnetic sensors were tested to find the best fit to the application requirements, but also to the specific features of the display area (e.g., presence of metal, thickness of walls, etc.). We have yet to find a tracking system giving sufficient frequency and accuracy of tracking data to allow for rendering with negligible delay and jitter. In the future, additional methods of viewer tracking will be studied.

3.4 Rendering and Compositing

According to the change-viewpoint requests originating from the tracking system the virtual room extension is rendered in real-time (currently 12.5 or 25 frames per second with a RE2). Conference participants are positioned in this extension by using transparent video textures. The separated video foreground of participants is texture-mapped on a grid with the corresponding transparency channel.

3.5 Hardware

The wall display is constructed from a pair of commercially available high-luminosity video projectors configured for rear-projection. Two projectors (NEC 10-PGs) – to generate reasonable brightness even when the display room is lit – are mounted on the ceiling and beams reflected on a mirror before they reach the wall-sized display. For capturing the local participant a small Panasonic camera is positioned in front of the screen. The display room is additionally equipped with an audio surround system and microphone inputs.

Since rendering and compositing introduces delay, an audio delay is used to assure lip synchronization. Currently, keying of the camera signal is performed by an Ultimatte System 7 keyer. Real-time rendering and compositing is performed on an SGI Onyx with two RealityEnginesII and Sirius video hardware.

3.6 Connectivity

A basic requirement for the operation of the TELEPORT is the availability of reliable high bandwidth communication networks such as ATM. However, since ATM networks are not yet widely available and not all users of TELEPORT might have access to broadband communication links, different options will be investigated and tested, e.g., internet, ISDN, VBN (a broadband network from German Telecom) and satellite links. This way we will be able to offer different alternatives for different applications, depending on the quality needed, operation costs, etc.

4 Field Trials and Usage

Concerning the usage of TELEPORT two directions have to be distinguished: The first addresses typical conferencing situations when participants should not be hindered by wearing any special devices and faces and eyes should not be occluded. The second direction comprises communication situations where people have to work in a shared distributed 3D environment. For these tasks the cooperation aspect and the possibility to view and manipulate objects in 3 dimensional space is considered to be more important than the loss of facial cues due to wearing glasses. Currently however, our work focuses on the videoconferencing aspects.

Examples of videoconferencing scenarios where a TELEPORT environment could be used include distributed negotiation, remote medical consultation, communication for the physically disabled, long-distance learning and cultural exchanges such as distributed rehearsing.

Distributed rehearsing enables actors or performers on different sites to rehearse a production. These trials will be performed within the context of "Distributed Video Production" (DVP), a project funded by the European ACTS program. For example, a small group of musicians will use TELEPORT to conduct distributed rehearsals.

5 Future Work

Future development of TELEPORT will take place along two main directions: image processing and 3D modelling. We plan to continue testing various delta-keying heuristics with the goals of achieving segmentation at the video frame rate and a more robust performance (e.g., adaptation to lighting changes). We also aim to apply image processing techniques to subject, and possibly viewer, tracking. In particular we would like to track subject facial features in order to texture map live video onto 3D facial models. In the area of modelling, we plan to utilize pre-constructed 3D models of TELEPORT subjects. The models will be animated and rendered by combining a sensor-based motion capture system for overall body movement with the mapping of facial features from video.

Acknowledgments

The authors acknowledge the support of Karl Matthias Könke who designed the display room and produced Fig. 1.

References

[1] Egido, C., Videoconferencing as a Technology to Support Group Work: A Review of its Failure, *Proc. CSCW'88*.

[2] Elrod, S., Bruce, R., Gold, R., Goldber, D., Halasz, F., Janssen, W., Lee, D., McCall, K., Pedersen, E., Pier, K., Tang, J., and Welch, B. Liveboard: A large Interactive Display Supporting Group Meetings, Presentations and remote Collaboration, *Proc. CHI'92*, pp599-607.

[3] Fish, R.S., Kraut, R.E., and Chalfonte, B.L. The VideoWindow System in Informal Communications. *Proc. CSCW'90*, pp. 1-11.

[4] Gaver, W., Smets, G., and Overbeeke, K. A Virtual Window on Media Space, *Proc. CHI'95*, pp. 257-264.

[5] Okada, K., Maeda, F., Ichikawaa, Y., and Matsushita, Y. Multiparty Videoconferencing at Virtual Social Distance: MAJIC Design, *Proc. CSCW'94*, pp. 385-393.

[6] http://www.hitl.washington.edu/projects/greenspace/background.html

[7] http://www.tnt.uni-hannover.de/tnt/project/eu/panorama/overview.html

Achieving Virtual Presence with a Semi-Autonomous Robot Through a Multi-Reality and Speech Control Interface

Kristian T Simsarian
kristian@sics.se
Ivan Bretan
ivan.bretan@sics.se
Niklas Frost
frost@sics.se

Jussi Karlgren
Jussi.Karlgren@sics.se
Emmanuel Frécon
emmanuel@sics.se
Lars Jonsson
jonsson@sics.se

Lennart E. Fahlén
lef@sics.se
Tomas Axling
axling@sics.se

Swedish Institute of Computer Science
S-16428 KISTA
Stockholm, Sweden
fax: +46 (8) 751-7230
tel: +46 (8) 752-1570

Abstract. This paper describes a model for a complex human-machine system where a human operator controls a remote robot through the mediation of a distributed virtual environment with a language interface. The system combines speech controlled graphical immersive environments with the live video from a robot working in a real environment. The worlds are synchronized and updated based on operator selections, commands and robot actions. This system allows the user to have a powerful tool with a high level of abstraction to create and control autonomous robots, thus making possible the realization of single and possibly multiple real-world autonomous robot applications.

1 Introduction

In this paper we describe our current work to construct a high-level remotely operated robot system. Control is acehieved via a high-level interface supplemented by language and gesture control within a graphical immersive environment containing live video of the remote space where the robot is situated.

The robot handles the *perception-action* of the human-machine system, the virtual environment is a model of the *world knowledge* of the system, and the interface, with both language and gesture interaction provides the tools for *interaction* thus manipulating the robot and the knowledge state of the entire system.

The virtual model is is able to display the current status of the system's awareness of objects and available actions and to specify high-level tasks, such as point-to-point navigation and pick-and-place manipulation, while the robot has the basic physical and perceptual skills to perform low level navigation in the form of path-planning and obstacle avoidance, and some vision processing. At the same time, the interaction between the user and the robot system is on a high level of abstraction facilitated by the combination of the use of a virtual environment, natural language and gesture interface. This releases the human operator from low-level tasks of robot control, and allows the operator to specify tasks in a high-level manner for possibly a number of robots.

The applications for completely autonomous robots are manifold; however, in the world today mobile robot high-level task planning is difficult. To have a robot perform complex tasks requires guidance or guided instruction from a human aide or controller. Designing a system to support a human guide for robot learning involves complex design decisions on several levels: firstly, the human guide needs information on the physical surroundings of the robot; secondly, the guide needs to be given a reasonable rendition of the robot's current awareness of those surroundings; thirdly, the guide needs to be given a useful and understandable mechanism to interact with the model and the robot's knowledge representation in order to be able to specify objects, entities, and tasks for the mobile robot. The above requirements are achieved by using the interface described in here.

This paper describes the framework we are using for the virtual and real world combination and demonstrates the principle which we are applying to performing remote tasks within a new immersive paradigm. This paradigm uses interaction mechanisms that will not limit the operator to low level manipulation.

2   Example Scenario

The human operator interacts with an immersive environment which represents a model of a remote real environment (see figure 2). In the virtual environment the operator has access to a mobile robot physically situated in the remote real environment. The robot is a vehicle that has the ability to carry the operator through both the virtual and remote-real worlds. The interface between user and robot in the virtual world consists of a real-time video view of the robot's real world environment accompanied by an interface control panel (figure in Appendix). The interface control panel consists of buttons, displays, and various data to aid the interaction. Some of the tools available can set robot speed, acceleration parameters, or command various image transforms. There are also additional displays that can give current real world robot and environment state, i.e. battery supply or radioactivity level. The robot has the ability to move through the world and can be controlled on a high level of abstraction by the operator through the interface. The operator gives simple instructions to navigate, such as "go there" accompanied by a pointing gesture in the virtual world. Or, alternatively, the user might give a more sophisticated command, such as "move toward the doorway" accompanied by the context of the robot's current view. Because the virtual model is at least roughly synchronized to the real world and information about specific doors are contained in the virtual environment model, this command can quickly be translated into navigational commands for the robot base.

One important difference in our model of robot control is that as the user

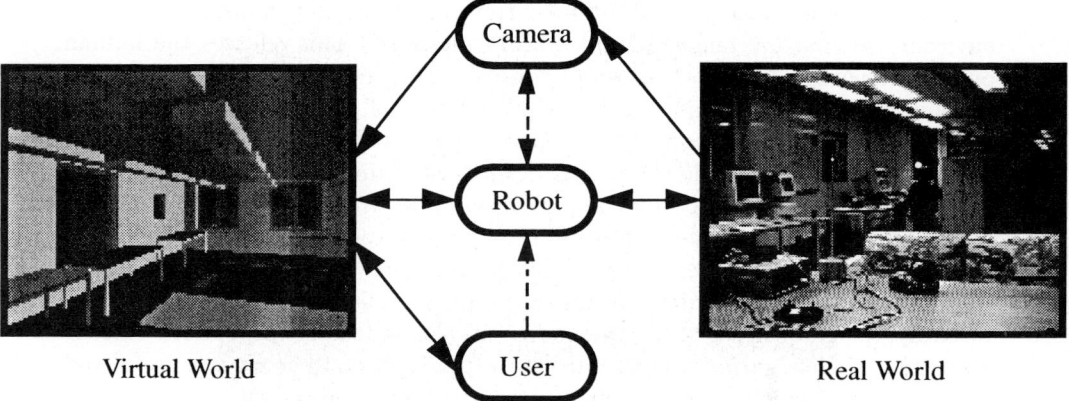

Figure 1: This figure shows the flow of information between the different system components. The solid lines indicate direct flow of information while the dotted lines indicate an indirect flow (see text).

interacts with this robot control interface, the machine is permitted to say "I don't know." The robot does not have to make high-level decisions, instead it performs as well as it can and always has the ability to return to the user with questions. Allowing this degree of relaxation in autonomy releases the system from many of the hardest problems in AI while simultaneously allowing us to build machines that can perform useful tasks and providing a novel platform for further research in autonomous robotics, sensing, man-machine interaction, and virtual environments.

For example, if our virtual model did not include a complete description for the real-world object that the user reference in the camera image, e.g. a book, then given a rough localization the robot could perform a vision process on the image to fit the right aspect ratios for a book at that distance and pose. When there is an ambiguity, the robot might ask "is this the book you mean?" while highlighting what it estimates to be the book boundary in the image. In some situations the robot might respond with a number of alternatives for the book including, among the alternatives, a box. These mistakes are, at least initially, allowed in the interface until visual recognition techniques have caught up with current needs. The selection of these alternatives would be part of the user-robot interaction. Thus the user would learn how to use the robot given its deficiencies. For future use, the user could segment out the book for future recognition and identification. The image texture of the book can also be used in the virtual world for aiding the identification by the operator and enriching the simulated environment, and also supplying visual features for the vision processes.

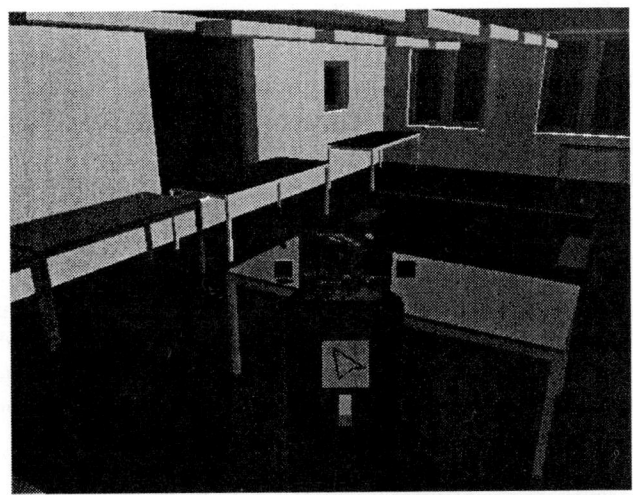

Figure 2: This figure displays a view of the immersive environment. It is a model of the laboratory space in which the robot is situated. In the center the virtual robot representation can be seen. On the robot sits a live camera view into the real world.

3 Robots, Operators, and Interaction

3.1 Autonomous Robotics

It is easy to see how having the capability to send autonomous robots into hazardous and remote environments (e.g. space, sea, volcanic, mine exploration, nuclear/chemical hazards), would be useful. Robotics can be built to stand higher environmental tolerance than humans, they can be built to perform specialized tasks efficiently and they are expendable. To this end there has been much research on fully autonomous robots that can navigate into an area, perform actions such as taking samples, performing manipulations, and return the information to base controllers without human assistance.

3.2 Teleoperated Robotics

Relatively independently from research in autonomous robotics, on the other end of mobile robot research, the field of teleoperated robotics has worked on the human-machine interface to enable an operator to control a robot remotely in space [24], and battlefield[4] applications and even used simulated environments for predictive task planning[20]. Some researchers have tried to bridge this gap from both directions. An autonomous robotics group has taken a schema-based reactive architecture and used this as a base-level for teleoperated control. In their architecture the mobile robot performs simple navigation while the operator's commands can be situated in the system either as another behavior that influences navigation or as a more global process that manipulates system parameters[2]. They have since extended this idea to allow the operator to control group behaviors in a multi-agent environment[3]. Other groups have recognized the need for tele-operators to move away from low-level robot movement control. One effort has created a multi-level architecture for robots to provide higher level navigation functions such as path-planning and obstacle avoidance with operator guidance[10].

3.3 Immersive Interfaces

Meanwhile, recent research in immersive virtual environments and human-computer interaction at SICS has worked on building a framework for natural interaction. One aspect of this work has been the study of interaction between agents, human and others *in* a shared virtual environment [5]. Another aspect has been the building of mechanisms for human users to interact *with* the virtual environment [17]. We are using an immersive virtual environment as the interaction paradigm with the real world and the robot. Specifically our work is an application in the SICS Distributed Interactive Virtual Environment (DIVE) system[12].

3.4 Augmented Reality

We incorporate on-board video from the robot into the virtual world. The video can subsequently be enhanced and augmented to communicate information to the operator. This is quite similar to work in *Augmented Reality*, which at is base is the concept of combining real world images (e.g. video) with graphic overlays. Augmented reality techniques have been demonstrated in a variety of practical applications. Examples of these are displaying graphical information in printer repair operations[15]. Or displaying information from a 3-D model base on a real world artifact [26]. Other applications include virtual tape-measurement on real scenes as well as graphical vehicle guidance[23], and enhanced displays for teleoperated control[22]. All of these separate applications are relevant for our robot application. Additionally the reverse operation can be performed, the virtual environment can also be augmented in a similar fashion by real-world images.

4 Integrating Perception, Knowledge, and Interaction

There are four main distributed computational subsystems in the complete system. These are the robot system – the physical layer; the computer vision processing system – the perceptual layer; the graphical object database and rendering system – the knowledge model; the speech and language processing and the graphical object manipulation system – the interaction layer. The information that is passed around can also be viewed as flowing between the real and

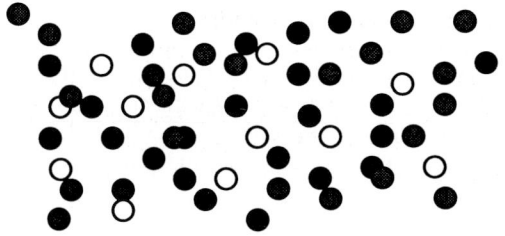

"Select the grey marbles."

Figure 3: An example where natural language commands have significant advantage over "point and click."

"Where is the paper about virtual reality and robotics I sent to the workshop in Monte Carlo last fall?"

Figure 4: Try this with gestures.

virtual worlds via the camera, the robot and the user. This flow of information can be visualized in figure 1.

4.1 Physical competence: Robotics

The robot exists in the real world. The robot is endowed with a basic model of the environment from an architectural-type drawing of the basic physical world structure and artifacts, and through movement and exploration, the robot has the ability to augment this model, with new objects, methods and descriptions that are more useful for comparison to its sensor data.

The robot that we are using for this system is a Real World Interface B21 robot with on-board processing and sensing. In this system this robot can perform basic tasks such as navigate around obstacles, recognize objects to the best of its ability and take its high level commands from a human, thus displacing the artificial high-level planner with a human one.

The robot can perform basic point-to-point navigation tasks and avoid basic obstacles while negotiating the indoor structured environment in which it is situated.

Using the robot encoders and periodic self-localization such as described in [28, 21] to account for drift, the robot can synchronize with the model represented in the virtual reality. Having access to a model of the environment as well as access to the operator's knowledge and assistance gives great leverage on the harder problems of robot navigation, such as localized sensor pitfall situations.

This type of hybrid human-machine system will give the operator something we are calling *virtual presence*, where the operator is present by way of a machine proxy, or by way of a virtual rendition of the surroundings, dependent on the perspective we take.

4.2 Perceptual processing: Vision

The robot sends the data it perceives to the vision processing system. The output from the vision processing system is sent further to the knowledge level of the system to be encorporated the virtual model of the world.

General visual segmentation of real world images continues to be a hard problem. However in this situation we are assisted in this tasks by both having some knowledge of appearance (through saved images of the real world such as texture maps), approximate location and the user. In many instances this harder problem of visual segmentation breaks down to an easier problem of verification and fine localization. The user can also interact with the vision processing to aid in the segmentation, identification and localization. Using graphical interaction tools such as "snakes" (an interaction method that allows a user to roughly identify a region which then shrinks to surround the nearest edge) the user can be facilitated in performing hand segmentation of the image. These images that are cut out the environment are used for both identification by the vision processor on the video images as well as identification by the user within the virtual environment. This part of the system is work in progress.

4.3 Knowledge model: The Augmented Virtual World

The video from the camera flows from the real world to the virtual world. These images represent the real-world from a robot-centered perspective. The user sends commands to the robot via the interface, thus these commands are made by the operator interacting with the virtual world. The commands may be as simple as updating velocity and orientation or may also be higher-level and more complex involving path specification, navigational targets, and grasping tasks.

The present interface takes video from the world and brings it into the virtual world which allows the possibility to superimpose graphics on video. Such an *augmented reality* interface can display information that may not be visible, but useful in the real world, thus augmenting the information present in the video channel with navigational aid information or nonvisual sensory data. It is also a convenient way of displaying to the operator what the current state of the system is: items in the environment could be graphically emphasized or deemphasized (dimmed), based on the needs of the operator, robot and task at hand. For example a book in the physical environment that is recognized and localized by the vision processor could be colored and emphasized for the operator to know that this object is known and could possibly be interacted with. If a object is not recognized, it is chance for the user to advise the system what the object in question is.

In addition to this standard notion of augmented reality, we also have the power to perform the complement operation, embellishing the virtual environment with real-world images. With the proper, possibly user-guided, feature extraction and image warping we can decorate the world with much of the richness of the real world. Thus, objects that the operator needs to interact with can be visually more informative than the pure virtual reality system would allow them to be.

Thusly the virtual world represents the knowledge state of the robot. It is not intended to be perfect or complete. Within this framework many of these methods for real and virtual world interaction for both the user and robot are embedded and distributed in the world itself (see section 4.4.2).

4.4 Interaction with the Operator

The virtual world serves as the communication medium between the robot and the user. It is through the interaction of the robot with the virtual environment and the operator with the virtual environment that interaction between the operator and the robot can take place. Thus bi-directional communication and command specification is achieved via the virtual world. In complement to operator commands, the robot can make queries of the operator regarding task direction as well as update the environment with objects and model features discovered in the course of exploration.

Our interface design is multimodal – meaning that it makes use of live video, 3-D graphics, gestures, menu choice, speech, and text as input and output channels. Language and graphics (or, indeed, any abstract and any analog manipulable representation) complement each other, in the sense that tasks of different types require different modalities [14], and that users have varying preferences for modalities or differing capacity to make use of them [16].

DIVERSE (DIVE Robust Speech Enhancement) is a speech interface to the virtual reality platform DIVE. DIVERSE is developed at SICS for use as a test system to experiment with multimodal interaction[17]. DIVERSE allows for spoken language control of operations that are normally carried out through direct manipulation in DIVE, such as transportation of objects, change of view, object creation, deletion, colouring etc, while still retaining the possibility to perform actions through direct manipulation whenever that is more suitable [16].

Interaction in DIVERSE is mediated through an animated agent to allow explicit modeling of the linguistic competence of the system, both in terms of output language and in terms of the gestures.

4.4.1 Spatial model

Inside the virtual environment that the DIVE system implements, there is a strong model of spatial interaction[7],[6]. This model provides a method of interaction for the operator, the robot, and the objects within the virtual and real worlds. In this section this spatial interaction model and the methods it suggests are described.

Here we summarize key concepts which constitute the DIVE and DIVERSE model of interaction, the details for this model can be found in [6] and [17]. The goal of the spatial model is to provide a small but powerful set of mechanisms for supporting the negotiation of interaction across shared virtual space. The spatial model, as its name suggests, uses the properties of space as the basis for mediating interaction. We briefly introduce the key abstractions of *space*, *objects, aura, awareness, focus, nimbus,* and *boundaries* which define part of the spatial model, and the concepts of *interlocutor* and *discourse compost* which are central to the linguistic interaction.

Aura is defined to be a sub-space which effectively bounds the presence of an object within a given medium and which acts as an enabler of potential interaction. Objects carry their auras with them when they move through space and when two auras collide, interaction between the objects in the medium becomes a possibility. It is the surrounding environment that monitors for aura collisions between objects.

Once aura has been used to determine the potential for object interactions, the objects themselves are subsequently responsible for controlling these interactions. This is achieved on the basis of quantifiable levels of **awareness** between them. Awareness between objects in a given medium is manipulated via **focus** and **nimbus**, further subspaces within which an object chooses to direct either its presence or its attention. More specifically, if you are an object in space the following examples help define the concept:

focus -the more another object is within your focus, the more aware you are of it;

nimbus -the more another object is within your nimbus, the more aware it is of you.

This notion of spatial focus as a way of directing attention and hence filtering information is intuitively familiar from our everyday experience (e.g. the concept of a visual focus). The notion of nimbus requires a little more explanation. In general terms, a nimbus is a sub-space in which an object makes some aspect of itself available to others. This could be its presence, identity, activity or some combination of these. Nimbus allows objects to try to influence others (i.e. to be heard or seen). Nimbus is the necessary converse of focus required to achieve a power balance in interaction.

Awareness levels are calculated from a combination of nimbus and focus. Aura, focus and nimbus may most often be implicitly manipulated through fundamental spatial actions such as movement and orientation. Additionally, aura, focus and nimbus may be manipulated through boundaries in space. Boundaries divide space into different areas and regions and provide mechanisms for marking territory, controlling movement and for influencing the interactional properties of space.

Language usage adds some complexity to the interface. Using language presupposes a *counterpart*, and the design of the dialog will hinge on how the counterpart is conceptualized. There are several conceivable models of the interlocutor [16, 17]. For the present application the robot itself is a natural counterpart for most tasks – the experiments in DIVERSE so far have involved a separately rendered **Agent** to anchor the discourse communicative competence of the system.

Determining what object an utterance refers to is non-trivial in the general case. Using the agent we model the system's conception of the world and the saliency of various objects by displaying a list of referents. This list – the **discourse compost** – is composed by the system giving each object present in the discourse a saliency grade, based on recent mention, highlightedness, gestural manipulation by the user, and above all, visual awareness. So, primarily, if the agent has a high degree of *awareness* of an object, it is a candidate for reference. This effect declines rapidly when the agent becomes less aware of it. Secondly, users can *manipulate* or *point at* an object. An object which the user points at gets a high saliency grade, with a rapid decline after the pointing gesture has been completed. Thirdly, we keep track of which objects have been mentioned. Objects in the recent *dialog history* are likely to be referred to again. The evidence from these different sources is compiled in the compost to determine which objects are likely future referents.

4.4.2 Methods

We use the interaction model to create an interactive and informationally rich immersive environment that stores the methods to aid the robots interaction in the real world. The concepts of aura, nimbus, focus are key to the way the robot interacts with the virtual and real worlds. Using the concepts of spatial boundaries and auras we can define interaction mechanisms and methods for sharing information between the robot and the environment.

For example using the concept of object aura we can define a means of transferring information for navigation and object identification. If the robot's aura collides with an object's aura that object may then open up a channel, i.e. the robot focuses and the object projects nimbus, thus enabling the object to pass information to the robot that would be pertinent to the mutual interaction. In this way each object stores information and methods about itself. This information can include: 1) object identification, 2) object function, 3) navigational approach method, 4) grasping method, 5) recognition method.

These last three types of information deserve special mention. An object may store the actual methods in which to perform a local interaction such as recognition. Given that the position of the object and the position of the robot are well known these methods can be rather specific.

Likewise, using the boundaries in space, various locations in the environment may store information and methods regarding navigation. For example there may be certain areas of the environment where great care must be taken, so crossing a boundary could then act like entering a 'speed control zone' and thus negotiate control for the robot's velocity. Similarly there could also be areas in the environment where certain configurations or specific paths should be avoided or taken. Crossing a boundary into such an area would open up a channel to transfer specific navigational commands to the robot.

Using this model of interaction unweights the robot control process from the need to have knowledge about the entire environment at all times. Using this spatial model we are distributing the processes and specific information throughout the environment. Also using the virtual world as a knowledge model in this way it makes it less necessary for a robot to have much knowledge about a new environment before actually entering it. Thus when the robot crosses the boundary into a new environment the new environment would contain all the necessary global information regarding that world.

4.5 How Do We Actually *Tell* The Robot What To Do?

Hitherto, controlling and manipulating a virtual or augmented reality has mainly been through *direct manipulation*, an interaction paradigm based on immediacy of control and tightly linked feedback between action and effect. Direct manipulation interfaces are generally share three main characteristics of 1. continuous representation of the object of interest, 2. physical actions or labeled button presses instead of complex syntax, and 3. rapid incremental reversible operations, whose impact on the object of interest is immediately visible [27].

These characteristics have usually been seen as standing in contrast to command based interfaces that build on more expressive forms of input such as formal command languages or human languages. While Shneiderman's points certainly have been understood as a justification for a completely analog interface representation such as pictures and graphs, and analog operations such as gestures, points one and three do not in fact in any way contradict the possibility of using text or other language input – indeed, any interface at all, be it language based or point-and-click based would do well to follow the principles. We will use language, in our case speech or typewritten text, as one of the mechanisms of interaction, thus relaxing the constraints posed by Shneiderman's second point, but continuing to observe points one and three. Language, as we will show below, is necessary to manage the level of complexity following from instructing a robot.

4.5.1 Why Charades Are Difficult

Virtual reality offers the user intuitively useful means of selecting and manipulating objects in the vicinity, much as gestures do in real life. Cognitive concepts like "this" and "that" are easily defined and formalized in virtual reality. Human languages are by design a step beyond deixis or the simple acts of ostentation behind "this" and "that". They allow the user to refer to entities other than concrete objects, using arbitrary conventions: abstract concepts ("air", "battery charge", "algorithm"), actions ("running", "picking up"), objects that are not present ("the tool kit in the other room"), objects that are no longer present ("my December salary"), objects that will be present ("Summer"), and objects and conditions that are impossible ("unicorn", "perpetuum mobile"), or objects with some specified property ("slow things").

Typical virtual reality tools constrain their users to the *here* and *now*, even if "here" and "now" may be defined differently than in physical reality. In figure 3, the reference to the grey marbles would be very difficult without the use of natural language. The idea that someone might want to refer to grey marbles if they are represented as in the picture ought not to be surprising: the concept of the set of grey marbles is not inherently complex. In figure 4, the reference to an object which is not actually present will pose a difficulty, unless there is a way of referring to objects that are not visible by their temporal location or their content. Referring to "virtual reality", as in the example, without using human language will of course be a considerable challenge.

The motive for including language in a robot-control interface is to add a level of abstraction to the system: to be able to specify goals on a higher-level than pointing at visible objects. This, of course, presupposes a level of representation abstract enough for symbolic reasoning: we have achieved this through the explicit model of the robot's real world knowledge in the virtual world.

5 Conclusions and Future Work

This paper describes the framework for including a human operator and a real robot in a remote environment in a virtual presence system. The virtual environment layer gives a natural level of representation for the world knowledge of the system; the robot is a natural repository for physical competence; the vision system for perceptual processing; and the multimodal interaction is an intuitive tool for control.

Besides consolidating the framework into a complete system and improving the various modules in it, there are some natural openings to continue development. The perceptual module (grounded on the remote physical layer) should accommodate higher level processing of other sensory data, both human-like speech or sound recognition and placement and non-human, such as temperature and other measurement interpretation; including renditions of information about various other actors and objects in the virtual environment; the interface must be capable of modeling more sophisticated knowledge that the robot learns – physical competence, among other things.

In addition to having tight temporal and causal coupling between virtual and real environments, the operator could move around the virtual environment freely, without involving the robot, and specify tasks for the robot to perform. As the operator navigates through the virtual environment the operator can specify point-to-point navigational tasks as well as pick-and-drop manipulation tasks. These then turn into batch-like higher-level goals – or in essence, programs by high-level example – to be submitted at some later time for the robot's navigational path-finding and grasping systems.

currsize

References

[1] Magnus Andersson, Lennart E. Fahlén, and Torleif Söderlund. A virtual environment user interface for a robotic assistive device. In *Proceedings of the second European Conference on the Advancement of Rehabilitation Technology*, pages 33–57, Stockholm, May 1993.

[2] Ronald Arkin. Reactive control as a substrate for telerobotic systems. *IEEE AES Systems Magazine*, pages 24–31, June 1991.

[3] Ronald Arkin and Khaled S. Ali. Integration of reactive and telerobotic control in multi-agent robotic systems. In *Proceedings of Third International Conference on Simulation of Adaptive Behavior: From Animals to Animats*, Brighten, UK, 1994.

[4] W.A. Aviles, T.W. Hughes, H.R. Everett, A.Y. Martin, and A.H. Koyamatsu. Issues in mobile robotics: The unmanned ground vehicle program teleoperated vehicle (tov). In *SPIE Vol. 1388 Mobile Robots V*, pages 587–597, 1990.

[5] S Benford, J. Bowers, L. Fahlén, and C. Greenhalg. Managing mutual awareness in collaborative virtual environments. In *Proceedings of VRST'94*, ACM, Singapore, 1994.

[6] S. Benford and L. Fahlen. A spatial model of interaction in large virtual environments. In *Third European Conference on Computer-Supported Cooperative Work*, pages 109–124. Kluwer Academic Publishers, 1993.

[7] Steve Benford, John Bowers, Lennart E. Fahlen, Chris Greenhalgh, John Mariani, and Tom Rodden. Networked virtual reality and co-operative work. *To appear in Presence*, 1995.

[8] Alan W. Biermann, Bruce W. Ballard, , and Anne H. Sigmon. An experimental study of natural language programming. *International journal of man-machine studies*, 18:71–87, 1983.

[9] Edwin Bos, Carla Huls, , and Wim Claassen. Edward: full integration of language and action in a multimodal user interface. *International Journal of Human-Computer Studies*, 40:473–495, 1994.

[10] S. Bouffouix and M. Bogaert. Real time navigation and obstacle avoidance for teleoperated vehicles. In *SPIE Vol. 1831 Mobile Robots VII*, pages 265–275, 1992.

[11] Ivan Bretan, Niklas Frost, and Jussi Karlgren. Using surface syntax in interactive interfaces. In *The 10th Nordic Conference of Computational Linguistics*, University of Helsinki, 1995.

[12] Christer Carlsson and Olof Hagsand. DIVE – a platform for multi-user virtual environments. *Computers and Graphics*, 17(6), 1993.

[13] R. Chandrasekar and S. Ramani. Interactive communication of sentential structure and content: an alternative approach to man-machine communication. *International Journal of Man-Machine Studies*, 30:121–148, 1989.

[14] Philip R. Cohen. The role of natural language in a multimodal interface. In *Proceedings of the ACM Symposium on User Interface Software and Technology (UIST)*, pages pp. 143–150, Monterey, CA, 1992.

[15] Steven Feiner, Blair MacIntyre, and Doree Seligmann. Knowledge-based augmented reality. *Communications of the ACM*, 36(7):52–62, July 1993.

[16] Bretan I. *Natural Language in Model World Interfaces*. Licentiate Thesis, Department of Computer and Systems Sciences. The Royal Institute of Technology and Stockholm University, Stockholm Sweden, 1995.

[17] Jussi Karlgren, Ivan Bretan, Niklas Frost, and Lars Jonsson. Interaction models, reference, and interactivity for speech interfaces to virtual environments. *Proceedings of Second Eurographics Workshop on Virtual Environments – Realism and Real Time*, 1995.

[18] Fred Karlsson. Constraint grammar for parsing running text. In Karlgren, editor, *Thirteenth International Conference On Computational Linguistics (COLING - 90)*, University of Helsinki, Helsinki, 1990.

[19] Fred Karlsson, Atro Voutilainen, Juha Heikkila, and Arto Anttila (eds.). *Constraint Grammar*. Mouton de Gruyter, Berlin, 1995.

[20] Jacqueline H. Kim, Richard J. Weidner, and Allan L. Sacks. Using virtual reality for science mission planning: A mars pathfinder case. In *ISMCR 1994: Topical Workshop on Virtual Reality*, pages 37–42, Houston, 1994. NASA Conference publication 10163.

[21] Eric Krotkov. Mobile robot localization using a single image. In *IEEE Proceedings of Robotics and Automation*, pages 978–983, 1989.

[22] M. Mallem, F. Chavand, and E. Colle. Computer-assisted visual perception in teleoperated robotics. *Robotica (10)*, pages 99–103, 1992.

[23] Paul Milgram and David Drascic. Enhancement of 3-d video displays by means of superimposed stereo-graphics. In *Proceedings of the Human Factors Society 35th Annual Meeting*, pages 1457–1461, 1991.

[24] NASA. *Proceedings of the NASA Conference on Space Telerobotics*. JPL Publication 89-7, Vol 1-5, Pasadena, Ca, 1989.

[25] Jane Robinson. Dependency structures and transformational rules. *Language*, 46:259 – 285, 1970.

[26] Eric Rose, David Breen, Klaus H. Ahlers, Chris Compton, Mihran Tuceryan, Ross Whitaker, and Douglas Greer. Annotating real-world objects using augmented vision. Technical report, European Computer-Industry Research Center GmbH, Arabellastrasse 17 D-81925 Munich, 1994.

[27] Ben Shneiderman. Natural vs. precise concise languages for human operation of computers: Research issues and experimental approaches. In *Proceedings of the 18th Annual Meeting of the Association for Computational Linguistics*, Philadelphia, 1980.

[28] K. T. Simsarian, N. Nandhakumar, and T. J. Olson. Mobile robot self-localization from range data using view-invariant regions. In *IEEE Proceedings of the 5th International Symposium on Intelligent Control*, pages 1038–1043, 1990.

[29] P.C Woodland, J.J. Odell V. Valtchev, and S.J. Young. Large vocabulary continuous speech recognition using htk. In *Proceedings of ICASSP'94, Adelaide*, 1994.

Editors' Note: See Appendix, p. 310 for coloured figures of this paper

Quick Elimination of Non-Interference Polytopes in Virtual Environments

Kelvin Chung and Wenping Wang
tlchung@cs.hku.hk   *wenping@cs.hku.hk*
Department of Computer Science
University of Hong Kong
Pokfulam Road, Hong Kong

Abstract

The problem of collision detection is fundamental to interactive applications such as computer animation and virtual environments. In these fields, prompt recognition of possible impacts is important for computing real-time response. However, existing algorithms do not eliminate non-interfence objects efficiently. This paper presents a practical algorithm to quickly eliminate most non-interference convex polyhedra when their bounding boxes overlap. The idea is to search for a proper separating plane between two polyhedra and cache this plane as a witness for the next time step. Temporal and geometric coherences are exploited in this algorithm so that it runs in expected constant time.

1 Introduction

The problem of collision detection has been extensively studied in many fields. Most of the research makes use of rectangular bounding boxes or a hierarchy of them as the first step to quickly eliminate most non-interference objects. For n bounding boxes, a sweep and prune technique [1] can achieve an expected $O(n + e)$ time by projecting the endpoints of three-dimensional bounding boxes onto the x, y, z axes and sorting them at each time instant. Other methods to reduce the complexity of testing the intersection of bounding boxes include spatial subdivision [3], octree [2], scheduling [4] and progressive refinement [14].

When the bounding boxes of objects overlap, usually an exact collision detection algorithm is called. In [5], a face octree is built for the faces of objects that intersect the overlapping region of bounding boxes to check for possible intersection. In [6] the rectangular box of an object is subdivided into cells with each cell containing a list of facets intersecting the cell. Intersection is done by considering only the facets in the overlapped cells. In [9], a data structure, called a "BRep-Index", is used for quick spatial access of polyhedra in order to localize contact regions between two objects. In [15], an expected linear time algorithm which computes the minimum distance and a separating plane of two objects is proposed. In [11] separating planes for pairs of objects are found by the above expected linear time algorithm and cached [10] to yield a reply of non-collision most of the time using temporal coherence. However, it also takes linear time in the following time frame to test the validity of the cached separating plane. In [16], a sub-quadratic running time algorithm is proposed. When the motion is restricted to be translation only, the best theoretical time is $O(\log^2 n)$, using the hierarchical representation of convex polyhedra [12]. Other methods to detect collision include octree ([1], [7]) and BSP tree ([3]), where each triangular patch is bounded by an axis-aligned bounding box. In [17], the ideas of [1] and [8] are extended to deal with concave polyhedra.

In [8], the closest points between pairs of convex polytopes are tracked. This method maintains a pair of closest features for each pair of convex polytopes and computes the Euclidean distance between the features to detect collisions based on Voronoi regions. The algorithm takes advantage of coherence and runs in expected constant time if the polytopes do not move swiftly. However, in most applications the closest features are not of great interest to the program when the polytopes do not collide. So it is not worth continuing to compute the closest features once it is known that a separating plane exists between the two polytopes. Moreover, this algorithm is complicated to implement.

Our algorithm is not for exact collision detection. It eliminates efficiently most non-interference object pairs by looking for a separating plane between two polytopes. It does not have to compute the closest features and is simple to implement. Moreover, it considers polyhedral vertices only but not edges and faces as in [8] and it either terminates when it finds a separating plane or stops after a prescribed number of iterations when it cannot find a separating plane. Temporal and geometric coherences are exploited so that it runs in expected constant time empirically. In essence, our algorithm extends and combines the ideas of [1], [8], [15], [11].

2 The Algorithm

2.1 The Algorithm Overview

The basic idea of our algorithm is to eliminate non-interference polytopes quickly using the fact that two polytopes are separated if and only if there exists a plane such that they belong to opposing half-spaces of this plane [18]. This algorithm acts as an intermediate step between the bounding box routine and the exact collision detection routine. It can eliminate nearly all the non-interference polytopes before a usually time-consuming exact collision detection routine must be called. We propose to handle collision detection of convex polytopes in a large-scale virtual environment in four steps :

1. Use spatial partitioning to eliminate non-interference objects that belong to different regions.

2. Within each region, use the sweep and prune technique [1] to quickly identify object pairs whose rectangular bounding boxes overlap.

3. Use our separating vector algorithm to eliminate non-interference objects whose bounding boxes overlap. Nearly all non-interference objects can be removed in this step to avoid further consideration.

4. When step (3) fails to eliminate a pair of polytopes as non-interference, they probably intersect. Then an exact collision detection algorithm proposed by Gilbert [15] is used. The two supporting vertices found in step (3) are used for initialization in that algorithm.

2.2 Searching for a proper separating vector

To illustrate the idea of our algorithm, the 2D version is shown in Figure 1(i), which shows two non-overlapping convex polygons P and Q.

Definition: *Let $\mathbf{V}$ denote the set of vertices of the convex polytope P. A supporting vertex of P in the direction $\mathbf{S}$ is $\mathbf{u} \in \mathbf{V}$ such that $\mathbf{S} \cdot \mathbf{u} \geq \mathbf{S} \cdot \mathbf{w}$ for all $\mathbf{w} \in \mathbf{V}$.*

Note that a supporting vertex of polytope P in a direction $\mathbf{S}$ always exists but may not be unique.

Initially a unit vector $\mathbf{S_1}$ is chosen and a supporting vertex $\mathbf{p_1}$ of P in the direction $\mathbf{S_1}$ is found. Similarly, a supporting vertex $\mathbf{q_1}$ of Q in direction $-\mathbf{S_1}$ is found. Then the following criterion with $i = 1$ is used to test whether P and Q collide. P and Q do not collide if

$$\mathbf{S_i} \cdot (\mathbf{q_i} - \mathbf{p_i}) > 0 \qquad (1)$$

for some direction $\mathbf{S_i}$, where $\mathbf{p_i}$ and $\mathbf{q_i}$ are supporting vertices of P and Q in the direction $\mathbf{S_i}$ and $-\mathbf{S_i}$ respectively. This is based on the following lemma.

Lemma 1: *Given a direction $\mathbf{S}$, let $\mathbf{p}$ be a supporting vertex of polytope P in the direction $\mathbf{S}$ and $\mathbf{q}$ be a supporting vertex of polytope Q in the direction $-\mathbf{S}$. If $\mathbf{S} \cdot (\mathbf{q} - \mathbf{p}) > 0$, then P and Q do not intersect.*

Proof: Since $\mathbf{p}$ is a supporting vertex of P in the direction $\mathbf{S}$, $\mathbf{S} \cdot \mathbf{p} \geq \mathbf{S} \cdot \mathbf{v}$ for all vertices $\mathbf{v}$ in P. Similarly, $\mathbf{S} \cdot \mathbf{w} \geq \mathbf{S} \cdot \mathbf{q}$ for all vertices $\mathbf{w}$ in Q. By the condition $\mathbf{S} \cdot (\mathbf{q} - \mathbf{p}) > 0$, we have $\mathbf{S} \cdot \mathbf{w} \geq \mathbf{S} \cdot \mathbf{q} > \mathbf{S} \cdot \mathbf{p} \geq \mathbf{S} \cdot \mathbf{v}$. Since $\mathbf{S} \cdot \mathbf{q} > \mathbf{S} \cdot \mathbf{p} \Rightarrow \mathbf{S} \cdot \mathbf{q} > \mathbf{S} \cdot (\mathbf{p} + \mathbf{q})/2 > \mathbf{S} \cdot \mathbf{p}$, we have $\mathbf{S} \cdot \mathbf{w} > \mathbf{S} \cdot (\mathbf{p} + \mathbf{q})/2 > \mathbf{S} \cdot \mathbf{v}$. Hence the plane with normal $\mathbf{S}$ and containing the point $(\mathbf{p} + \mathbf{q})/2$ separates P and Q properly; that is, they belong to the opposing half-spaces of this plane. □

A vector $\mathbf{S}$ is called a *separating vector* of the two polytopes if it is the normal vector of a separating plane of the two polytopes. Note that the vector pointing from the closest point of P to the closest point of Q is a separating vector of the two polytopes.

If condition (1) does not hold, P and Q may still not collide. Then we find another direction $\mathbf{S_2}$ based on $\mathbf{S_1}$ and supporting vertices $\mathbf{p_2}$ and $\mathbf{q_2}$ of P and

Q, respectively, in this new direction S_2. The direction S_2 is defined by the following expression with $i = 1$.

$$S_{i+1} = \langle ((q_i - p_i) \times S_i) \times (q_i - p_i) \rangle \qquad (2)$$

where $\langle x \rangle$ denotes $x/\|x\|$. Note that S_{i+1} is perpendicular to the vector $q_i - p_i$ (see Figure 1(iii)).

The vector S_{i+1} is chosen by Eqn. (2) because a separating vector is most likely to be in this direction. Moreover, in Section 3 we will prove that this direction S_{i+1} is guaranteed to be closer to any separating vector of P and Q than S_i is, provided that P and Q do not collide.

To locate p_2 and q_2, it is sufficient to use local search since the polytopes are convex. Thus this searching step takes expected constant time due to geometric coherence. Details of this local search is given in the next section. Once p_2 and q_2 are found, condition (1) is tested again. If $S_2 \cdot (q_2 - b_2) > 0$ then the procedure returns non-colliding pairs P and Q. If condition (1) fails, the above procedure is repeated.

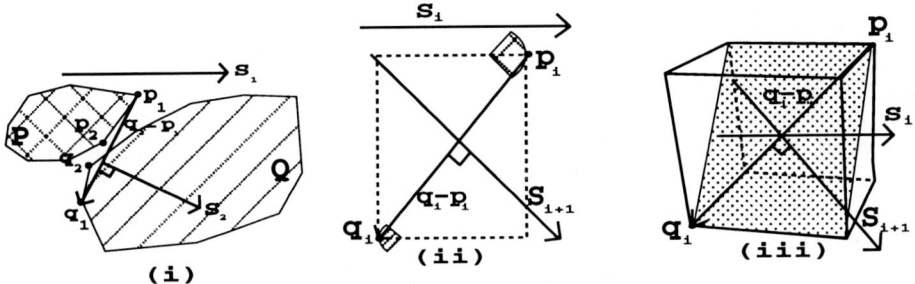

Figure 1: Searching for separating vector (i) idea (ii) in 2D (iii) in 3D.

If the procedure cannot determine a proper separating plane after k iterations for some prescribed k, it is most likely that P and Q intersect. In this case an exact collision detection routine proposed by Gilbert [15] is called with initial vertices p_k and q_k for P and Q, respectively. These special initial vertices guarantee that Gilbert's algorithm can terminate quickly because they are very close to the actual closest vertices between the two polytopes. Thus the effort spent on finding p_k and q_k is not wasted.

Experimental results show that, with $k = 3$, more than 95% of non-colliding polytopes are eliminated by this algorithm before a time-consuming exact collision detection routine has to be called and this performance is almost independent of the number of vertices of polytopes.

2.3 Searching for a supporting vertex

The searching algorithm outlined in [1] is used to find the supporting vertex. Basically, the current vertex is compared to the neighboring vertices to see if its dot product with **S** is the largest. If not, this vertex is replaced by a neighboring vertex with the largest dot product with **S**, and the process is repeated. This local search can find a supporting vertex eventually due to convexity. To speed up the searching process, we use a timestamp for each vertex to remember which vertices have already been considered. This timestamp is a counter which increments by one every time the local search is performed. When searching for the new supporting vertices, a vertex is ignored if its timestamp matches the current timestamp. Otherwise the dot product is evaluated and its timestamp is set to the current timestamp.

When searching for a supporting vertex of a polytope, the vector $\mathbf{S_i}$ is transformed to the local coordinate system of the polytope by the inverse of the rotation matrix of the polytope. After a supporting vertex is found, the vertex is transformed back to the world coordinate. Hence only two coordinate transformations are required for each search. This searching process runs in expected constant time because of the temporal and geometric coherences and the convexity of polytopes.

2.4 Choosing the initial searching direction

When the bounding boxes of two polytopes overlap for the first time, there are three cases in general (see Figure 2). In each of these cases, an initial searching direction $\mathbf{S_1}$ is chosen to be the normal vector of the plane formed by some contact points between the two bounding boxes. This vector is chosen, instead of the direction of the line connecting the two polytopes' centers, because the separating vector is most likely to be in this direction when the two bounding boxes of polytopes overlap for the first time. For the less likely case where one bounding box is completely contained inside the other, the line segment connecting the two bounding boxes' centers is chosen.

Although the above method gives a good estimate of a separating vector, for polytopes with a small number of vertices, the line segment connecting the two polytopes' centers may be a better choice. That is because both methods may end up with the same supporting vertices $\mathbf{p_1}$ and $\mathbf{q_1}$ for simple polytopes, and the overhead of computing the initial searching direction as in Figure 2 may be large.

2.5 Caching

In each time frame, the separating vector and the two supporting vertices found are cached. If the polytopes collide in this time frame, the separating vector and the two supporting vertices of the last time frame in which polytopes do not collide are cached. The previous separating vector is used as the initial searching direction $\mathbf{S_1}$ in the next time frame. Since the objects do not move swiftly in a virtual environment, this vector is likely to be a separating vector in the current time frame. Similarly, the supporting vertices found in the previous

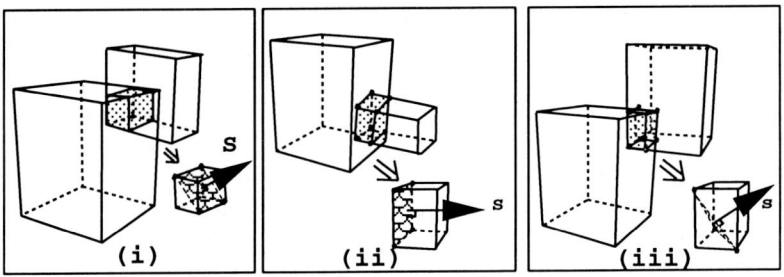

Figure 2: Three cases to find the initial separating vector

time frame are used to search for the new supporting vertices in the current time frame. Due to temporal and geometric coherences this searching step runs in expected constant time.

2.6 Preprocessing

When for the first time bounding boxes overlap, an arbitrary vertex can be used to start the searching algorithm to find the supporting vertex. To be more efficient, we precompute supporting vertices in various directions and store them in a 2D table. Given a supporting direction, this initial vertex can be retrieved in constant time from the array. The larger is the size of this 2D table, the closer is this initial vertex to the true supporting vertex and, the more quickly does this searching algorithm perform.

3 Proof of Convergence

Lemma 2: *Given a unit vector S_i, let p_i and q_i be the supporting vertices of polytopes P and Q in the direction S_i and $-S_i$ respectively. Suppose that P and Q do not collide and w is any separating vector of P and Q. If $S_1 \cdot w > 0$ and $S_i \cdot (q_i - p_i) < 0$, then*

$$S_{i+1} \cdot w > S_i \cdot w > 0, \quad i = 1, 2, \ldots \tag{3}$$

where S_{i+1} is defined as in Eqn.(2).

Proof: Let $r_i = \langle q_i - p_i \rangle$, where $\langle x \rangle = x/\|x\|$. Then we have $r_i \cdot S_i < 0$.

$$\begin{aligned} S_{i+1} \cdot w &= \langle (r_i \times S_i) \times r_i \rangle \cdot w \\ &= \langle S_i - (r_i \cdot S_i) r_i \rangle \cdot w \\ &= ((S_i \cdot w) - (r_i \cdot S_i)(r_i \cdot w))/L_i \end{aligned}$$

where $L_i^2 = ((r_i \times S_i) \times r_i) \cdot ((r_i \times S_i) \times r_i) = 1 - (S_i \cdot r_i)^2$.

Because for any separating vector w, $(q' - p') \cdot w > 0$ for any point $p' \in P, q' \in Q$, $r_i \cdot w > 0$. Since $r_i \cdot S_i < 0$,

$$L_i(\mathbf{S_{i+1}} \cdot \mathbf{w}) - \mathbf{S_i} \cdot \mathbf{w} = -(\mathbf{r_i} \cdot \mathbf{S_i})(\mathbf{r_i} \cdot \mathbf{w}) > 0$$

So

$$L_i(\mathbf{S_{i+1}} \cdot \mathbf{w}) > \mathbf{S_i} \cdot \mathbf{w}. \tag{4}$$

Since $0 \leq L_i \leq 1$ and $\mathbf{S_1} \cdot \mathbf{w} > 0$, we have, by induction, $\mathbf{S_{i+1}} \cdot \mathbf{w} > \mathbf{S_i} \cdot \mathbf{w} > 0$. □

Hence if the two polytopes do not collide and $\mathbf{S_i}$ is not a separating vector, then $\mathbf{S_{i+1}}$ given by Eqn.(2) is closer to any separating vector than $\mathbf{S_i}$ is, since by Lemma 2 the angle between $\mathbf{S_{i+1}}$ and $\mathbf{w}$ is smaller than the angle between $\mathbf{S_i}$ and $\mathbf{w}$. Choosing the initial vector to be the line segment connecting the two polytopes' centers ensures that $\mathbf{S_1} \cdot \mathbf{w} \geq 0$. We also assume that the polytopes do not move swiftly so that the condition $\mathbf{S_1} \cdot \mathbf{w} \geq 0$ holds for the cached vector $\mathbf{S_1}$, which is the supporting vector of the previous time frame.

Another property of the algorithm is that if the pair $\mathbf{p_i}$ and $\mathbf{q_i}$ appear in two consecutive steps, then P and Q do not collide, as indicated by the following lemma.

Lemma 3: *If* $\mathbf{S_i} \cdot (\mathbf{q_i} - \mathbf{p_i}) < 0$ *and* $\mathbf{p_{i+1}} = \mathbf{p_i}$, $\mathbf{q_{i+1}} = \mathbf{q_i}$, *then* $\mathbf{S_{i+1}} \cdot \mathbf{r_{i+1}} > 0$, *i.e.* P *and* Q *do not collide.*

Proof: Let $\mathbf{r_i} = \langle \mathbf{q_i} - \mathbf{p_i} \rangle$ and $\mathbf{r_{i+1}} = \langle \mathbf{q_{i+1}} - \mathbf{p_{i+1}} \rangle$, we have $\mathbf{r_i} = \mathbf{r_{i+1}}$.

$$\begin{aligned}
\mathbf{S_{i+1}} \cdot \mathbf{r_{i+1}} &= \mathbf{S_{i+1}} \cdot \mathbf{r_i} \\
&= \langle (\mathbf{r_i} \times \mathbf{S_i}) \times \mathbf{r_i} \rangle \cdot \mathbf{r_i} \\
&= \langle \mathbf{S_i} - (\mathbf{r_i} \cdot \mathbf{S_i})\mathbf{r_i} \rangle \cdot \mathbf{r_i} \\
&= ((\mathbf{S_i} \cdot \mathbf{r_i}) - (\mathbf{r_i} \cdot \mathbf{S_i})(\mathbf{r_i} \cdot \mathbf{r_i}))/L_i \\
&= 0
\end{aligned}$$

where $L_i^2 = 1 - (\mathbf{S_i} \cdot \mathbf{r_i})^2$.

Hence we have $\mathbf{S_{i+1}} \cdot (\mathbf{q_{i+1}} - \mathbf{p_{i+1}}) = 0$. This means that P and Q do not overlap. Note that P and Q may touch each other in this case but we consider the touching case as non-collide. □

4 Experiments

Experiments have been carried out to investigate how the number of searching steps k is related to the percentage of non-interference objects eliminated by this algorithm. The simulation uses 100 polytopes of the same size moving in a closed environment for 1000 frames. Each object has its translational velocity equal to 5% of its radius and rotational velocity of 10 degrees per time frames. A precomputed table for the supporting vertex of size 8x16 is used. When there is a collision between two polytopes, their rotational and translational velocities are reversed. Three different types of polytopes are used: an ellipsoid, a long thin rod and a flat circular plate. Points are randomly sampled on the surface

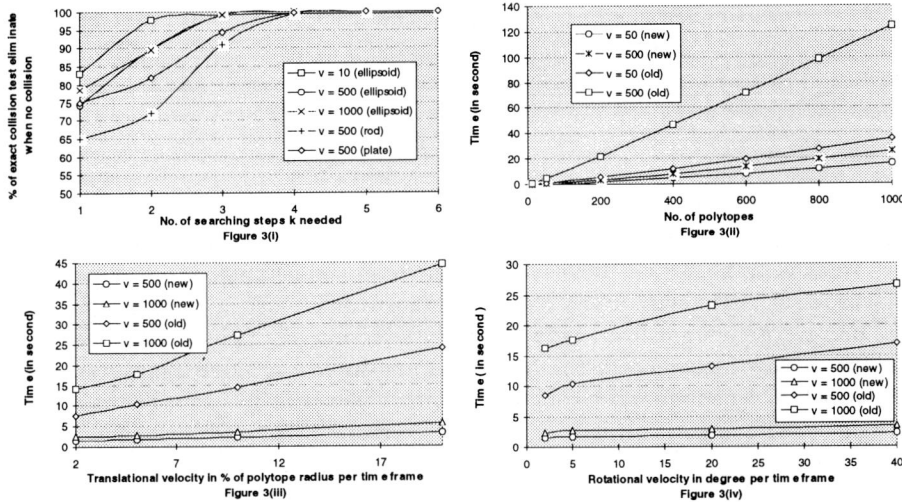

Figure 3(i)
Figure 3(ii)
Figure 3(iii)
Figure 3(iv)

of these objects to give the vertices of the polytope; the number of vertices is indicated in Fig.3. Fig.3(i) shows that, when $k = 3$, more than 90% of pairs of non-interference objects with overlapping bounding boxes are reported as non-interference by this algorithm. In the case of ellipsoids, this figure increases to 99%. This collision test is called only when the tightest rectangular bounding boxes of two polytopes overlap [1].

However, we have found some cases where supporting vertices found during the searching step repeat themselves alternately between two pairs of fixed vertices, though the two polytopes do not collide. As a result, this algorithm does not guarantee that a separating vector can be found in a finite number of steps.

We also compared our algorithm with the closest features tracking algorithm, which is the fastest algorithm so far [1]. The comparison is carried out under the following conditions : (1) different number of polytopes; (2) different speeds for translational movement; (3) different speeds of rotational movement. The experiments are carried out by using our algorithm to replace the lowest layer of the I_COLLIDE[1] source code which detects collision between two polytopes using the closest features tracking algorithm. The simulation is done on SGI/Reality Engine and there are 100 polytopes in the environment. The shape of an ellipsoid is used. Fig.3(ii) shows the simulation time with different no. of polytopes and different complexity of polytopes in the environment. The results show that our algorithm is much faster in all cases. In Fig.3(iii), when the translational velocity is changed from 2% to 20% of object radius per time frame, the simulation time of our algorithm increases slightly, while the simulation time for the closest features tracking algorithm increases substantially. That is because when the translational velocity increases, the closest features tracking algorithm needs more time to locate the closest points between polytopes. Moreover, the I_COLLIDE library needs to call another linear programming algorithm for exact collision detection every time when there is a recycling of features. Similarly, when the rotational velocity is increased from 5 degrees to 40 degrees per time frame we can see (Fig.3(iv)) that our algorithm takes only a little longer time while the closest features tracking algorithm takes substantially longer time to finish.

5 Conclusion

We have proposed an efficient algorithm to quickly eliminate non-interference polytopes in virtual environments. This algorithm closely integrates the bounding box algorithm and the exact collision detection algorithm and serves as an additional layer between them. Nearly all non-interface polytopes can be eliminated before a usually more time-consuming exact collision detection algorithm is called. This algorithm is fast and simple to implement. With caching, preprocessing and local searching, this algorithm takes advantage of coherence to run in empirically expected constant time.

References

1. D. J. Cohen, M.C. Lin, D. Manocha, M. Ponamgi. I-Collide: An interactive and exact collision detection system for large-scale environments, *Proceeding of Symposium of Interactive 3D Graphics*, pp. 189-196, 1995.
2. M. Moore and J. Wilhelms. Collision detection and response for computer animation, *ACM Computer Graphics*, Vol. 22, No. 4, pp. 289-298, 1988.
3. W. Thibault and B. Naylor. Set operations on polyhedra using binary space partitioning trees, *ACM Computer Graphics*, 4, pp. 153-162, 1987.
4. A. Foisy., V. Hayward, and S. Aubry. The use of awareness in collision prediction, *International Conference on Robotics and Automation*, pp. 338-343. IEEE, 1990.
5. A. Smith, Yoshifumi Kitamu, Haruo Takemura and Fumio Kishino. A simple and efficient method for accurate collision detection among deformable polyhedral objects in arbitrary motion, *Virtual Reality Annual International Symposium*, pp. 136-145, IEEE, 1995.
6. A. Garcia-Alonso, N. Serrano and J. Flaquer. Solving the collision detection problem, *IEEE Computer Graphics and Applications*, 13(3), pp. 36-43, 1994.
7. Y. Yang and N. Thalmann. An improved algorithm for collision detection in cloth animation with human body, *First Pacific Conference on Computer Graphics and Application*, pp. 237-251, 1993.
8. M. Lin and J. Canny. Efficient collision detection for animation, *Proceedings of the Third Eurographics Workshop on Animation and Simulation*, Cambridge, 1991.
9. W. Bouma and G. Vanecek. Collision detection and analysis in a physical based simulation, *Eurographics Workshop on Animation and Simulation*, pp. 191-203, September, 1991.
10. D. Baraff. Curved surfaces and coherence for non-penetrating rigid body simulation, *ACM Computer Graphics*, Vol. 24, No. 4, pp. 19-28, 1990.

11. Rich Rabbitz. Fast collision detection of moving convex polyhedra, *Graphics Gem IV*, AP Professional, pp. 83-109, 1994.

12. D.P. Dobkin and D.G. Kirkpatrick. A linear algorithm for determining the separation of convex polyhedra. *Journal of Algorithms*, pp. 381-392, 1985.

13. M. C. Lin. Efficient Collision Detection for Animation and Robotics, *PhD thesis*, Department of Electrical Engineering and Computer Science, University of California, Berkeley, December 1993.

14. Philip M. Hubbard. Collision Detection for Interactive Graphics Applications, *IEEE Transactions on Visualization and Computer Graphics*, Vol. 1, No. 3, pp. 218-228, 1995.

15. E. G. Gilbert, D. W. Johnson, and S. S. Keerthi. A fast procedure for computing the distance between complex object in three-dimensional space, *IEEE Journal of Robotics and Automation*, 4(2):193-203, 1988.

16. Elmar Schomer and Christian Thiel. Efficient collision detection for moving polyhedra, *Proceedings of the 11th Annual Symposium on Computational Geometry*, pp. 51-60, 1995.

17. M. Ponamgi, D. Manocha and M. Lin, Incremental algorithms for collision detection between solid models, *Proceedings of ACM/Siggraph symposium on Solid Modeling*, pp. 293-304, 1995.

18. R. T. Rockafellar, *Convex Analysis*. Princeton University Press, 1970.

Integrating Graphics Into Video
Image-Based Camera Tracking and Filtering

Peter Wißkirchen, Klaus Kansy, Günther Schmitgen
GMD – German National Research Center for Information Technology
53754 Sankt Augustin, Germany
E-mail: wisskirchen@gmd.de

Abstract. In virtual studios, most of the setting is not constructed in reality but generated synthetically by a graphics computer and mixed into the camera image. A convincing mixing requires very precise coordination of the real camera with the graphics pipeline, especially in the case of camera moves. This process is called camera tracking.

The paper describes an image-based algorithm for camera tracking. The algorithm uses real world reference points which are identified interactively in the first image and tracked in the image sequence in real-time. Based on these measurements, the camera data is calculated. The most demanding task is the smoothing of measurements and camera data to achieve stable and coherent camera moves. Kalman filtering methods are used to eliminate jitters from the calculated camera data.

Keywords. Virtual studio, visual effects, synchronization, image processing, Kalman filtering, camera tracking.

1 Introduction

In the last years, computer graphics has been successfully applied for enriching movies. Several movies have been produced that integrate computer-generated animations with real scenes. "Jurassic Parc" is a well known and often cited example. Animations in such movies have been generated by highly specialized artists and computer scientists who spent a lot of time on the careful design and compilation of individual scenes. The integration is usually performed individually frame by frame. In a static situation where the camera settings (position, pan, tilt, roll, zoom) and the lighting conditions remain unchanged, the setting of the graphics pipeline and the surface attributes have to be established only once for all frames. If camera settings or lighting conditions are allowed to change dynamically, the synthetic objects have to be generated differently for each individual frame.

In contrast to the above interactive approaches, recent activities favor *real-time integration* of synthetic computer graphics and video. Real-time implies that the integration has to be performed automatically on the fly in a time close to the video frame rate ($\frac{1}{25}$ sec). This prohibits manual assistance—with the possible exception of the initialization phase. The current settings of camera and lighting have to be recorded on-line and transformed into a corresponding setting of the synthetic camera and the synthetic world. The changes have to take effect immediately.

There are a number of interesting application scenarios for these techniques [Kansy et al. 1995, 1996], mainly in virtual studios currently introduced into the TV industry. Rather than building different studios with characteristic settings for each single TV show, the video will be captured in front of a blue background which can be replaced with any desired synthetic background. Blue screen technology is currently used extensively in studios. It allows the use of hopefully less expensive virtual settings and could re-use one real studios for different shows by changing the set with one

Fig. 1. View into the virtual studio   **Fig. 2.** Merge of real and virtual scene

computer command. Figure 1 shows a look into a virtual studio from the camera perspective. The blue background can be automatically replaced by any synthetic image (Figure 2).

Usually, the camera is static: it does not change its position, zoom, and other camera parameters. The benefits of a real three-dimensional background, however, can be exploited only when the camera setting is allowed to change arbitrarily. For a realistic result, the camera parameters have to be tracked precisely such that no distortion between real and synthetic image becomes visible. The three-dimensional background has to be rendered in real-time to be coherent with the real scene.

Virtual props extend the classical props used in theater: they are synthetic objects included into the video image and share the capabilities of real props and computer controlled items. Props close to real items have to be positioned very precisely to avoid the impression of a relative movement (floating effect). In a medical discussion, a three-dimensional and partly transparent heart could be integrated into the scene. In an outdoor setting, synthetic objects could be inserted into a landscape, e.g., a bridge into a valley or a new building into a city view. In all these cases, the viewing parameters of the camera may vary and have to be tracked in real-time such that real and virtual objects move coherently without visible delays.

2 State of the art

The settings of the real camera can be measured directly by putting sensors on the camera. One of the first sensor system was the Ultimatte Memory Head; currently one can choose among several different sensor systems [Sommerhäuser 1966]. However, sensor systems imply special equipment which is expensive, clumsy, and not available everywhere—for instance not outside of studios. The precision of the sensors is a limiting factor which restricts the allowable camera moves. For instance, the camera typically does not change its place during one shot.

Within the RACE II project MonaLisa, the ELSET system has been developed with a real-time camera tracking server [Routsis et al. 1994] where the setting of the real camera is determined solely by analyzing the video image. For each frame, pattern recognition in the video is performed to derive the current view direction and the zoom factor of the camera. The camera position cannot be calculated by this system and, therefore, the camera has to remain at a fixed position.

The aim of our work [Kansy et al. 1995, 1996] was to develop a scheme where the camera is allowed to move freely without restrictions and, even, to support shoulder cameras. It was clear that only an image-based approach could provide sufficient precision because it allows for a feed-back from the camera image and, hence, can position objects with pixel precision and maintain this precision over long camera moves. To calculate the camera position, it is necessary to recognize a three-dimensional structure within the images. Standard algorithms [Bogart 1991] require at least four reference positions with known world coordinates within each frame, to calculate all seven geometric camera parameters (i.e., camera position (3 coordinates), camera orientation (3 angles), and the zoom factor). The reference positions have to be spread over all dimensions of the three-dimensional space to allow the calculation.

The need for known reference points in the video image is not a big problem in a virtual studio where respective reference structures can easily be provided within the blue background or by furniture within the studio. On the contrary, such reference points can provide additional functionality as they can be used as anchor points for precise positioning of synthetic objects within the video scene relative to real objects.

The Israelian company ORAD [ORAD 1995] is developing a competing product called "ORAD's Virtual Set". Their prototype system provides a "virtual set solution that enables moving the cameras or even using a shoulder camera." It is based on a careful chosen pattern of light blue stripes on the dark blue wall rather than individual points and uses the new DSP processors TMS320C80 (MVP) of Texas Instruments for analysing the pattern and deriving the seven geometric camera parameters. The pattern on the wall is automatically removed when the synthetic scene overwrites all blue portions in the real scene. However, different blues in the blue screen limit the quality of the merged image.

Finding a three-dimensional reference structure within the video is only one part of the solution. The camera image tends to jitter especially during camera moves; as a consequence, the reference structure will jitter also; finally, the calculated camera parameters tend to exaggerate the jitter of the reference structure. For a virtual studio, this jitter is not tolerable as the human eye immediately recognizes even slight differences in the movement of the real and the virtual world. Standard smoothing techniques like least square fit, by far, are not sufficient to suppress the jitter. Kalman filtering seems to be the most appropriate technique to smooth the statistically disturbed measurements of the reference structure and to control the calculated camera moves. This paper reports about the current state of our work.

3 The CaTS camera tracking system

We have implemented a unique camera tracking system CaTS which uses objects in the scene with known geometry for calculating the geometric camera parameters in real time. Figure 3 shows the components of the CaTS system.

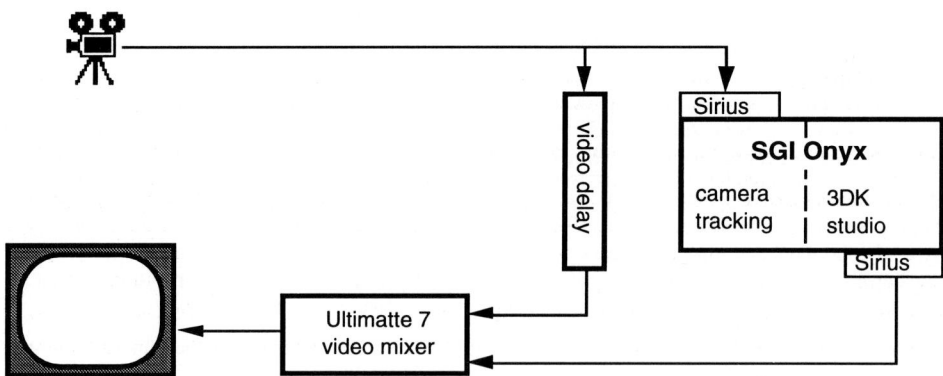

Fig. 3. Configuration of the CaTS camera tracking system

A camera within the virtual studio captures the scene before a blue background. The video signal is sent to two destinations: a Sirius board and a video delay unit.

The Sirius board transfers each frame in the video signal into the memory of a multi-processor SGI Onyx computer. To be more precise, the video signal transfers one frame as two fields: one field containing all odd-numbered lines and the other the even-numbered lines of the video frame. One processor of the Onyx processes the image, identifies the position of the given reference objects, and calculates the camera parameters. The camera parameters are then used by the rendering process (3DK studio) to generate the synthetic scene.

Currently, no special image processing or pattern recognition board is used which limits the recognition process to simple point and edge detection. This is a weak point in the current CaTS implementation. The quality of the derived position data would benefit from image enhancement and edge detection processes. Figure 4 shows a magnified view of a black dot with dissolving pixels and widely varying colour values which illustrates the difficulty of assigning a unique position to the dot. It is planned to replace this part of the system by specialized processors.

Figure 5 shows the edges of a desk during a pan action which shows that the two fields of even- or odd-numbered lines belong to different points in time and, hence, define different images. This figure illustrates that it will be better to base the object tracking and position finding on fields rather than full frames.

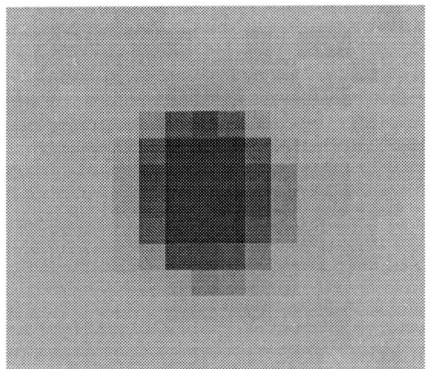

Fig. 4. The dissolving pixel image of a black dot.

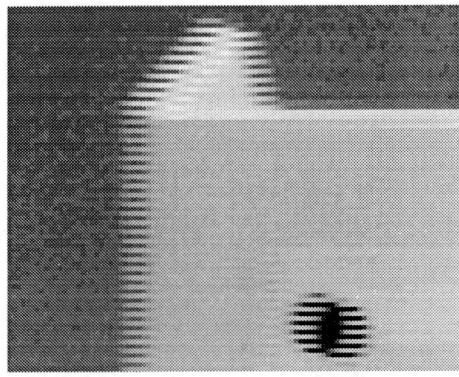

Fig. 5. Edges of a desk during camera pan

The camera parameters are written to shared memory where they can be retrieved by the rendering process which occupies two further processors. The synthetic background is generated independent of the tracking process and uses always the most recent camera parameters in shared memory.

The processing of the image data within the computer consumes time. To achieve high video quality, the CaTS system operates with 50 Hz frequency, i.e., with the field rather than the frame rate of the video signal. The tracking and the rendering process consume less than 20 msec each. This means that they can keep pace with the incoming video signal. Figure 6 shows that the synthetic background is ready to be mixed with the video signal with 3 fields delay. Additional hardware-specific delays extend this value to a typical 4 frame delay (i.e., 160 msec). The video signal has to be delayed by this amount to allow the synthetic background to be mixed with the appropriate video image. The blue screen mixing is performed using a Ultimatte 7 which generates the final video signal for storage, display, or dissemination.

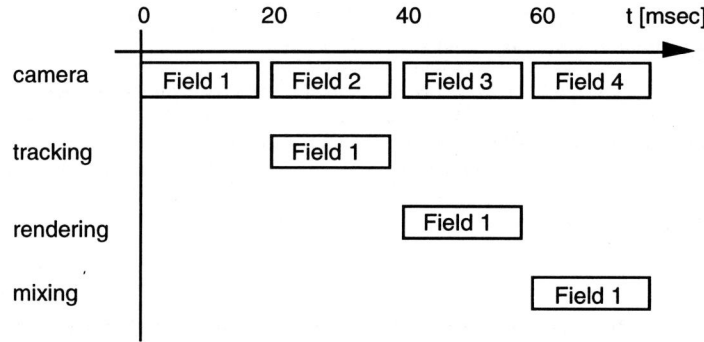

Fig. 6. Delay between original video signal and synthetic background by tracking and rendering

4 Calculation of camera data

To calculate the geometric camera parameters *eye_point, pan, tilt, roll,* and *zoom*, the positions of some reference points must be known in real world together with their corresponding screen points in the video frame (see Fig. 7). The positions of the reference points in world coordinates (*wpts*) have to be measured carefully. With permanent reference points in a studio or a fixed set up of real objects, this measurement can be done precisely. The positions of the corresponding screen-points (*scrpts*) within the first image are identified interactively, e.g., by mouse clicking on their images.

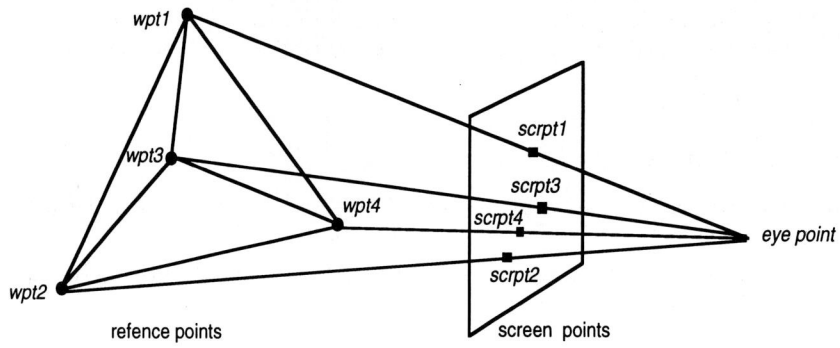

Fig. 7. Projection of four reference points (*wpt1–4*) onto a screen

Using standard mathematical methods, the camera parameters *cam = (eye_point, pan, tilt, roll, zoom)* are calculated from four or more reference points. For this calculation we use Bogart's algorithm published in the Graphics Gems [Bogart 1991]. A slight adoption of Bogart's C-package, in sequel called BOGART, works as shown in Fig. 8. Note that BOGART delivers besides the projection map h also its jacobian H (used below to calculate the covariance matrix of the sensor data *bog_cam*).

Digital image processing algorithms exist for 3D reconstruction of scenes from different views. They allow the calculation of both, the positions of the reference points and the camera parameters. These combined algorithms include direct [Faugeras 1993] as well as iterative approaches [Azerb 1993; Broida 1986] using the well known Kalman Filter described below. However, as precision is a crucial point for camera tracking, these combined methods may be used only in a preprocessing step for

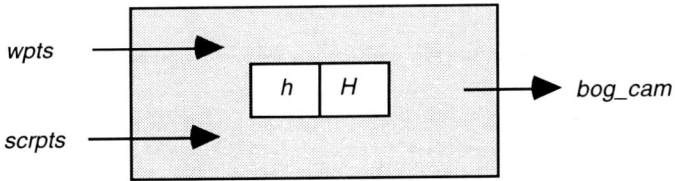

Fig. 8. The BOGART algorithm calculates camera data from world points and their image on screen

getting the world coordinates of a set of reference points. According to our experiences, they are not sufficient precise for calculating camera data.

Having calculated the camera position at the start point, the video camera can be moved and the camera settings be changed. The reference points are automatically tracked in real-time in all subsequent frames. In a production system, this task would be performed by a specialized chip. Currently, the video signal is grabbed into computer memory and simple colour tests are performed in the neighborhood of the previous positions to find the new positions of the reference points in the new frame. For each step, we use again BOGART to get data bog_cam_k used as measurement data used for further processing by Kalman filtering.

The jittery video signal leads to errors in the reference points which generates unstable transformation parameters. This affects especially parameter changes with similar effect like moving the camera closer to the scene versus zooming. By choosing more than the minimum number of reference points, the stability can be increased. Additional reference points also make the algorithm to a certain extent immune against single reference points leaving the image area. Nevertheless, the camera data achieved by this reconstruction process have to be filtered considerably to achieve the precision required by our application. This filtering is performed by a specific Kalman filtering technique described in the sequel.

5 Kalman filtering

For a detailed description of the mathematical basis of Kalman filtering and its various uses we refer to the respective literature [Chui et al. 1987; Lewis 1992; Meditch 1969].

Mazuryk and Gervautz [1995] applied Kalman filtering to a scenario similar to our setting: head tracking in a virtual environment. It is their aim to calculate stable transformation parameters for generating the virtual environment appropriate to the current head position and looking direction. For this application, only position and orientation of the head is needed, zoom is not a concern. Furthermore, not precision but consistency and timeliness is crucial to give people within the virtual environment a reliable and immediate feed back. We are aiming at a seamless integration of virtual and real worlds where precision and coherence are very important whereas a fixed delay of, say, 3 frames is admissible even for a live TV show. Video delays are available to retain the video signal for some frames until the virtual world has been produced.

Kalman filtering is based on linear stochastic system theory. With Kalman filtering, a predicted system state $\tilde{x}_{k+1}$ is corrected by using measurements y_{k+1} which are noisy, resulting in a final value x_{k+1} (see below). The state-space description is given by

(1) $\quad x_{k+1} = A_k x_k + w_k$

(2) $\quad y_k = C_k x_k + v_k$

where

x_k state vector at time t_k (i.e., k^{th} iteration)

y_k state vector measurement at time t_k

w_k process noise vector

v_k measurement error

A_k transition matrix between states x_k and x_{k+1} in the absence of noise

C_k relation between measurement and state x_k

Kalman filtering requires for each step an estimate of the error covariance matrix Q_k to represent the process noise w_k as well as an estimate of the error covariance matrix R_k representing noise in measurements v_k. Together with an error estimation P_0 at start time (in our case set to the zero matrix), the algorithm is defined by [Chui, Chen 1987]:

$$(3) \quad \tilde{P}_k = A_{k-1} P_{k-1} A_{k-1}^T + Q_{k-1}$$

$$(4) \quad S_k = C_k \cdot \tilde{P}_k \cdot C_k^T + R_k$$

$$(5) \quad K_k = \tilde{P}_k \cdot C_k^T \cdot S_k^{-1}$$

$$(6) \quad P_k = (I - K_k \cdot C_k) \cdot \tilde{P}_k \cdot A_k^T + Q_k$$

$$(7) \quad \tilde{x}_k = A x_{k-1}$$

$$(8) \quad x_k = \tilde{x}_k + K_k (y_k - C_k \cdot \tilde{x}_k)$$

The term

$$(9) \quad y_k - C \cdot \tilde{x}_k$$

is called *innovation*.

In our case, we have modeled the system as a simple kinematic model with constant velocity as follows:

The system state vector consists of the camera position and the velocity vector

$$(10) \quad x_k = (cam_k, \dot{cam}_k)^T$$

Matrix A_k predicts the camera data (with constant velocity) and is defined by:

$$(11) \quad A_k = \begin{bmatrix} I & \Delta t \\ O & I \end{bmatrix}$$

The vector of measurements y_k contains the camera position data delivered by the BOGART algorithm:

$$(12) \quad y_k = bog\_cam_k$$

Note: We do not use the original measurements, i.e., the found screen points, in the Kalman filtering but interpret the BOGART algorithm as a sensor which delivers for each time t_k a measurement of the camera position. Thus, the nonlinear relation between measurements in the image and the camera data are moved completely into the BOGART algorithm.

Now, when relating only on position data, C becomes

(13) $C = \begin{bmatrix} I & 0 \end{bmatrix}$

and the innovations are given by

(14) $innovation_k = y_k - C_k \tilde{x}_k = bog\_cam_k - (cam_{k-1} + \dot{cam}_{k-1} \Delta t)$

Thus, the innovation measures the *difference between camera extrapolation and camera measurement*.

The covariance matrices Q_k and R_k are established as follows: We determine by experiment $Q = Q_k$ as diagonal matrix with a constant value q_1 for the variances of the extrapolated camera position data and $q_2 = 10 \cdot q_1$ as the variances of the extrapolated camera velocity. The measurement noise R_k can be calculated by using the pseudo inverse of the jacobian matrix H_k used by the BOGART algorithm from (uncorrelated) variance of the screen points.

Figure 9 shows a camera move from frame 120 to 200 which represents a pan from 0 to -8 degree. The single tracks represent the camera data delivered by the BOGART algorithm. Figure 10 shows the same sequence with camera data filtered by the Kalman filtering.

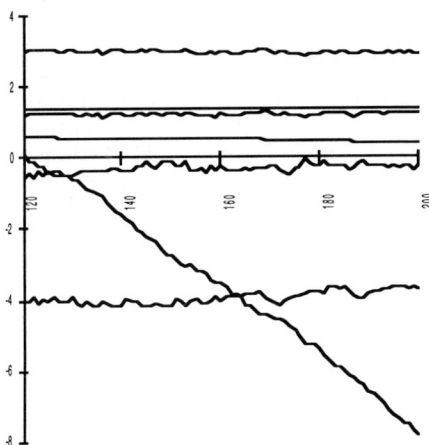

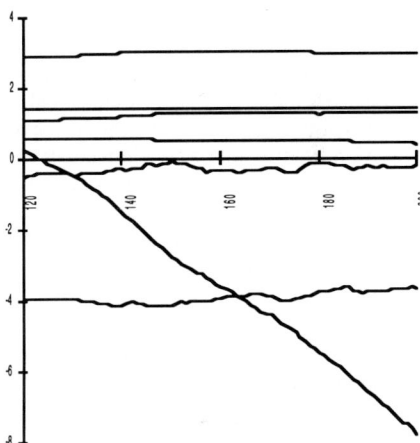

Fig. 9. Seven camera parameters as calculated by the BOGART algorithm

Fig. 10. Seven camera parameters smoothed by the Kalman filtering

6 Adaptive filtering

The integration of graphics into video requires a high precision and stability of the camera data, as the human eye immediately notices slight shifts and uncorrect moves within the combined image.

The above Kalman filtering is sufficient only for smooth camera movements. Sudden changes in speed and direction will lead to the well known overshooting effect. The following Figures 11 and 12 show a sudden change of *zoom factor* which leads to an unmotivated temporary change of *tilt angle*. This problem is well known in practical applications of Kalman filtering. To avoid it, we use *adaptive filtering*, a strategy often used in practical applications and described in our special one as follows.

In many cases, including our own, the errors Q_k and R_k are (partly) unknown and changing in time. Therefore, these data have to be adaptively optimized due to heuristic criteria. This leads to *adaptive*

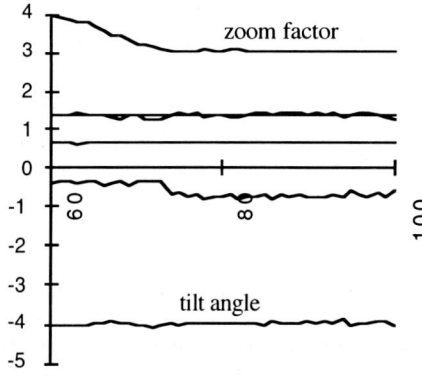
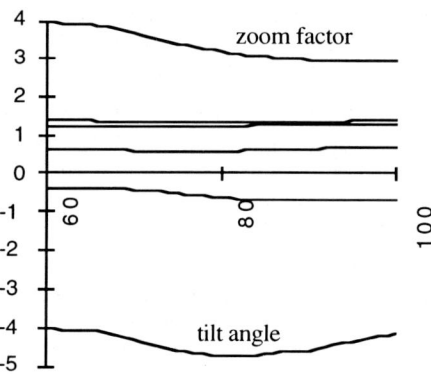

Fig. 11. Camera parameters for zoom as calculated by the Bogart algorithm

Fig. 12. Camera parameters for zoom smoothed by the Kalman filtering

filtering, a strategy which can be described in our case as follows. When the camera is moving smoothly, we keep Q_k as small as possible. This will effect in a small value for K giving the extrapolated value $\tilde{x}_{k+1}$ more weight, and is thus resulting in a good smoothing effect (nearly constant velocity) (cf. (8)). Problems with this strategy generating overshooting effects such as illustrated in Fig. 12 may arise after a certain number of steps or suddenly, when the camera is jerked vehemently. Fortunately, upcoming overshooting effects can be detected by an indicator. In these cases, the difference between camera extrapolation and camera measurement, i.e. the innovation (cf. (14)) exceeds a certain limit. As soon as this happens, a higher value for Q_k is selected resulting in K_k closer to identity matrix I. This then leads to a result in (8) with a filtered camera position closer to

$$y_k = bog\_cam_k.$$

Note: We apply the above strategy, but measure the amount of the innovation in a slighty other way as is described in [Bar-Shalom, Fortmann 1988]. Instead of evaluating the criterion

(15) $innovation_k \geq \varepsilon_0$

we use a better suited definition called *normalized innovation* squared. Its value requires S_k^{-1} (calculated by inverting (4)) and leads to a selection criterion for K_k depending on ckecking whether an empirically defined boundary ε_1 will be exceeded by

(16) $innovation_k^T \, S_k^{-1} \, innovation \geq \varepsilon_1.$

7 Implementation aspects

Kalman filtering, in general, requires matrix inversion at runtime to calculate K_k. When the values of Q_k and R_k are estimated by constant values, K_k can be precalculated. Under slight conditions, K_k converges against a constant value resulting in *steady-state filtering* [Chui, Chen 1987]. To be able to apply adaptive filtering, we precalculate and store for different values of Q^i a complete sequence of S^{i-1} (used in (16)) and K^i with $0 \leq ... \leq K^i \leq K^{i+1} \leq ... I$. Starting with a rather small K^* to achieve good smoothness, we check at each step (16) and decide which precalculated K should be selected for further processing. In this way, a adaptive filtering is possible without any costly matrix inversion at runtime. What should be finally noted is that the measurement error R_k is not really a constant matrix because the jacobian H_k is depending on the position of the camera. But we have made the experience that for a normal video recording, a constant value $R_k = R$ will be a sufficiently good choice for evaluating term (4) above.

We have performed experiments with many modifications of the above mentioned filtering procedure. In particular, we have selected a higher degree of the kinematic model (constant acceleration model, thus extending (11)), but with no real improvements of the final result.

8 Future work

Currently we implement an extension of Kalman filtering called *fixed-lag smoothing* described by [Meditch 1969]. With this approach, the live video is delayed by a fixed timelag (ca. 3-5 frames). This allows to *look into the future* to anticipate sudden changes within a camera move. With this approach we hope to master problems which may occur when recording scenes with shoulder cameras. The price to pay for such a procedure is a delay which may sum up to about 5-8 frames.

The performance of the overall system is dictated by the requirements of the TV application: precisely 25 images per second have to be generated. Considering the field mode of TV, 50 images per second are required. The calculation of the camera parameters and the Kalman filtering as described above are non-critrical processes which could even keep pace with 100 images per second on an SGI Indigo computer. The limiting processes are the recognition and measurement of reference objects in each image and the high quality rendering of the virtual world which has to be done within 20 msec each to keep in pace with the video signal. As a consequence, currently only simple reference objects are supported which can be located fast enough. It is intended to use signal processors in future versions which would allow to recognise and locate more complicated and natural reference objects. The virtual world is designed such that it can be rendered within the given time frame. By adding powerful graphics boards to the system and distributing the task over several CPUs, the complexity of the world in terms of polygons and lighting effects can be increased.

References

[Azerb et al. 1993] Ali Azarbayejani et al.: Recursive estimation of structure and motion using relative orientation constraints. *IEEE Conference on Computer Vision and Pattern Recognition*, June 1993, 294-299.

[Bar-Shalom, Fortmann 1988] Yaakov Bar-Shalom, Thomas E. Fortmann: *Tracking and Data Association*. Academic Press, San Diego, 1988

[Bogart 1991] Rod G. Bogart: View correlation. In: *Graphics Gems II*, Academic Press (1991) 181-190.

[Broida, Chellappa 1986] T. J. Broida, R. Chellappa: Estimation of object motion paramters from noisy images. *IEEE Trans. Pattern Analysis andd Machine Intelligence*, 8(1):90-99, January 1986.

[Chui, Chen 1987] C.K. Chui, G. Chen: *Kalman Filtering with Real Time Applications*. Springer Series in Information Sciences 17. Springer Verlag, Berlin, 1987.

[Faugeras 1993] Olivier Faugeras: *Three-Dimensional Computer Vision*. MIT Press Cambridge, Massachusetts, USA, 1993.

[Kansy et al. 1995] Klaus Kansy, Thomas Berlage, Günther Schmitgen, Peter Wißkirchen: Real time integration of synthetic computer graphics into live video scenes. *Proc. Interface of Real and Virtual Worlds*. Montpellier, France, June 26-30, 1995, pp. 93-101

[Kansy et al. 1996] Klaus Kansy, Günther Schmitgen, Peter Wißkirchen: Bildbasierte Kameraführung im Virtuellen Studio – Pixelgenaues Mischen von Realität und Virtualität. *Fernseh- und Kinotechnik* 50, Heft 1-2, pp. 27–32 (1996)

[Lewis 1992] Frank L. Lewis: *Applied Optimal Control and Estimation*, Prentice Hall, 1992.

[Mazuryk, Gervautz 1995] Tomasz Mazuryk, Michael Gervautz: Two-Step Prediction and Image Deflection for Exact Head Tracking in Virtual Environments. *Computer Graphics Forum* 14(1995) C-29–C-41.

[Meditch 1969] J. S. Meditch: *Stochastic Optimal Linear Estimation and Control*. McGraw Hill, New York, 1969.

[ORAD 1995] ORAD Hi-tec Systems Ltd: *ORAD's Virtual Set*. Data sheet by ORAD Hi-tec Systems Ltd., 40 Ravutski Street, Ra'anana, POBox 695, Israel 43106. URL: http://orad.co.il/

[Routsis et al. 1994] D. Routsis, P. Le Floch, A.V. Sahiner: Real-Time Camera Tracking Server on the ELSET Accelerator. In *Proc. European Workshop "Combined Real and Synthetic Image Processing for Broadcast and Video Production"*, 23.-24.11.1994, VAP Media Centre, Hamburg, Germany (1994)

[Sommerhäuser 1966] F. Sommerhäuser: Das virtuelle Studio – Grundlagen einer neuen Studioproduktionstechnik. *Fernseh- und Kinotechnik* 50, Heft 1-2, pp. 11–22 (1996)

3D-Morphing and its Application to Virtual Reality

Peter Astheimer, Christian Knöpfle

Fraunhofer-Institute for Computer Graphics (IGD)
Wilhelminenstr. 7, D-64283 Darmstadt, Germany
phone: ++49 6151 155 121
fax: ++49 6151 155 199
email: knoepfle@igd.fhg.de
http://www.igd.fhg.de/~knoepfle

Abstract: This paper describes the principles and problems of 3d-morphing in real-time applications. Several known morphing-algorithms will be discussed and a new algorithm will be presented, which works on arbitrary polyhedra. Furthermore this paper presents 3d-morphing as an application for smooth transition between different level-of-detail (LOD).

1 Introduction

First generation virtual worlds consisted of mostly static scenarios where only limited interaction was possible. This was due to limited processing power and lack of sophisticated systems. The traditional way to experience these worlds was by walk-throughs or fly-bys. The objects were also static, so human explorers of these worlds soon became bored.

Today available graphics and computation hardware allow virtual worlds to potentially react to user actions quite well, as well as to comprise interesting dynamic objects or artificial creatures, including their special behavior and emotional expression. One possibility to realize a living world is by transforming (morphing) objects, e.g. a friendly character turning into a menacing, outraged sorcerer.

An important technique to conquer complex scenarios, especially when viewed from a bird's position, is level-of-detail. Many different algorithms exist which are optimized for certain object features [2]. Morphing can provide a smooth transition between two levels-of-detail of an object.

Morphing can be used for design-studies to combine different features of different objects. It is also possible to determine the development of a shape in the future by means of parameter extrapolation, e.g. to predict the shape of a next-generation car [5]. Another application is the visualisation of the evolution of the human race [9].

2 Morphing

The lay audience has become aware of the possible effects and benefits of morphing in the entertainment sector. Well known examples are Michael Jackson's music video "Black and White" [4] and films like "Indiana Jones 3: The Last Crusade" and "Terminator 2". Whereas "Terminator 2" has been realised using 3D-morphing, the others have been realised using 2D image-based techniques.

The advantages of 3D-morphing compared to 2D-morphing are:
- 3D-morphing is independent of camera position and light sources. Thus a scene object has to be modeled only once and then different camera and light positions can be applied. When using 2D-morphing for every change in camera/light position the morphing has to be recalculated.
- 2D-morphing can't handle shadows, lights and invisible objects correctly because of the lack of spatial information.

2.1 Principles and Problems

Two objects (source and destination) are needed to apply 3D-morphing. With a morphing algorithm a morph-object is generated which interpolates between these two objects. The difficult part is to set up a meaningful correlation between two totally different objects (with respect to number of points and faces, topology, visual attributes). The process of 3D-morphing can be subdivided into two steps:
- In a preprocessing step the morph-object and a correspondence list have to be computed. The correspondence list contains information regarding which point and which face of one object will be mapped onto which point and which face of the other object.
- At runtime the morph-object has to be constructed and displayed according to user actions or story requirements, e.g. by interpolating the vertices of the source and destination objects. This task has to be processed in real-time.

3D-morphing also encounters several difficulties and problems:
- Different numbers of faces and vertices of the two involved objects
- Different topology of the objects
- In-between morphs should resemble both objects (e.g. possible degeneration into several objects)
- Potential degeneration of faces (to lines, points)
- Coplanar in-between faces resulting in flickering display
- Interpolation of textures might not be supported by the hardware
- Different triangulation of faces resulting in shading flicker

3 Algorithms

In [7] the PIP algorithm (Parametrized Interpolating Polyhedron) is described which generates morph-objects or PIPs and calculates the correspondence between the vertices. This algorithm can handle every kind of object and respects the topology of the involved objects. The basic idea is similar to blending between two objects by means of transparency. This 'blending' is done with the Minkowski-operator:

$$PIP(A,B) = (1-t) \cdot A \oplus t \cdot B$$

A: source object
B: destination object
t: blending parameter, 0 .. 1
$\oplus$: Minkowski-operator

The described algorithm generates the needed faces for the morph-object. These faces belong to one of the following types:
- Faces, which evolve from a single point of object A to a face of object B.
- Faces, which evolve from a face of object A to a single point of object B.
- Faces, which evolve from an edge of object A to an edge of object B.

To determine the vertex correspondence is simple (fig. 1).

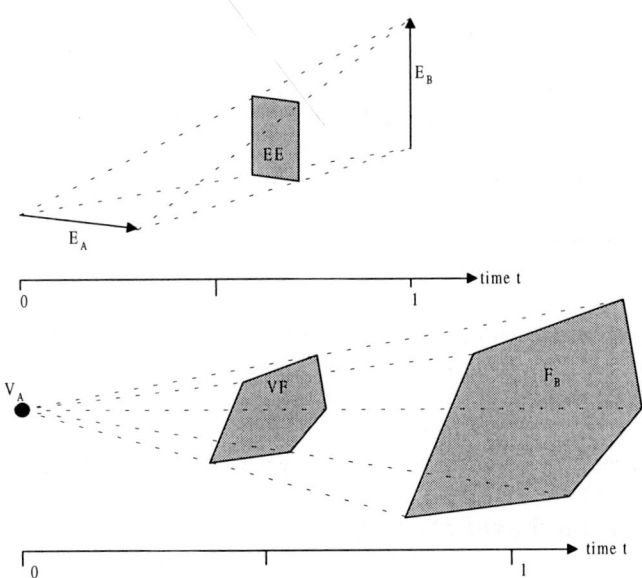

Fig. 1. Edge to edge correspondence and vertex to face correspondence

Unfortunately, this algorithm works only for polyhedra in 'general position', so that no faces of an object are parallel to an edge of the other object. A very simple but effective approach to solve this problem is to slightly rotate one of these objects until 'general position' is reached. For the interpolation step the original, unrotated objects are used. An advantage of this algorithm is that the face normals remain constant during the interpolation process. One of the major problems using this algorithm is that the morph object can have up to m*n faces, where m and n are the number of faces of the initial objects.

Another approach is the NoTop algorithm ([8]), which ignores the topology of the initial objects. Here, only corresponding faces are specified. The correspondence is determined by the minimum distance between two faces. For this purpose, both objects are translated in the origin and scaled on the same bounding sphere. The maximum number of faces of the morph-object is m+n. This method is well suited for explosion effects, because the in-between morph often consists of a number of unordered and unconnected faces. The visual effect resembles the output of a particle system.

Another algorithm suitable for VR applications is described in [10], which only works with polyhedra without holes. Basically the algorithm is divided in 3 steps:
- Projection of the topologies of the initial objects onto a unit sphere.
- Merging the two projected topologies.
- Creating new initial objects by projecting the unified topology onto the inital objects using barycentric coordinates.

The vertex correspondence is simple to determine, because the two new inital objects are topologically equal. The main disadvantage of this algorithm is the heavily increased complexity of the generated objects. See [10] for further details.

Many other morphing algorithms cannot be used, because they work on data representations, which are not suitable for real-time applications. [5] works on a pseudo 3D representation and [3] only on implicit surfaces. [6] describes a method using the Fourier-transformation, which only works on solid models. [9] describes a way to define features on each object, which are then morphed into each other. So the appearence of the morph can be controlled. Unfortunately this algorithm works only with solid models.

The interpolation step is straight-forward. Except for linear interpolation between two vertices and visual attributes also hermite curves and ease-in- / ease-out-functions result in special effects.

3.1 Morphing for Level-of-Detail representations

One of the major problems when using level-of-detail representations is the continuous, unnoticable transition from one level to another, e.g. depending on the distance to the viewer. A widely used technique in VR systems is simply switching the visibility between two levels of detail, which leads to a noticeable break/leap during the animation.

Another approach is blending in the transparency domain between two representations. The disadvantage of this solution is that two objects must be rendered simultaneously and their faces depth-sorted. Thus the "best" solution and smoothest transition is to apply 3D-morphing techniques (see fig. 2).

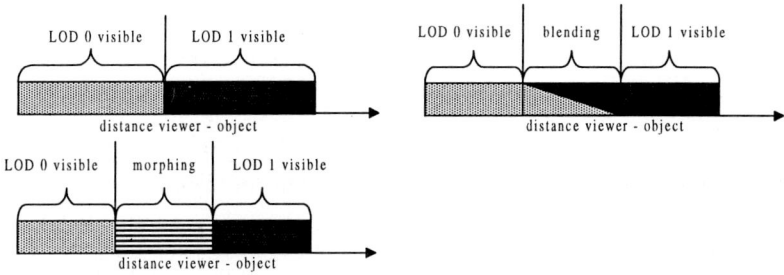

Fig. 2. Different lod-techniques: switch, blend, morph

The level-of-detail representations can be generated either by hand or by an algorithm. A common algorithm collapses a number of vertices into one unique point. Doing this, the number of vertices and faces of an object decreases. Because the lod algorithm implies this 'correspondence-step' between the vertices of two following levels, the difficult step of finding the vertex-correspondence is implicitly solved too (see fig. 3).

See also [2] for a discussion of several lod algorithms.

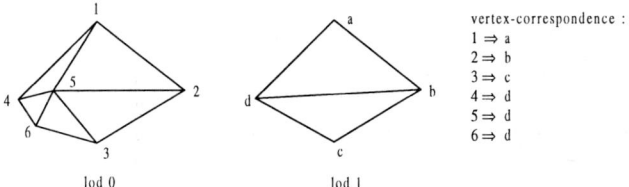

Fig. 3. Vertex-correspondence using lod algorithms

4 Morph Tool

The implementation of the morphing capabilities is based on the real-time renderer Y. Y is the FhG's real-time rendering system applied in VR applications. It uses a hierarchical scene graph, level-of-detail, viewer, lights, environment (ambient, background colour, etc.) and callback nodes for user-defined actions. Y is based on OpenGL graphics library and includes multipipe culling and drawing and arbitrary windows.

A GUI allows morphs to be created, saved, loaded and played back. Also different parameters can be set, e.g. ease-function, interpolation type (linear, hermite curve) and number of steps between two initial objects. While the morph is played back, vertex position, texture coordinates, colors and normals are interpolated according to the specified interpolation-type. Unfortunately textures cannot be interpolated due to hardware-respective time constraints.

The geometry of the initial and morph-objects can be stored in any standard data format (e.g. FHS, CGRG, Inventor), where the point order is not altered. The correspondence table and morph parameters are stored in a special morph-format (fig. 4).

```
MORPH simple_morph              % name of the morph
{
        OBJECTS triangle1 triangle2     %name of the intial objects
        MOBJECTS triangle3              %name of the morph-object
        LINEAR 50                       %interpolation-type and num. of steps
        EASE 0.2 0.0 0.2 0.0            %ease-in 0.0-0.2, ease-out 0.8-1.0
                                        %start- and endspeed is 0.0

        CONSTFNORMAL                    %don't interpolate face-normales
        CORRESPONDENCE 3                %correspondence table follows
        {
                (1,3) (3,1) (2,2)       %correspondence (index_1, index_2)
        }
}
```

Fig. 4. Example of morph data structure

In the GUI the PIP and the NoTop algorithm are applicable, as well as the creation of morph-lod's based on the lod-algorithm described in [12]. The user can specify the initial objects by picking them with the mouse-cursor. In a dialog-window parameters can be set and the correspondence-calculation started (fig. 6).

5 Results

In the color section (see Appendix) a figure depicts the morphing of a torus into a beethoven bust, processed by the PIP algorithm. Another color figure presents an example of the NoTop algorithm, which transforms a Ficus Benjamini tree into a Beethoven-bust..

As discussed earlier, the main problem of the PIP algorithm is the possibly enormous number of faces of the morph-object, but practically the numbers are lower (table 1).

Table 1. Number of generated faces using the PIP algorithm

initial objects	number of faces of object A (m)	number of faces of object B (n)	max. number of faces (m*n)	Σ generated faces	percent of max. number
pyramid torus	5	400	2000	537	26%
torus beethoven-bust	400	2.802	1.120.800	34.536	3,08%
screwer hammer	119	64	7616	720	9.5%

Another important fact is how fast 3D-morphing can be performed. Our benchmarks are done on a SGI Onyx with 4xR4400 250 MHz and a Reality Engine^2. For the interpolation step only one processor was used (see table 2).

Table 2. Morph-benchmarks

initial objects	morph-object Σ faces	morph-object Σ points	msec/frames without rendering	msec per point
screwer hammer	720	2457	4.73	0.0019
lod-chair lod-chair	502	317	0.51	0.0016
pyramid torus	537	2144	2.91	00014
apple tree	8290	24870	65.93	0.0026

A way to speed up the interpolation-process is by paralleling it. The speedup is shown in fig. 5.

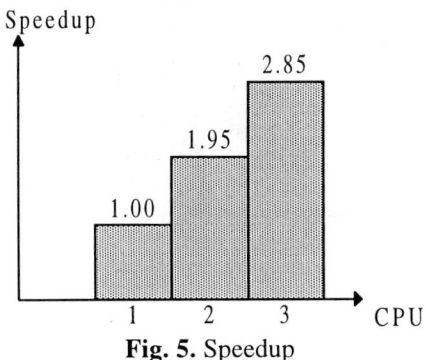

Fig. 5. Speedup

Assuming the hardware platform described above and only one processor available for the interpolation, then for an application with 20 frames / sec. a morph-object with approx. 15000 points can be interpolated and rendered.

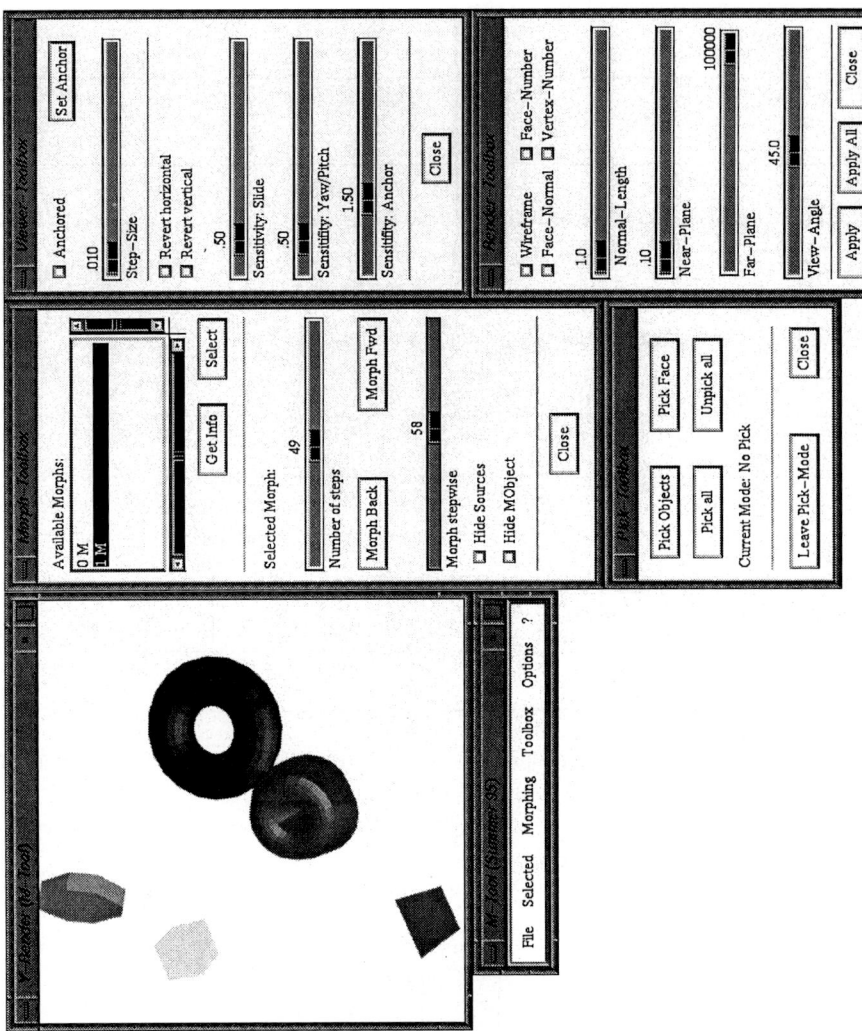

Fig. 6. The Morph-Tool

6 Conclusion and Future Work

3D-morphing is a powerful tool to either animate static VR scenarios (e.g. special effects or for artifical life scenarios) or to provide smooth transitions between different levels-of-detail of an object.
When objects have multimodal attributes, e.g. in the visual or haptic domain, these attributes will also have to be considered for morphing in future.

References

1. Astheimer, P., Göbel, M.: Virtual Design II, an advanced VR development environment, in: M. Göbel (ed.): Virtual Environments, Springer, Wien, 1995
2. Astheimer, P., Pöche, M.L.: Level-of-Detail Generation and its Application in Virtual Reality, in: Singh, G., Feiner, S.K., Thalmann, D. (eds.): VRST '94 Proceedings, World Scientific, Singapore, August 1994, pp. 299 - 309
3. Beier, T.: Practical uses for implicit surfaces in animation, Notes from ACM SIGGRAPH '90 Course 23 - Modelling and animating with implicit surfaces, pp. 20.1-20.11
4. Beier, T., Neely, S.: Feature-based image metamorphosis, Proceedings of ACM SIGGRAPH '92, pp. 35 - 40
5. Chen, S.E., Parent, R.E.: Shape Averaging and its applications to industrial design, IEEE Computer Graphics & Applications, Januar 1989, pp. 47 - 54
6. Hughes, J.F.: Scheduled fourier volume morphing, Proceedings of ACM SIGGRAPH '92, pp. 43-45
7. Kaul, A., Rossignac, J.: Solid-Interpolating Deformations: Construction and animation of PIPs, Proceedings of Eurographics 91, pp. 493 - 505
8. Knöpfle, C.: 3D-Morphing für VR-Anwendungen, diploma thesis (in german), FH Darmstadt, October 1995
9. Lerois, A., Garfinkle, C.D., Levoy, M.: Feature-based volume metamorphosis, Proceedings of ACM SIGGRAPH 95, pp.
10. Kent, J., Carlson, W., Parent, R.: Shape transformation for polyhedral objects, Proceedings of ACM SIGGRAPH 92, pp. 47-54
11. Reiners, D., Zachmann, G.: The Y System, Fraunhofer-IGD internal report 1996
12. Schaufler, G., Stürzlinger, W.: Generating multiple levels of detail from polygonal geometry models, Virtual Environments (Monte Carlo, MC), Jan. 1995, pp. 53-62

Editors' Note: See Appendix, p. 311f. for coloured figures of this paper

Motor functions in the VLNET Body-Centered Networked Virtual Environment

Igor-Sunday Pandzic[1], Tolga K. Capin[2],
Nadia Magnenat Thalmann[1], Daniel Thalmann[2]

[1]MIRALAB-CUI
University of Geneva
24 rue de Général-Dufour
CH1211 Geneva 4, Switzerland
{Igor.Pandzic, Nadia.Thalmann}@cui.unige.ch
http://cuisg13.unige.ch:8100/HomePage.html

[2]Computer Graphics Laboratory
Swiss Federal Institute of Technology
CH1015 Lausanne, Switzerland
{capin,thalmann}@lig.di.epfl.ch
http://ligwww.epfl.ch

Abstract

The participant's sense of presence within a Virtual Environment becomes an even more important issue within networked, multi-participant Virtual Environments. In such environments this issue extends to the perception of presence of others in the environment and the ability to communicate and interact with them. This interaction, as well as the interaction with the other objects in the environment, further increases the participant's own sense of presence. In the Virtual Life Network (VLNET) system we address these issues using a highly realistic human body model for participant representation together with the set of motor functions giving behaviors to these virtual actors and to other objects in the virtual world.

Keywords: networked virtual environments, virtual humans, virtual life, computer animation, multimedia

1. Introduction

In the past few years we have seen an increasing number of research efforts for building networked Virtual Environments, and solutions were proposed for building toolkits for communication in networked virtual worlds [Amselam 95][Carlsson 93][Macedonia 95][Singh 95], and special-purpose applications [Maxfield 95] [Stansfield 95][Gisi 94][Broll 95].

Any Virtual Environment is supposed to give the user the sense of presence, i.e. the subjective state of awareness and involvement in a non-present environment. The important factor for the sense of presence is the interaction with the environment. This interaction should be effected in an intuitive way and the objects in the virtual environment should behave in a natural, expected manner, thus diminishing the barrier between the user and the VE. In networked, multi-user VEs this question extends to the interaction with other participants in the environment. We can observe a mirror effect: the perception of presence of others within the VE together with the interaction and communication with them strongly increases our own sense of presence. A more realistic representation of participants and their behaviors is likely to reinforce this effect.

There has been similar research to represent virtual humans in virtual environments [Granieri 95][Yoshida 95]. In the VLNET (Virtual Life Network) system we use a highly realistic-looking deformable body model for the participant representation together with the motor functions that generate a natural motion of the virtual body corresponding to the user's activities. W extend and generalize the concept of motor functions and use them to attach behaviors to any object in the scene.

The following section discusses the issues of participant representation. Next we describe the use of motor functions for object behaviors and interaction with the environment. We present the network structure of the VLNET system and finally pass to the results and the conclusion.

2. Representation of Participants

The participant representation in a networked VE system has several functions:

- convey the information of the participant's presence

- identify the participant

- visualize the participant's position and direction of interest

- visualize the participant's actions

- enable communication between the participants

The user representation in VLNET is based on the HUMANOID articulated body model [Boulic 95], At the core of this model there is a skeleton structure resembling the anatomical structure of a real skeleton, consisting of a 3D articulated hierarchy of joints, each with realistic limits of movement. Through its 74 degrees of freedom (with an additional 30 degrees of freedom for each hand) this structure allows the full control of the body model.

The body envelope (skin) is attached to the skeleton in the form of 16 deformable surfaces representing the body parts: head, pelvis, thorax, abdomen, left and right upper leg, lower leg, foot, upper arm, lower arm, and hand. As the skeleton is animated, these surfaces follow the movement and are deformed appropriately at the seams to form a realistic-looking deformed body.

Besides the realistic visual representation, the believable body model must incorporate the natural body motion corresponding o the user actions.

Each user sees the virtual environment through the eyes of her body, and can control the movement of the body by various sensor devices (varying from spaceball and dataglove, to numerous sensors attached to body). In addition to her eye position, the user also has control of her virtual hand to interact with the environment (pick and reposition objects). We selected these two modes of control, as most conventional input devices sense position and orientation of the head (e.g. head-mounted displays) and the hand (e.g. dataglove).

In the VLNET system, we provide a set of motor functions that are responsible for different human motion: walking motor for *navigation*, and arm motor for *manipulation* of objects. These motor functions are based on approximations coming from biomechanical experiments, and they attempt to consider different parameters of the motion they are responsible for, in order to give parametrized motion (for example step length in walking as a function of velocity).

When the user navigates through the environment, the walking motor is used to perform a natural walking motion. The participant uses input devices (e.g. spaceball, dataglove with gesture interpretation) to update the eye position of the virtual actor. Based on this control, the incremental change of the eye position is computed and the rotation and velocity of the body center is estimated. The walking motor uses the instantaneous velocity to compute the length and duration of the walking cycle, from which it computes the joint angles of the body. The walking motor is based on the HUMANOID walking model [Boulic 90], guided interactively by the user or automatically generated from the given trajectory. Figure 1 (see Appendix) shows an example of the walking motion in real time.

For object picking and the arm motion in general, the arm motor has to compute the joint angles of the arm based on the 6 degrees of freedom of the hand determined by user input. Figure 2 illustrates the complexity of the degrees of freedom of the joints in the arm. There are multiple solutions of joint angles reaching the same hand position, and the most realistic one has to be chosen. At the same time the joint constraints have to be taken into account. These considerations make the arm motor much more complicated then a simple inverse kinematics problem. For the arm motor we use the captured data obtained using sensors and stored into a precomputed table of arm joints. This table divides the normalized volume around the body into a discrete number of subvolumes (e.g. 4x4x4) and stores the mapping from subvolumes into joint angles of the right arm. Figure 3 (see Appendix) shows an example of arm motion produced by this mechanism.

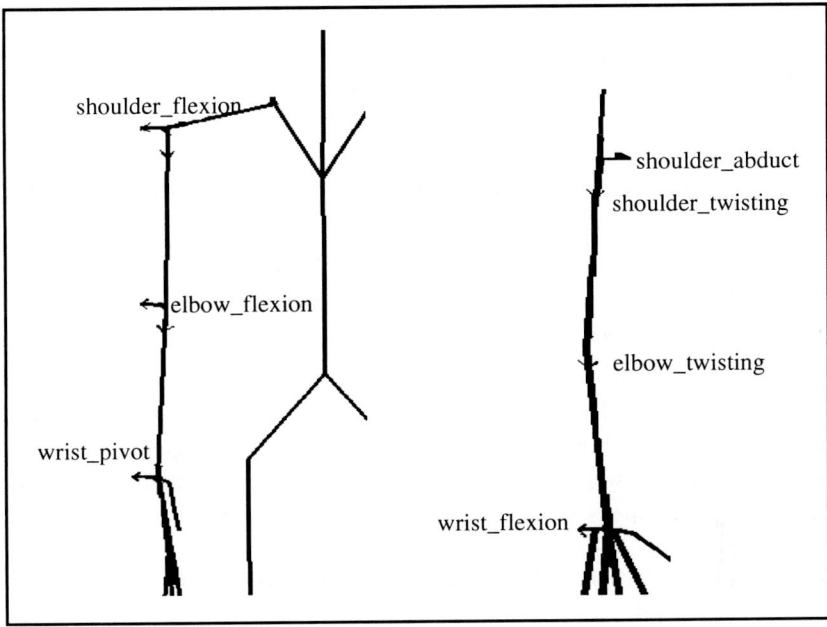

Fig. 2. Degrees of Freedom for the Right Arm

To enhance the usefulness of the virtual body as means of communication between participants, we try to provide within the virtual *self* the same means of communication that we use with our real body. Among those means of communication are gestures, body postures and the facial expressions.

The users can select a posture for the upper body to express different emotions: tiredness, happiness, paying attention, etc. Currently, the user explicitly selects one emotion, using commands similar to *smileys* that are used commonly in text messages to express different emotions. The emotion motor sets the body joints at the vertebrae ending at the shoulders, based on this input. There is a need to define an emotion motor function that automatically recognizes the appropriate motion using data sensed from the real user. This developed motor function is an introductory step to building an automatic emotion motor. Figure 4 (see Appendix) shows body postures for some example emotions set by this motor.

Facial expressions are among the most important means of human communication, expressing intentions, thoughts and feelings. Therefore we include the facial communication in our multi-user virtual environment to enhance the communication between the users [Pandzic 94].

We implement the facial communication by capturing the user's face using a camera and distributing it in real time to other users to be texture-mapped on the face of the virtual actor. Thus the virtual actor has the real moving face of the remote user.

The original images captured by the camera are first processed to extract the subset of the image containing the user's face. This processing is based on a comparison with an initial background image (the requirement is that the background is static). The extracted facial image is compressed at each frame and distributed to other users. At the receiving side, an additional service process is charged with the receipt and decompression of the images. The main application gets the decompressed images through shared memory from the service process, decoupling the facial video frame rate from the application frame rate.

The facial images are texture-mapped on a simplified model of a human head with attenuated features. This is a compromise between mapping on a simple shape (e.g. box, ellipsoid) which would give unnatural results and mapping on a full-featured human head model where more precise image - feature alignment would be necessary. The texture mapping is illustrated in figure 5 (see Appendix).

3. Interaction with Virtual Environment and Object Behaviors

It is expected that the participants feel a higher degree of presence if the environment *reacts* to their actions in a realistic way. For example, the user should be able to interact with the environment, reposition objects by picking them up with her virtual hand, and releasing them, making them fall. In order to pick up an object, the user moves her hand near the object and explicitly requests picking (e.g. by clicking spaceball button, closing dataglove). The objects stay picked until released explicitly by the user.

Typically the VEs are created by bringing together different models, possibly with different scalings and even different formats. These models lack any corresponding interaction information between objects. This makes it difficult to manipulate the scene. A dynamics simulation with collision response would partly solve this problem. However, even for medium-sized environments this is a time-consuming solution, resulting in unwanted delays in the simulation. Also, this solution still wouldn't give the possibility of adding specific behaviors, such as hands of a watch showing time. Therefore, we adopt a solution which compromises between realistic appearance and goal-oriented behaviors. We propose three classes of motor functions that can be attached to the objects, and include efficient communication schemes. We present the classification in this section, and network issues for executing these motor functions in multi-user VEs, in the next section.

A set of behaviors can be associated dynamically with any object in the environment. The object behaviors are implemented as different motor functions which give them a means of interacting with the users and the other objects. The types of motor functions can be divided into 3 classes:

- *continuous motor functions:* these functions require transformation update of the object regularly, within a specific period of time without any delay. For example, hands of a clock to show the time are in this category.

- *user-dependent motor functions:* these functions depend on the user input. This can be an explicit user input (for example, request for changing servers, see below); or implicit input (for example, automatic door behavior driven by position of the user).

- *environment-dependent motor functions:* these functions are dependent on the environment as well as the object itself. We define different built-in motor functions corresponding to this category: magnet, vertical displacement, horizontal displacement, axis alignment. Magnet allows to attach different objects to each other with a predetermined transformation matrix (e.g. the watch body and bracelet are always attached with one transformation). Vertical displacement is called when the object is released; and is used for making the objects fall until it collides with an object, simulating gravity.

A subset of these behaviors can be added optionally to the objects during the scene creation. Different motor functions can be appended together to obtain more complex behaviors. For example, when an object is released; the vertical displacement motor is activated until a collision occurs with another object (e.g. table); after that the axis-alignment motor, that orients the object in a vertical position with respect to the collided object, becomes active.

A motor function is attached dynamically to an object through a pointer to the motor function structure. This structure contains the necessary internal data of a particular motor function and the pointers to the subroutines to be executed in defined situations (e.g. the Update subroutine is executed in each time step, the Save subroutine is activated when the user saves the scene configuration to a file). When the subroutines are executed, they get as a parameter the pointer to the object to which the motor function is attached. Using this mechanism the user can dynamically attach motor functions to objects, change their parameters or detach them.

4. Network Structure

The communication is based on a client/server model as illustrated in figure 6. Each server handles one virtual world and is meant to run continuously, providing a permanent virtual world to which the VLNET clients can connect, a kind of virtual meeting place.

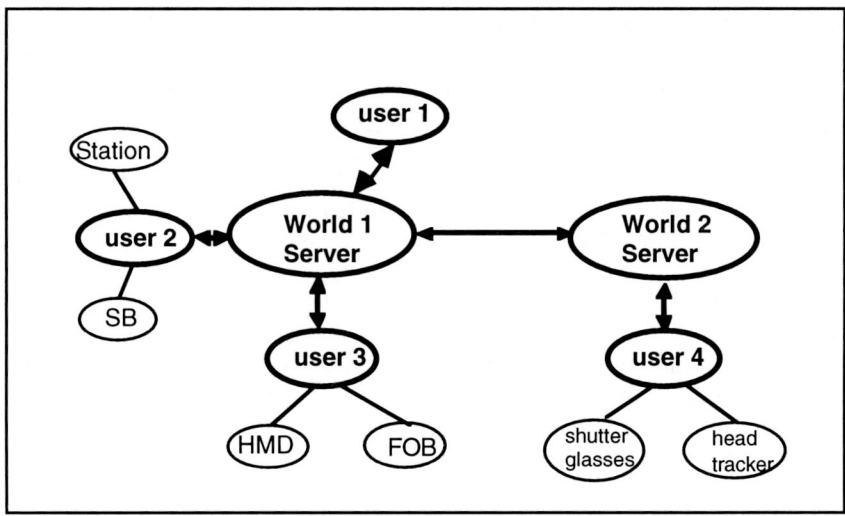

Fig. 6. Communication Architecture of the VLNET System is based on a client/server model with links between the servers

When the client establishes connections with the server, the server first provides the scene description to the new client, including all the object files necessary to build and visualize the virtual environment. All the other clients are informed that a new user entered the virtual world. The user representation information (body description, face) is exchanged between all the users, passing through the server. This insures that each user can provide his own body and face description and thus be recognized by others.

Once this initial information exchange is finished, all information exchange is done through the server using uniformly sized packets which are not more than the Maximum Transfer Unit of the protocol being used. The content of each packet is interpreted according to its type - new transformation of an object, body skeleton angles, grouping/ungrouping information, entry/exit messages etc. The packet is a data structure comprising a header which contains the message type and the sender id, and the body which is a union of data structures - one for each message type. All geometrical information is sent in absolute, rather then incremental values, insuring the coherence of the shared virtual environment even if a packet is lost.

When a user quits her VLNET session, the server cancels her from the client list and informs all other clients, thus insuring that this user disappears from the environment.

Links to other servers (i.e. other virtual worlds) can be established in a similar fashion as VRML or WWW links. These links can be attached to any object using a specialized motor function. When the user approaches such an object (it makes sense to make it look like a door), she is disconnected from the current server and connected to another one following the link. This gives the user the impression of "walking into another world". The user can take any objects with her when going to a different world. The linking mechanism, providing the possibility to carry objects through different worlds and allowing virtual actors to walk freely through the worlds, actually provides a hyper-world consisting of multiple servers scattered across the network.

The motor functions can be handled in different ways in the networked application.

The simplest mechanism is to execute the motor function locally on each host. This is appropriate for motor functions that do not put much strain on the CPU and where there is no danger of loosing the coherence of the shared environment. Time dependent motor functions are generally handled in this way.

The second way to handle the motor functions in a networked environment is to execute the function only on the host on which it has been triggered, and distribute the object position updates to other hosts. The standard communication packets are used for this distribution. This approach has two advantages: it distributes the processing, which is convenient for the more power-consuming motor functions, and it guarantees the coherence of the shared environment. This approach is used in general by the user- and environment-dependent motor functions (although some of them can be handled by the first, simple approach).

An extension of this second approach is provided for the motor functions that need to communicate some function-specific data. To this end a general-purpose communication packet can be used by the motor function. As an example of this approach, we have implemented a virtual slide show. When a user changes the slide, the slide show motor function distributes the slide number to other hosts, insuring that everybody sees the same slide.

5. Results

We have built experimental worlds for different applications such as teleshopping, game-playing, architecture and medical education, and have made tests between multiple users located in Switzerland, Belgium, Singapore and Japan over the Internet or using ATM. Snapshots from some of these sessions are presented in figure 7 (see Appendix). The system was demonstrated at the Telecom 95 fair in Geneva with a teleshopping application running over a dedicated ATM connection with Singapore.

6. Conclusion and future work

In this paper we have presented the VLNET system which provides a shared environment with virtual humans and their interactions. The motor functions provide powerful and efficient tools for increasing realism of body-centered interactions. In addition, they allow parallel animation of objects in the multiple-user VEs, improving the speed of interaction.

Future work remains for including deformable objects in the shared environment. There is also a need to build an emotion motor that automatically recognizes the emotion of the real participant, and updates the body realistically corresponding to this emotion. Currently the motor functions are coded in software. However further research will continue building general motor functions by combining low-level motors or allowing external scripts to control the objects in the world. Our future work will also aim at the compatibility with the VRML standard.

Acknowledgments

The research was partly supported by ESPRIT project HUMANOID (P 6079), Swiss National Foundation for Scientific Research, Silicon Graphics, Federal Office of Education and Science, and Department of Economy of City of Geneva. We would like to thank assistants of LIG and MIRALAB for the models and libraries.

References

[Amselam 95] Amselem D., "A Window on Shared Virtual Environments", *Presence: Teleoperators and Virtual Environments*, Vol. 4, No. 2, 1995.

[Boulic 95] Boulic R., Capin T., Huang Z., Kalra P., Lintermann B., Magnenat-Thalmann N., Moccozet L., Molet T., Pandzic I., Saar K., Schmitt A., Shen J., Thalmann D., "The Humanoid Environment for Interactive Animation of Multiple Deformable Human Characters", *Proceedings of Eurographics '95*, 1995.

[Boulic 90] Boulic R., Magnenat-Thalmann N. M.,Thalmann D. "A Global Human Walking Model with Real Time Kinematic Personification", *The Visual Computer*, Vol.6(6),1990.

[Broll 95] Broll W., "Interacting in Distributed Collaborative Virtual Environments", *Proceedings of IEEE VRAIS'95*, 1995.

[Bukowski 95] Bukowski R.W., Sequin C.H., "Object Associations: A Simple and Practical Approach to Virtual 3D Manipulation", *Proceedings of ACM Symposium on Interactive 3D Graphics*, Monterey, California, 1995.

[Capin 95] Capin T.K., Pandzic I.S., Magnenat-Thalmann N., Thalmann, D., "Virtual Humans for Representing Participants in Immersive Virtual Environments", *Proceedings of FIVE '95*, London, 1995 (to appear).

[Carlsson 93] Carlsson C., Hagsand O., "DIVE - a Multi-User Virtual Reality System", *Proceedings of IEEE VRAIS '93*, Seattle, Washington, 1993.

[Gisi 94] Gisi M.A., Sacchi C., "Co-CAD: A Collaborative Mechanical CAD System", *Presence: Teleoperators and Virtual Environments*, Vol. 3, No. 4, 1994.

[Gobbetti 93] Gobbetti E., Balaguer J.F., Thalmann D., "VB2: An Architecture for Interaction in Synthetic Worlds", *Proceedings of ACM UIST '93*, Atlanta, 1993.

[Granieri 95] Granieri J.P., Becket W., Reich B.D., Crabtree J., Badler N.I., "Behavioral Control for Real-Time Simulated Human Agents", *Proceedings of ACM Symposium on Interactive 3D Graphics*, Monterey, California, 1995.

[Macedonia 94] Macedonia M.R., Zyda M.J., Pratt D.R., Barham P.T., Zestwitz, "NPSNET: A Network Software Architecture for Large-Scale Virtual Environments", *Presence: Teleoperators and Virtual Environments*, Vol. 3, No. 4, 1994.

[Maxfield 95] Maxfield J., Fernando T., Dew P., "A Distributed Virtual Environment for Concurrent Engineering", *Proceedings of IEEE VRAIS '95*, 1995.

[Pandzic 94] Pandzic I.S., Kalra P., Magnenat-Thalmann N., Thalmann D., "Real-Time Facial Interaction", *Displays*, Vol 15, No 3, 1994.

[Singh 95] Singh G., Serra L., Png W., Wong A., Ng H., "BrickNet: Sharing Object Behaviors on the Net", *Proceedings of IEEE VRAIS '95*, 1995.

[Stansfield 95] Stansfield S., Miner N., Shawver D., Rogers D., "An Application of Shared Virtual Reality in Situational Training", *Proceedings of IEEE VRAIS '95*, 1995.

[Yoshida 95] Yoshida M., Tijerino Y., Abe S., Kishino F., "A Virtual Space Teleconferencing System that Supports Intuitive Interaction for Creative and Cooperative Work", *Proceedings of ACM Symposium on Interactive 3D Graphics*, Monterey, California, 1995.

Editors' Note: See Appendix, p. 313 for coloured figures of this paper

Crowd Simulation in Immersive Space Management

Eric Bouvier
ArSciMed, 207, rue de Bercy, 75012 Paris, France [1]
Institut de Recherche en Informatique de Toulouse,
Université Paul Sabatier, France
Pascal Guilloteau
I.B.M. - European Virtual Reality Buissness Unit, Paris-La Defense, France
Centre d'Infographie, Université de Marne La Vallée, France [2]

Abstract

We present here an immersive application specifically oriented to the visualisation of urban space dedicated to transportation. To the "usual" constraint of urban / architecture walkthrough, we add the dimension of rapid transit of large numbers of people and vehicles, which we manage by a dedicated tool of "crowd simulation", using statistical algorithms such as are used in the realm of physics. This enables us to have a fast and realistic simulation of a complex environment, to be used for urban assessment and planning, on a dedicated graphics-accelerated PC based workstation "Elysium".

1 Introduction

Various projects have recently improved the immersive impression in Virtual Environments. Some consist of enhancing the ergonomics of Virtual Reality devices while others try to get more image quality. The results are sometimes very impressive but there is still an enormous difference between Virtual Environments and real world, mainly due to the absence of life. In space management, the presence of crowd has much more importance than just enhancing immersion because it can be used as a conception tool: the presence of people will change the perception of the signs so that arrangement will be possible to improve their position, dimensions of corridors could be adjusted according to the expected pedestrian flow, organization of emergency planning could be simulated... The application that we present here consists of navigating in a full 3d geometry with movable objects and autonomous pedestrians. The next section presents the architecture of the application, and then each module is described in detail. We finish with a concrete application : the planning of a subway station.

---

[1] email: ascm@world-net.sct.fr
[2] email: Pascal.Guilloteau@univ-mlv.fr

2 Program Architecture

2.1 Presentation of the modules

The application is made of four modules built around a main loop which includes all shared information. The main loop gets data from the input module and spreads the information to the others units that compute the valid position of the observer (navigation module), the positions of the pedestrians (crowd module), the modifications of the objects (movements, creation, destruction), and finally send the updated positions to the graphics unit.

These four modules are :

- The input module
- The navigation and interaction modules
- The crowd simulation module
- The graphics module

2.2 Input / Output Module : Flexor, Voice, Network

The input module scans various devices like the keyboard, the flexor (a kind of mouse with six degrees of freedom, buttons and sensors under the fingers). It also includes network facilities (used for a remote control, or a collaborative review), and the voice recognition (obviously the most natural way of communication for humans).

2.3 Navigation Module : Collision, Level of Detail, Visible Objects, Priority of Drawing

The navigation unit manages the displacement of the user preventing him from passing through walls, objects or other persons, generates the list of visible objects and updates their priority of drawing [6]. A level of detail of the pedestrians geometric model is managed by this module to accelerate the display rate when the user is in motion. This module will be described in section three.

2.4 Crowd Simulation Module

The crowd simulation module controls the movements of each individual of the crowd has it is described in section four. It communicates to the main module all information necessary for display : a list of the pedestrian positions and orientations (to determine the direction of sight) and the kind of individual with its associated geometry. This information can be updated at display frame rate or eventually at a lower rate (in this case intermediate positions and orientations are linearly interpolated). The main module may also communicate to the crowd module interactive modifications in the behaviors of various kinds of people.

2.5 Graphics Module

All objects are loaded in the memory of the graphic board at the beginning of the simulation, and thus the graphics module just has to send to the graphics unit the modified information during run time. This enables the graphics pipeline to run at full speed without the bottleneck of transmitting the whole 3D database for each frame - only short updates are sent.

3 Navigation and Interaction

In the real world, moving and manipulating objects is very easy, but it exploits the natural human ability to perform many manipulations at the same time. So the idea is to try to interact as easily in the immersive world as we proceed in real life. It is common in Virtual Reality to change the viewpoint by tracking the positions and the orientations of the head, and to move objects by tracking the hand, but this would require that the user move as freely in the virtual world as he does in reality. As present immersive equipment does not allow that, we use the sensors under the fingers of the flexor to move forward and backward. The speed of marching is indicated by the pressure of the finger on the sensor. In this way the user can walk in a huge area without moving from his or her position, we just track the rotation of the head to compute the direction of sight. The user can also press the buttons of the flexor to rotate his viewpoint without turning his head so that problems with the helmet cable are avoided.

In our system, more than a passive observer, the user can be part of the simulation. In this case, he is considered as a special pedestrian in the simulated crowd, let's say a "super-pedestrian" that can move in the scene according to user actions and create or erase objects in his visible area. His presence will nevertheless be interpreted like other autonomous pedestrian, for instance the people he encounters will avoid him just like if he was himself a part of the crowd.

3.1 Metaphor of Navigation and Paradigm of Interactions

The interface between the user and the computer is managed by the input module, which gets data from all the input devices. Different metaphors are available through this module depending of the current function of the user. When he navigates in the world, he can create an object at any time of the experiment (by the voice command for example), but at this moment he stop walking and puts the new created object at its valid place, by moving his hand in the three directions. The orientation of the object could be modified by rotating the hand along one of the three axes.

3.2 Collision Detection

The navigation of the user needs to be realistic, and take care of the presence of walls, objects, or pedestrians. The description of the scene is a hierarchical tree where each room and the bounding boxes correspond to a node of the tree, so we can easily know where the user is. With the bounding box of the room, we can compute collisions with his environment only in a smaller part of the tree, without travelling throught the whole tree. If the position of the user is not valid we keep the old one and add a noise to his position so that he can understand that he can't go forward.

3.3 List of visible objects, and priority for rendering

The hierarchical tree is also used to compute the invisible objects from the current point of view, and remove them from the viewing list to accelerate the rendering rate of the graphics board. But we need to know which node is visible from any other one (for example if a door is openned in a room, we can see outside). A database has been created before the experiment to simplify the computation, but there are different ways to automatically precompute this information [7]. The graphics card that we use in the implementation is a fast 3D one, supporting texture mapping, but doesn't have Z-Buffering facilities, so at definition time of the scene the designer has to specify the priority of each object in each room. Then the program manages the problem when many rooms are visible at the same time.

3.4 Low Level of Detail

In the creation of a big scene, many pedestrians could be inside, so if there are one hundred people in the crowd, the graphics rate is not the same when there are ten faces, or three hundred faces for the representation of one pedestrian. So we use three levels of detail for the people depending of the action of the user. Full detail is automatically available when the user doesn't move, and we switch to low detail graphic representation of people when the user starts walking, or erase pedestrians if needed. We could imagine generalizing this method to all objects, or changing the detail as a function of the distance to the observer.

4 Crowd Simulation

A crowd is a complex dynamics system in which global evolution depends on the movements of a great number of actors that have various behavior patterns. There are two main ways to model crowd's movements, the first one is a global approach that consists of analyzing the global evolution of the crowd, modeling it as a continuous fluid. The second approach is to consider each individual of the crowd as an independent entity in a microscopic way. We present here a microscopic approach based on a physical model known as Particle Systems [1]. Particle Systems where first introduced by W.T. REEVES [3] to model natural phenomena like water, gases, fire, clouds... Such fuzzy objects are modeled as a collection of elementary dynamic primitives instances of a certain number of generic classes which define their physical properties (mass, color, lifetime, size...). The movements are computed according to the presence of external forces. The equations of motion for a particle of position P and velocity V with external acceleration A :

$$V = V_0 + \int A(t)dt$$
$$P = P_0 + \int V(t)dt$$

where

P_0 is the initial position and V_0 is the initial velocity.

P, V are integrated in [5] with Euler's method of integration :

$$V(t + \Delta t) = V(t) + A(t)\Delta t$$
$$P(t + \Delta t) = P(t) + \frac{V(t) + V(t + \Delta t)}{2}\Delta t$$

In crowd simulation we cannot be satisfied with such a simple physical based model for two reasons. First the interaction between people in the crowd is very important for the evolution of the system, and usual Particle System engines don't consider them. Secondly, the movements of individuals are not only produced by physical forces as they are described in solid mechanics. "Subobject System" are introduced in [4] as a generalization of Particle System to model flocks of birds, herds and schools. The particles are substituted by a geometrical shape with an orientation, and a behavioral model is associated to them.

Behavior model is based on the perception/action model : each subobject is able to get information from its environment and adapt its reaction according to what it perceives. Interaction between subobjects is described as a particular component of behavior consisting for each of them to look for the position of each other subobject of the system and deciding if it has to modify or not its trajectory. The implementation that was used by Reynolds used a brute force algorithm with a $O(n^2)$ complexity that is not suitable in real-time simulation of great number of subobjects. We use the same kind of approach with different behavior patterns, considering that humans are different than animals, and apply a more efficient model of avoidance. We have implemented people interactions exploiting the fact that a collision may only occur between two people in a period of time Δt if the distance between them is smaller than a certain value r that can be computed by :

$$r = V_1 \Delta t + V_2 \Delta t$$

r is bounded by r' defined with :

$$r' = 2V_{\max} \Delta t$$

where
V_{max} = Maximum velocity of all people.
We use a special data structure with a dynamic sorting of people so that we always maintain a list of possible collisions for a given person. We choose a person in the list with a heuristic function depending on the size of the people, their direction of walk and their speed. The other behavioral rules can be defined and associated to different kinds of individual so that we can simulate a crowd of heterogeneous people including groups. They are divided in two levels. The reflex reactions that enable people to physically avoid obstacles (walls or other persons) and a higher level behavior consisting of more intelligent pattern of behavior. This second level of behavior is modeled by a kind of transition network : We define several states for each kind of individual and determine transitions between them. The different kinds of transition are listed here :

- Timing transition : the state changes after a certain period of time.

- Visiting transition : the state changes when an individual has reached a certain point.

- Density transition : the state changes when the local density of people has reached a certain threshold. Global transition : the state changes when a global event has been activated (for instance an alert). These few elementary transitions can model a complex behavior as a man trying to escape from a high density place (" Density transition ") and giving up after a few minutes realizing that he can't escape (" Timing transition "). In our model, the states are implemented, with analogy to solid mechanics, by a set of decision charges reacting to a set of decision fields. For more details see [1].

5 Example : Space Management for the metro station 'Grand Stade'

We present here an application that we have created to illustrate these concepts. The application has been used in a project consisting of arranging a metro station to adapt it to an increasing traffic due to the construction of a stadium for the Soccer World Cup in 1998. Two points made that situation particularly suitable for our application . First, the teams that traditionally work on this kind of project are compound of various professions with various practices of work which have to work together in a very interactive way. Secondly, the steady flow of the traffic was a constant preoccupation in this project as the metro would be one of the main way to reach the stadium. Our application answer to the first point by the concept of collective use of a virtual environment. The first plans of the station are integrated in the virtual environment so that it is immediately possible for the architects to navigate inside, and detect very soon errors of conception and validate the different ways of circulation for the public. Then the different teams can integrate their respective work interactively: the signs are added, several kind of covering can be proved, the advertising are installed in the most attractive points, the tickets machine can be moved to the most useful place,... However, it is hard to understand the real dimensions of an area if we don?t consider it in the operating situation, where the influence of the presence of the subway travelers is very important. The simulation of the presence of crowd will grant a better perception of the volumes and above all, will permit to verify that the dimensions and the geometry of the place are compatible with the expected pedestrian flows.

The application has been developed on the 'Elysium', a full integrated Immersive Virtual Reality System from I.B.M. and Virtuality(U.K.), which includes a development toolkit, and all devices needed for an immersive experience: a helmet, trackers, sounds and a flexor (a kind of glove that is easier to use and very powerfull). In the final application we have implemented an ergonomic multi-modal interface with voice recognition and voice command that is used to select the kind of operation to proceed or a current object. Then the flexor is used to move the current object that can be a trash can, a maps of the subway network or a tickets machine. This kind of interface has proved to be sufficiently easy to use and intuitive, that no education is necessary to use it. We have also implemented network facilities to give the possibility to walk through the database from any other PC connected with visio-conference. The crowd simulation module has proven to achieve several goals :

- Fill the space : architectural digital mock-ups look much more lively with a dense crowd in it. Besides, crowd bring to virtual digital mock-ups a dimensional unit, a kind of calibration of the space.

- Studying the visibility of signs, advertisement, shops in presence of crowd.

- Improving the traffic and the security. For example, the application has permit to detect that putting a map of the subway network just before the entry of an escalator would increase congestion of the traffic.

In this particular implementation, the behaviors of the crowd are limited : some people are exiting from the subway wagons and reaching the exists or correspondences while other are arriving in the station, buying a ticket at the tickets machine and then walk in the corridors until they reach the wagons. An interactive modification of the position of a tickets machine is linked to a modification of the position of the associated goal and so results in a new behavior of the entering people. A more generic crowd simulation software called KINEMAWAY is actually developed by ArSciMed and will allow a fully control of the definition of the behavior of the crowd.

References

[1] E. Bouvier, E. Cohen, *Simulation of Human Flow with Particle Systems*, Simulators International XII, 27(3), April 1995, pp 349-354

[2] J.L. Pajon, V.Bui Tran, P Vuyslteker, P. Guilloteau, J. David, *Immersive Visualization for Simulations in Earth Sciences*, 2nd Eurographics Workshop on Virtual Environments, Feb. 1995, pp. 12-19

[3] Reeves, W. T., *Particle Systems - A technique for Modeling a Class of Fuzzy Objects*, ACM Transactions on Graphics, 2(2), April 1983, reprinted in Computer Graphics 1983, pp. 359-376.

[4] Reynolds Craig W, *Flocks, Herds, Schools : A Distributed Behavioral Model*, Computer Graphics, 21(4), 1987, pp. 25-34

[5] K. Sims, *Particle Animation and Rendering Using Data Parallel Computation*, Computer Graphics, 24(4), 1990, pp. 405-413.

[6] S.J. Teller, C.H. Seqin, *Visibility Preprocessing for Interactive Walkthroughs*, Computer Graphics, 25(4), July 1991, pp 61-69

[7] T. A. Funkhouser, C. H. Séquin, *Adaptative Display Algorithm for Interactive Frame Rates During Visualization of Complex Virtual Environments*, Computer Graphics, Annual Conferences series 1993, p 247-254.

Editors' Note: See Appendix, p. 315 for coloured figures of this paper

Collaborative Geometrical Modeling in Immersive Virtual Environments

Martin Usoh and Mel Slater[1],
Department of Computer Science,
University College London,
Gower Street,
London WC1E 6BT, UK.

Tzwetomir I. Vassilev[2],
Department of Computer Science,
QMW University of London,
Mile End Road,
London E1 4NS, UK.

Abstract. Although single person virtual environment systems can aid the individual in particular aspects of work they do not address issues of interaction and collaboration between participants and how these can enhance productivity. We present a system for geometrical modeling which permits collaboration between designers at physically separated sites to build and modify objects composed of free-form surfaces. The system is immersive therefore allowing workers not only to be in the same environment as the objects they're designing, but to come together and interact in the same extended space. In this context higher levels of interaction between workers must be used to cooperatively design and modify complex objects. We realise the importance of appropriate behaviour and provide tools which are intuitive in their use. These tools enable the designer to use natural hand and body motion to sweep out complex surfaces and to interactively deform and reshape them. These objects can in turn be seamed together and used as components for more complex and higher level structures.

Keywords. Collaborative virtual environments, distributed virtual environments, virtual reality, virtual classroom, information retrieval, geometrical modeling.

1. Introduction

This paper describes an application for multi-participant geometric design that is being constructed under the DEVRL project (Distributed Extensible Virtual Reality Laboratory). This project is a collaboration between four UK universities to establish a distributed virtual reality laboratory initially exploiting the Internet (in particular SuperJANET) as the communication channel for constructing multi-participant applications. The philosophy of the project as a whole, and its various applications are described in [1].

---

[1]m.usoh@cs.ucl.ac.uk, m.slater@cs.ucl.ac.uk
[2]Permanent address for correspondence: ceco@ait.tu-rousse.bg

In [2] we described an initial system for creating and modifying free-form geometric surfaces in immersive virtual environments. This was based B-Spline surfaces, and exploited an interaction model that we refer to as "body centred interaction" (BCI) [3]. This interaction model is designed in an attempt to maximise the sense of presence of individuals in immersive environments. In this new work we have extended the sophistication of the underlying geometrical model, and have correspondingly extended the application of the BCI paradigm. A major purpose of the work is to provide the ability for shared modeling, where a (small) number of designers simultaneously inhabit a virtual space for collaborative/cooperative work. This raises a number of interesting problems for the shared environments in which there is a high degree of interaction and necessity of collaboration between participants working together on complex objects. For instance, in creating a design what should be the relationship between the participants? Should it be hierarchical whereby each designer is able to modify his/her own segment of the design but the chief designer is able to affect changes to the whole design? How will the system deal with such a structure and how can communication be facilitated between the different groups. Since the mid 1980s such issues have been debated in Computer Supported Co-operative Work (CSCW) [4]. Investigations have been conducted using video and audio links where users can interact with a viewpoint from their own space. Now in the mid 1990s issues are being considered relating to participants whose viewpoints are from within the same extended virtual space. We note, however, that such issues are most effectively investigated using systems which are able to deliver immersive capabilities.

In describing the UNISURF CAD system, Pierre Bezier distinguished three classes of surface design problem [5]:

- Objects that require great accuracy, that are of major technical importance for the product being designed, such as turbine foils or boat hulls;

- Objects that are used only as part of an assembly, for example, to separate other parts, and which do not require such great accuracy as the first;

- Objects created by stylists, where their aesthetic appearance is the most important characteristic.

In this research we restrict attention to the third type of design, only because it is recognised that with virtual environments available today, it is not feasible to create objects with the precise accuracy required for the first two. However, concepts that relate to the third type of design will invariably be relevant to the other two. Our work is also mainly focused towards immersive environments without precluding application to non-immersive desktop systems. We note, however, that given an environment which is capable of including participants as integral and embodied parts of the virtual world their productivity can become increased since there is less of a need to learn new and often inappropriate paradigms originally developed for desktop systems. The designers can be placed in the same space as the object they are creating and are able to utilise natural movements of their body in creating the design. In addition they can relate more directly to the objects which are being modeled in terms of size and spatial characteristics.

In Section 2 we briefly describe the deformable B-Spline surface model and its capabilities. In Section 3 we discuss how these capabilities are mapped to the interaction paradigm, and in Section 4 the particular collaborative aspects. Conclusions are presented in Section 5.

2. Deformable B-Spline Surface

For designers to effectively utilise a modeling system they must be aware of the properties and behaviour of the materials used in the system. The virtual materials must exhibit constant and repeatable deformations following a set of characteristics such as rigidity, cohesiveness, elasticity and plasticity. We assume that the properties of each surface will allow it to:

- be deformed when a force or a set of forces is applied in an appropriate manner;

- be split or broken into a set of component surfaces;

- regain its previous shape after a deformation;

- seam with other surfaces given appropriate adhesive and cohesive forces.

In [2] we used a simple CAGD scheme based on B-Spline surfaces, represented by control points to create deformable surfaces. In order to change the surface the control points would have to be manipulated. As was pointed out, and as has been pointed out by others before, this does not provide for an elegant method for deforming a surface. If the surface is complex, there are too many control points to manipulate, and the relationship between the surface and the control points becomes non-intuitive. For a single bi-cubic Bezier patch we must deal with sixteen control points. Even in this simple case parts of the patch will occlude some control points and the spatial relationship between control points and the patch is difficult to understand. Given the capability of an immersive virtual environment system, however, a designer can become more aware of this relationship when in comparison to viewing through a desktop display without stereo. It nevertheless remains impractical for the designer to use direct manipulation of the control points to achieve a desired shape since the effect on the surface of manipulating a group of control points must be well understood [6].

In line with our theory of body centred interaction, direct manipulation of the surface became a goal. However, in order to provide an added sense of "reality" to the deformation process we opted for a mixed geometrical-physical model, the underlying paradigm being that of the application of forces to a surface that would deform elastically as a result. In order to achieve this the method of minimising appropriate functionals was exploited, which is briefly described below.

Let $w(u,v) = [x(u,v), y(u,v), z(u,v)]$ be a B-Spline surface parameterized by u and v, and let $f(u,v)$ denote the applied sculpting forces on it. The energy functional for surfaces was employed [7] shown in Eq. (1).

$$E = \iint_{surface} [c_1 w_u^2 + c_2 w_v^2 + c_3 w_{uu}^2 + c_4 w_{uv}^2 + c_5 w_{vv}^2$$

$$+ c_6 w_{u^2v}^2 + c_7 w_{uv^2}^2 + c_8 w_{u^2v^2}^2 - 2f\,w] du dv, \qquad (1)$$

where the suffixes mean partial derivatives in respect to the parameters u and v.

The integral (1) has the following advantages over the other functionals described in the literature [8, 9, 10, 11]:

(a) Its minimisation leads to a linear system $KuVKv = CuFCv^T$ where V is the matrix of spline control points matrix, Ku and Kv are stiffness matrices, Cu and Cv are coefficients and F is the force matrix. As one can see the two dimensionality of control points and forces is preserved and due to this fact the system can be solved very efficiently.

(b) Most of the functionals in the literature referenced above have two parameters to control the physical properties of the surface; resistance to stretching and to bending. Here it is also possible to control the hardness of the material thus affecting the degree of spread of the deformation across the material.

(c) The new proposed fairness norm has two stiffness matrices, one in direction of the parameter u and another one for v. This gives users the opportunity to design nonisotropic materials, i.e. with different properties in the different directions.

The following actions can be performed on the surface:
- Applying a single force or a set of forces;
- Deforming a curve embedded on the surface;
- Deforming an area of the surface;
- Moving a single point from the surface to a new position;
- Moving a surface curve to a new target curve in the space.

3. Interactive Surface Creation

One of the important aspects of our model for the enhancement of presence in immersive virtual environments (for example, [12]) is that there should be a strong correlation between sensory data (e.g., the visual input) and proprioception (correspondingly, the proprioceptive information generated by head movements). This match requires that the internal mental representation of the movement and disposition of a participant's body correspond to the sensory data generated by those body movements. So when, for example, proprioceptive feedback is generated as a result of an arm moving, then correspondingly the participant should see the arm move, and ideally hear the effect of the movement, and (even more ideally) feel any (virtual) objects with which the arm comes into contact as a result of this movement. The maximisation of this match between proprioception and sensory data is one of the dimensions that, in our model, increases the sense of presence that an individual has of being in the virtual environment.

The concept in the BCI paradigm for interaction derives from this idea. BCI requires that appropriate whole body gestures be employed for the realisation of actions in a VE. For example, it is certainly possible to move through a VE by using a 3D mouse, or by making simple hand gestures. However, this reduces the match between proprioception and sensory data - since the visual flow does not match the proprioceptive information about movements of the body. Hence the idea of "walking in place" [12] to simulate real walking was used, and experimental studies confirmed that this method does, other things being equal, increase the reported sense of presence.

Now this approach can also be used to carry out actions that are not possible in everyday life - such as creating surfaces out of nothing. The designer holds a virtual wand-like tool. As s/he sweeps out a shape in space the surface is correspondingly visually created as an interpolated surface through the space that has been swept out. The wand itself can be extended or retracted, and can be bent to various curved shapes - thus the shape of the surface to be swept out is itself variable, and under control of the designer (see Plate 1). This process is essentially transforming the kinetic energy of the designer into visible surfaces, making a relationship between body moves, and visual appearance - turning a sweeping gesture into something concrete.

Having swept out a surface the designer can also deform it. This can be achieved in various ways:

- selecting a point on the surface and applying a force.

- marking out a curve on the surface, and applying a force to the interior of the curve. This is achieved by the designer using the wand to mark out the surface, and then specifying the force and the direction in which it is applied. Only the part of the surface inside this curve will be deformed.

- directly grabbing hold of part of the surface and moving it.

At all times the designer has a virtual body representation - being able to see the trunk of the body, the left and right hands and the legs. In the current system, only the right hand is tracked, so that the left hand is immobile. However, we still make use of the left hand. Rather than the tools for creation and deformation of surfaces being available as 3D icons or "menu" items, a way of thinking appropriate to 2D interfaces, the designer always has the tools literally "to hand". Tools not in use can be placed in the left hand, and so are always quickly available during the design process. Plate 2 illustrates the deformation of a flat swept out surface after applying a force to it.

Since the geometrical representation of the surfaces is based on B-Splines, it is not difficult to seam surfaces together with a desired degree of continuity along the edge through appropriate interpolation of the control points at the joining edges. Where the number of control points on two edges differ a knot insertion algorithm can be used to equalise the number of points. This aspect of the work is being implemented at the time of writing.

3.1 System Architecture

The system is implemented on the DIVISION ProVision100 VPX (PixelPlanes) system under dVS 2.0.4. Although much faster than the ProVision200 used for our original system, this still has problems with updating the model fast enough for the kind of interaction that we would like. For example, when a force is applied we would like the surface to deform continuously (rubber band fashion) as the force is being defined. Unfortunately, the system cannot keep up with this so that it is necessary to first fix the force, and then the surface will jump to the new shape specified by the force. It is hoped that this problem will be resolved with a future version (dVS 3.1).

The dVS operating system is based on a distributed client/server architecture. It consists of a set of independent modules or actors which provide a set of services in the environment. The actors are overseen by a director which maintains the distributed model database. Each actor has a local copy of the database with elements appropriate to it. For instance the visualisation actor would contain copies of model elements relating to visualisation and rendering such as the material properties of the surface. The collision actor in turn would contain data relating to object positions and bounding volumes. Each actor is free to modify its local database but updates to the global database are performed via the director. The system provides an application actor for user programming. Objects can be defined and modified at this user level and changes then relayed to the director for lower level processing. This, however, can be also be a source of bottlenecks in the system processing, manifesting itself in the form of reduced model update rates. In attempt to overcome this we have moved the model creation and manipulation functions from the user level to the lower visualisation level. In addition we are able to make some direct calls to the renderer level. However, we are still restricted from direct access to the polygons at the renderer level - something which is important in fast creation and manipulation of dynamic objects.

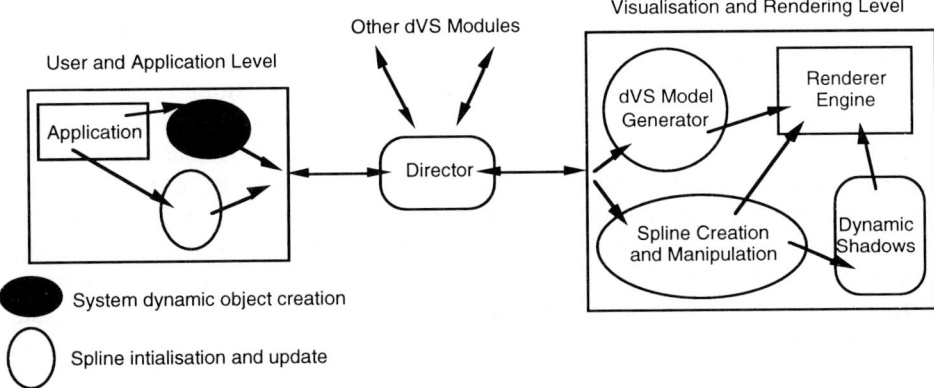

Fig. 1. The modeling architecture

Figure 1 illustrates schematically the system model of dVS with the spline module at the visualisation level. At this level it is also possible to include other modules requiring fast dynamic modifications of polygons to aid model creation. In [13], for example, we have noted the importance of dynamic shadows on presence and spatial awareness. Depth cues obtained from shadows cast by the virtual body or tool onto the sculpted surface or, one surface onto another, can enhance spatial perception and increase model awareness.

4. Collaborative Aspects

The major focus of the DEVRL project is collaboration in shared environments. The DEVRL surface design system will allow several designers to create free form surface shapes in the same environment. The particular features that we are aiming for in this regard are that designers:

• can pass surfaces between one another;

• can merge the objects that they have created into one combined object;

• can create shapes jointly - e.g., stretching surfaces by pulling at different edges, thus allowing them to collaboratively design objects in a novel way;

- can stretch surfaces around other objects (and around each other), thus creating a basic form of "virtual clothing".

Imagine a virtual world consisting of one plane forming the ground. Our goal is that a group of designers can virtually "terraform" such a world - by deforming the ground plane itself, by creating new shapes and combining them together.

There are significant problems in designing a system for effective collaboration in this context. Designers must be able to inform each other of their intentions: for example, when a designer grabs hold of a shape currently being held by another designer, is this an attempt to take the shape away or to stretch it, or for some other purpose? A secondary channel of communication, such as voice, appears to be essential. When several designers are simultaneously attempting to deform a shape, what is the protocol that decides how exactly the shape deforms? This is made easier with the method described in Section 2, since several forces can be simultaneously applied to a surface to deform it. But the precise interaction method to be used to allow the designers to accomplish this have not been decided as yet.

5. Conclusions

At the time of writing the creation and deformation of surfaces by a single designer in the manner described in Section 3 has been implemented. Curved surface generation has been made capable in three ways:

(a) creating a surface and applying a force (direction and magnitude) to deform it;
(b) creating a surface and manipulating it by directly displacing its control points;
(c) deforming the sweeping tool and then using it to create a curved surface.

We have noted that point (b) is not the desired method of deforming parametric surfaces since it is non-intuitive. The system must provide for an elegant and direct procedure which can allow the designer to utilise real world processes which they are generally familiar with. Of course the designer can also be given appropriate 'magical' tools for enhancing the design, e.g. for smoothing and closing the model.

Using dVS's facility for shared worlds across WANs it has been possible to have two participants simultaneously in the VE and able to see each other's actions. However, at the time of writing the work on full-scale collaborative design is in progress.

References

1. Slater, M., Usoh, M., Benford, S., Snowdon, D., Brown, C., Rodden, T., Smith, G., Wilbur, S.: Distributed Extensible Virtual Reality Laboratory - A

Project for Cooperation in Multi-Participant Environments, Proc. of Eurographics Workshop on Virtual Environments, Monte Carlo, Feb. 19-20 (1996). Also this volume.

2. Slater, M., Usoh, M.: Modeling in Immersive Virtual Environments: A Case for the Science of VR, International Conference on Applications of Virtual Reality, 7-9 June, (1994), Leeds, UK, and in Huw Jones, Rae Earnshaw, John Vince, Virtual Reality Applications Academic Press, (1995).

3. Slater, M., Usoh, M.: Body Centred Interaction in Immersive Virtual Environments, in N. Magnenat Thalmann and D. Thalmann (eds.) Artificial Life and Virtual Reality, John Wiley and Sons, 125-148 (1994).

4. Rodden, T.: A Survey of CSCW Systems, Interacting with Computers, December, Butterworth-Heinemann, 3(3), 319-354 (1991).

5. Bezier, P.: The Mathematical Basis of the UNISURF CAD System, Butterworth & Co., (1986).

6. Hsu, W.M., Hughes, J.F., Kaufman, H.: Direct Manipulation of Free-Form Deformations, Computer Graphics (SIGGRAPH), 26(2), July, 177-182 (1992).

7. Vassilev, T.: A Method for Fair B-spline Interpolation and Approximation by Insertion of Additional Data Points, in press (1996).

8. Celniker, G., Gossard, D.: Deformable Curve and Surface Finite Elements for Free-Form Shape Design, Proceedings of SIGGRAPH, 25(4), 257-266 (1991).

9. Celniker, G., Welch, W.: Linear Constraints for deformable B-spline surfaces, Proceedings of the 1992 Symposium on Interactive 3D Graphics, March 165-170 (1992).

10. Halstead, M., Kass, M., DeRose, T.: Efficient, fair interpolation using Catmull-Clark Surfaces, Proceedings of SIGGRAPH, Annual series, 35-44 (1993).

11. Terzopoulos, D., Qin, H.: Dynamic NURBS with Geometric Constraints for Interactive Sculpting, ACM Transactions on Graphics, 13(2), 103-136 (1994).

12. Slater, M., Usoh, M., Steed, A.: Taking Steps: The Influence of a Walking Metaphor on Presence in Virtual Reality, ACM Transactions on Computer Human Interaction (TOCHI), September (1995).

13. Slater, M., Usoh, M., Chrysanthou, Y.: The Influence of Dynamic Shadows on Presence in Immersive Virtual Environments, 2nd Eurographics Workshop on

Virtual Environments, Monte Carlo, Jan. 31 - Feb. 1st, Eurographics Workshop Proceedings, ISSN 1024-0861 (1995).

Editors' Note: See Appendix, p. 316 for coloured figures of this paper

Multi-user interactions in the context of concurrent virtual world modelling

Patrice Torguet, Frédéric Rubio,
Véronique Gaildrat, René Caubet

I.R.I.T., Paul Sabatier University,
118, Route de Narbonne, 31062 Toulouse Cedex, France
e-mail: {torguet I rubio}@irit.fr
URL: http://www.ensica.fr/~torguet

Abstract. Distributed virtual reality, thanks to newly proposed paradigms, offers interesting perspectives to virtual world modelling. Our main interests are in applications which allow users to edit and deform existing shapes. This paper presents a concurrent virtual world modelling application based on those ideas. Herein is shown how concrete manipulations of tools (such as a hammer) are transformed into free form deformations of existing shapes. We also present a first implementation based on VIPER (VIrtuality Programming EnviRonment) a generic distributed virtual reality development platform.

1 Introduction

First virtual reality (VR) applications were mainly architectural walk-through with symbolic representations of more complex elements (e.g. a cube instead of a house). As soon as basic virtual reality paradigms were defined, software designers turned their attention towards interactivity problems.

Therefore, recently, proposed interfaces were improved thanks to technology advances (workstation power, new and reliable peripherals...) and virtual reality interactivity studies. Moreover, distributed virtual reality, adds multi-user interaction and co-operation to virtual environments. Those aspects are the main interests of our current works.

We focus on distributed virtual reality applied to interactive world modelling. Our final objective is to offer high level metaphors for co-operative world modelling. We wish to provide users a set of tools used to interact in a virtual environment in the most natural way: they can model shapes by doing natural gestures they would make in a real situation (i.e. hammer an object, dig a hole...).

In this paper we present an application where users model virtual worlds by interacting with modelling tools. Section 2 is an overview of VIPER [1], our generic distributed virtual reality programming platform. Section 3 presents the modelling application. Section 4 details the distribution of such an application based on

VIPER. Finally we conclude our paper with some perspectives on either our modelling application and VIPER.

2 VIPER: a VR application programming environment

Developing distributed virtual environments is a complex time consuming task. In order to develop such environments the programmer has to be proficient in network, graphics, device handlers and user interface programming. Moreover, network based programs are inherently more difficult to program and debug than sequential ones. In order to simplify this task, we have developed VIPER (VIrtuality Programming EnviRonment) which enables the rapid and easy development of distributed VR applications.

2.1 The virtual environment model

VIPER is aimed for the design of every application based on a virtual environment which can be modelled by exchanges (symbolised by *stimuli*) between *entities*, in a *virtual universe* (Fig. 1).

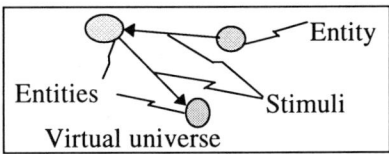

Fig. 1. Virtual environment structure

The entity paradigm allows uniform management of virtual worlds scenery, virtual objects and *avatars* (an entity which behaves as an interface between a user [2], an application [3, 4] or a robot and the virtual universe). Entities are autonomous and own a set of attributes and behaviours. They are conceptually grouped in *families* (a set of entities which own the same attributes and behaviours). Our system is best suited for homogeneous virtual environments (few families made of many instances).

The purpose of this structure is to simplify the definition of distribution schemes. Autonomous entities lead to a perfect encapsulation of the behaviour and state of an entity, and therefore facilitates distribution of entities: such an entity can execute its behaviour on any site communicating with other entities through well defined stimuli.

Interactions between entities, modelled by the *stimulus* paradigm (phenomenon or event perceptible by an entity), cross media, called *stimuli spaces*, which allow communications between many entities simultaneously. Each stimuli space is in fact a projection of the environment along a specific type of stimulus (3D shape space, sound space...). An entity receives perceptible stimuli (visible shapes, near sounds...) through *sensors* and acts on its environment through *effectors* (producing new stimuli) (Fig. 2). Sensors and effectors also manage interaction with the real world (e.g. a glove and a tracker sensors which track user movements and a HMD effector which presents two images to an user).

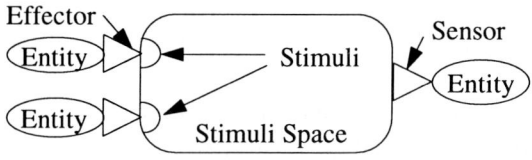

Fig. 2. Interaction model

Each entity owns a set of behaviour components which modify its internal state (the set of its attributes) and commands actions to its effectors. Behaviour components are triggered by sensors (there is a time sensor which allows timed behaviours) or by other components.

2.2 The software architecture of VIPER

In order to better suit the structure of our applications, we have adopted an object oriented design for our system. Classical advantages of object oriented languages (encapsulation, reuse...) and most of all, inheritance are very interesting to model our entity families. The C++ programming language has been chosen because of its availability on most hardware platforms (from low-end PCs to multiprocessors).

In order to simplify the developer task we decided to offer the programmer a set of generic classes of concurrent aggregates [5]. Those aggregates encapsulate object distribution mechanisms for their elements and remote access over a network. A number of distribution models used in distributed VR have been implemented into aggregate classes: active replication [4], replication on demand [6], topologically optimised distribution schemes [7, 1]... Virtual universes and stimuli spaces have been defined respectively as concurrent aggregates of entities and stimuli.

The software architecture of VIPER consists in four layers (Fig. 3).

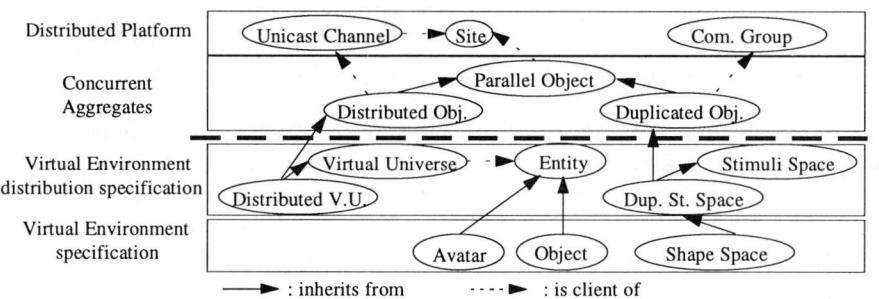

Fig. 3. Layers and example classes of VIPER

The two first layers are the kernel of VIPER:

- The first layer, the distributed platform, is composed of a set of sites (workstations, multicomputers...) which create a virtual machine based on a message passing system like PVM [8] or RMP [9]. This layer encapsulates the communication system used by our system. VIPER requires that such a communication system provides reliable (even though unreliable communication can be used in some part of the system) point to point (unicasting) and group (multicasting) communications.

- Using this layer, an object-oriented concurrent programming environment encapsulates data distribution and an SPMD (single program multiple data) model (cf. [5] for details). This layer proposes aggregates classes (also called parallel object classes).

The two last layers are the API (Application Programming Interface) of VIPER and define two programming levels:

- The third layer allows the definition of specific virtual environment distribution schemes. Distribution and remote access mechanisms can be chosen or redefined from a library of existing classes of parallel objects (from the second layer). Thus, the developer defines new stimuli spaces and new virtual universes. And therefore, he/she is able to optimise thoroughly his/her application.

- Using the last layer, a developer can describe a virtual environment (entities and their interactions) as if his/her application was a sequential object oriented program. He/she defines new classes of entities (or stimuli, stimuli spaces, sensors, effectors) that inherit from existing ones. In fact, this programming level totally hides the distributed aspects of the application.

3 An example application: multi-user world modelling

The first application we have developed is a multi-user world modeller. In this part, we will describe the design and implementation of this application.

We think that interactive world modelling can benefit a lot from distributed virtual reality in term of ergonomics, conviviality and efficiency (two or more users can co-operate to model a large virtual world). In order to better apprehend the problems of this domain, we have studied some existing multi-user modelling applications.

The first application, we know of, is built over Shastra, an architecture for development of collaborative applications [10]. Several users can co-operate in order to smooth a polyhedral model. The session master (a specific user) distributes certain areas of the object to smooth to other users. However, those tasks are performed through a 2D classical GUI, which is not the best suited environment for 3D manipulations.

Within the Virtuosy project [11], a collaborative design application has been initiated in the domain of the fashion industry. This application allows several designers to visualise and modify clothes, negotiating and discussing their properties. Those designed objects are manipulated and changed in a 3D real-time virtual environment. Moreover, animated mannequins wear those clothes and move in a realistic way.

According to those studies and our previous application domain (declarative multimodal modelling) [12], we have decided to design an interactive multi-user world modelling application.

We wish to introduce high level metaphors for co-operative world modelling. We offer users a set of tools used to interact in a virtual environment in the most natural way: they can model shapes by doing natural gestures they would make in a real situation (i.e. hammer an object, dig a hole...). Our aim is to make modelling more intuitive. Therefore our tools have a double role: their shape gives a hint on both their function (hammer, nippers...) and their use (to hammer, to pinch...).

We have currently developed two deformation tools: a hammer and a hook which can be used to interactively deform surfaces (the user catch some part of an object with the hook and then move or rotate it to produce surface deformations). Tools are available on tables which exist in the environment. Of course, the user can also directly manipulate objects in order to move them, to arrange them...

3.1 The mathematical model of deformations

Let us describe first, the mathematical model used by our deformation tools. The deformation model we use, is called FFD (Free-Form Deformation) [13]. FFD deforming consists in enclosing an object (or a part of it) in a parallelepiped of clear, flexible plastic. The object is imagined to also be flexible, so that it deforms along with the plastic that surrounds it.

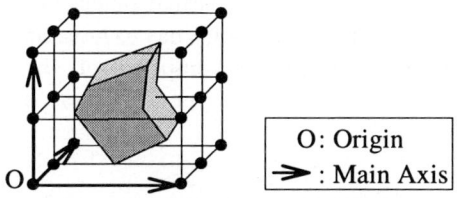

O: Origin
➤ : Main Axis

Fig. 4. An example of lattice

Deforming consists in a number of steps. First of all, the parallelepiped is defined by providing its origin, main axes and the number of control points on each axis (Fig. 4). Then, we compute the object point co-ordinates in the lattice local co-ordinate system. Thereafter, every lattice deformation (moving one or many control points) can create an object deformation according to a Bézier or B-Spline interpolation. We illustrate this with an interpolation based on trivariate Bernstein polynomials:

$$P_{ffd} = \sum_{i=0}^{l} \binom{l}{i}(1-s)^{l-i} s^i \left[\sum_{j=0}^{m} \binom{m}{j}(1-t)^{m-j} t^j \left[\sum_{k=0}^{n} \binom{n}{k}(1-u)^{n-k} u^k P'_{ijk} \right] \right]$$

where (s, t, u) are local co-ordinates of the processed point (P_{ffd}) and P'_{ijk} are control points after deformation of the lattice.

However it is, sometimes difficult to obtain specific effects (such as flattening a bump). We, therefore, decided to design a system which would mask completely the mathematical functions used to deform objects.

We propose a set of tools based on this deformation model [14]. The only parameters of those tools are natural (the part of the object which is to be modified, the size of a hammer head...). Moreover, those high level parameters are a concise definition of the deformation which, when transmitted over a network, keep the bandwidth usage low.

The lattice used to deform with a hammer is created as follows: as soon as the hammer head (in fact a point of the head) enters an object, a lattice is automatically generated according to hammer and object specific parameters. The lattice length and width are computed so that they closely enclose the hammer head (this allows us to perform a local, isolated deformation). The lattice depth and control point density are defined taking into account the object flexibility. This feature is not currently physically based and only acts as a deformation parameter.

Then the lattice is oriented in relation to the hammer head trajectory (two last positions) and translated to the impact point. Lattice local co-ordinates of the object points are computed. The lattice is modified (according to the hammer head size and the speed of the blow) and the object deformed.

3.2 Introducing modelling tools in VIPER

Within VIPER all manipulations (grabbing, moving...) are modelled by exchanging orders (a subclass of stimuli) between entities within the framework of a specific stimuli space called an order space. Each virtual object has an order sensor which receives its given orders. Moreover, an entity has to have an order effector in order to manipulate other entities. An order is composed of: the id of the manipulated entities, the id of the manipulator, the type of order and specific parameters (depending on the order type).

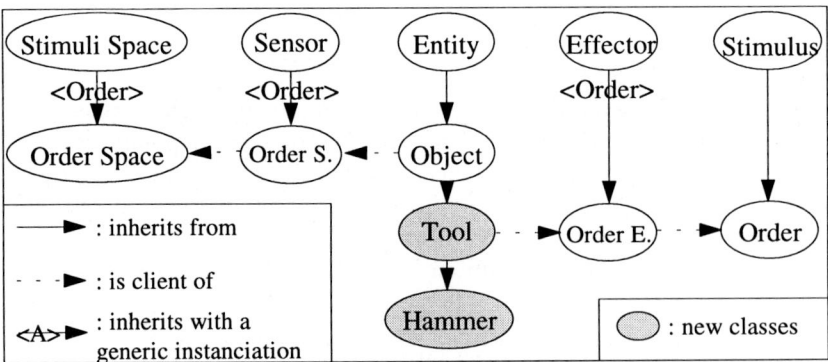

Fig. 5. Extending VIPER with new classes

A modelling tool is an entity (in fact it is an object which is in turn an entity). It is manipulated by one or many entities and it, also, manipulates one or many entities. Therefore, a tool owns at least an order sensor (inherited from the object class) and an order effector which allows him to send manipulation orders (Fig. 5).

For example, when a user manipulates a hammer so as to deform an object (Fig. 6), the user's avatar entity sends manipulation orders (grabbing, releasing) to a hammer entity. This entity analyses such orders and its surrounding environment (through a shape sensor) in order to detect any collision. Whenever a collision is detected, the hammer entity sends a deformation order to the hit object. As soon as the target object entity receives the deformation order, it builds a lattice (see section 3.1 for details), deforms it as required by the deformation order high level parameters (the last two hammer positions and the size of the hammer head) and then computes the new shape.

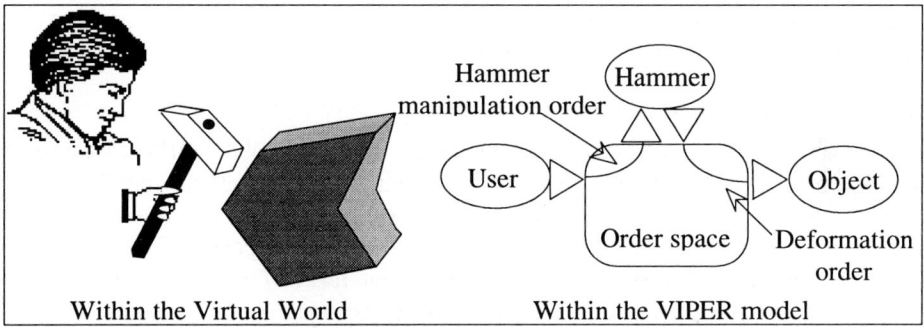

Fig. 6. Hitting with a hammer

4 Application distribution

We will now describe, the distribution of this application using VIPER. Showing how distributed virtual universes and distributed image spaces can solve groupware problems of the application.

4.1 Managing distributed entities

Within a Distributed VR application, obviously, the first distributed data are entities. This distribution is managed by distributed virtual universes (DVU). Each DVU is a concurrent aggregate of entities. It defines a naming function for entities (an entity Id is composed of its DVU Id followed by its creation site Id and a sequential number), a distributing function which tells where (on which site) each entity is stored and possibly some remote access functions for entities.

The simplest class of DVU is the passive distributed virtual universe. This universe holds entities that cannot move from site to site. New entities can be added dynamically on specific sites and new sites can join the DVU. Avatars obviously belong to this type of universe. Such a DVU only provides a simple distribution function which extracts the site Id from an entity Id.

However, in order to better deal with the high latency of wide area networks, we have designed another type of DVU called the active distributed virtual universe (Fig. 7). This DVU tries to minimise the distance between interacting entities. For example, when an user manipulates a virtual object which happen to reside on a distant site, the DVU will as soon as possible move the virtual object entity to the manipulating user site. Such a DVU provides a distribution function (implemented by a replicated synchronised table which contains for each entity of the DVU: an entity Id and the Id of the site which currently owns the entity) and remote access methods used to send and receive entities (using point to point communication).

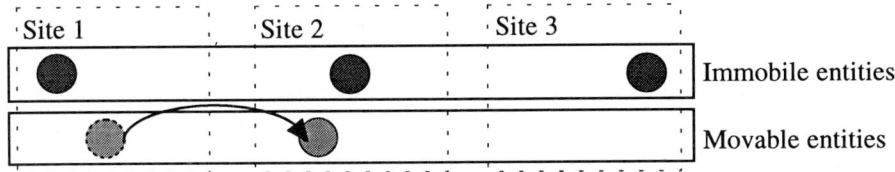

Fig. 7. Distributed virtual universes

4.2 Interactions between distributed entities

As soon as two or more users enter the modelling space, a problem arises. Each user must see other users in order to interact with them. VIPER solves this problem with a distributed stimuli space, called the shape space, which uses an active replication distribution model. Each entity owns a *shape* which is composed of one or many geometric 3D shapes (which are used as different *level of details* or as multiple views of a same entity), a position, an orientation and a scaling factor in relation to a father object co-ordinate system (the shape space is a hierarchy of shapes). Each time an entity modifies its shape (movement, change of parent or deformation) the stimuli space replicates those changes on any site using a stimuli space dedicated communication group. Then each entity which owns a shape sensor can use this hierarchy in order to present a view of the world to its user (avatar) or to detect collisions with other objects (avatars, hammer entities...).

It is important to note that all communications are hidden in the stimuli space and therefore an entity, as well as the programmer of the entity class, is not concerned with communication management.

Direct interaction (i.e. when an entity manipulates other entities) in a distributed context is another problem: interacting entities may happen to reside on different sites. We have decided to model those interactions by exchanging orders (a new class of stimuli) between entities within the framework of a specific distributed stimuli space called the order space. We could have solved this problem with the previously exposed replicated stimuli space. However we can optimise the application by defining a new stimuli space which sends only orders to interested entity sites using point to point communications (Fig. 8). Indeed, as each entity Id can be translated to a site Id where the entity is stored (thanks to DVU distribution functions), we can only send orders to those sites.

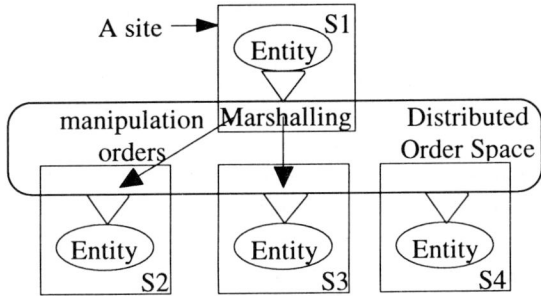

Fig. 8. A distributed order space

4.3 Access management

In our application, access management problems may occur when two or more users want to access the same object in order to manipulate it.

In the current version of VIPER, we state that a new deformation can be started on one object if and only if the lattice to create doesn't intersect with an existing lattice. For other manipulations (e.g. moving an object, rotating it), a manipulation can only be started if no other manipulations are being performed.

5 Conclusion and future works

We have implemented the ideas presented here within the context of a countryside modelling application (see Appendix). Users can do terrain modelling like digging lakes, growing hills... They can also place scenery elements (trees, houses...) on the terrain. Multi-user aspects are very interesting in this application, because they accelerate a lot large terrain modelling.

Currently, we are improving the collaborative aspects of our modelling system. Indeed we are developing multi-user deforming tools (e.g. a tool to co-operatively bend, twist, stretch or flatten objects). These tools are based on the same mathematical model. However, in this case, multiple users are able to manipulate simultaneously the same lattice.

We are also further developing VIPER with interpreted behaviours. Those behaviours will allow us to dynamically add behaviours to objects in our virtual world modelling application. Thus, using an enchanter's wand metaphor, users will be able to select objects and add interpreted behaviours to them.

Moreover we intend to develop multimodal modelling (which will allow combination of voice and gestures to command orders) and general purpose tools (e.g. brushes to paint objects, connectors to allow hierarchical objects to be defined).

References

1. Torguet P., Caubet R., "VIPER (VIrtuality Programming EnviRonment): A virtual reality applications design platform", 2nd Eurographics Workshop on Virtual Environments, Jan. 1995.
2. Mouli R., Duthen Y., Caubet R., "In VitrAm (In Vitro Animats, a behavioural simulation model)" 2nd IEEE International Workshop RO-MAN'93, Tokyo, 3-5 November 1993.
3. Snowdon D. N., West A. J., "The AVIARY VR-System. A Prototype Implementation", 6th ERCIM workshop, 1-3 June 1994, Stockholm.
4. Carlsson C. and Hagsand O. "DIVE - a Platform for Multi-User Virtual Environments", Computer & Graphics, Vol. 17, N° 6, November/December 1993.
5. Moisan B., Duthen Y., Caubet R., "Tools for SPMD object-oriented programming" EUROMICRO'93 Barcelona 6-10 September 1993.
6. Singh G., Serra L., Png W., Ng H., "BrickNet: A Software Toolkit for Network-Based Virtual Worlds", Presence, Vol. 3, No. 1, Winter 1994.
7. Macedonia M.R., Zyda M.J., Pratt D.R., Barham P.T., "Exploiting Reality with Multicast Groups: A Network Architecture for Large-Scale Virtual Environments". In proceedings of VRAIS'95. IEEE Computer Society Press, Los Alamitos, CA, March 1995.
8. Sunderam V., "PVM : A framework for Parallel Distributed Computing", Concurrency: Practice & Experience Vol. 2 N° 4, December 1990.
9. Whetten B., Montgomery T., Kaplan S., "A High Performance Totally Ordered Multicast Protocol", In Theory and Practice of Distributed Systems, N° 938 in LNCS, Springer Verlag 1994.
10. Anupam V. and Bajaj C., "SHASTRA - An Architecture for Development of Collaborative Applications", Proceedings of the Second IEEE Workshop on Enabling Technologies : Infrastructures of Collaborative Enterprises, Morgantown, West Virginia, IEEE Computer Society Press, p. 155-166.
11. Benford S., Bowers J., Gray S., Leevers D., Rodden T., Rygol M., Stanger V., «The Virtuosi Project», Proceedings VR'94 (London Virtual Reality Expo 1994), Meckler, London, Feb. 1994.
12. Gaildrat V., Caubet R., Rubio F., "Declarative Scene Modelling with Dynamic Links and Decision Rules Distributed Among the Objects", IFIP International Conference on Computer Graphics ICCG93 Bombay, February 1993, p. 165-178.
13. Sederberg G. T. W., Parry S. R., "Free-Form Deformation of Solid Geometric Models", Siggraph 86 Conference Proceedings, Vol. 20, N° 14.
14. Rubio F., Torguet P., Gaildrat V., Caubet R., "Déformations de formes libres à l'aide d'outils de réalité virtuelle", Interface to Real and Virtual Worlds, Montpellier, France, June 1995.

Editors' Note: See Appendix, p. 320f. for coloured figures of this paper

System integration of VR-simulated surgical support system

Hiroshi Oyama, M.D.

Head of MedVR project,
National Cancer Center Hospital,
5-1-1, Tsukiji, Chuo-ku, Tokyo 104, Japan.
E-mail: hoyama@medvr.res.ncc.go.jp

Abstract. We describe here a virtual reality simulated surgical support system and how to use a technology of virtual reality in medicine. We made a virtual operation room and 3D organs with cancer in a virtual environment. The simulated organ image was composed of approximately 15,000 polygons and the frame rate was about 10-15/sec. The system may be used to plan surgical procedures and to educate medical staff. We discuss here the purpose of the system, its current implementation, its current limitations and future applications.

1. Introduction

The Medical Virtual Reality (MedVR) Project is advancing in the National Cancer Center Japan. It is part of the Cancer Information and Supercomputing Programs: Supercomputing Projects for Integrated Research and Innovative Treatment (SPIRIT) which consist of several sub-projects, including an AI expert-consultation system, high-level medical image processing for diagnosis and treatment, genetic and molecular analysis, and cancer information services available through a nationwide network.[1] There are three goals in the MedVR program: (1) to develop a surgical edutainment and preoperative surgical planning support system in virtual space, (2) to develop a new diagnostic method using medical imaging, and (3) to improve the living conditions of in-patients with limited physical activity by providing them with a virtual experience. [2,3] The advantages of simulating surgical procedures using VR techniques include; (1) repeated practice of the surgical procedure and image training are possible, (2) the surgical procedure can be planned prior to the actual operation in individual patients with VR images modeled using the patient's preoperative CT or MR images, (3) objective evaluation of the procedure by a supervisor is possible, and (4) patients and their families can comprehend more precisely and adequately better understand the surgical procedure before and after the operation. (Fig. 1)

Preoperative evaluation of surgical procedures is now evolving from surgical planning based on spatial relationships of planar or 3D images into simulated surgical training in a virtual environment. For the benefit of patients with cancer, we should evaluate the pros and cons of the virtual simulation of a surgical operation. Video and high-definition TV (HDTV) have been used to aid discussion at surgical conferences. Both technologies have been valuable because the surgeon can reconstruct 3D images of the cancer and normal organs by observing planar CT or MR images. However, a surgical simulation which uses actual 3D photographs may be more effective, since delicate operative manipulations can be simulated and spatial relationships of internal organs can be more precisely recognized. We recently reported a surgical simulation support system and its prototype application for removal of brain tumors. [4] However, as we have used the system for presurgical planning for various cancers, it has become evident that the system is useful not only for presurgical evaluation for the removal of various cancers, but also for evaluating the effectiveness of the operative method after the surgery. To further improve the effectiveness of this simulation system, we have constructed an enhanced surgical conference system that can simultaneously employ 3D operative imaging and the virtual surgical simulation support system. The system is referred to as a virtual reality (VR)- enhanced surgical conference system, and allows us to make a precise evaluation of delicate operative hand skills before and after surgery. Surgeons can simulate the surgery in a virtual environment before and after the operation, and can examine the operative procedure while watching a 3D image of the surgical manipulation. In this report, we describe the configuration of a system that can provide an operative simulation using a virtual environment and actual 3D operative imaging simultaneously at a surgical conference. The clinical usefulness of this VR-enhanced surgical conference system is evaluated by analyzing the decision-making process of the surgeon regarding an operative procedure.

2. System Configuration

We mainly use Boom 3C for observation of the surgical simulation due to its high resolution and pseudo-colonization. A fastrak, a pointing device, is used as a tool in virtual space and represents surgical instruments such as a knife, bipolar coagulator, tweezers, air drill and so on. High-performance image processing Image data are drawn from an image database in which the data format is based on DICOM 3. 3D texture-mapping and isosurfacing are achieved by high-performance image processing with parallel AVS (Advanced Visualization Software) on a massive parallel supercomputer (SP2). The organ or cancer image data is extracted from an image database composed of MR and CT slice images in DICOM 3 format with the use of CliPSS software. The volume of the 3D texture is limited to 128X128X64 and the shape data are limited to about 9000 triangles. FDDI switch and HIPPI switch were used to transport the enormous volume of image data from the image database to the high-performance WS. The background sounds during a surgical operation were edited with an Indigo II sound-server to increase the reality of the simulation. (Fig. 2)

A VR image database uses an icon-based hierarchical file management system created by Indigo Magic. We can input a 3D organ image into the virtual surgical field from this image database very easily. We also use a switching system to exchange an image of a 3D color video system and a virtual view of the surgical simulation support system. The 3D camera consists of right and left CDD cameras with a resolution of 410,000 pixels, which can be enlarged six times. The camera has an electrically-driven zoom lens (F 1.2 ~ 22). The camera measures 65 x 25 x 130 mm and weighs approximately 3.5 kg. The simulation system presents virtual organs and cancers interactively using head-tracked display devices. In addition, the system allows interactive surgical procedures to be performed on a cancer model. The cancer model is generated from CT or MR images using a 3D texture method. Using this method, it is possible to visualize the internal structure of the organ as the simulated resection takes place. The hardware system is composed of three high-performance graphic workstations (two Onyx/RE2 and one Indigo-II Extreme) and a 3D video editing system. The software system for developing the VR environment is structured so that computations are distributed on the three workstations. Using the two Onyx computers to generate the image, the simulated system achieves frame-rates of 11-12 frames/sec for monocular viewing and 6-7 frames/sec for binocular-stereo viewing of a scene with 15K visible triangles. The VR database is constructed for each patient after editing polygon images of the cancer and related organs from CT or MR images. The simulated environment for a patient is referred to as a virtual reality environment file (vef). The surgeon can select the individual vef for a patient from a menu window. The 3D images are stored on VHS or 8-mm videotape.

3. Methods

3.1. Analysis of the surgical decision-making process

We attempted to analyze how a surgeon plans a surgery for a patient with cancer. The surgeon begins with a preoperative evaluation of the location of the cancer, the extent of infiltration and the presence of swelling lymph nodes or distant metastases using CT or MR images of the patient. The surgeon develops a preoperative surgical plan after considering the physical condition of the patient. For example, the surgeon evaluates whether the patient can stand an extended operation, and decides which procedure to perform based on this evaluation. This process is mainly based on the experience of the particular surgeon. At the lower level of such a knowledge base, there is medical knowledge generally obtained from medical textbooks. The surgeon's personal knowledge base is limited by his clinical experience and his medical education at medical school. The surgeon's knowledge is further reinforced by training and acquisition of knowledge from medical specialists with vast clinical experience. If a surgeon thinks that some surgical procedures exceed his skill and his personal knowledge, he or she may ask for an expert opinion from a more experienced surgeon. Thus, a consultation is thought to expand surgical knowledge and to guide the surgeon to make proper decisions. In actual surgery, this process is repeated instantly and a decision is made quickly. A characteristic of an actual operation is that the surgeon is required to respond to operative problems immediately. When a surgeon can not adequately respond to an operative problem with his or her personal experience and knowledge, it is often valuable to consult with other surgeons who have more experience with the particular procedure in progress. Based on this analysis, it is clear that there is a need for two types of surgical simulation. In one type, the goal is to make an accurate model of the cancer with precise spatial relationships for preoperative planning, without any interactive simulation. In the second type, the goal is to expand a surgeon's personal experience with various procedures through virtual surgery using an interactive surgical simulation, thus reducing the danger to patients. A virtual environment is very important in realizing both of these types of simulation. The purpose of the present system is to expand the knowledge base of surgeons through personal surgical experience using both a real 3D operative picture and virtual surgical images, and thus correct misconceptions that can easily develop during self-taught VR simulation.

3.2. Methodology

Phase 1: The surgeon runs a preoperative surgical simulation (Simulation 1) when he plans an operation. (Fig. 3)

The simulation can be used to construct a well-planned operation in virtual space. The surgeon can see 3D images of virtual organs and cancer, which are segmented from images using CliPPS software and isosurfaced using AVS, without any simulation of surgical manipulation. Both images can be observed from various angles during real-time rendering using Performer software. About 50,000 polygons are needed to generate an image of the desired quality. (Fig. 4)

Phase 2: After reducing the number of polygons in the image, the model for surgical simulation begins to run in the virtual operation room. (Simulation 2). Surgeons can now interact with the virtual operation. Our system is insufficient to fully simulate the actual operation because small blood vessels and nerves around the cancer can not yet be drawn. We now use the present system to evaluate the sequence and extent of the excision needed to remove the cancer. (Fig. 5)

Phase 3: After surgeons are trained to perform the operation in a virtual environment, the actual operation is 3D-imaged in an operation room. Using the 3D stereo camera, we particularly concentrate on operative scenes which could not be examined preoperatively and on scenes of delicate surgical manipulations. At a postoperative conference, when surgeons wear shutter glasses and watch the 3D surgical picture, they can more easily appreciate the surgical skills used. In this way, their surgical knowledge can be enhanced. When surgeons want to examine a manipulation which was considered technically difficult during surgery and simulate other approaches to the operation, they can change to a surgical-simulation mode and simulate the surgical procedures with a 3D picture. Using this system, we expect that less-experienced surgeons will be able to learn various surgical skills more easily and expand their surgical knowledge base without performing many operations on actual patients.

4. Summary and Conclusion

The actual usefulness of the current system is now being evaluated. The advantage of the present system is that it composes individual VR images by connecting images from an enormous image database based on preoperative CT or MR images using a supercomputer. These data are transmitted directly from the image database to the VR-producing system, and the parallel AVS with a supercomputer can compose VR images quickly. We have developed a surgical simulation support system particularly for cancer surgery for several reasons. First, spatial perception is of cardinal importance in cancer surgical operations to precisely determine the location of the tumor. Second, this system can provide a surgeon with a virtual operational field in a particular patient preoperatively. Third, with the use of this system, surgeons can train themselves to perform procedures in advance. Finally, this system can provide a virtual experience for trainees who have very limited opportunities to experience actual surgery to remove cancer. Our surgeons' initial impression is that the VR simulation alone is not sufficient to analyze actual operative procedures. However, by watching both the actual 3D pictures and the simulated surgical images, they can easily understand the details of the spatial position of the cancer and its relationship to normal structures. To further evaluate the usefulness of the present system , an objective evaluation must be carried out. We plan to systematically evaluate the number of operative cases, the time required for pre- and postoperative simulations, and the number of simultaneous evaluations using 3D imaging and VR simulation. (Fig. 6)

In addition, we will record the operative methods, the operative time, bleeding volume, nature and extent of complications, duration of hospitalization and recurrence rate in subsequent actual operations. Such an evaluation of objective data is necessary to determine the advantages and disadvantages of this kind of system for analyzing various types of surgery. We think that this system will be able to enhance a surgeon's personal surgical experience. Medical science was once an art of learned experience. Medicine gradually became a science when it incorporated qualitative and quantitative methods. Surgery represents a practical aspect of clinical medicine. Qualitative analysis in medicine has made rapid progress through the introduction of various modalities of image diagnosis, and quantitative analysis of various pathophysiological conditions has been advanced by the development of various analytical equipment. However, medicine has failed to advance as a practical science because of the lack of proper tools. The technology of VR is expected to contribute to solving some, if not all, of these problems. It is often very difficult to perform cancer surgery. Surgeons must be experienced and well-prepared. Refined surgical technique is the most important factor in determining the outcome of the procedure. The present system was constructed to enhance a surgeon's knowledge through experiencing virtual surgery. At present, 3D imaging is used to evaluate endoscopic surgery and for diagnosis. Although this method is useful for simplifying the operation itself, it is not suitable for pre- or postoperative evaluation. If surgeons evaluate the operation at a post-surgical conference using our system, a more detailed examination of the surgical manipulation can be performed in a VR environment. We are continuing our research and selecting proper disease examples for the system. We hope that the combined system will become a useful training and planning tool for clinical applications.

Parts of this paper were submitted for the Health Care in the information Age on Medicine Meets Virtual Reality IV in 1996.

Acknowledgments : This work was supported in part by a Grant for Scientific Research Expenses for Health and Welfare Programs, by a grant from the Foundation for the Promotion of Cancer Research, and by the Comprehensive 10-year Strategy for Cancer Control.

References

1. Oyama H., Miyazawa T., Aono M., Ohbuchi R. and Suda S.: VR medical support system for cancer patients. Cancer edutainment VR theater (CEVRT) and psycho-oncological VR therapy (POVRT). R. M. Satava et al. (eds.): Interactive Technology and Healthcare: IOS Press and Ohmsha 1995 (Medicine Meets Virtual Reality. pp. 433-438).

2. Satava R.M.: Virtual reality surgical simulation: the first steps, Surgical Endoscopy 7 (3), 203-205 (1993).

3. Bricken W.: Virtual Environment Operating System: Preliminary functional architecture," Technical Memorandum M-90-2, Human Interface Technology Lab, University of Washington (1990).

4. Oyama H., Nomura K., Miyazawa T., Aono M., Ohbuchi R. and Suda S.: Surgical simulation support system. R. M. Satava et al. (eds.): Interactive Technology and Healthcare: IOS Press and Ohmsha 1995 (Medicine Meets Virtual Reality. pp. 439-444).

Editors' Note: See Appendix, p. 317 for coloured figures of this paper

Distributed Extensible Virtual Reality Laboratory (DEVRL):
A Project for Co-operation in Multi-Participant Environments[1]

Mel Slater and Martin Usoh, University College London, UK
Steve Benford, Dave Snowdon and Chris Brown, University of Nottingham, UK
Tom Rodden and Gareth Smith, Lancaster University, UK
Sylvia Wilbur, Queen Mary and Westfield College, London, UK

Abstract. This paper describes an ongoing project in the UK to establish a framework for distributed virtual reality applications. The paper describes the aims of the project, the three applications (physics teaching, collaborative information browsing, and geometric design), the methodology for evaluation, and the network infrastructure.

Keywords
Collaborative virtual environments, distributed virtual environments, virtual reality, virtual classroom, information retrieval, geometrical modeling.

1. Introduction

Collaborative Virtual Environments (CVEs) involve the use of distributed virtual reality to support interaction and collaboration between people. The concept of CVEs has emerged from two threads of research. First, the virtual reality community has begun to explore multi-participant VR, either as an extension to single user systems which exploit distributed processing architectures or for supporting specific collaborative activities such as multi-player games and battle simulations. Second, the Computer Supported Cooperative Work community has been developing notions of shared space through technology such as media spaces which have raised issues of social interaction and mutual awareness in computer systems.

This paper describes the work of the project known as **DEVRL**, Distributed Extensible Virtual Reality Laboratory. The major purpose of this project is to investigate the formation of a distributed virtual reality (VR) laboratory to support research into CVEs. The principle objectives of the distributed laboratory are :-

- the development of a distributed hardware, software and networking infrastructure for constructing and evaluating CVEs over wide area networks;

---

[1] This work has been sponsored by the UK's Engineering and Physical Sciences Research Council (EPSRC)

- demonstration of the potential of a variety of CVE applications;

- conduct of experiments with three initial CVE applications in order to explore the issue of multi-participant presence and the underlying network requirements of CVEs and also the relationship between the two (i.e. how does network performance influence the sense of multi-participant presence).

The paper presents a snapshot of DEVRL one year into the project and discusses progress towards each of these three objectives. Section two provides a brief overview of the current DEVRL infrastructure. Section three then describes each of our three demonstration applications: the virtual classroom, collaborative information retrieval and shared geometric design. Finally, section four introduces the issues of multi-participant presence and network requirements and outlines proposed experimental work.

2. The DEVRL infrastructure

We begin with a brief overview of the DEVRL infrastructure. At the core of DEVRL are three universities: University College London, The University of Nottingham and Lancaster University, each with an existing local VR laboratory. These three sites are separated by distances of several hundred kilometres. They are all connected via the UK's SuperJANET research network. At present, SuperJANET provides bandwidths of up to 10 Mbs^{-1} using the SMDS protocol, although migration to ATM is planned within the next eighteen months, providing bandwidths of 55 Mbs^{-1} and upwards.

Between them, the four sites provide access to a number of VR workstations including a ProVision100 VPX, one SGI ONYX RE^2 and several Indigos and Indies. At present, it is possible to conduct experiments with over ten simultaneous participants spread across the three sites. The sites support immersive access (enabling three participant immersive applications to be run over the wide area) and one supports a projection interface. The software infrastructure is provided by a number of VR platforms including Division's dVS, DIVE and MASSIVE.

Three CVE applications are currently under development (see below). However, some initial testing of the infrastructure has been carried out using the MASSIVE VR-teleconferencing system. MASSIVE has been used to hold a number of project meetings in distributed VR with several participants engaged in simultaneous graphical, audio and textual interaction. Some of these meetings have included participants from other non-core sites; the most notable having spanned five organisations in three countries (The UK, Sweden and Germany). The results of these early experiments with MASSIVE have been reported in [5].

3. The DEVRL applications

Next, we describe the three CVE applications which are being developed for DEVRL. From the outset the DEVRL project has aimed to be informed by the practical difficulties encountered in constructing applications. We can characterise such applications on three dimensions:

- The number of participants simultaneously engaged in the application as low (less than 10), medium (in the 10s) or high (in the 100s or more).

- The complexity of the objects and their behaviours as low (representation of relatively static data), medium (representation of objects which change in response to a user interaction) or high (representation of objects which can dynamically change of their own volition).

- The degree of interaction between participants as low (they see each other and can exchange information), medium (same as low, but they can be engaged in complex activities that must be visible to others), and high (same as medium, but users may engage in synchronised activities relating to high complexity objects in order to achieve a common task).

Table 1
A Characterisation of the DEVRL Applications

Application	Number of Participants	Complexity of Objects	Degree of Interaction
Virtual Classroom	M	H	M
Information Retrieval	H	L	L
Geometric Modelling	L	M	H

DEVRL is constructing three different CVE applications. These are the virtual classroom, a collaborative simulation for learning physics; collaborative information retrieval, a 3-D information visualisation which supports data sharing and chance encounters with other people; and geometric modelling, which supports collaborative and interactive design of complex geometric shapes. We may then approximately characterise these three applications as shown in Table 1. We now describe each of the three applications in turn.

3.1. The Virtual Classroom

The virtual classroom provides access to a number of interactive simulations of basic physical laws. A major advantage of virtual reality based simulation is that it is possible to support physical experiments which cannot be readily reproduced in real classrooms, such as the change in gravitational force exhibited by an object when its mass in changed. Another advantage is the possibility of providing users with viewpoints that are not normally possible in the real world, such as viewing the path of a projectile from the projectile's point of view. Each simulation is different in terms of both its functional and intended cooperative semantics. Physical simulations currently under investigation include gravitational, linear momentum and rotational momentum based experiments. The following paragraphs briefly describe the two of these which have been implemented to date, both as applications of DIVE.

Projectile simulation. A projectile application exists where a virtual cannon fires a virtual cannon ball into free space. The cannon ball is acted upon by a simulated uniform gravitational field, which pulls the flying ball down as it travels. During its flight the cannonball leaves a trail denoting its path. Users may alter the initial velocity of the cannon ball and the cannon's angle of elevation, from which it is fired. The experimental task involves two participants who must co-operate to hit a target using the cannon. The first user cannot see the target as it is obscured by a wall, which the cannon ball must clear. This user controls the cannon, allowing them to alter the initial speed of the cannon ball and its angle of elevation. The other user is 'strapped' behind the cannon ball and follows its trajectory. This user may freely look around the cannonball while the ball is in flight. It is the task of the moving user to tell the controlling user how far away from the target the cannonball landed, and between them the two users must derive the correct settings to hit the target.

Centre of gravity. A 3D pivot application allows a number of spheres with differing mass to be moved on a hinged plane. This plane rotates about its centre in the X and Z axis. The plane automatically pivots to represent the sum of the moments exerted by each of the masses placed onto it. The aim of the experiment is to balance the plane so that it is flat. Each participating user may only move their allocated sphere and must work cooperatively to balance the plane.

3.2. Collaborative Information Retrieval

Our second application involves the construction of a shared 3-D information visualisation to allow users to browse, search and share on-line document repositories. Given the rapid spread of the World Wide Web, coupled with the recent emergence of the Virtual Reality Modelling Language (VRML), this application is being constructed as a front end to WWW. However, unlike VRML which currently only supports single users navigating relatively static 3-D scenes, our application provides a number of interactive and multi-user visualisations. At the time of writing, the following components have been developed as applications of the DIVE system with embedded links into the Web.

Map tool. The map tool supports browsing of the WWW through the construction of 3-D graphs of a given region of the Web as defined by a starting node and an adjacency distance (i.e. a radius from this node expressed in terms of a number of links). The tool explores the Web within the defined region and then draws a 3-D graph using the Force Directed Placement algorithm [2]. Users may then navigate the resulting graph, selecting nodes in order to see summary details of the contents or further selecting them in order to launch Mosaic.

Search tool. This tool is based on the previously reported VR-VIBE visualisation [3] and supports interactive searching of a document store through the manipulation and comparison of multiple search queries. A number of queries can be defined each consisting of several text keywords. These are positioned in a virtual space to form a spatial framework. Document icons are positioned within this framework according to the strengths of their relative attractions to each query (i.e. the more strongly an individual document matches an individual query, the closer it is placed to it). The size and shade of document icons also shows their overall attraction to all of the queries. Users may dynamically interact with the visualisation in a number of ways: selecting documents displays summary details or launches Mosaic to view the document; raising a relevance filter removes all documents whose overall score falls blow a threshold value from the display; grabbing and dropping queries dynamically deforms the space; switching queries on and off also changes the space and, finally, new queries may be defined dynamically. As with the map tool, the visualisation in DIVE provides links for retrieving actual WWW documents.

Awareness and communication support. In addition to DIVE's standard multi-user facilities , we have introduced a number of further communication mechanisms. First, both visualisations represent the presence of non-VR users as they wander across WWW information. Thus, a Mosaic user who happens to be accessing some of the pages that appear in either the map and search tools will be shown as a simple embodiment located next to the relevant document icon and their changes in location will be animated as they wander over the pages being visualised. Second, additional mechanisms are provided to request meetings with other people of to send them email. For example, on coming across some interesting information, it is possible to invite its author into the visualisation in order to discuss it as part of a virtual meeting.

3.3. Geometric modelling

Out third application builds on previous work in geometrical modelling in VR for single participants [11]. A single designer has the problem of constructing initial shapes, modifying them and seaming them together. In the context of an environment shared by several designers, each may design a part of the final product, and then merge the parts together. Designers and clients may evaluate the product and engage in collaborative modification of the combined shape.

The underlying model uses a new method for deformable B-Splines based on minimising an energy functional [16]. This allows the application of forces to deform the shape very precisely and rapidly. Our specific approach is based on the notion of "body centred interaction" [12]. This builds on the notion that the match between sensory data and proprioception enhances the sense of personal presence. Therefore actions are based on appropriate mobilisations of the participant's whole body, rather than on interactive techniques borrowed from 2D display systems, or alternatively, a large number of individual hand gestures. This is based on the belief that immersive systems require their own repertoire of interaction techniques, and a new interaction paradigm.

In a multi-participant environment there are difficult problems to overcome - if two designers have each grabbed a corner of a shape, does this signify a contest for control of the shape or a desire for them to simultaneously stretch (or even tear) it? At the time of writing single designers may create shapes which may be observed by others, but the collaborative aspects are not yet implemented. This application is discussed in the companion paper [15].

3.4. DEVRL Town

In order to promote awareness of our work and research into CVEs in general, we are constructing a project wide virtual environment called DEVRL Town. Eventually, several versions of DEVRL Town will be realised in DIVE, dVS, MASSIVE and even VRML (at least a limited single user version for the latter). DEVRL Town is obviously based on the metaphor of a virtual town and will provide a general source of project related information as well as a common project entry point for accessing the applications (as buildings within the town). We wish to encourage other researchers and projects to establish their own presence in DEVRL Town.[2]

4. Experimental work

So far, we have described the DEVRL infrastructure and applications. We conclude the paper by previewing the experimental work to be carried out in the later stages of the project. Clearly, there are no results to report at present. Instead, we concentrate of a detailed description of the issues to be explored and the underlying theory that will be driving this work. There are three components to our experimentation:

1. developing and validating a theory of multi-participant presence - i.e. understanding the factors which affect people's sense of shared presence.

2. developing and validating a model of network performance - i.e. understanding the kinds of network traffic generated by our applications and, conversely, predicting the effects of bandwidth and latency limitations on application performance.

3. exploring the relationship between (1) and (2). More specifically, understanding how network and hence system performance affect notions of shared presence and also how users' actions (presumably influenced by the sense of shared presence) affect the underlying system performance.

The following sections touch on each of these issues in turn.

4.1. Multi-participant presence

First we consider the notion of *presence* as applied to CVEs.

Categories of Presence. In a shared virtual environment there are two related but conceptually different forms of presence: *personal presence* and *shared presence*. The first relates to the sense of "being there" in the VE, and has been explored in [1,6,7,8,10, 13]. Personal presence itself has two manifestations: *subjective* presence relating to the individual's state of mind, which can be elicited to some extent through questionnaires, and interviews. The second is *behavioural* presence, where the individual acts as if they

---

[2] DEVRL town URL:
http://www.comp.lancs.ac.uk/computing/research/cseg/projects/devrl/town.html

were present in the environment, and exhibits behaviour concomitant with this. Again subjective and objective presence are logically orthogonal, but related in practice.

Shared presence, to our knowledge not yet discussed in the literature, similarly has two aspects. For each individual: first, the sense of the presence of other individuals in the VE; and second, the sense of being part of an entity and a process which is more than just the "sum of the individuals", i.e., being present in a group and in the process which the group is unfolding during the course of the group meeting. Once again, we can separate the subjective and objective aspects of each of these: the subjective relating to each individual's state of mind, and the objective relating to the observable behaviour of each member of the group, and the overall group behaviour. By "overall group behaviour" we mean such phenomena as the group as a whole gradually drifting spatially across a virtual room, without this being the conscious decision of any particular individual.

Theories of Presence. Although there are no well-established fully worked out theories of presence, having some theoretical framework is essential in order to carry out meaningful experiments and take useful measurements. In previous work we have developed an approach to individual presence which is maybe the beginnings of an theory with some empirical backing, and a theory that leads to insights about interaction techniques within immersive virtual environments. This theory (most fully explained in [14]) is based on the notion of immersion, as a description of a technology, leading to a potentially quantifiable measure of the degree of immersion offered by a system, and the match between proprioception and sensory data.

We postulate that personal presence is a prerequisite for shared presence. The following additional factors seem relevant:

- The notion of a Virtual Body is perhaps even more important for shared presence than for personal presence. An individual requires some spatial, acoustic, and ideally tactile information to establish and maintain the presence of other individuals in the environment.

- The static existence of others is almost certainly not enough, there must be a sense of the possibility of interaction and the exchange of information.

- The representation of others is again crucial: It has been found that different individuals respond differently to the different modalities: visual, auditory, kinaesthetic. Some might find it easy to maintain the sense of presence of others with just crude visual representations of Virtual Bodies, and text interaction only. Others might require fully functioning Virtual Bodies.

- Immersion: Almost all of our previous studies have been based on a visually immersive system. In this project with the use of the MASSIVE and DIVE systems we have the possibility of exploring non-immersive environments.

Experimental approach. Progress was made in earlier work on understanding the factors that enhance personal presence by choosing a small number of parameters that were measured subjectively using experimentation: the sense of "being there", the sense of having been in the *place* specified by the VE rather than having just seen images depicting a place; and the extent to which the participant "forgets" that s/he is really in a laboratory wearing a HMD in favour of the virtual world [14]. There is an intention to develop a similar set of parameters for "subjective shared presence". The simplest types of questions to elicit this form of presence that we are currently exploring, and that will form part of our experimental strategy are of the form:

- To what extent did you have a sense that you were in the same place as [person X] during the course of these events?

- To what extent did you have a sense that [person X] was in the same place as you during the course of these events?

- To what extent did you have a sense of the emergence of a group/community during the course of these events?

- To what extent did you have a sense of being "part of the group"?

There is similarly a need for a set of observable behaviours that can be compared as between the "real" and "virtual" worlds.

- It is well known that in repeated real world meetings, people tend to arrange themselves around a desk, or spatially in a room, in approximately the same places, meeting after meeting. Does this recur with virtual meetings - do they arrange themselves in the same place relatively as in the real meetings, and also in subsequent virtual meetings?

- Do virtual meetings unfold in the same way as real meetings? The same people speaking, in responding to the same kinds of events and information as tends to happen in real meetings?

- In the course of events that require motor skills - passing objects around, playing physical games, etc., do the events unfold in the same kinds of ways?

- Is there observable group phenomena which occurs whether or not the environment is virtual - for example where the group as a whole acts under the influence of some social gravity, and physically drifts spatially, without this being the conscious intention of any individual?

We are currently designing a series of experiments to explore these parameters.

4.2. The network requirements of CVEs

Next we consider the networking issues raised by CVEs. DEVRL addresses two major networking issues: scale and synchronisation. The following paragraphs discuss each of these in turn, touching on some of the technical approaches that have been adopted by current distributed VR systems.

Scale. As the number of simultaneous inhabitants of CVEs grows beyond a few tens towards hundreds or thousands of people, so issues of scale will become paramount. We identify four distinct dimensions of scale:

- Bandwidth - coping with increasing network traffic as the population and complexity of virtual worlds increases;

- Computational - even if the network can deliver the information, techniques need to be developed to ease the computational load of processing it (especially rendering).

- Perceptual - even if the information can be displayed, techniques need to be developed to help participants manage the cognitive load of understanding it (e.g. how would one follow a conversation involving several hundred people speaking all at once?).

- Geographical - physical distance introduces its own constraints. In particular, the speed of light imposes a lower limit on network latency which may become significant over wide areas (even without the further delays introduced by switching and transmission technologies).

A number of solutions have been proposed to deal with these issues. The use of multi-cast protocols has been widely discussed as a means of minimising network traffic (e.g. [9]). In addition, various spatial scoping mechanisms have been implemented in order to reduce both computational and network load by limiting mutual knowledge between objects to specific regions of space. These include the aura mechanism from the DIVE [4] and current MASSIVE [5] systems and the cellular spatial sub-division technique proposed for future versions of NPSNET and MASSIVE. Considering perceptual scale, distancing techniques provide a means of filtering out the detail of more distant and therefore less interesting objects. Of particular note is the generalised spatial model of interaction as implemented in the MASSIVE system, where the notion of mutual awareness, controlled through the further concepts of focus and nimbus, allows for flexible and extensible distancing between objects across media such as graphics, sound and text.

Synchronisation. The issue of synchronisation concerns the degree to which different participants' versions of a shared virtual world need to be kept consistent and the mechanisms by which this can be achieved. This problem becomes apparent to end users when significant latencies occur in the system. However, it is important to be aware that the synchronisation issue is in fact always present. Indeed, relativity tells us that there is no absolute notion of synchronicity in the real world even if we don't perceive the consequences of this for everyday interactions. At the heart of the synchronisation issue is whether to enforce synchronisation or whether to allow different participants' world states to diverge under certain circumstances. Systems which take the former approach may be based on a centralised client-server model or may employ a distributed database locking model to keep different world databases in step with one another (see the DIVE system for an example of the latter). The impact of latency on such systems is likely to be an overall reduction in system performance and an increased perception of lag (in essence, everyone perceives the world at the rate of the slowest person). Such approaches may not work well over wide areas or in highly heterogeneous systems involving machines with radically different capabilities.

An alternative approach involves the use of predictive techniques. Instead of transmitting changes in position, objects exchange higher level models of behaviour which allow their positions and representations to be calculated independently at different nodes of the distributed system. Such techniques seem particularly suited to environments which contain objects whose behaviours are both constrained and predictable (e.g. the path of a missile or vehicle) and have been widely used in battle simulation systems (e.g. NPSNET). However, it is not clear what overhead might be incurred for less predictable environments.

Experimental approach. The overall aim of the network level experimentation is therefore to construct and validate a predictive model of network traffic. Two factors need to be considered. First, the network traffic generated will be application dependent. Second, the network traffic generated will be closely tied to the number of simultaneous users and their on-going actions (e.g. how often to people move, talk etc.). As a result, we propose that network evaluation should proceed as follows:

1. Each application and underlying system needs to be profiled. This involves conducting a formal analysis of communication protocols, resulting in a list of all possible application events and associated network messages combined with a discussion of the amount of traffic generated for each.

2. User behaviour needs to be profiled. This means gathering statistics about patterns of usage allowing us to confidently predict the relative frequencies of the different events described in (1). This requires the construction and use of event logging tools for each application.

The network traffic model arises as a combination of (1) and (2). Specifically,

network traffic generated = traffic generated by each event×frequency of events occurring

Once constructed, the model can be validated by comparing predicted traffic against actual measured traffic (using network monitoring tools) for different numbers of users.

5. Summary

This paper has provided an overview of the UK's Distributed Extensible Virtual Reality Laboratory Project (DEVRL). The paper has described initial results in relation to all three of the project's objectives, namely establishing a distributed infrastructure for testing CVE applications; constructing three examples of such applications; and conducting experiments with these applications in order to explore the issue of multi-participant presence and the effects of network latency and bandwidth constraints on their operation.

At the time of writing the infrastructure has been established and tested through a series of virtual meetings and the three applications (the virtual classroom, collaborative information retrieval and geometric modelling) are under development. The next stages of the project will involve experimentation with these applications.

DEVRL is open to new participants who might want to test their own applications and systems over its infrastructure, take part in experiments or establish a presence in DEVRL Town. Please contact: *devrl@cs.nott.ac.uk* for more details.

References

1. Barfield, W. and S. Weghorst (1993) The Sense of Presence Within Virtual Environments: A Conceptual Framework, in Human-Computer Interaction: Software and Hardware Interfaces, Vol B, edited by G. Salvendy and M. Smith, ElsevierPublisher, 699-704, 1993.

2. Benford, S., Snowdon, D., Greenhalgh C., Ingram, T., Knox, I. and Brown, C. (1995) VR-VIBE: A Virtual Environment for Co-operative Information Retrieval, in Proc. Eurographics '95, Maastricht, The Netherlands, September, 1995, North-Holland.

3. Benford, S., Snowdon, D. and Mariani, J. (1995) Populated Information Terrains: First Steps, in Virtual Reality Applications, pp. 27-39, Academic Press Ltd, 1995.

4. Carlsson, C. and Hagsand, O., DIVE (1993) A Platform for Multi-User Virtual Environment, Computer & Graphics Vol 17, No. 6, 1993, pp. 663-669.

5. Chris Greenhalgh and Steve Benford (1995) MASSIVE: A Virtual Reality System for Tele-conferencing, ACM Transactions on Computer Human Interfaces (TOCHI), ACM Press, 239-261.

6. Heeter, C. (1992) Being There: The Subjective Experience of Presence, Presence: Teleoperators and Virtual Environments, 1(2), spring 1992, MIT Press, 262-271.

7. Held, R.M. and N.I. Durlach (1992) Presence: Teleoperators and Virtual Environments, 1, winter 1992, MIT Press, 109-112.

8. Loomis, J.M. (1992) Presence and Distal Attribution: Phenomenology, determinants, and assessment, SPIE 1666 Human Vision, Visual Processing and Digital Display III, 590-594.

9. Macedonia, M. R., Zyda, M. J., Pratt, D. R., Barham, P. T. and Zeswitz, S., NPSNET: a network software architecture for large scale virtual environments, Presence, 3(4), MIT Press, 1994.

10. Sheridan, T.B. (1992) Musings on Telepresence and Virtual Presence, Presence: Teleoperators and Virtual Environments, 1, winter 1992, MIT Press,120-126.

11. Slater, M. and Usoh, M. (1994) Modeling in Immersive Virtual Environments: A Case for the Science of VR, International Conference on Applications of Virtual Reality, 7-9 June, 1994, Leeds, UK, and in Huw Jones, Rae Earnshaw, John Vince, Virtual Reality Applications Academic Press, 1995.

12. Slater, M., M. Usoh (1994) Body Centred Interaction in Immersive Virtual Environments, in N. Magnenat Thalmann and D. Thalmann (eds.) Artificial Life and Virtual Reality, John Wiley and Sons, 125-148.

13. Slater, M., M. Usoh, A. Steed (1994b) Depth of Presence in Immersive Virtual Environments, Presence: Teleoperators and Virtual Environments, MIT Press 3(2), 130-144.

14. Slater, M., M. Usoh, A. Steed (1995) Taking Steps: The Influence of a Walking Metaphor on Presence in Virtual Reality, ACM Transactions on Computer Human Interaction (TOCHI), 201-219.

15. Usoh, M., M. Slater, T.I. Vassilev (1996) Collaborative Geometrical Modeling in Immersive Virtual Environments, 3rd Eurographics Workshop on Virtual Environments, Martin Goebel ed., Monte Carlo, 21-23rd February, 1996, reprinted in this volume.

16. Vassilev, T.I. (1996) Fair Interpolation and Approximation by Energy Minimization and Points Insertion, Computer Aided Design, in press.

DYNAMIC MANAGEMENT OF GEOGRAPHIC DATA IN A VIRTUAL ENVIRONMENT

Hans Jense and Kurt Donkers

TNO Physics and Electronics Laboratory
P.O. Box 96864, 2509 JG, The Hague, The Netherlands
Email: {jense|donkers}@fel.tno.nl
URL: http://www.tno.nl/instit/fel/

Abstract. In order to achieve true 3D user interaction with geographic information, an interface between a virtual environment system and a geographic information system has been designed and implemented. This VE/GIS interface is based on a loose coupling of the underlying geographic database and the virtual environment system via a dynamic data-translator. This process monitors events initiated by the user in the virtual environment. Based on these events, appropriate queries are generated and sent to the geographic database. On the other hand, the data-translator receives GIS data as a result of queries, and converts these data into appropriate representations for the virtual environment. Moreover, the VE/GIS interface performs data-management tasks in order to efficiently utilize the limited amount of data that can be kept on-line in the virtual environment. To this aim, an object caching mechanism has been devised. The dynamic data-translator supports both explicit and implicit access to the geographic database. These concepts are illustrated in a virtual environment based user interface that provides basic interaction facilities for the intuitive exploration of geographic information. The approach chosen leads to a layered data management scheme where issues related to collaborative VE experiences, such as guaranteed performance, synchronization, concurrent access, and network traffic limitations, can be handled at an appropriate system level.

1. Introduction

1.1 Geographic Information Systems

Geographic information systems (GIS) are defined as the common ground between information processing systems, e.g. traditional databases, and the many fields of expertise that use spatial analysis techniques. These spatial analysis techniques can be used as powerful tools to collect, store, retrieve, transform and display spatial data from the real world. In general, Geographic Information Systems (GISs) are designed to support
1. the storage of large quantities of heterogeneous spatial data,
2. database queries for the presence, location, and properties of various kinds of spatial objects, and
3. a high amount of interactivity in query composition and processing, as well as handling access to the database.

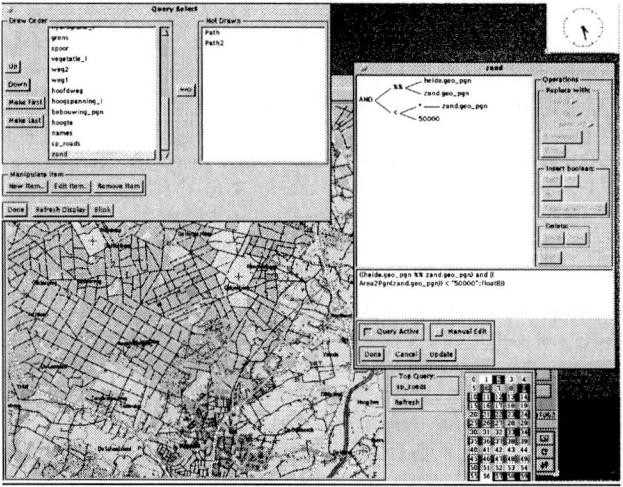

Fig. 1. The GEO++ user interface.

In order to provide this support user interfaces for GISs until now have relied on conventional, 2D graphical interaction techniques. A good example of a GIS based on such an interface is GEO++, a geographic information system developed at TNO-FEL, based on the Postgres database management system [1, 2].

The user interface of GEO++ offers facilities for the viewing of Postgres relations, the addition and editing of Postgres tuples ("objects"), graphic query composition, graphic display of query results on maps, map entity labeling, picking of graphic objects, zooming and panning of displayed maps, etc. The user can interactively compose queries via 2D mouse based interaction. 2D windows-based presentation facilities are available to display query results (see fig. 1.)

Recently, extensions to the display facilities of GEO++ have resulted in the GEO3D system [3]. Its 3D display capabilities can produce static and semi-interactive projections of 3D geographic data on a 2D screen. The 3D display extensions are based on [4].

1.2 Virtual Environments

Virtual Environments on the other hand, offer facilities for advanced man-machine interaction through 3D image presentation, and direct manipulation of (virtual) objects [5, 6]. To this aim, the user is immersed in the 3D computer generated environment using peripheral devices such as head-mounted displays, and position/orientation sensors. VE technology is expected to have a big impact on future developments of interactive systems for applications such as education (training simulators), tele-manipulation, design (CAD), scientific visualization and decision support information systems.

Virtual environments would, at least in theory, allow a more natural interaction with the inherently spatial data in a GIS. Related work in the area of data visualization in VEs has been described by others. Fairchild has done work on VE based visualization for information management [7], while McGreevy has reported extensively non the use of virtual environments for planetary face exploration [8]. In the Sequoia 2000 project, advanced visualization techniques are being investigated, although virtual environments have not been mentioned explicitly [9]. The use of virtual environment techniques for the interactive visualization of remote sensing data has been reported by Bagiana and Jense [10].

This paper describes some aspects of the development of a VE based user interface for geographic information systems. We have designed and implemented software that provides facilities to interrogate a geographic information system from within a virtual environment simulation. In section 2 we discuss how differences between the data representation in a GIS and the data representation in a VE system lead to problems that have to be solved in the interface. Section 3 then described the high-level architecture of the interface. The interaction facilities provided to the user are described in section 4. The results of our work are provided in section 5, and we conclude by discussing these results, and giving suggestions for future work.

2. Background

2.1 GIS architecture

GEO++ is a GIS with a so-called integrated architecture. This means that its capabilities for handling spatial data are implemented in an open, extensible Data Base Management System (DBMS). This is in contrast to some other approaches, where the spatial data are stored and processed separately from the non-spatial data. These so-called dual or layered architectures most often use a relational DBMS to handle the non-spatial data In the case of GEO++, the underlying relational DBMS is Postgres, which has built-in support for spatial data types. The Postgres query language is called Postquel.

2.2 Geographic data types

Geographic data can be divided into *spatial* and *thematic* data. The spatial data can be further subdivided into *geometrical* and *topological* data. The geometrical data describes the spatial properties of the geographic information in terms of points (coordinates), lines (e.g., line equations), and polygons (e.g., plane equations, normal vectors, etc.). The topological data are used to represent spatial properties of, and relationships between, the geometrical data such as connectivity, adjacency, inclusion, etc. Finally, thematical data are application dependent attributes related to the geographical entities. Typical examples are: city names, road capacities, and population density figures.

2.3 Basic interaction facilities

Roughly speaking, three basic interaction facilities can be distinguished that every GIS must support: map display, object selection, and spatial calculations. These operations are of course closely interrelated. For instance: before a spatial calculation can be performed, the user must first select the object(s) on which it is to be performed, while the result of the calculation should be displayed in a meaningful manner.

2.4 VE system architecture

On the VE systems in use at TNO-FEL, the software platform of choice is dVS (distributed virtual environment system), developed by Division Ltd. [11]. dVS provides an open and extensible software environment for the development of advanced VE applications. It enhances the basic operating system (in our case UNIX) with various components that handle tasks that occur in almost all VE applications, e.g., position/orientation tracking, collision detection, image generation, audio, etc. A wide range of VE peripherals, such as head-mounted displays, positions sensors, etc. are supported. dVS provides a high-level interface to programmers that allows abstraction of hardware specific implementation details, and thus enhances the portability of applications.

The architecture of dVS adheres to the so-called Actor model in which functionality related to specific elements of the VE simulation., e.g., visual aspects, audio, collision detection, etc. is encapsulated in separate components, called Actors, that communicate with each other in a truly parallel, distributed environment. User code is wrapped in an application Actor that runs in parallel with the standard dVS Actors.

Communication between Actors is supported by an infrastructure that consists of a shared data space (the VL database). Actors can place shared objects in this dataspace, that are then monitored by other Actors. Actors can update shared objects and also react to changes in objects they monitor. In order to prevent the entire VL database from being replicated in the address spaces of all Actors, these can subscribe to certain shared objects in which they are interested. For instance, the Visual Actor that is responsible for image generation, is usually only interested in the shared objects that represent geometric properties of elements in the Virtual Environment.

2.5 Requirements for interaction with geographic data in a VE

The visualization and manipulation of geographic data using virtual environment techniques puts several requirements on the interface between the GIS and the VE system. The requirements are determined by
1. the performance capabilities of the VE system, e.g., image generation rate, amount of data that can be handled,
2. the differences in data representations in the GIS and the VE system,
3. the communication channel between GIS and VE system, e.g., its throughput.

These requirements dictate the use of some form of data management that should have the following properties:

- the VE system should keep running at "full speed", without having to wait for data that have been requested from the GIS,
- the limits of the VE data representation capabilities should be respected when more and more data are coming in, e.g., by discarding data that are no longer relevant,
- on the other hand, repeated requests to the GIS for the same data should be prevented
- conversion from the GIS representation to the representation required by the VE system should be supported.

In the next section we describe the architecture of an interface that supports all of the above mentioned features.

3. Architecture of the Gis2Ve interface

The software that implements the interface has been named Gis2Ve (GIS-to-VE). Fig. 2 depicts the major components of the Gis2Ve software, as well as its relationship with the VE system on one hand, and the geographic database on the other.

The Gis2Ve interface consists of a number of cooperating independent processes. This architecture allows several interface activities to be handled concurrently. The processes communicate using the standard UNIX Inter Process Communication (IPC) facilities, through shared memory, shared message queues, and semaphores. Each of the processes can spawn child processes to handle subtasks. One of our computers (a Silicon Graphics PowerSeries/VGX) is based on a multiprocessor architecture and has 4 CPU's. On this machine the Gis2Ve processes can run in true parallel mode. Other advantages of this process decomposition is that it allows tuning of the overall performance of the system by allocating processes to processors based on their performance requirements, and that it is easy to change the implementation of individual processes, provided the IPC protocol is adhered to. The various processes of the Gis2Ve interface are described in more detail below.

The event handler is the central entity of the system. It handles the control flow between the several processes, monitors events, and takes the appropriate actions. The relationships between events and responses are defined the "production" rules, stored in the rule base.

The rule base is a database of production rules. It gives production rules belonging to a certain action. Although not implemented at the current time, the intention is to make these responses context sensitive and user specific.

The object cache acts as a secondary store for the dVS database. It manages a certain amount of data objects, partly in shared memory, and partly on disk, which has been used by the dVS database and may later be used again. Data objects which have been used recently stay in memory, after a certain time they are swapped to disk and finally they are deleted.

The query generation process despatches database queries to the GIS whenever new data is needed. The query generation process relies on certain rules for generating appropriate queries based on various events. It composes the required queries in child processes, which also send the query to the geographic database.

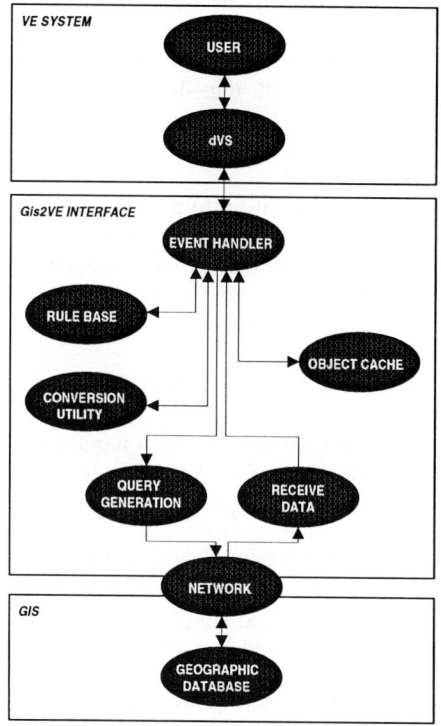

Fig. 2. Architecture of the VE/GIS interface.

The receive data process monitors the child processes generated by the query generation process. Each child processes places its received data in shared memory. When this has been done, the receive data process notifies the conversion utility and destroys the child process that received the geographic data.

The conversion utility transforms each received GIS data object to the format required by dVS. Rules for the conversion are stored in the conversion utility. Each conversion is carried out by a child process of the conversion utility. Several of these conversions may be going at a given time in parallel.

4. Interaction with geographic data in a virtual environment

4.1 Explicit and implicit query generation

From the point of view of interaction facilities, VE based user interfaces offer a rich environment for the user to manipulate and explore his data in a highly intuitive manner. The challenge for the UI designer lies in the choices and trade-off that have to be made in order to provide the user with a concise and meaningful set of interaction tools. For the interaction with a Geographic Information System the most important tool for the user is the query mechanism of the Database Management System. In conventional information systems, a basic set of query primitives can be used to create higher level composite queries to select from the database data that meet a whole set of criteria. This query composition process usually amounts to the programming of a composite query in the provided query language.

4.2 3D menu and area selections

In our VE based user interface the user can generate queries, for instance by pointing at an area and selecting a thematic attribute type from a 3D menu. The thematic attribute value for the indicated area is then retrieved from the database and visualized in an appropriate way. We have called this type of queries *explicit queries*, mainly to distinguish them from *implicit queries*, which are queries that are not initiated by explicit actions of the users, but instead are implied by his actions in the virtual environment.

4.3 Implicit panning

An example of implicit query generation is the automatic visualization of only those areas that lie within the direct vicinity of the user. The spatial data that meet a certain "closeness" criterion are automatically retrieved from the database and displayed. A the user moves around in the environment, areas that get farther away are removed from the virtual environment (but remain in the cache, see above!). This interaction technique can be compared to the panning facilities provided to the user of a conventional 2D screen based GIS. An additional benefit of this "implicit panning" mechanism is that, the limited resources of the virtual environment system (i.e., the maximum number of objects that can be present in the VE, as well as the performance capabilities) are automatically managed. In this sense it is a cruse form of level-of-detail management.

5. Results

The Gis2Ve interface was implemented as an application on top of the dVS software platform. At our laboratory we have dVS running on several machines, one of which is a Silicon Graphics 4D240VXG machine. This system has 4 CPU's and a high performance graphics subsystem for real-time rendering.

Two implementations of the basic Gis2Ve interface has been realized. Both implementations adhere to the conceptual system decomposition outlined in section 3. In the first version, the functionality of most of the system components has been implemented in separate processes. In that version, two of the processes are not complete: the query generation process does not produce actual Postquel queries to the database, and the rule base is only very rudimentary [12].

In a later, second version, the query generation process does produce Postquel queries has, and the interface has been implemented as a single process. The motivation for this decision was that we suspected that the interprocess communication between the individual processes consume a significant amount of overhead processing time which tends to negate the performance improvement expected of this parallel implementation. Initial experiments indicate that the performance loss of the single process version w.r.t. the multiprocess version is limited. Additionally, in this version the query generation module has been implemented. It can now generate basic Postquel queries to the underlying Postgres DBMS (which incidentally can reside on a different machine, accessible though a network connection).

For testing purposes, we have used two datasets.
1. The ETOPO5 dataset, which contains a global elevation map with a resolution of 12 samples per degree longitude or latitude. This amounts to about 18 Mbytes of data. ETOPO5 was used to test the first version of the interface and thus was not stored in a Postgres database, but as a "flat" file instead.
2. A dataset covering the United States, consisting of county borders with the associated population counts. This dataset was used to evaluate the second implementation of the interface. Therefore it was stored in a Postgres database.

The sizes of these datasets are of course nowhere near the amount of data in an actual GIS, but sufficient for testing the Gis2Ve functionality and performance.

Based on the virtual environment system, a basic user interface was implemented that allows the navigation of the datasets. As the user "flies" over the ETOPO5 dataset, appropriate parts (1 degree x 1 degree grid sectors) of the dataset are automatically loaded and become visible in the virtual environment (implicit queries). Additionally, the user can select a region from the global dataset to start a fly-through sequence. Queries to retrieve the initial sectors from this region are then generated explicitly. Table 1 provides some quantitative results of the effectiveness of the Gis2Ve interface. The figures indicate the advantage of keeping the grid sectors in secondary storage (the cache) once they have been retrieved from the database but are currently not visible in the virtual environment.

Table 1. Performance figures.

Nr. of grid sectors	First retrieval from database	Retrievals from object cache
3 x 3	~ 30 s	< 1 s
5 x 5	70 - 80 s	< 1 s

Around the second implementation of the interface, the single process version, a simple 3D menu structure was implemented to provide the user with a basic selection mechanism. The menu supports the following facilities:
- Session: supports session management, e.g., New database, New session, Load previous session, Save session, Quit session
- Edit: select and change visual attributes, object types and navigation beacons;
- View: provides a global overview of the dataset for orientation and rapid position changes)
- Options: set system parameters
- Help: provides context sensitive help

An impression of how the geographic data is currently presented is shown in figure 3. It shows both the actual data and several 3D icons for user interaction.

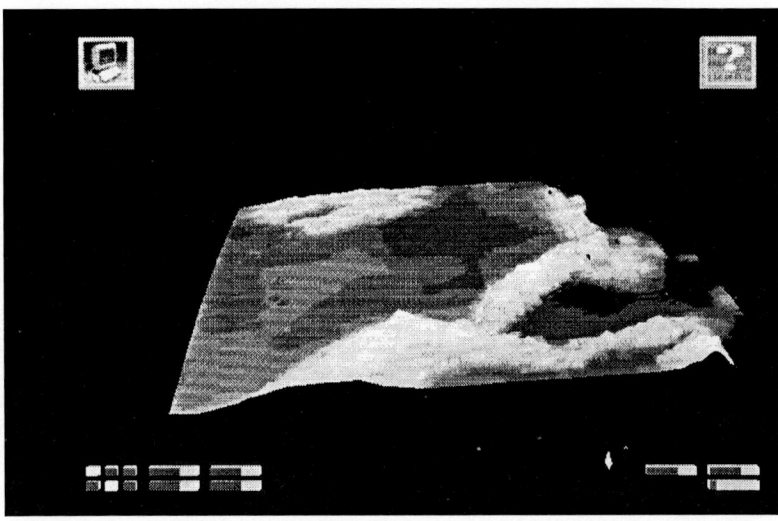

Fig. 3. Geographic data presentation in a virtual environment.

6. Conclusions and further work

The first measurements of the performance of the Gis2Ve interface, both of the multiprocessing implementation and the single process version, indicate that it provides an effective low-level building block for the development of VE based interaction facilities. After the implementation of the Gis2Ve interface has been completed and fully tested, it will be used to investigate how the 3D interaction can be used to enhance the user's perception and understanding of the structure and relations of spatial data. The basic user interface developed around the second version is a first attempt in this direction. Additional research will be performed in order to develop useful interaction techniques that will allow the user to effectively query the database using the direct manipulation facilities of the virtual environment. In particular we intend to evaluate the prototype system that is now available in the context of a real-world application of Geographic Information Systems.

The Ve2Gis interface provides a framework that can easily be extended to support multiple simultaneous users. Areas that have to be addressed in this case are: guaranteed performance, synchronization, data consistency, data persistency, and network traffic limitations. The approach chosen for the Ve2Gis interface, with three data representation layers (runtime VE database, local object cache, end underlying database) allows each of these issues to be handled at the appropriate system level. For instance, concurrent access by multiple local users can be handled by the mechanisms incorporated in the runtime VE database (in our case VL), whilst the underlying Postgres database offers facilities to handle concurrent access by remote users as well as persistent data storage. Techniques to guarantee the performance of networked VE applications under conditions of (sometimes severe) network bandwidth limitations are currently being studied. The basis for this work is the expertise at TNO-FEL in the area of Distributed Interactive Simulation (DIS) [13]. Although the concepts of DIS were originally developed to support the internetworking of military simulators, they provide a starting point for distributed immersive VE applications as well.

Another context for further work on multi-user concepts is provided by a project, in which TNO-FEL participates, in the area of Advanced Communications Technologies and Services under the European 4th Framework Programme. In this project, COVEN (COllaborative Virtual ENvironments), methods and techniques will be developed to support multiple simultaneous users in the collaborative exploration of, amongst other things, geographic information. The w we have done so far on the Gis2Ve interface has laid the foundation for further research into the technical issues of providing dynamic access to databases for several, possibly large numbers of simultaneous users.

References

1. Tom Vijlbrief and Peter van Oosterom, The GEO++ System: An Extensible GIS. Proc. 5th Int. Symp. on Spatial Data Handling, pp. 40-50, Aug. 1992.
2. M. Stonebraker, L. Rowe, and M. Hirohama, The Implementation of POSTGRES. IEEE Trans. Knowledge and Data Engineering, 2(1), pp. 125-142, 1990.
3. P. van Oosterom, W. Vertegaal, M. van Hekken, and T. Vijlbrief, Integrated 3D Modelling within a GIS. Proc. Advanced Geographic Data Modelling workshop, Delft (NL), 12 -14 Sep. 1994.
4. T. Gaskins, PEXlib Programming Manual. O'Reilly & Associates, Inc., Dec. 1992.
5. H. Rheingold, Virtual Reality, Summit Books, New York, 1991.
6. G. Burdea and P. Coiffet, Virtual Reality Technology, Wiley, new York, 1994.
7. K. M. Fairchild, Information Management Using Virtual Reality-Based Visualisations. In: A. Wexelblat (ed.), Virtual Reality - Applications and Explorations. Academic Press, Cambridge, MA, 1993.
8. M. W. McGreevy, Virtual Reality and Planetary Exploration. In: A. Wexelblat (ed.), Virtual Reality - Applications and Explorations. Academic Press, Cambridge, MA, 1993.
9. M. Stonebraker, Sequoia 2000: A Reflection on the First Three Years. IEEE Computational Science and Engineering, pp. 63-72, Winter 1994.
10. F. Bagiana and G. J. Jense, Virtual Environment Techniques for the Exploration of Earth Observation Data, Proc. 2nd EUROGRAPHICS Workshop on Virtual Environments, Monte Carlo (Monaco), Feb. 1995.
11. dVS Technical Overview. Division Ltd., Bristol, UK, 1993.
12. L. H. van der Schee and G. J. Jense, Interacting with Geographic Information in a Virtual Environment. Proc. Joint European Conference on Geographic Information, The Hague (NL), March 1995.
13. DIS Steering Committee, The DIS Vision, Technical Report IST-SP-94-01, Institute for Simulation and Training, May 1994.

VRML for LHC Engineering

Jean-Francis Balaguer

CERN

Computer & Network Division
CH-1211 Geneva 23

```
    E-mail: balaguer@cern.ch
WWW: http://www-venus.cern.ch/~balaguer/
```

Abstract. CERN is about to start building the LHC (Large Hadron Collider), which at its completion, in the year 2004, will be the world's largest machine for High Energy Physics. The LHC-system will be designed, engineered and manufactured in a distributed manner by about three hundred institutions around the world. One of the challenges to be taken up will be that of the technical information exchange for design and documentation purposes, between all the partners involved. In particular, being able to access current or previous designs, in a seamless manner, is essential. By combining into a single tool, called i3D, the 3D input and high-performance rendering capabilities of high-end VR systems with the data-fetching capabilities of network browsers, we are able to handle the distributed nature of the LHC project and address some of its information management issues. In particular, by accessing individual parts and subsystems directly from the site where they are being designed, we are able to reflect the distributed structure of the design process and make available virtual prototypes that are always in sync with the latest design. The browsing capabilities of the system allows us to attach documents of any kind of media to each three-dimensional objects, offering a means to structure technical information and to present it under the most suited media.

1. Introduction

CERN exists primarily to provide European physicists with accelerators that meet research demands at the limits of human knowledge. In the quest for higher interaction energies, the Laboratory has played a leading role in developing colliding beam machines.

The next research instrument in Europe's particle physics armoury is the Large Hadron Collider (LHC), a project similar in duration and budget size to a huge off-shore drilling platform [2]. In keeping CERN's cost-effective strategy of building on previous investments, this new equipment is designed to share the 27-

kilometre tunnel of the existing Large Electron-Positron collider (LEP), and be fed by existing particle sources and pre-accelerators. CERN is about to start building the LHC (Large Hadron Collider), which at its completion, in the year 2004, will be the world's largest machine for High Energy Physics. The LHC will require huge investments in effort and funding from all the CERN member states, and it is of capital importance that each single aspect of this huge project can be analyzed in every little detail, so that errors in the design of the premises and equipment can be determined as soon as possible. This will require the most efficient organization and technology at every stage of the design process.

In order to evaluate and promote the use of virtual environment technology as a tool to help design, build and maintain the LHC premises and equipment, a pilot project was started in January 94 by the Computer & Network and the Accelerator Technologies divisions, under the name VENUS (Virtual Environment Navigation in the Underground Sites). In order to respond to the needs of LHC designers and engineers, the VENUS project is composed of the following applications:

- Virtual prototyping;
- Networked design integration;
- Territory impact study;
- Assembly planning and control.

In this paper, we will present only the virtual prototyping and the networked design integration applications since both projects are based on the i3D system [1], a Virtual Reality Modeling Language (VRML) [3] capable tool that incorporates the 3D input, stereo output and high-performance rendering capabilities of high-end VR systems with the data-fetching abilities of network browsers. More details about the territory impact study and the assembly planning and control applications can be found in [9].

2. The i3D System

i3D is a tool allowing the exploration of three-dimensional scenes described using VRML, where each 3D object can be annotated with a document of any kind of media documents that can be accessed on the World Wide Web [4]. Using a 3D device, the user can explore its three-dimensional data and request access to other documents. Three dimensional data is handled directly by i3D while the handling of other types of media is currently delegated to NCSA Mosaic or

Netscape. The first version of i3D has been developed at CRS4[1], by the author and Enrico Gobbetti. Its development is currently being pursued at CERN.

2.2 User Interaction

When exploring three-dimensional environments, navigation using interactive control of virtual camera motions is often the most important of three dimensional interaction [8, 11, 16]. Multiple degree-of-freedom input devices allow interactive 3D viewing with continuous viewpoint control, allowing the simulation of motion parallax, one of the most essential visual cues with binocular perception for the understanding of the three-dimensional structure of the visualized data [5, 6, 14].

A Spaceball is used for the continuous specification of the camera's position and orientation, LCD shutter glasses for binocular perception, while the mouse is used to select objects and access media documents. Additionally, abstractions of the 2D mouse motions into 3D transformations are also provided so that navigation be possible when no Spaceball is available. A pop-up menu as well as keyboard commands are used to control various visibility flags and rendering modes. Figure 1 shows the two-handed input capabilities of i3D's input device configuration.

Figure 1. i3D's input device configuration

To explore three-dimensional worlds, the user can free fly using an eye-in-hand metaphor [15] or a walk metaphor where tilt rotation is locked. Alternatively, the user can inspect the scene or the currently selected object by dragging the world

---

[1] Center for Advanced Studies, Research and Development in Sardinia, Cagliari, Italy.

with a trackball around the object's selection point or the center of the object's (or scenes) bounding box.

While navigating inside a three-dimensional scene, the user can request additional information by accessing media documents associated with geometrical data. Since annotated geometries are drawn with a blue silhouette, they can be easily identified. Selecting an annotated geometry by clicking on its visual representation with the mouse triggers the document retrieval and display. For three-dimensional scenes, i3D maintains a stack of active worlds. Using keyboard commands, the previous or next world in the stack can be made current, thus providing a mean to quickly switch between active worlds.

2.3 World Model

i3D's database manager stores the representation of three-dimensional scenes as a collection of 3D objects, including light sources and cameras. From the set of world's objects, the database manager builds an octree spatial subdivision to be able to answer rapidly to spatial queries, as for example when selecting objects by tracing a ray from the mouse position. The generic 3D object possesses the following attributes:
- a 3D transformation that defines the object's spatial position, orientation and scaling;
- a list of geometries representing the different levels of complexity that can be used to render the object;
- a material, that defines the way the object behaves with respect to lighting;
- a texture, defining the image to be mapped on the object's geometries;
- an URL, that locates the media document associated with the 3D object.

Geometric, material and texture objects can be shared by multiple 3D objects of a same scene. Worlds can be described to i3D either using a proprietary file format or VRML.

2.4 Rendering

The task of the i3D's rendering manager is to display a visual representation of the current world at high and constant frame rates. During navigation, the rendering manager is activated at regular intervals by the main i3D event loop and is requested to refresh the screen while adhering to the user-specified timing constraint. To satisfy this requirement, the rendering manager must be able to trade rendering complexity with speed [8].

At each activation, the rendering manager renders a single frame by executing the following steps:

- *visibility determination*: first, the database is traversed and the objects visible from the observer's viewpoint are identified. This task is accelerated by first hierarchically determining the visibility of portions of the scene through a traversal of the spatial subdivision maintained by the database manager. This process takes into account both viewpoints when stereo rendering is enabled to limit the number of visibility tests;
- *display list construction*: each visible objects is then compiled into a sequence of device-dependent commands. During this conversion, geometries are optimized by building structured triangular meshes from their triangle lists to reduce their rendering time. To avoid recreating compiled versions at each frame, i3D caches the graphical descriptions generated for each database object and reuses them until they become invalid;
- *level of detail selection*: to reduce the number of polygons rendered in each frame, so as to be able to meet the timing requirements, the rendering manager traverses the generated display list and selects the level of detail at which each of the objects will be represented. Level of detail selection is based on the importance of each object for the current frame (which is determined by computing an approximation of its size projected on the screen) and on feedback regarding the time required to render previous frames. The feedback algorithm is similar to the one presented in [12];
- *display list optimization*: once the levels of details are selected, the system has all the information required to render the frame. To exploit coherence, the display list is sorted to optimize the rendering speed. In particular, objects sharing the same texture and/or material are grouped together. In other visual simulation systems, this task is left to the user, that has to encode this information together with the scene description [10, 12, 13];
- *display list rendering*: the sorted display list is finally traversed and rendered by executing each of the compiled command sequences. Rendering statistics for the current frame are updated and stored so as to be used when selecting the level of detail selection for the next frame.

3. Application

3.1 Virtual Prototyping for LHC

In any project of the scale of LHC, the design phase is probably the most delicate one, as this is when some critical choices are to be taken which could dramatically affect the final results, timing and costs. Unlike in commercial manufacturing, accelerator designers and engineers don't have a chance to improve their product on a "second generation". Each instrument is built once with very small possibilities of modifications. This implies that it must be perfect on the first and unique trial.

The ability to visualize the model in depth is essential to a good understanding of the inter-relationships between the parts. Interactive navigation is a powerful method for reviewing, confronting and refining designs, that allows specialists to focus on items of interest, and simplifies identification of geometry in any section of the model. Colors assigned to engineering disciplines help examine design integration, look for gaps, part interferences and mismatches. Since the premises and equipment can be electronically preassembled, all fixing interferences can be visually checked, even clearances necessary for installations or moving parts and, all this accomplished well before the final design is released for construction. Since changes made in the later phase of production cost many times more than those caught in the prior phases, savings are inevitable.

Figure 2. Virtual prototype for the ALICE experiment set-up.

Virtual prototyping allows managers and engineers to critique design as when watching physical mock-ups, but better and earlier. Physical mock-ups, usually take several weeks to construct, and proved, in previous CERN projects, to be rather inflexible to modifications (each design iteration requiring major rebuilds), ill suited for ergonomic considerations and dynamic simulations, sometimes inaccurate and finally rather costly. Virtual prototypes (see Figure 2), on their side, can be made available easily and immediately, at no extra cost, since each part has already a three-dimensional computer representation inside the CAD database. Since it can easily be kept in sync with the current design, virtual prototyping gives us much more of a responsive ability to study how the various parts and assemblies fit together; it helps reduce risks and costs, and shorten schedule.

The visual capabilities of present CAD tools are much too limited to allow interactive navigation and, with these systems, it takes a fair amount of time and imagination to isolate eventual design errors. For this reason, the virtual prototypes are entirely extracted from the EUCLID CAD database and converted to VRML or i3D's file format. The conversion process is carried out in two steps: each EUCLID part is converted to Wavefront OBJ format and placed in a directory structure reflecting the assemblies' structure. EUCLID models being usually defined with CSG trees, evaluating the CSG representation at various resolutions provide us with an efficient way to generate multiple representations of a single part at various levels of complexity. However, this is not always possible, in particular when the CSG representation has been converted to a facet representation. We are investigating the use of decimation techniques to process these geometries when encountered. Once the model has been successfully extracted from the CAD system, various filters are applied to the individual geometries to convert them into one of i3D's readable formats and to apply geometrical processing such as smoothing normal vectors. Finally, the directory structure is traversed and a scene is created in each directory of the structure. By systematically inlining children directories in the parent's scene file, the virtual prototype is composed.

In order to allow design group meetings, the VENUS project has set up a meeting room where a Silicon Graphics Reality Engine2 workstation with an Multi-Channel Option is used to render the stereograms that are fed into a VRex 2000 stereo projector. Binocular perception is obtained by wearing cheap polarizing glasses that perform the proper image separation. That way, we provide each participant with a better perception of the complex spatial relationships between parts of the virtual prototype. An operator is responsible for controlling the viewpoint using a Spaceball or a mouse, on request of members of the group. The ability of the i3D system to rapidly switch between different prototypes loaded in memory is a powerful feature when confronting the current design with earlier versions.

3.2 Networked Design Integration

The LHC-system will be designed, engineered and manufactured in a distributed manner by about three hundred institutions around the world. One of the challenges to be taken up, in order to guaranty the success of the LHC project, will be that of the technical information exchange for design and documentation purposes, between all the partners involved [2]. In particular, being able to access current or previous designs, in a seamless manner, is essential.

The World-Wide Web has added a universal organization to the data made available on the Internet allowing to view all hosts as a unique data source, and to treat all of this data as part of a single structured document. By composing the descriptions of each part or subsytem, and accessing them directly from the site where they are being designed, we are able to retrieve virtual prototypes reflecting the status of the latest or some previous version of the design. This behavior can be easily obtained by exploiting the inlining capabilities of both VRML and i3D's file format.

Figure 3. Using the 3D model to access distributed data.

The browsing capabilities of the i3D system allows users to interactively recall and view information attached to 3D models, by selecting objects of interest during navigation. Annotations can refer to text, still images, technical drawings, sound, animations or even other 3D models, exploiting in this way all of the digital media capabilities of current workstations (see Figure 3 for an example session of data browsing using i3D). Annotating each three-dimensional model with an HTML page provides us with the basic ability to structure the available technical information. Soon, we will be able to build such pages automatically when exporting the prototype from EUCLID. In the future, we plan to investigate the association of multiple URLs with each three-dimensional model and to provide context sensitive selection to determine which URL needs to be retrieved.

4. Conclusions and Future Work

In this paper, we have presented how, by combining into a single tool the 3D input and high-performance rendering capabilities of high-end VR systems with the data-fetching capabilities of network browsers, we are able to handle the distributed nature of the LHC project and address some of its information management issues. In particular, by accessing individual parts and subsystems directly from the site where they are being designed, we are able to reflect the distributed structure of the design process and make available virtual prototypes that are always in sync with the latest design. Thanks to stereo real-time video projection and 3D input devices, managers and engineers can meet to evaluate the current design, taking advantage of binocular perception and motion parallax simulation to better understand the complex spatial relationships between the parts of the prototype. The browsing capabilities of the system allows us to attach documents of any kind of media to each three-dimensional objects, offering a means to structure technical information and to present it under the most suited media.

Future work will concentrate on improving the i3D system, in particular its data-fetching capabilities by using the W3 library of common code [7]. We also plan to improve the visual cues for media annotation and to offer context sensitive selection to handle multiple URLs per object.

5. References

1. Balaguer J-F, Gobbetti E (1995) i3D: a High Speed 3D Web Browser. Proceedings VRML'95, San Diego, California.

2. Bachy G, Hameri A-P, Mottier M (1995) Engineering Data Management: a Tool for Technical Coordination. CERN MT/95-07, LHC Note 345.

3. Bell G, Parisi A, Pesce M (1995) The Virtual Reality Modeling Language. Available through WWW at http://vrml.wired.com/vrml.tech/vrml10-3.html.

4. Berners-Lee TJ, Cailliau R, Groff JF, Pollermann B (1992) World-Wide Web: The Information Universe. In Electronic Networking: Research, Applications, and Policy 2(1): 52-58.

5. Brooks FP Jr, Frederick P (1986) Walkthrough - A Dynamic Graphics Systems for Simulating Buildings. Proc. SIGGRAPH Workshop on Interactive 3D Graphics: 9-22.

6. Bryson S, Pausch R, Robinett W, van Dam A (1993), Implementing Virtual Reality, SIGGRAPH Course Notes 43.

7. Frystyk H, Lie WH (1994) Towards a Uniform Library of Common Code. Proc. WWW Conference, Chicago, USA.

8. Funkhouser TA, Séquin CH (1994) Adaptive Display Algorithms for Interactive Frame Rates During Visualization of Complex Virtual Environments. Proc. SIGGRAPH: 247-254.

9. de Gennaro S (1995) Virtual Prototyping at CERN. Proc. CHEP'95, Rio de Janeiro, Brasil.

10. Ghee S, Naughton-Green J (1994) Programming Virtual Worlds. SIGGRAPH Tutorial Notes on Programming Virtual Worlds: 6.1-6.58.

11. Mackinlay JD, Card S, Robertson G (1990) Rapid Controlled Movement Through a Virtual 3D Workspace, Computer Graphics 24(4) : 171-176.

12. Rohlf J, Helman J (1994) Performer: A High Performance Multiprocessing Toolkit for Real-Time 3D Graphics. Proc. SIGGRAPH: 381-395.

13. Strauss PS, Carey R (1992) An Object-Oriented 3D Graphics Toolkit. Proc. SIGGRAPH: 341-347.

14. Upson C, Fulhauber T, Kamins D, Laidlaw D, Schlegel D, Vroom J, Gurwitz R, van Dam A (1989) The Application Visualization System: A Computational Environment for Scientific Visualization. IEEE Computer Graphics and Applications 9(4): 30-42.

15. Ware C, Osborne S (1990) Exploration and Virtual Camera Control in Virtual Three Dimensional Environments. Proc. SIGGRAPH Workshop on Interactive 3D Graphics: 175-183.

16. Watson V (1989) A Breakthrough for Experiencing and Understanding Simulated Physics. SIGGRAPH Course Notes on State of the Art in Data Visualization: IV-26 - IV-32.

Virtual Housing System

Junji NOMURA

Virtual Reality R & D Group, Information System Center,
Matsushita Electric Works, Ltd.
1048, Kadoma, Osaka 571, Japan

Abstract: This report is a description of a software application to construct a whole house or living space in a virtual world and to experience it through the application of virtual reality technology. In the virtual house we can preview the appearance, convenience, safety, comfort level, and other factors such as temperature, air flow, and outside noise by using results from simulations. For developing the virtual housing system, four major goals have been defined. These goals are to keep the graphics drawing speed at better than 10 frames/sec. (which we call real time animation), to use texture-mapping on almost all surfaces in the house where texturing with appricable, to develop a user interface to check the house's utility, and to use a multi display large screen environment in which more than 30 people can participate at the same time. This virtual housing system is a subsystem of the Japanese Ministry of International Trade and Industry (MITI) project called "Housing Development Project for the 21st Century".

1 Introduction

A number of research projects stemming from virtual reality (VR) [1] or artificial reality technology [2] are being developed these days. In Japan there are new publications describing research such as the Virtual Dome [3] or the Application of Human Models in VR [4]. The former is being developed to construct a more realistic world and the latter to aim more effective information by using the human model. In the industrial world there are publications from automobile, steel, and building industries.

We are developing a software application to construct a living environment and to experience the environment through the use of virtual reality technology. In a virtual house we preview the appearance, convenience, safety, comfort level, and other factors such as temperature, air flow, and outside noise by using results from simulations. We have already developed a kitchen VR system (we call it the ViVA system, "Virtual Reality for Vivid A&i space" system) [5], and it is in use by customers in our showroom. We will progress to widen the domain from a kitchen to a house composed of some rooms and develop the functions necessary to experience the house.

In this paper the concepts are described relevant to our VR system for living environments and we explain how we will apply these newly developed functions.

2 Concept of VR System for Living Environments

The advantage of experiencing a virtual house is that the person who would live there can examine how much they will be satisfied with the appearance, convenience, and functions. When building a house, a plan or a floor plan is normally drawn by the professional. It is impossible for the person who knows nothing about the building to imagine the completed house. Further more there is not a single system by which the person can determine whether or not the completed house will be satisfying enough.

To help to solve these problems, we propose 3 important factors in VR system for living environment.

(1) We should make the realistic house data. The house data is composed of 3 dimensional geometry data and material data. The latter includes the texture, shininess, and reflection data which give the users a greater feeling of realism. When we add the lighting effects of different kinds of illumination and sunshine, we can get more realistic images.

(2) By using computer graphics we can construct a virtual world wherein we can interact, and get some level of immersion. The virtual reality system operates by sensing the position, direction, movement, and orientation of the user and, in the future, by getting the user's thinking and mental condition. The user can move and look around quite naturally. They can interact with nearly all objects. For instance they can pick a pencil up or open a door. And these objects react in accordance with natural phenomenon or physical laws.

(3) The user can experience not only the house but also factors essential to comfort. By changing the living environment, they can create a more comfortable living space. We will add a factor to influence on the level of comfort such as cutting down on outside noise, efficient air flow, and good thermal condition.

3 The ViVA System as an Application of VR for the Kitchen Environment

We announced the ViVA system at our Shinjuku showroom in October 1990. The system configuration is shown in Fig. 1 above and composed of sensor parts, a graphics computer, acoustic equipment, and a head mounted display (HMD). We will explain to what extent we were able to implement our concepts.

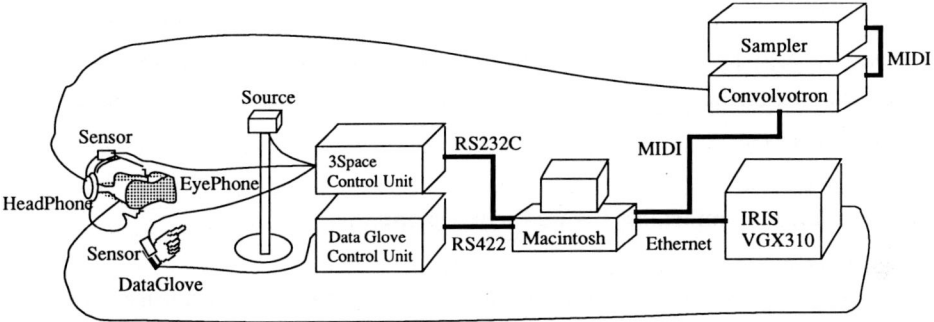

Fig.1. System Configuration of ViVA

3.1 Making Database of the Kitchen

First a kitchen plan including a floor plan is made by an arrangement between a customer and our planner, a person who is employed to assist with the initial plan of the living space. We convert the information to geometry data. We developed the system with a graphical user interface (GUI) to give doors thickness, an opening angle, and an axis of rotation shown in Fig. 2. These features were necessary to experience the doors in the virtual kitchen. We also texture-mapped materials onto kitchen doors.

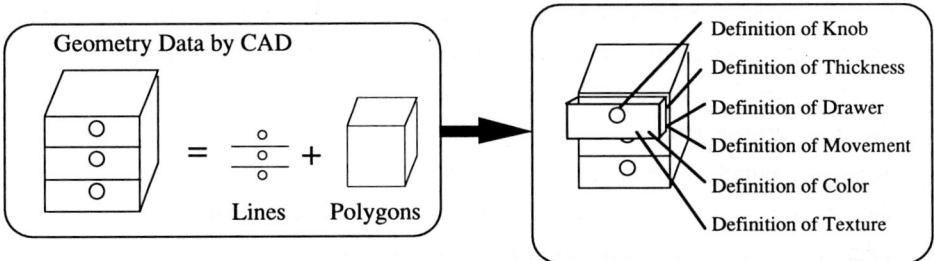

Fig.2. Data Exchange from CAD to VR

3.2 Immersive Feeling

Wearing an HMD, the view beyond the virtual kitchen is cut off and the user is always able to see an image in front of them. Tracking the position and the orientation of the head/right hand by magnetic sensors, the head and right hand in the virtual world were displayed at correct position and direction. By obtaining the joint angles of the user's fingers from a Data Glove, their hands were also rendered correspondingly. In response to their motion, for instance walking or making a fist, the scene and the hand shape in the graphics were changed. They could pick a dish or a cup up and put them into the cupboard. When they released the dish they'd picked up, it fell and was broken. When they grasped the faucet, they could turn on the water. We wanted to create an environment which has governed by the physical laws.

3.3 Creation of Comfortable Living Environment

The user could get a sense of the dimensions and configuration of the kitchen environment which has derived from the plan. By changing the color and texture of doors and comparing configurations one by one, they could select what they really liked. We added the acoustic function to this system, so they could experience the sound simulation results of attenuation of outside noises through the walls [6].

4 Consideration of ViVA System

The following are the problems we could not solve in the ViVA system.
(1) With data we prepared we could not get fully realistic feel. Rendering speed decreased in proportion to the volume of geometry data. We regarded real-time rendering, (more than 10 frames per second (Hz)), as more important than realistic drawing. We limited the data to under 5000 polygons. We studied that the user could notice the delay of drawing speed when it was under 10 Hz and that they might feel discomfort when under 2 Hz. After adding texture mapping functionality, rendering became as slow as 1 or 2 Hz. Therefore, we made it possible for the users to set their positions first and then select a texture-mapping function.
(2) We were limited by the number of objects with which the user could interact. When they went through the wall, they lost their positions. To stop going forward when colliding with a wall, the collision between all walls and a part of the user's bodies should be computed. But we could only compute collisions between the user and 4 or 5 walls because of rendering speed limitations. We could not compute the collision between

objects.

(3) In the virtual world the user was limited to controlling only their positions and orientations. Changing the color or texture, had to be operated by another person from outside of the virtual world.

5 VR System Applied for a House

We have developed the following system to widen the domain from the kitchen to an entire house, and several users can experience the house at the same time by watching stereo graphics and listening to stereo sound. The system configuration is in Fig. 3.

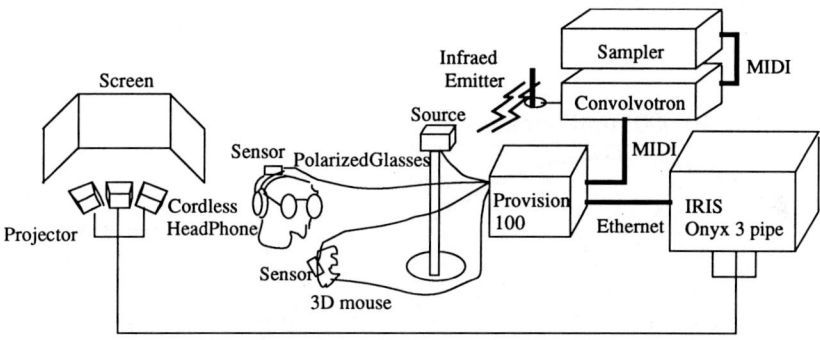

Fig.3. Developed System Configuration

5.1 Virtual House Shared by Several Persons

In ViVA only one user could experience the virtual world. To create a better living environment, not only a customer but also a planner and a constructor should discuss the configuration together. Our goal is for each person to experience the virtual world by wearing a HMD and a glove, but it is too difficult now. So one person experiences it as mentioned, and the graphics are simultaneously displayed on 3 continual arch shaped screen after being made into a stereo image pair as described in Fig. 4. The audience wears polarized glasses and cordless headphones, so they can also experience the 3 dimensional image and sound. By using 3 synchronized projectors, about 30 people can watch it with a view angle 90 degrees in the horizontal direction and 30 in the vertical direction.

5.2 Creation of Realistic Data for Living Environment

We have defined the data format of objects specially for VR. We have developed the system (IOESS, Interactive Organizing and Editing of Space System) by which we can connect several CAD systems as shown in Table 1. We have developed functions in IOESS to merge and distribute the CAD data, to define the door's angle and axis to open, and to define the coordinates of mapping textures. We divide a house into closed rooms. Each closed room has a layer structure given above in Fig. 5. We defined the floor at the top of nodes. The furniture is made separately in the local coordinate system and should be described as independent nodes. Each node is distributed into the absolute coordinate system by translation and rotation. Finally the house consists of closed rooms. Almost all objects are texture-mapped to give more realistic feel. Though the total size of the texture data is 7.3 mega-bytes, the rendering speed is fast even with texture mapping because of the improvement of the hardware performance.

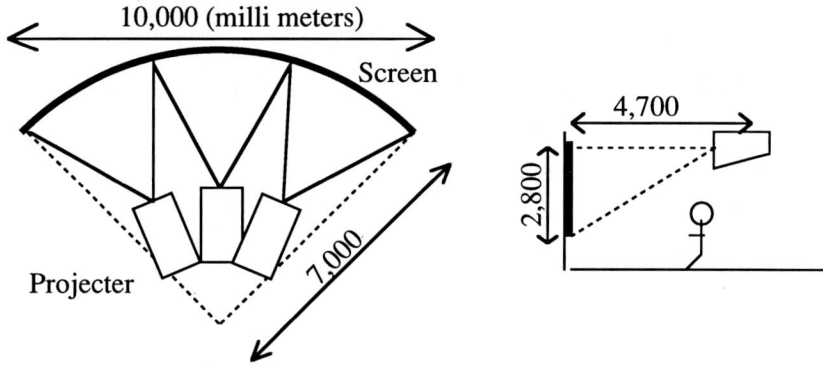

Fig.4. Screen and Projectors

Table1. Available CAD

CAD	CopyRight	Valid Data
Auto CAD	AutoDesk Inc.	Geometry,Hierarchy,Position
A+E	IBM	Geometry
SigmaArris	Sigma Design Inc.	Geometry
SuperBuild	Fujitu	Geometry,Position,Texture

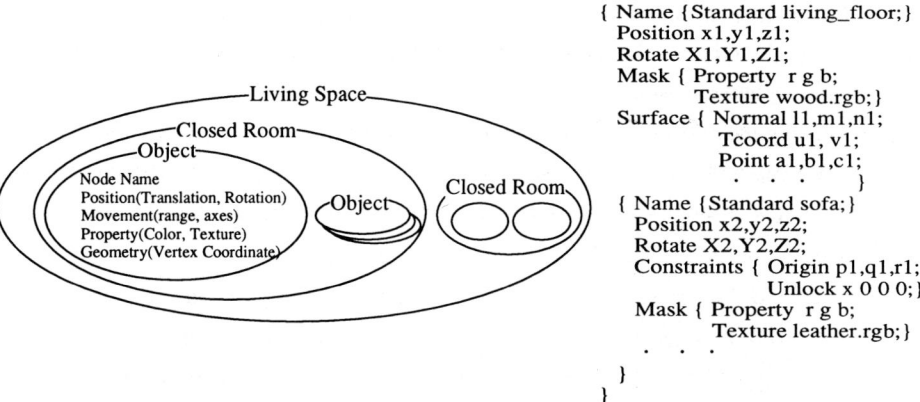

Fig.5. Hierarchy Structure of Data

5.3 Immersive Feeling

(1) As described earlier, the user data is obtained from a magnetic sensor and a 3D mouse. Using this data the user is put into the virtual world.

(2) We developed the functionality to render only the current room to keep the rendering speed at real time. We named this function "Room Switching". Through trial runs we discovered that the rendering machine can draw 19000 polygons faster than 10 Hz. The size of the house data is 37000 polygons. By Room Switching the drawing speed depends not on the total volume but only on the rendered room.

When the users are in room A in Fig. 6, room B is not rendered. As they open the door, room B is rendered. After they go into room B and shuts the door, room A is not rendered. To realize this feature, we defined the boundary data shown in Fig. 7. The boundaries are put on the floors and under the doors. The user is forbidden to move between the floor boundaries and permitted to move from the floor boundaries to the door boundaries. They can open the door there and move to the neighboring floor boundaries. To observe the position of the boundary and the person, we can query the room where they are and forbid them not to move out of the boundary. When the door is open, this function is not effective, so the function was added that the open door is automatically shut after the appropriate time except when the users are on the door boundary.

We can keep rendering speed at real time as shown in Fig. 8. The "Room Switching" function takes advantage of the layered data structure and divided closed rooms. Though faster rendering hardware has been developed, the demands of data size and features such as texture-mapping make it necessary to use, so "Room Switching" func-

tion maintains the frame rate.
(3) By using boundaries, the user cannot walk through walls but must go to an adjacent room by opening a door.
(4) By keeping the eye at an appropriate height, the user can climb stairs easily.
(5) The user can have interaction with all objects. By distributing collision detection computation to a separate CPU, we can reduce the speed loss from collision computation

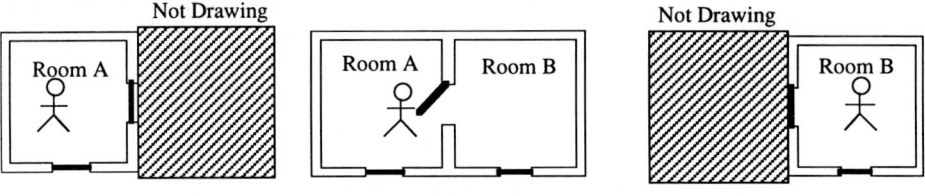

Fig.6. Room Switching Function

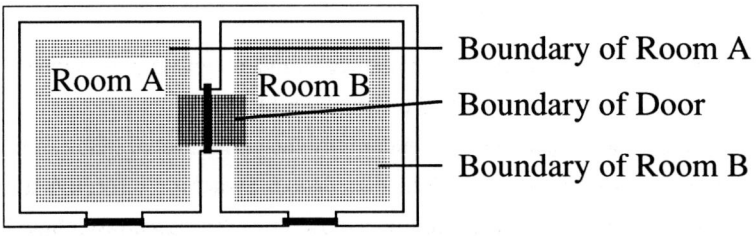

Fig.7. Boundary Data

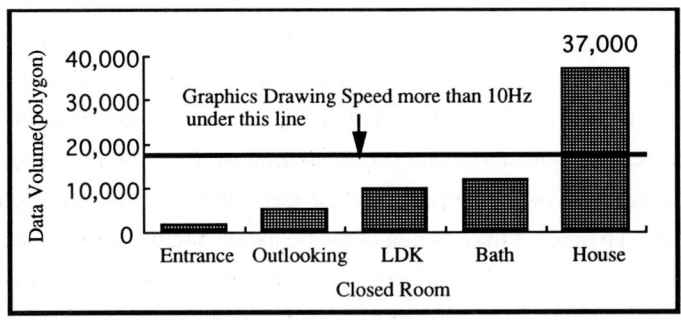

Fig.8. Data Volume of Closed Rooms

5.4 Creation of Comfortable Living Environment

We have made a menu in the virtual world. The menu contains icons and has sub-menus.

The user can change the virtual world and pull down functions by selecting menus and create more comfortable living environment. The menu functions are shown in Table 2.

Table 2. Function of 3D menu

Function	Purpose	Icon
Color Change	Change rgb color separately using sliders	RGB
Texture Change	Change textures by selecting a icon	
Delete Object	Delete objects by selecting a object	
Read Object	Read objects by selecting a icon	
Quit 3D Menu	Quit 3D menu	STOP

6 Conclusion

To implement our concepts for a VR system for living environment, we have made a realistic house from several kinds of CAD data and developed the Room Switching function to keep drawing speed at real time. We have developed the system where several users can share the virtual house experience by stereo graphics and sound. Furthermore the user can interact with all objects and go to the next room by opening doors. He can change the virtual world by changing color and texture, removing or creating objects.

References

[1] Kruger, M.: Artificial Reality, Addison-Wesley, 1982.
[2] Kelly, K.: Virtual Reality: an interview with Jaron Lanier, Whole Earth Review, No. 64, 1990.
[3] Hirose, T., Sato, S.: Synthesis and Transmission of Realistic Sensation Through Virtual Reality Technology: 9th Symposium on Human Interface, pp. 111-116, 1993.
[4] Hukui, M., et al.: Workspaces Evaluation by Virtual Subjects: 9th Symposium on Human Interface, pp. 111-116, 1993.
[5] Nomura, J.: System Kitchen Planning Process in Virtual Space: JSEP-57-08, pp. 44-47, 1991.
[6] Shinomiya, Y.: A Quasi-experience Acoustic System using Virtual Reality Technology: Dynamics & Design Conference Symposium 2, pp. 49-5, The Japan Society of Mechanical Engineers, 1991.

DiscMC: an interactive system for fast fitting isosurfaces on volume data

Paola Criscione[†], Claudio Montani[†], Riccardo Scateni[‡], and Roberto Scopigno[*]

[†]IEI–CNR, Pisa, Italy – [‡]CRS4, Cagliari, Italy – [*]CNUCE–CNR, Pisa, Italy

Abstract. This paper describes the architecture of DISCMC, an interactive system which supports isosurfacing on regular volume datasets. DISCMC adopts a discretized fitting algorithm that considerably reduces the number of polygons generated by a Marching Cubes-like scheme while presenting shorter running times. The extracted surfaces are composed of polygons lying within a finite number of incidences, thus allowing simple merging of the output facets into large coplanar triangular facets. A pyramidal representation of the volume dataset has been adopted to speed-up isosurface fitting, by avoiding *empty* volume traversal, and to support multiple level of resolution fitting. The system has been implemented in a Unix environment, using a *de facto* standard graphics library. The functionalities and the user interface of the system are described in detail.

1 Introduction

The use of *Marching Cubes* (MC), a technique originally proposed by Lorensen and Cline [3], is nowadays considered the standard approach to the problem of extracting isosurfaces from a volumetric dataset. As a member of the large class of surface tracking techniques, Marching Cubes is a very practical and simple algorithm, and many implementations are available both as part of commercial systems or as public domain software.

Despite its extensive use in many applications, shortcomings of the approach have been pointed out regarding *topological ambiguities*, algorithm *computational efficiency*, and excessive output *data fragmentation*. The DISCMC system is an attempt to overcome these shortcomings.

Standard MC produces no consistent notion of object connectivity; the *local* surface reconstruction criterion used allows a number of *topological ambiguities*, and therefore standard MC may output surfaces which are not necessarily coherent. Many solutions have been proposed recently [5, 7, 9, 11].

MC is characterized by its *computational efficiency*, but in the case of high resolution dataset fitting times are not interactive. The most common speed-up technique is to avoid the traversal and classification of empty sub-volumes; octrees and other data structures have been used to prevent fruitless exploration of regions of the volume [2, 12].

Excessive fragmentation of the output data can prevent interactive rendering when high resolution datasets are processed. Equipments able to generate volumetric datasets as large as $512 \times 512 \times [\leq 512]$ are now generally available. Although an isosurface does not usually cross more than a small subset of all the voxels, we can understand how easy it is to generate surfaces defined by millions of triangles. State-of-the-art hardware is not yet fast enough to manipulate such masses of data in real time.

In this work we present DISCMC, a fast and approximated isosurface fitting system. The aim of the paper is twofold: to present the implementation and functionalities of the DISCMC system and to evaluate the pyramidal representation adopted in DISCMC to speed-up fitting and to support multi-resolution isosurface extraction.

The fitting algorithm at the base of DISCMC has been proposed in a previous paper [4]; it is situated half-way between the *cuberille* method, which assumes constant value voxels and directly returns the voxel faces (orthogonal to the volume axes) [1], and the *cell interpolation* approach of MC. The DISCMC approach leads to: fast approximated fitting, by replacing edge interpolation with midpoint selection; interesting reductions in output fragmentation, by applying a very simple merging approach; and lower running times, when compared with classical MC. Moreover, the use of an unambiguous triangulation scheme [5] allows the extraction of isosurfaces without topological anomalies. We have recently proposed a new, revised version of the algorithm [6] generating geometries composed only by triangles, thus resulting in a consistent speed-up in the rendering process. For any detail and explanation about the algorithm we advice to consult reference [6].

Section 2 presents the algorithm. The basic ideas of the algorithm, the organization and contents of the new lookup table and the data structures used to store the extracted facets are briefly described. We then introduce the *merging* phase, where coplanar facets are merged into larger convex polygons that are triangulated. In Section 3 we describe in details why a *pyramidal representation* has been adopted to speed-up cell classification and to support multiple level of resolution fitting. The architecture and the graphical user interface of the DISCMC system are presented in Section 4. Results and conclusions are discussed in Section 5.

2 The Discretized Marching Cubes Algorithm

The Discretized Marching Cube [4] is a derivation of MC based on midpoint selection.

In a number of applications where approximated isosurfaces could be acceptable, linear interpolation is not critical to extract meaningful isosurfaces since the maximal approximation error involved in midpoint choice rather than interpolation is 1/2 of the cell size.

The set of vertices that can be generated by DISCMC is finite: there are only 13 different spatial locations on which a new vertex can be originated (12 cell-edge midpoints plus the cell centroid). Moreover, applying midpoint selection allows for a *finite set of planes* where the generated facets lie. We have only 13 different plane incidences onto which a facet can lie, and for each incidence the algorithm generates a limited number of different facets.

The following points characterize the DISCMC algorithm:

- each facet can be simply classified in terms of its shape and plane incidence; vertex coordinates are not necessary: they can be reconstructed by the coordinates of the cell the facet belongs to;

- the limited number of different plane incidences increases the percentage of coplanar adjacent facets and therefore allows a drastic reduction in the number of returned polygons while preserving small, but possibly significant, roughnesses;

- the algorithm does not require interpolation of the surface intersections along the edges of the cells; this implies it works in integer arithmetic (except for the computation of normals) at a considerably higher speed than standard methods.

2.1 A new lookup table

DISCMC requires a simple reorganization of the standard MC LUT. Due to midpoint selection the number of different facets returned by DISCMC is fixed, and we have only a constant number of different output primitives for each plane incidence: only right triangles are generated on planes $x = c$, $y = c$ and $z = c$; only rectangles on planes $x \pm y = c$, $x \pm z = c$ and $y \pm z = c$; only equilateral triangles on planes $x \pm y \pm z = c$. Moreover, using midpoint interpolation means that the geometrical location of facet vertices depends on the cell vertices configuration and the cell position in the dataset mesh.

Under these assumptions, the resulting facet set returned by DISCMC for each of the canonical MC configurations is reported in Figure 1. With respect to the original proposal by Lorensen and Cline we omit configuration 0 (the empty cell) and configuration 14 (which can be obtained by reflection from configuration 11, i.e. configuration k in Figure 1). Furthermore, three more configurations (configuration n, o and p in Figure 1) have to be managed in order to prevent topological ambiguity [5]. The adopted disambiguation policy implies the DISCMC LUT is not always symmetric.

Each facet is coded in the *DiscMC* LUT by using a *shape code*, which codifies the shape and position of the facet (1..4 for right triangles, 1..2 for rectangles and 1..8 for equilateral triangles), and an *incidence code*, i.e. the plane on which the facet lies. Geometrical information on the facet vertices isn't explicitly stored in the *DiscMC* LUT.

2.2 Isosurface extraction and merging phases

The data structures used to store the fitted facets are designed to guarantee efficient access during the following merging phase, even if this causes a loss of

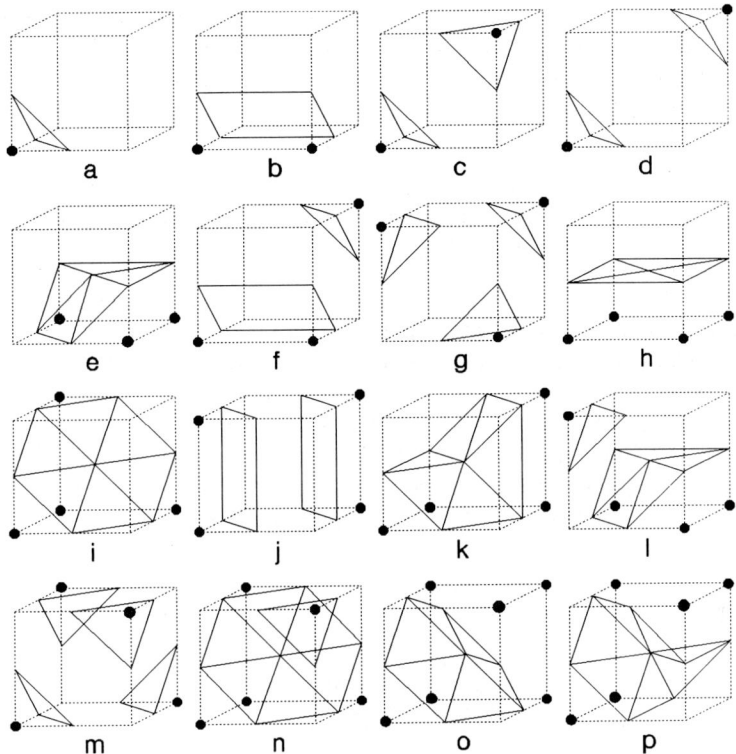

Figure 1. The sets of facets returned by DISCMC for each cell vertex configuration.

efficiency in memory usage.

The data representation used is a two-level bucketed structure. For each facet extracted from the volume data, it's quite trivial to identify the plane it lies over: it depends on the incidence code and the spatial coordinates of the cell containing the facet.

At the end of the extraction process we are ready to merge adjacent coplanar facets, and each list contains only those facets which are eligible to be merged.

The real kernel of the algorithm is the merging phase. The goal of this phase is to merge all the adjacent sets of coplanar facets in larger elements. The original DISCMC merging approach, as described in [4] was completely revised, in order to increase its efficiency and to produce triangles instead of polygons[1]. The new merging phase is described in details in a recent paper [6]. Basically, it splits the polygons, generated by merging coplanar facets, into the largest possible convex sub-polygons, and then triangulates them.

An important advantage of this surface simplification approach is its *geo-*

---

[1] We chose to transform via software the polygonal n-sided facets into triangle strips to produce output data in a format which guarantees faster visualization on the current state-of-the-art graphics workstations.

metrical robustness. Most of the process relies on the use of look up tables and combinatorial rules; any choice is based on geometrical computations, which might be affected by the numerical limited precision.

The merging process here briefly described returns triangle strips representing the isosurface in what we call **Draft** quality.

2.3 Computation of normals and *Proof* modality

For many applications and for high-resolution datasets *Draft* quality isosurfaces are sufficient. Normals are computed as the gradient in the vertices location, in order to render Gouraud or Phong shaded faces.

One problem may arise while rendering the isosurface. The generated triangular patches are absolutely correct from a geometrical point of view (and C^0 continuous, apart from the facets that lie on the volume dataset border). Nevertheless, we built them without taking into account the neighbor patches, so some of the vertices produced might be T-vertices (see Figure 2). This would lead to aliasing problems while Gouraud-shading the facets.

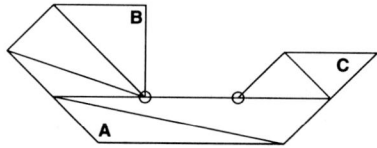

Figure 2. T-vertices (the circled vertices in the figure) returned in Draft modality.

To avoid this problem we developed a slightly different merging and triangulation process, called ***Proof*** modality, which detects the presence of T-vertices in the fitted surface and then triangulates all of the polygons taking care of the potential T-vertices lying on their border [6].

The *Proof* modality triangulation algorithm can triangulate polygons with three or more vertices aligned. T-vertices management involves very low overheads in processing time but leads to an increase in the number of triangles generated.

3 Pyramidal representation

A well known problem in isosurface fitting is that a large percentage of the processing time is spent to analyze and classify cells not crossed by the isosurface (*empty* cells). Solutions based on the use of hierarchical representation are generally proposed to avoid empty cells test. A hierarchical representation based on an octree structure (BONO, Branch On Need Octree) has been proposed by Wilhelms and Van Gelder [12].

We decided to adopt a simpler representation, a pyramid of regular volumes, in order to simplify the data structure management and to reduce storage costs.

The main goal of the pyramidal representation is to speed-up isosurface fitting. Therefore, our pyramid consists of a set of $3D$ arrays whose elements contain min - max intervals of the corresponding underlying block of cells.

Each element of the array at the base level of the pyramid contains the min - max interval of, at most, the corresponding 8 cells into the data volume (see Figure 3); the array at the top level (it is just one element) contains the min - max interval of the eight elements of the array of the underlying level; this is also the min - max interval of the whole dataset. Depending on the dimensions of the original dataset, border elements of each array of the pyramid can refer less than 8 underlying cells or elements. This permits to work with dataset whose resolution is not $2^n \times 2^n \times 2^n$, avoiding the problems that arise when an octree is used.

The pyramid is visited recursively: we may start from the root level (which contains a single cell), or from an intermediate level. For each cell, then, if the value of the isosurface we are extracting falls within the cells min - max interval we recursively go down the pyramid visiting the corresponding 8 (or less if the cell is on the border of the dataset) cells in the level immediately below; otherwise, we stop the recursion and avoid the visit of these cells.

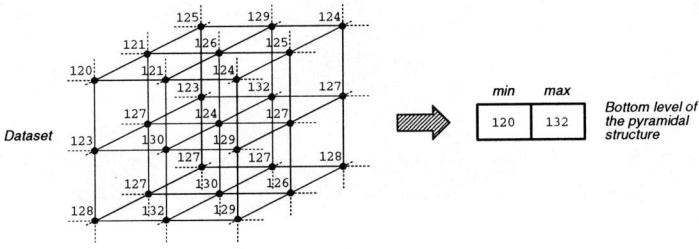

Figure 3. A sketch of the dataset to pyramid representation mapping.

The pyramidal representation has several advantages:

- the pyramid storage cost is usually lower that the octree cost because no pointers are needed and the links between levels are implicit with the cells indices; the space saving for which octrees have been introduced is usually lost while using them to classify volumetric datasets since, due to small variations of the scalar fields even in isovalued regions, complete octrees are needed;

- the storage needed to represent the pyramidal representation increases less than 50% the storage needed to represent the dataset: given a dataset with n cells, the pyramid requires

$$\sum_{i=1}^{\lceil \log_8 n \rceil} \frac{n}{8^i} < \frac{n}{4}$$

cells, and each entry contains two field values (min, max);

- given a pyramidal representation, it is very easy to select sub-volumes of interest and to limit the isosurface fitting to these volumes only.

Another great advantage of the pyramidal representation is the possibility to easily implement a multiple level of resolution fitting.

We can stop the visit of the data structure at a user-defined level, and extract approximated representations: these approach allows for a significant reduction of the isosurfaces complexity: experiments on a 256^3 dataset showed that fitting surfaces on level 7 (the next to the last level) gives sufficiently good approximations while reducing the surface complexity to a fourth of the original (see Figure 4 for an example).

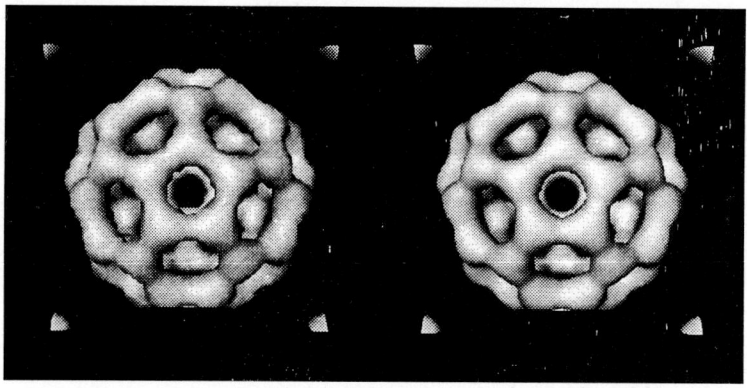

Figure 4. Isosurfaces fitted on the dataset (right, 62,508 triangles) and on the bottom level of the pyramid (left, 20,164 triangles).

4 DiscMC system implementation

The DiscMC algorithm is at the very base of our isosurface fitting system. The system has been designed to run on Unix workstations, rendering the extracted isosurfaces using the OpenGL graphics library [8] and having a graphical user interface based on a portable toolkit built over X11. These choices assure a good DiscMC portability on many different platforms (including PC's running Linux), even if for the time being our distribution includes only SGI binaries.

The system GUI was implemented using **XForms** [13], a toolkit built over X11 (Xlib). We looked for a very simple-to-use toolkit, which should not require an in deep knowledge of X11. We chose to adopt XForms, a very handy library (usable from C) with all the common widget necessary to design a standard GUI (button, sliders, input field, dials, file system browser *forms*, using the toolkit terminology).

The library provides also a program, the *Form Designer*, which lets the user interactively design the interface layout and generate the corresponding C code. A limitation of the XForms toolkit is that the user cannot configure or extend the library, defining new interactive forms. This important feature, available in other graphical user interface toolkits (e.g., SGI RapidApp and ViewKit products), did not result critical in the design and implementation of the DISCMC user interface, because the set of widget provided was enough for our purposes.

4.1 System's Functionalities

We chose to give the user the possibility to either render the fitted geometries in an OpenGL window, or to save them on disk. The geometries (lists of triangular facets) are saved on disk using the SGI Open Inventor [10] format. The saved isosurfaces can therefore be visualized using any Inventor viewer (e.g., ivview), which probably will provide a more sophisticated interface than the DISCMC viewer that has been designed as an extremely simple tool, providing a single light source, Gouraud shading or wire-frame rendering, and a basic control of the viewpoint.

We dedicate the rest of this section to briefly summarize the functionalities available in the system using the GUI layout as a guide.

Main Window We have two buttons managing the interactions with the disk (the two uppermost buttons, see figure 6 in Appendix). One to LOAD a dataset from disk and the other to SAVE on disk the triangle mesh. The format used to store the dataset on disk is a very simple one (in fact, we named it .sds, simple dataset): it uses one byte for each fields value and contains no other information. The size of the dataset and their physical dimensions are instead stored in a .sdh file (simple data header). All the information is stored as binary values.

There are two fields showing the name, the resolution and the voxel shape of the loaded dataset.

The user may choose between two different *data output modalities*:
DRAFT: gives faster surface extraction and also best results in terms of simplification; on the other hand, triangle meshes with T-vertices may be returned and this may originate aliasing problems in Gouraud-shaded rendering;
PROOF: at the cost of both some more processing time and lower simplification factor, T-vertices are detected and removed.

Based on the results of simulations made on several datasets at different thresholds, we realized that the PROOF modality gives in output roughly 5% triangles more than the DRAFT modality.

The FAST EXTRACTION mode forces the construction of the $min - max$ pyramidal representation previously described and use this data structure to speed-up isosurface fitting.

The threshold value (iso-level) is selected with the slider provided in the main window. The START button is used to fire the fitting process.

To help the user in selecting the desired threshold, an **Image Browser** window allows the interactive, slice-by-slice analysis of the dataset.

Info Window The *Info Window* (see figure 6 in Appendix) helps the user to keep under control at a glance a number of information on the isosurface currently fitted. They are:

1. the VOLUME bounded by the isosurface (measured in cell units; the real dimension of each cell is defined in the *.sdh* file and it is shown in the Main Window);

2. the number of TRIANGLES that would be generated by a standard implementation of Marching Cubes (with ambiguous configuration management);

3. the number of TRIANGLES that are generated by our discretized approach (BEFORE MERGE), and the number of those which are produced after the merging process (AFTER MERGE);

4. the elapsed TIMES, relative to:

   LOADING: loading the dataset and data structures allocation;
   MARCHING: discretized fitting on the dataset cells;
   REDUCING: merging facets in larger triangle strips;
   COMPLETING: T-vertices management (if in PROOF mode), isosurface storing onto disk (if graphics output is OFF);

5. the surface simplification obtained as a percentage on the standard MC mesh (REDUCTION).

The current values in the Info Window may be saved on disk at any time for comparison and statistic purposes.

Image Browser Window We considered a primary need for an interactive system to have the chance to interactively decide, on the basis of a dataset browsing facility, the threshold of interest to compute the isosurface. For these purposes the *Image Browser Window* (see figure 7 in Appendix) allows the interactive, slice by slice, analysis of the dataset.

A selected list of the main functionalities provided in this window is as follows:

SLICE ORIENTATION: selection of the slicing plane (XY, YZ or ZX) to be used while browsing the dataset;
SELECTED PIXEL INFO: when the user selects a pixel on the image, its position (coordinates on the plane) and value are shown in this field;
HIGHLIGHT: to paint the selected pixels with the current highlight color; while the highlighting, obviously, does not affect the original image all the pixel in the plane with the same value are colored by the selected color to let the user identify better where such a value appears in the dataset.

Multi-resolution Window The pyramidal data structure provided allows the extraction of isosurfaces at multiple level of resolution. Using the counter contained in this window user chooses the level onto which isosurfaces are extracted.

5 Results and conclusions

We tested DISCMC on a number of different datasets and compared it with a public domain regular Marching Cubes algorithm[2] (hereafter *Classic* MC). We modified its original lookup table in order to avoid ambiguous configurations [5].

The results in Table 1 refer to the two different merging-modalities of the DISCMC algorithm: the *Draft* mode and the *Proof* version, with the T-vertices removed.

Name	Resol.	Thr.	MC Classic		DISCMC Draft			DISCMC Proof		
			Triang.	Time	Triang.	%	Time	Triang.	%	Time
Bucky	128^3	127.5	183,480	9.26	48,638	26.5	4.42	62,508	34.0	5.89
		215.6	48,584	4.17	18,660	38.4	3.32	22,412	46.1	3.85
		65.1	223,264	10.43	55,243	24.7	4.68	70,738	31.6	6.33
Head	$256^2 \times 34$	41.7	138,252	7.05	42,381	30.6	4.03	52,201	37.8	5.13
		105.1	250,369	9.40	71,197	28.4	5.77	87,562	35.0	7.68
Hydro	127^3	127.5	44,704	3.21	9,448	21.1	2.02	11,512	25.7	2.33
		40.1	124,736	6.65	26,592	21.3	2.51	32,496	26.0	3.27
Sphere	128^3	50.1	135,464	6.91	27,088	19.9	3.19	32,800	24.2	4.02

Table 1. Number of triangles produced, simplification percentage and times of a public domain implementation of the Marching Cubes algorithm and of the two versions (*Draft* and *Proof*) of DISCMC.

Table 1 reports the numbers of triangles generated by *Classic* MC and by DISCMC. Five datasets were used during testing: *Bucky* (128^3) is the electron density around a molecule of C_{60}[3]; *Head* ($256^2 \times 34$) is a CAT scanned dataset[4]; *Hydro* (127^3) is the electron density around a molecule of H_2; *Sphere* (128^3) is a voxelized sphere. The thresholds (*Thr*) used are shown in the table. In Table 1, percentage values (the number of triangles produced by *Draft* or *Proof* DISCMC over the number of triangles in the *Classic* MC) represent a measure of the compression in space obtained with our method. The running times of *Classic* Marching Cubes and of Discretized Marching Cubes in *Draft* and *Proof* mode are also presented. Times (in CPU seconds) do not take into account I/O operations (i.e. dataset reading, output vertices, normals and triangles rendering or writing on disk). Tests were performed on an R4400 Indigo2 Silicon Graphics workstation.

Note that the times of the *Draft* (*Proof*) version are between 21% and 63% (8% and 51%) shorter than *Classic* MC: this is mainly due to the use of integer arithmetic and to the fast algorithm adopted for the merging phase. The Classic MC and the DISCMC times in Table 1 are measured with any optimization of the marching step (e.g. via octree or pyramid data structure).

---

[2] Written and kindly provided by Brian Tierney of the Lawrence Berkeley Laboratory, E-mail: bltierney@lbl.gov.
[3] Courtesy of AVS International Centre.
[4] Courtesy of Niguarda Hospital, Milan, Italy.

Table 2 reports timing results for each phase in the *Proof* DISCMC algorithm. Times (in CPU seconds) do not take into account I/O operations and relate to: non optimized (*NoOpt*) and optimized (*Pyramid*) *marching* times (cells classification, facets extraction, volume computation); *merging* times (construction of 2D convex polygons, update of the 3D array of vertices); *completion* times (T-vertices management, computation of normals, triangulation).

Name	Resol.	Thr.	Proof DISCMC March		Merge	Complete
			No Opt.	Pyramid		
Bucky	128^3	127.5	2.62	0.75	1.66	1.61
		215.6	2.45	0.24	0.81	0.59
		65.1	2.65	0.86	1.85	1.83
Head	$256^2 \times 34$	41.7	2.63	0.53	1.33	1.17
		105.1	2.82	0.94	2.79	1.97
Hydro	127^3	127.5	1.86	0.16	0.19	0.28
		40.1	1.97	0.43	0.53	0.77
Sphere	128^3	50.1	2.49	0.49	0.64	0.89

Table 2. Running times of *Proof* Discretized Marching Cubes (in CPU seconds).

The speed-up introduced by the adoption of the pyramidal representation is impressive.

The efficiency of the DISCMC merging and retriangulating steps is high. This is crucial because the design goal of DISCMC was to give simplified meshes **with** high efficiency, to be used, for example, while interactively searching for the correct threshold. Once such a threshold has been selected, a more sophisticated method can be used as well to obtain the best approximated mesh.

Other characteristics which differentiates DISCMC from other simplification approaches are as follows: it does not entail managing a geo-topological representation of the triangle mesh; its algorithmic robustness, because we do not have to handle complex situations (e.g. triangles degenerating into points) which have to be taken into careful consideration in the Classic MC and other simplification approaches; it uses mostly integer arithmetic, and restricts the use of floating point computation to the computation of normals.

The results obtained and the good quality of the output images (Figure 5) support our claim that DISCMC represents a valid tool for the rapid reconstruction and visualization of isosurfaces from medium and high resolution datasets.

6 Acknowledgements

DISCMC is available at the Visual Computing Group WWW site of the CNR in Pisa (http://miles.cnuce.cnr.it/cg/homepage.html).

We gratefully acknowledge the great job done by T.C. Zhao and M. Overmars in implementing the XForms Library and thanks them for having released

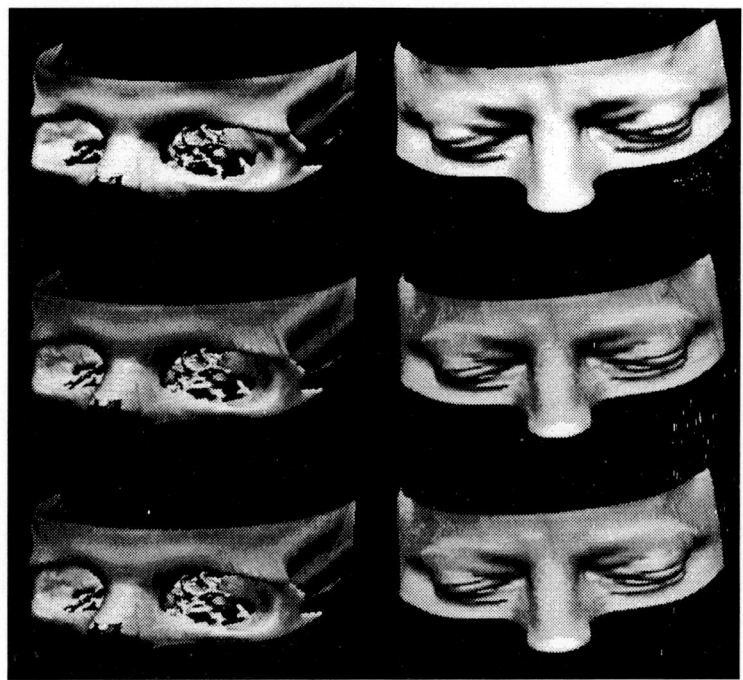

Figure 5. Results from the *Head* dataset (two different thresholds) for the *Classic* Marching Cubes, *Draft* DISCMC and *Proof* DISCMC (upper, middle and lower images, respectively).

it as a nearly-public domain software. Info on XForms may be requested to: zhao@csd.uwm.edu.

This work was partially financed by the Sardinian Regional Authorities and by Progetto Strategico "Conoscenza per Immagini: un'applicazione ai Beni Culturali" of the Italian National Research Council.

References

[1] Gordon, D., Udupa, J. Fast surface tracking in 3D binary images. Computer Vision, Graphics and Image Processing, (45), 196–214 (1989).

[2] Itoh, T., Koyamada, K. Isosurface generation by using extrema graphs. In: IEEE Visualization '94 Proc., pp. 77–83 (1994).

[3] Lorensen, W., Cline, H. Marching cubes: a high resolution 3D surface construction algorithm. ACM Computer Graphics (Proceedings of SIGGRAPH '87), 21(4), 163–170 (1987).

[4] Montani, C., Scateni, R., Scopigno, R. Discretized Marching Cubes. In: R. Bergeron, A. Kaufman (eds.), Visualization '94 Proceedings, pp. 281–287. IEEE Computer Society Press (1994).

[5] Montani, C., Scateni, R., Scopigno, R. A modified look-up table for implicit disambiguation of Marching Cubes. The Visual Computer, 10(6), 353–355 (1994).

[6] Montani, C., Scateni, R., Scopigno, R. Decreasing iso-surface complexity via discretized fitting. Tech. Rep. B437, I.E.I. – C.N.R., Pisa, Italy (1995).

[7] Natarajan, B. K. On generating topologically consistent isosurfaces from uniform samples. Visual Computer, 11(1), 52–62 (1994).

[8] Neider, J., Davis, T., Woo, M. OpenGL Programming Guide. Addison Wesley (1993).

[9] Payne, B., Toga, A. Surface mapping brain functions on 3D models. IEEE Computer Graphics & Applications, 10(2), 41–53 (1990).

[10] Wernecke, J. The Inventor mentor: programming Object-oriented 3D graphics with Open Inventor. Addison Wesley (1994).

[11] Wilhelms, J., Gelder, A. V. Topological considerations in isosurface generation. ACM Computer Graphics, 24(5), 79–86 (1990).

[12] Wilhelms, J., Gelder, A. V. Octrees for faster isosurface generation. ACM Transaction on Graphics, 11(3), 201–227 (1992).

[13] Zhao, T., Overmars, M. Forms Library – a graphical user interface toolkit for X. Tech. Rep. 95-, Department of Computer Science, Utrecht University, Utrecht, NL (1995).

Editors' Note: See Appendix, p. 318 for coloured figures of this paper

Nearest Neighbour Search for Visualization Using Arbitrary Triangulations

Frank Weller and Robert Mencl

Universität Dortmund
Informatik VII (Computer Graphics)
D–44221 Dortmund
Germany

Abstract. In visualization of scattered data, one is often faced with the problem of finding the nearest neighbours of a data site. This task frequently occurs in an advanced stage of the visualization process, where several data structures have been created during run time. Many applications compute a triangulation of the data for their visualization purposes. To take advantage of this previously allocated data structure we propose an algorithm for determining the k nearest neighbours in a triangulated point set. As a benefit, this algorithm dynamically computes exactly as many neighbours as necessary for the specific application and does not assume a particular kind of triangulation. Furthermore, it works in any finite-dimensional, metric affine space.

1. Introduction

In visualization of scientific data, the raw input usually undergoes a large number of processing steps before an actual image can be computed. Structural analysis of complex shapes, visualization of multivariate scattered data, and computer tomography, for example, demand the efficient solution of a multitude of geometric problems.

A frequent approach for treating these different problems is the application of independent modules for each problem separately. Although their data structures are not necessarily disjoint, the various modules often make no use of previously created data structures of other modules. This leads to an overhead of storage and computing time requirements, which should evidently be avoided.

This paper adresses one fundamental geometric problem, the k nearest neighbours query: Given a particular data site $\mathbf{p}_i$ from a set P, find the k nearest sites in P. Immediate applications within the field of visualization are gradient and derivative estimation, clustering, and surface extraction (cf. [7, 8]), to name only a few.

In previous work on nearest neighbour problems [2, 1], regular space subdivisions play an important role. These subdivisions perform well on uniformly distributed data, but are somewhat less suited for data sets of strongly varying density. Triangulations, on the other hand, are an irregular data structure which adapts easily to all kinds of data distributions. They are fundamental in many geometric algorithms. Several authors have used triangulations for visualizing point sets in 3-space (see, e.g., [4, 5, 6].)

The aim of this paper is, as a result of the above considerations, to present an algorithm for solving the k nearest neighbours problem by taking advantage of a previously computed triangulation. The algorithm can process multivariate data, as it functions in spaces of arbitrary finite dimension. Furthermore, it does not assume a particular metric. Many triangulation-based algorithms will work only with triangulations that possess certain properties, such as Delaunay triangulations. Our algorithm makes no such requisites. Thus, it can operate on any triangulation that another module has 'left behind.' In determining the k nearest neighbours, our algorithm explores only a part of the triangulation. While this part contains more vertices than just the k nearest ones, it is in general considerably smaller than the complete triangulation. The neighbour points are reported in order of increasing distance from the query point. In some applications, this order presents useful additional information. Implementation of the algorithm is straightforward. Apart from distance computations and the triangulation, only standard operations and data structures are needed.

With only minor modifications, the algorithm becomes applicable to slightly different types of queries. Thus, it is easy to find the data points lying within a certain radius from the query point. Not only vertices of the triangulation, but arbitrary points in the respective space can be used as query points. A query can be suspended after a certain number of neighbours have been determined, to be resumed later if further neighbours are needed. This is particularly useful for interactive graphical techniques where additional demand for neighbourhood information arises as a result of feedback from the user.

2. Terminology

Let $\mathbf{A}^d$ be a real-affine space of dimension d with metric $\mathrm{dist}\,(\cdot,\cdot)$. A m-*simplex* $\mathbf{s}$ is the convex hull of $m+1$ points, called vertices, which are not contained in a $(m-1)$-dimensional subspace. A *subsimplex* of $\mathbf{s}$ is the convex hull of a proper subset of the vertices of $\mathbf{s}$. A $(d-1)$-subsimplex of a d-simplex is called a *facet*. Two d-simplices are called *incident* if one of them is a subsimplex of the other. Two d-simplices are called *adjacent* if they have d vertices in common and their intersection is a facet.

We define the distance of a simplex $\mathbf{s}$ from a point $\mathbf{p}$ as

$$\mathrm{dist}\,(\mathbf{s},\mathbf{p}) := \min_{\mathbf{q}\in\mathbf{s}} \mathrm{dist}\,(\mathbf{q},\mathbf{p})\quad .$$

Let the point set $P = \{\mathbf{p}_1, \ldots, \mathbf{p}_n\} \subset \mathbf{A}^d$ not be contained in a proper subspace of $\mathbf{A}^d$. A *triangulation* T of P is a tesselation of the convex hull of P into d-simplices whose vertices are in P. We denote the subsimplices of all d-simplices of T collectively as the subsimplices of T. In particular, the points in P are the 0-subsimplices of T.

3. The Algorithm

The basic concept of our algorithm is a ball which is centered at the query point $\mathbf{p}_i$ and whose radius increases continuously. As the ball expands, it encounters the vertices of T in order of increasing distance from $\mathbf{p}_i$. Our algorithm registers not only the vertices, but also the d-simplices of T in the order in which the ball encounters them. To this end, an appropriate subset of the d-simplices and vertices is stored in a heap, which is sorted by distance from the query point. The element closest to $\mathbf{p}_i$ is found at the top of the heap.

The expanding ball will, in general, encounter several d-simplices and/or vertices simultaneously. The algorithm, on the other hand, processes these elements one after another. At any given time during the expansion process, we call a d-simplex or vertex of T *intersecting* if the algorithm has determined that it intersects the ball. All other d-simplices and vertices are called *non-intersecting*, even if they do intersect the ball. The term closest is used with respect to distance from the query point.

Lemma 1 *Let $\mathbf{p}_i$ be contained in at least one intersecting d-simplex. Then one of the closest non-intersecting d-simplices is adjacent to (i.e., shares a facet with) an intersecting d-simplex.*

Proof: Let $\mathbf{t}$ be a closest non-intersecting d-simplex, and let $\mathbf{q}$ be the point of $\mathbf{t}$ closest to $\mathbf{p}_i$. Since T covers a convex volume, it must cover the line segment $\overline{\mathbf{p}_i\mathbf{q}}$. By choice of $\mathbf{t}$ and $\mathbf{q}$, it is clear that each interior point of $\overline{\mathbf{p}_i\mathbf{q}}$ is contained in some intersecting d-simplex. Since we consider closed d-simplices, $\mathbf{q}$ is also contained in an intersecting d-simplex, say, $\mathbf{t}'$. (If the line segment has no interior points, then $\mathbf{q} = \mathbf{p}_i$ is contained in an intersecting d-simplex by hypothesis.) Now consider two interior points, $\mathbf{p}$ and $\mathbf{p}'$, of $\mathbf{t}$ and $\mathbf{t}'$, respectively. We choose these points sufficiently close to $\mathbf{q}$ that the line segment $\overline{\mathbf{p}'\mathbf{p}}$ is covered by d-simplices containing $\mathbf{q}$. If necessary, we perturb the points such that $\overline{\mathbf{p}'\mathbf{p}}$ does not intersect any subsimplex of T of dimension less than $d-1$. At some point between $\mathbf{p}'$ and $\mathbf{p}$, the line segment must pass from an intersecting into a non-intersecting d-simplex. This point is interior to a facet $\mathbf{f}$, which is shared by the two d-simplices. Since the non-intersecting d-simplex contains $\mathbf{q}$, it is a closest non-intersecting d-simplex. ∎

The algorithm starts by inserting one d-simplex incident on $\mathbf{p}_i$ into the empty heap. It then keeps processing simplices from the top of the heap until it has found the k nearest neighbours. If the simplex from the heap is a vertex, it is reported as the next neighbour. When a d-simplex $\mathbf{t}$ is taken from the heap, it becomes intersecting. The d adjacent d-simplices and the vertices of $\mathbf{t}$ are inserted into the heap. A flag for each d-simplex and each vertex prevents multiple insertion into the heap. The flag is set when its corresponding simplex is inserted. A simplex whose flag is set will not be inserted again.

As mentioned above, the heap is ordered by distance from the query point. As a secondary ordering criterion, vertices are given priority over d-simplices: If a vertex and a d-simplex are equally distant from $\mathbf{p}_i$, the vertex will appear at the top of the heap first. This prevents the algorithm from unnecessarily processing d-simplices which are as far from $\mathbf{p}_i$ as the k-nearest neighbour. The complete algorithm is described in Algorithm 1.

Theorem 2 *Algorithm 1 reports k nearest neighbours of $\mathbf{p}_i$ in order of increasing distance.*

Proof: Let us first consider the case $k = n-1$, i.e., all other vertices are requested. In this case, we have to show that the vertices are reported in the correct order. Assume that vertex $\mathbf{q}$ is reported before $\mathbf{p}$, but $\mathbf{p}$ is strictly closer to $\mathbf{p}_i$ than $\mathbf{q}$. This can only happen if $\mathbf{q}$ appears at the top of the heap before $\mathbf{p}$ has been inserted. There exists a d-simplex $\mathbf{t}$ which is incident on $\mathbf{p}$. Now $\mathbf{t}$ must be non-intersecting, or $\mathbf{p}$ would have been inserted into the heap. On the other hand, $\mathbf{t}$ is not further from $\mathbf{p}_i$ than $\mathbf{p}$, and therefore strictly closer than $\mathbf{q}$. By Lemma 1, there exists a closest non-intersecting d-simplex $\mathbf{t}'$ which is adjacent to an intersecting d-simplex. Because of this adjacency, $\mathbf{t}'$ must be in the heap. On the other hand, $\mathbf{t}'$ is closer than $\mathbf{q}$, a contradiction. Therefore, $\mathbf{q}$ cannot be reported before $\mathbf{p}$. To prove the case $k < n-1$, we simply note that the algorithm runs in exactly the same way as for $n-1$ neighbours, but stops after the k nearest neighbours have been found. ∎

Figure 1 shows two snapshots of the algorithm working on a planar triangulation. The intersecting triangles and vertices are drawn in white and black, respectively. The triangles and vertices in the heap are drawn in gray. In the left diagram, the algorithm has just deleted a vertex from the heap. In the right diagram, it has also processed the triangles that are incident on this vertex.

Algorithm 1 (k **Nearest Neighbours Query**)
Input: Triangulation T of point set $P = \{\mathbf{p}_1, \ldots, \mathbf{p}_n\}$,
  query point $\mathbf{p}_i \in P$,
  and integer k.
Variables: heap H ;
  simplex **s** ;
  d-simplex **t** ;
  vertex **v** ;
  integer j ; (* number of neighbours found so far *)
begin
$j := 0$;
find a d-simplex **t** which is incident on $\mathbf{p}_i$;
insert **t** into H ;
set the flag of **t** ;
repeat
  delete simplex **s** from the top of H ; (* we now call **s** intersecting *)
  if s is a d-simplex **then**
    for each vertex **v** of **s** with flag of **v** not set **do**
      compute $\text{dist}(\mathbf{v}, \mathbf{p}_i)$;
      insert **v** into H ;
      set the flag of **v** ;
    endfor
    for each d-simplex **t** adjacent to **s** with flag of **t** not set **do**
      compute $\text{dist}(\mathbf{t}, \mathbf{p}_i)$;
      insert **t** into H ;
      set the flag of **t** ;
    endfor
  else (* **s** is a vertex *)
    $j := j + 1$;
    report s as the jth neighbour ;
  endif
until $j = k$;
end

4. Complexity

We assume that the data structure of the triangulation allows us to carry out the following operations:

- Given a vertex, find an incident d-simplex in constant time.
- Given a d-simplex, find its vertices in time $O(d)$.
- Given a d-simplex, find the $d + 1$ adjacent d-simplices in time $O(d)$.

One elementary step in Algorithm 1 is the distance computation between a d-simplex and the query point. The time complexity of this step depends on the dimension and on the metric being used. In d-dimensional space, it takes time proportional to d to determine the Euclidean distance between two points alone. In the following, we let δ denote the worst-case complexity of distance computations, both between two points and between a point and a d-simplex.

Let $|T|$ denote the number of d-simplices in T, and let $|H|$ be the number of simplices contained in H. We note that $n \in O(|T|)$. In the planar case, we also have $|T| \in O(n)$.

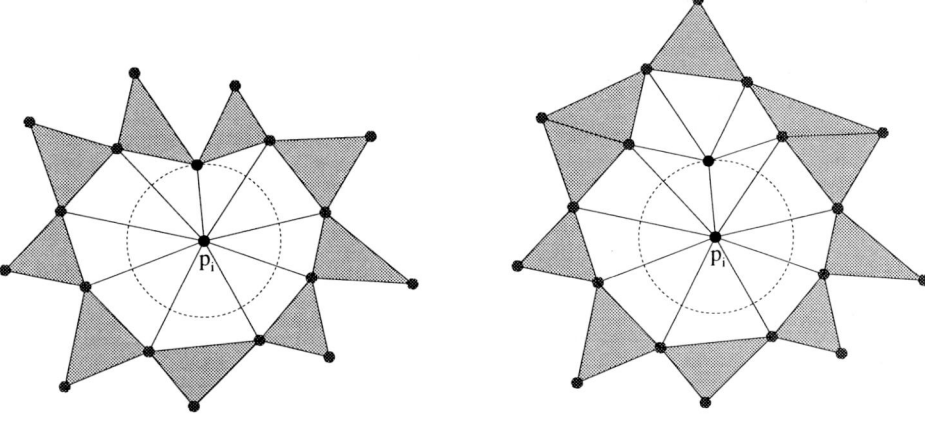

Fig. 1. Two phases of the algorithm as the expanding ball encounters a vertex and, simultaneously, three triangles.

In 3-dimensional space, triangulations with $|T| \in O(n)$ exist and can be constructed in $O(n \log n)$ time (cf. [3]).

To analyze the time complexity of the algorithm, let us first look at the time spent on heap operations. An insertion or deletion takes $O(\log |H|)$ time. Each vertex and each d-simplex is inserted into, and, likewise, deleted from, the heap at most once. Therefore, both the number of heap operations and the heap size are bounded by $O(|T|)$. The total time for all heap operations is $O(|T| \log |T|)$ in the worst case. Distance computations are carried out only for those simplices which are inserted into the heap, and only once per simplex. Therefore, the total time for distance computations is bounded by $O(\delta |T|)$.

Next, we will look at the two for-loops. Disregarding the heap operations and distance computations, for which we have already accounted above, the body of each for-loop consists only of setting a flag. This can be done in constant time. Within one execution of the repeat-loop, each for-loop is run at most $d+1$ times. The loop overhead consists of finding $d+1$ vertices or d-simplices and testing their flags, which takes time proportional to d. Thus, the for-loops cost $O(d)$ time. All other steps that we have not considered so far require constant time. Each time the repeat-loop is executed, a simplex is deleted from the heap. This bounds the number of executions of the repeat-loop with $O(|T|)$. Thus, the time for all executions of all constant-time steps is bounded by $O(d|T|)$. This results in a total execution time of $O(|T|(d + \delta + \log |T|))$ in the worst case.

Figure 2 shows a planar example which causes worst-case behaviour of the algorithm. The dots in the diagram indicate that the left and right boundaries have $n/2-1$ vertices each, where n may be arbitrarily large. We consider a query with $k = 2$ at the time when the nearest neighbour of $\mathbf{p}_i$ has just become intersecting. The heap contains the $n/2 - 1$ vertices left of $\mathbf{p}_i$. Before the next neighbour can be found, $n/2 - 2$ triangles and $n/2-1$ vertices lying to the right of the nearest neighbour are inserted. Since these new simplices are closer to $\mathbf{p}_i$ than the $n/2 - 1$ vertices already contained in the heap, the summed cost for the insertions is proportional to $n \log n$. Note that this extreme behaviour of the algorithm occurs only if $\mathbf{p}_i$ or its nearest neighbour is used as the query point. For any other vertex, at most 6 triangles and 7 vertices are inserted into the heap before the second neighbour is found. In fact, as long as k is small compared to n, the time complexity averaged over all vertices depends on k rather than on $\|T\|$.

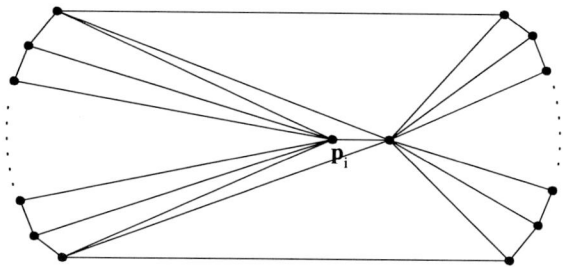

Fig. 2. Triangulation causing worst-case behaviour of the algorithm.

We conjecture that dependency on k only will be the case for most triangulations. This conjecture is strongly supported by the experimental results which are presented in the next section.

5. Experiments

In order to investigate the algorithm's behaviour in practice, it was measured on various point sets. The experiments were set up as follows. For each point p_i in a data set P, a query for the 2000 nearest neighbours of p_i is carried out. When the query finds the jth neighbour, $1 \leq j \leq 2000$, two quantities are recorded: the current heap size, denoted by $\|H\|(p_i, j)$, and the number of heap insertions which the query has executed up to this point, denoted by $\#I(p_i, j)$. Note that these quantities reflect not only the current state of the actual query for 2000 neighbours, but also the final state of a hypothetical query for only j neighbours of p_i.

The measurements were carried out on eight two-dimensional data examples:

- 3 sets of uniformly distributed random points, containing 2500, 10000, and 100000 points,
- 3 square grids of sizes 50 × 50, 100 × 100, and 200 × 500, and
- 2 sets of 8700 and 13687 points, scanned from real objects and exhibiting strong variation in point density due to previous data reduction.

In each case, T was a Delaunay triangulation of P.

We were interested in the worst-case behaviour of the algorithm on each particular data set, so the maxima

$$|H|(j) := \max_{p_i \in P} |H|(p_i, j) \text{ and } \#I(j) := \max_{p_i \in P} \#I(p_i, j)$$

over all queries within the same data set P were computed. Figure 3 shows the graphs of $|H|(j)$ and $\#I(j)$ as funcions of j. Two observations can be made in the graphs. The first is that $\#I(j)$ is strongly correlated to j. In other words, it appears to depend on j linearly. The second observation is that, although the underlying data sets vary in size by a factor of up to 40, the corresponding function graphs in Figure 3 almost coincide. This indicates that, as far as our examples go, the time complexity is in fact independent of $|T|$.

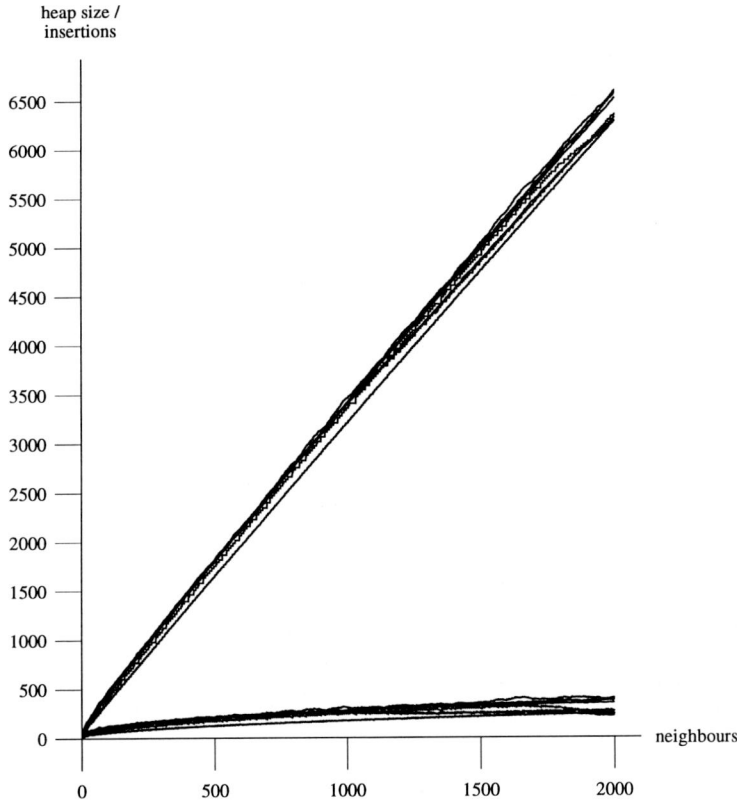

Fig. 3. Number of heap insertions (upper set of curves) and current heap size (lower set of curves).

6. Variations of the Basic Algorithm

This section describes four possible modifications of Algorithm 1. The first one is a speed-up, whereas the others aim at performing different, similar tasks.

6.1. Equidistant Stack

Whenever the expanding ball encounters a new subsimplex of dimension less than $d-1$, it intersects a number of d-simplices simultaneously. This holds for the very first 0-simplex, the query point $\mathbf{p}_i$, too. Let r be the current radius of the ball. Suppose we have taken d-simplex $\mathbf{s}$ from the heap and find an adjacent d-simplex $\mathbf{t}$ with dist$(\mathbf{t}, \mathbf{p}_i) =$ dist$(\mathbf{s}, \mathbf{p}_i) = r$. Algorithm 1 will insert $\mathbf{t}$ into the heap at a cost of $O(\log |H|)$. Now the heap cannot contain any d-simplex with a distance less than r at this point, nor a vertex of distance less than or equal to r. Therefore, only d-simplices which are equidistant to $\mathbf{t}$ can appear at the top of the heap before $\mathbf{t}$ does. These equidistant d-simplices, including $\mathbf{t}$, may be processed in an arbitrary order without affecting the correctness of the algorithm. Instead of inserting $\mathbf{t}$ into the heap, we may set it aside to be processed

> **Algorithm 2 (Modifications for Equidistant Stack)**
>
> - (∗ as in Algorithm 1 ∗)
>
> **Variables:** stack S ;
>
> - (∗ as in Algorithm 1 ∗)
>
> **repeat**
>   **if** S not empty **then**
>   pop d-simplex **s** from S ;
>   **else**
>   delete simplex **s** from the top of H ;
>   **endif**
>   **if s** is a d-simplex **then**
>
>   - (∗ as in Algorithm 1 ∗)
>
>   **for** each d-simplex **t** adjacent to **s** with flag of **t** not set **do**
>   compute dist $(\mathbf{t}, \mathbf{p}_i)$;
>   **if** dist $(\mathbf{t}, \mathbf{p}_i)$ = dist $(\mathbf{s}, \mathbf{p}_i)$ **then**
>   push **t** onto S ;
>   **else**
>   insert **t** into H ;
>   **endif**
>   set the flag of **t** ;
>   **endfor**
>
>   - (∗ as in Algorithm 1 ∗)

immediately after **s**. Since we will find several equidistant d-simplices in general, we use a stack S for setting them aside. A new simplex is deleted from the heap only when S is empty. Algorithm 2 shows the changed parts of the algorithm.

6.2. Radius Query

Instead of looking for k nearest neighbours, one may be interested in all neighbours within a ball of some radius r centered in $\mathbf{p}_i$. For this kind of query, the algorithm does not count the neighbours it finds, but stops when it realizes that no more neighbour within distance r can be found. This is the case when a vertex **s** with dist $(\mathbf{s}, \mathbf{p}_i) > r$ or a d-simplex **s** with dist $(\mathbf{s}, \mathbf{p}_i) \geq r$ appears at the top of the heap.

6.3. Arbitrary Query Points

In principle, Algorithm 1 works not only for vertices, but also for an arbitrary query point, **p**. The problem lies in determining the first d-simplex, **t**, which is inserted into the heap before the repeat-loop. If **p** lies in the convex hull of P, this process is known as point location and yields a d-simplex **t** containing **p**. For **p** outside the convex hull, all d-simplices which are visible from **p** are inserted at the beginning of the computation.

6.4. Suspended and Concurrent Queries

In some applications, one does not know a priori how many nearest neighbours of a query point will be required. After looking at the k nearest neighbours, one may find that another ℓ neighbours are necessary. In such a situation, it is an easy matter for Algorithm 1 to resume the query where it left off before. The cost for searching first k and then the next ℓ neighbours is the same as for searching $k + \ell$ neighbours in a single query. Some information must be saved in order to resume a query. This comprises the heap H, the flags, and the number k of previously found neighbours.

It is also possible to run queries in a concurrent manner, e.g., find k_i neighbours of $\mathbf{p}_i$, then k_j neighbours of $\mathbf{p}_j$, then another ℓ_i neighbours of $\mathbf{p}_i$, etc. Multiple suspended queries require a separate heap and a separate set of flags for each query point. Suppose that concurrent queries are carried out for all n vertices, then the space requirement for the flags is proportional to $n|T|$. However, if the average number of neighbours computed per vertex is small, most of the flags will never be used. Storage space can be reduced if we replace the flags by a hash table. Instead of setting a flag, we insert a pair of the form (query point, 'flagged' simplex) into the table. By the very nature of concurrent queries, the required number of neighbours in a single query is not known in advance. Thus, it may be impossible to make an appropriate choice for the size of the hash table, which has a strong influence on the table's efficiency. As an alternative, we can substitute a sorted tree (e.g., AVL or SBB tree, cf. [9]) for each heap, i.e., one per query. We insert s' into the tree if it is not contained in the tree and was not processed before s. Containment in the tree can be tested efficiently. Simplices are processed in order of increasing distance from the query point. Therefore, if s' is strictly closer than s, it has been processed before, and if s' is strictly further than s, it has not been processed before. Equidistant simplices that have been processed are stored in an auxiliary tree, and can be found there. A simplex is inserted into the auxiliary tree as soon as it is processed. The auxiliary tree is cleared when the intersecting sphere expands, i.e., when a simplex of greater distance is processed.

7. Conclusion

We have presented an algorithm for computing the k nearest neighbours of a vertex in a triangulated point set. The algorithm does not expect any particular kind of triangulation and computes only as many neighbours as are needed for the application. It operates in spaces of any (finite) dimension and with arbitrary metric. The output is sorted by increasing distance from the query point, which is a benefit for various applications. The algorithm is easy to implement and uses only very simple data structures in addition to the triangulation.

The principle of the algorithm, a ball expanding through the triangulation, is flexible enough to cover a variety of similar tasks. Radius queries, arbitrary query points, and suspended and concurrent queries require only small adjustments in the algorithm. This flexibility makes our algorithm a useful tool in a wide range of visualization applications.

References

1. S. Arya, D.M. Mount, N.S. Netanyahu, R. Silverman, and A. Wu. An optimal algorithm for approximate nearest–neighbour searching. In *Proceedings 11th Annual Symposium on Discrete Algorithms*, pages 573–582, 1994.

2. P.B. Callahan and S.R. Kosaraju. A decomposition of multi-dimensional point-sets with applications to k-nearest-neighbours and n-body potential fields. In *Proceedings 24th Annual ACM Symposium on the Theory of Computing*, pages 546–556, 1992.
3. H. Edelsbrunner, F.P. Preparata, and D.B. West. Tetrahedrizing point sets in three dimensions. *Journal of Symbolic Computation*, 10:335–347, 1990.
4. Herbert Edelsbrunner. Weighted alpha shapes, 1992. Technical Report UIUCDCS-R-92-1760, Department of Computer Science, University of Illinois at Urbana-Champaign, Urbana, Illinois.
5. Herbert Edelsbrunner and Ernst Mücke. Three-dimensional alpha shapes. *ACM Transactions on Graphics*, 13(1):43–72, 1994. Also as Technical Report UIUCDCS-R-92-1734, Department of Computer Science, 1992, University of Illinois at Urbana-Champaign,USA.
6. T.A. Foley, H. Hagen, and G.M. Nielson. Visualizing and modeling. *The Visual Computer*, 9:439–449, 1993.
7. Pascal Fua and Peter T. Sander. Reconstructing surfaces from unstructured 3D points. In *Proc. Image Understanding Workshop*, pages 615–625, San Diego, CA, 1992.
8. Hugues Hoppe, Tony DeRose, Tom Duchamp, John McDonald, and Werner Stuetzle. Surface reconstruction from unorganized points. *Computer Graphics*, 26(2):71–78, July 1992. Proceedings of Siggraph '92.
9. Niklaus Wirth. *Algorithmen und Datenstrukturen mit Modula–2*. B.G. Teubner Verlag, 1986.

Fast ray-tracing of rectilinear volume data

Miloš Šrámek

Institute of Measurement Science, Slovak Academy of Sciences,
Dúbravská cesta 9, 842 19 Bratislava, Slovak Republic
e-mail: miloss@umhp.savba.sk

Abstract. Tomographic devices often produce data with directionally and spatially dependent resolution. Resampling to cubic voxels is possible at the cost of a significant increase of data volume and rendering time. We present an algorithm for direct ray tracing of rectilinear grids, which enables the implementation of surface rendering with subvoxel surface detection based on local interpolation, as well as different volume rendering techniques (color compositing, reprojection, maximum intensity projection). Further we present a faster version of the basic algorithm, based on cubic macro-regions assigned to each background voxel. Each macro-region is defined by its chessboard distance to the nearest foreground voxel and can be skipped during the scene traversal. The speed-up is thus gained by increasing the step along the ray, maintaining 6-connectivity of the ray in the object vicinity, which is necessary for correct surface detection.

1 Volume visualization by ray tracing

Ray tracing is now common in the field of computer graphics, and the technique has also gained popularity in volumetric visualization. This is due to its ability to enhance spatial perception of the scene using such effects as transparency, mirroring and shadow casting. Correct understanding of the nature of the processed data further necessitates usage of various visualization techniques. In the framework of its basic scheme, ray tracing enables the implementation of various surface as well as volume rendering techniques (color compositing, reprojection, MIP), which makes it an ideal tool for data exploration.

The term *surface rendering* denotes a set of 3D data visualization techniques where only object surfaces contribute to the rendered image. One possibility is to build a *surface model*, i.e., to define a set of patches approximating the surface. These patches can then be rendered by some standard technique, usually with a hardware support. The *binary volume rendering* techniques represent an alternative. Although the image is still only contributed to by surfaces, no explicit surface model is defined. Instead, a trivariate implicit function $\mathcal{F} = \mathcal{F}(P, P_\sigma)$ is given, depending on voxel position P and data samples in some neighborhood P_σ. A continuous surface description can be then obtained by thresholding this function at some level T.

In order for there to be a possibility to specify various surface properties (color, reflectivity etc.) for different objects, an *object identifier* can be assigned to a voxel, either directly during the scan conversion of an analytical object description or as a result of *segmentation* in the case of scanned data. Voxels with no identifier assigned belong to *background* and can be ignored during the processing, since they do not contribute to the rendered image.

Due to the fact that the scene is defined within a 3D discrete raster, the ray should be represented as a *discrete ray*, i.e., as an ordered sequence of voxels pierced by the ray, with the following properties:

1. to enable supersampling and recursivity, the ray should be able to start at any point outside of the scene, or inside, and with arbitrary direction and

2. to get correct images, no object voxels along the ray should be missed. Therefore, the ray should, at least in the vicinity of an object, fulfill the demands of 6-connectivity[1].

Traversal of the ray voxels usually has more phases. Background voxels, surrounding the objects, are usually found first. Their traversal stops either when the ray leaves the scene or when the first object voxel is found. In the second case a *hit-miss test* should be performed in order to know if the ray should continue further by the following object or background voxel, or if a *ray-surface intersection* should be searched for. The hit-miss test can be performed by evaluation of the interpolating function $\mathcal{F}$ at one or more points lying in the voxel and comparing the results with the threshold value. In order to detect the ray-surface intersection point exactly, a system of equations defined by the ray and the surface $\mathcal{F}(\mathcal{P}, \sigma) = T$) should be solved either analytically or numerically[2].

The *probabilistic volume rendering* techniques represent an alternative to the surface approaches. Rather than segmenting the scene into objects and background, an *opacity* and *color* are assigned to each voxel, based on local properties of the data. The opacity reflects a measure by which the given voxel can contribute to the rendered image. A *culling* function can be defined, identifying the voxels which cannot contribute to the rendition and which can be discarded from consideration, alike to the background voxels in the surface rendering. Among others, techniques tracing primary rays (*ray casting*) through the scene were proposed, accumulating color and opacity of voxels or data samples obtained by interpolation along the ray.

We can see that visualization of volumetric data by ray tracing is a task which is algorithmically similar to standard ray tracing of analytical objects, if some space subdivision speed up method is used. In this case the object space is subdivided, either hierarchically or uniformly, again into voxels, which can be empty or can contain a list of contributing objects. The primary goal of the subdivision is to limit the number of ray-object intersection tests, which are themselves costly operations, by only performing tests with objects belonging to voxels pierced by a ray.

Ray traversal algorithms designed for the subdivision speed up techniques can therefore also be also for ray tracing volumetric data. However, one difference still exists, namely the voxel scene size. While the optimal subdivision rate for the speed up techniques was found to be low (only hundreds of voxels[3]), data sets which are orders of magnitude larger are processed in visualization tasks. Therefore applicability of these algorithms is only moderate and special techniques for ray tracing volumetric data were developed.

2 Macro-region based voxel traversal algorithms

Not all voxels along the ray contribute to the rendered image with the same weight. Only some of them belong to the interesting objects or surfaces, while the others can be traversed rapidly or even totally skipped. This capability is called *space-leaping*[4] and exploits some kind of *coherence* inherent to the object and/or image space as well as to a sequence of consecutive images.

The macro-region based voxel traversal algorithms exploit the object space coherence, i.e., the tendency of object (background) voxels to occupy connected regions of the space. In this case, background voxels are gathered into cubic, parallelepipedal or spherical macro-regions, which can be skipped in one step thus reducing the number of steps and therefore also the total rendering time. Various schemes for the macro-region definition are possible. Some of them are based on hierarchical encoding of the scene space, others define the macro-regions directly in the original voxel scene.

2.1 Distance based speed up techniques

Distance transforms convert a 2D (3D) binary image into an image, where each background pixel (voxel) is assigned a value corresponding to its distance to the nearest object pixel (voxel). Although computing the distances is in principle a global operation, algorithms were developed for approximating the global distances by propagating distances between neighboring pixels[5].

The idea to exploit the distance transforms to speed up the background traversal was introduced by Zuiderveld *et al.*[6]. The proposed Ray Acceleration by Distance Coding (RADC) scheme works in two phases:

Preprocessing: The volume is segmented and the distance information is added to background voxels by a 3D distance transform.

Rendering: The floating point 3D DDA algorithm defining the ray as a sequence of equidistant samples is used, exploiting the distance information for skipping empty regions.

Since objects in volumetric data sets tend to be centered in the middle of the volume, rays usually skip rapidly the off-center parts and slow down until they hit an object. For parallel projection, if the ray totally misses the object, the minimal distance along its path can be utilized for further speed up. In such a case, this distance defines a region in the image plane, where it is not necessary to fire new rays, because they all miss the object. The RADC algorithm works with various digital approximations of the ideal Euclidean distance. Since different shapes of thus defined free regions were not taken into account, highest speed has been obtained with the chamfer distance, which is the best approximation of the Euclidean distance.

A similar technique was proposed by Cohen and Sheffer[7]. The authors call the free zones defined by the distance transform *proximity clouds*. Once a ray enters a cloud cell, it can safely skip the distance determined by the cell's value. The algorithm is also based on the floating point 3D DDA algorithm and it differs from the RADC in that it takes the shape of the free zone into account: the step size depends not only on the distance value, but also on the kind of the distance and the ray direction. If the ray is defined by its direction vector $\vec{r} = (r_x, r_y, r_z)$ and the assigned distance is d then the coordinate increment should be

$$\left(\frac{d\, p_x}{D(\vec{r})}, \frac{d\, p_y}{D(\vec{r})}, \frac{d\, p_z}{D(\vec{r})} \right) \qquad (1)$$

where $D(\vec{r})$ is size of the projection vector in the corresponding metrics (Euclidean metrics is used in the case of chamfer distance):

$$D(\vec{r}) = \begin{cases} |p_x| + |p_y| + |p_z| & \text{for the city block distance} \\ \sqrt{(p_x^2 + p_y^2 + p_z^2)} & \text{for the Euclidean distance} \\ \max(|p_x|, |p_y|, |p_z|) & \text{for the chessboard distance.} \end{cases} \qquad (2)$$

Authors have shown that the average step for the city block distance can even be a few percent longer than for the Euclidean distance. Another advantage of the city block distance is that its computation is easier than computation of the chamfer distance, which is usually used instead of the Euclidean distance.

The proposed technique has two drawbacks:

1. The distances are calculated for the cell centers, while the current location along the ray is not necessarily in the center. Therefore, to avoid skips beyond the free zone, the computed distance d is decreased by 1.

2. The sequence of cells generated by the floating point 3D DDA algorithm does not fulfill the condition of 6-connectivity, which may cause some of the object voxels to be missed. Therefore, in the object's vicinity, the algorithm is switched to the incremental cell traversal algorithm[3] generating the 6-connected sequence.

A different method, the CD voxel traversal algorithm[2], relies exclusively on cubic macro-regions defined by the chessboard distance (CD). In this case, the ray is defined as a sequence of nonuniform samples at its intersections with the macro-region walls. This precision allows the utilization of the full size of the macro-region and overcomes the first drawback of the previous "proximity clouds" technique. In the close vicinity of an object, where CD equals zero, the macro-regions are identical to single voxels. Since the samples lie on their faces, a 6-connected sequence of voxels is defined, overcoming the second drawback.

The algorithm has two control variables: *faceType* (face is X type if it is perpendicular to the x axis) and relative position $\mathcal{P} = (p_x, p_y, p_z)$ of the sample with respect to the voxel vertex. Its main loop is based on the following observation: for each ray direction and each assigned CD there is some threshold $t_y^x(n)$ (assuming X is the actual face type and n is the assigned CD) of the p_x coordinate. If $p_x < t_y^x$, then the macro-region exit face is also X type, otherwise it is Y type. The algorithm therefore distinguishes between two step types, those with equal and those with different entry and exit face types. The fact that the sample coordinate is maintained during the traversal can speed up detection of the ray-surface intersection point[8].

3 Traversal of rectilinear grids by cubic macro-regions

In the previous section we described algorithms speeding up a binary scene traversal by exploiting distance information, assigned to each background voxel. Their common feature was that they assumed cubic voxels. In this section we introduce an algorithm which speeds up the traversal of scenes defined by a rectilinear grid. It is similar to the CD algorithm described above, in that it is also based on cubic macro-regions. However, in this case we assign the distances to background voxels of a secondary scene with cubic voxels and the same dimensions. Thus, parallelepipedal empty regions are defined in the original scene. The exact voxel dimensions are taken into account during the traversal.

Let **G** be a 3D grid of $(N_x + 1) \times (N_y + 1) \times (N_z + 1)$ points p_{ijk}:

$$\mathbf{G} = \{p_{ijk} = (S_x^i, S_y^j, S_z^k) : 0 \leq i \leq N_x, 0 \leq j \leq N_y, 0 \leq k \leq N_z\}, \tag{3}$$

where i, j and k are integers,

$$S_\nu^m = \sum_{i=1}^{m} \Delta_\nu^{i-1}, \quad \nu = x, y \text{ or } z \tag{4}$$

are sample coordinates ($S_\nu^0 = 0$) and $\Delta_x^0, \Delta_x^1, \ldots, \Delta_x^{N_x}, \Delta_y^0, \Delta_y^1, \ldots, \Delta_y^{N_y}$ and $\Delta_z^0, \Delta_z^1, \ldots, \Delta_z^{N_z}$ is the spacing between samples along each coordinate axis.

Let a voxel be a tuple $V_{ijk} = (v_{ijk}, h_{ijk})$, where $v_{ijk} = (S_x^i, S_x^{i+1}) \times (S_y^j, S_y^{j+1}) \times (S_z^k, S_z^{k+1})$ is voxel volume and $h_{ijk} \in \{0, 1\}$ is its value. Grid points p_{ijk} are defined in voxel vertices, and therefore the voxel scene **V**:

$$\mathbf{V} = \{V_{ijk} : 0 \leq i < N_x, 0 \leq j < N_y, 0 \leq k < N_z\}, \tag{5}$$

has one element less along each axis than **G**. The voxel value $h = 1$ means that the voxel can contribute to the image: either an object surface passes through its volume (binary volume rendering) or it can contribute with nonzero color and opacity in probabilistic volume rendering. The value $h = 0$ means, that the voxel cannot contribute, and therefore it can be skipped during the traversal without processing. We denote voxels with values equal to 0 (resp. 1) 0-voxels (resp. 1-voxels).

Let the secondary voxel scene **V**' consist of the same number of unit cubic voxels along each axis and let the corresponding voxels have equal values:

$$h'_{ijk} = h_{ijk} \tag{6}$$

If we assign now to each 0-voxel V_{ijk} its chessboard distance n to the nearest 1-voxel, we define a cubic macro-region in **V**':

$$\mathcal{O}'_n(V_{ijk}) = \{h'_{pqr} = 0 : i-n \leq p \leq i+n, j-n \leq q \leq j+n, k-n \leq r \leq k+n\} \tag{7}$$

with its center in V_{ijk} and with side size $2n+1$. A corresponding macro-region is defined in **V**:

$$\mathcal{O}_n(V_{ijk}) = \{h_{pqr} = 0 : S_x^{i-n} \leq p \leq S_x^{i+n}, S_y^{j-n} \leq q \leq S_y^{j+n}, S_z^{k-n} \leq r \leq S_z^{k+n}\}, \tag{8}$$

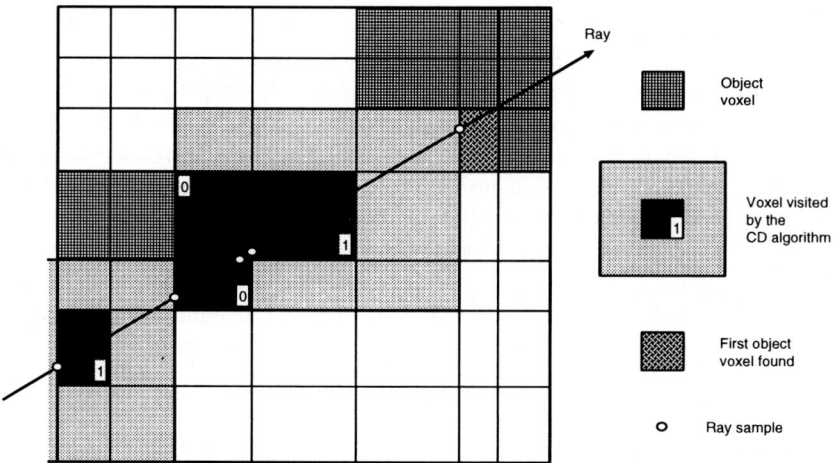

Fig. 1. Rectilinear grid traversal by cubic macro-regions

which is, of course, not cubic and voxel V_{ijk} is not situated in its center.

The voxel scene **V'** corresponds to the form of our data as stored in main memory or in a file. We do not care about the grid spacing and therefore the necessary distance transform is done in exactly the same way as for the cartesian scenes. The grid spacing should be taken into account during the ray definition, as will be shown in the next section.

3.1 The algorithm

We know that there are no object voxels within $\mathcal{O}^n(V)$, so we can jump from V directly to the first voxel outside of $\mathcal{O}^n(V)$. The traversal speed up is thus increased by reducing the number of visited voxels (Figure 1). We shall assume that the direction vector has only nonnegative coordinates. Generalization to all possible directions is done by proper initialization of some variables.

Let us imagine that the ray has reached voxel V with coordinates $V = (v_x, v_y, v_z)$ and assigned chessboard distance n, at an entry point $\mathcal{P} = (p_x, p_y, p_z)$ positioned at one of its walls. It is necessary to find the nearest intersection of the ray $\mathcal{X} = \mathcal{P} + t\vec{r}$ with the planes:

$$x = S_x^{v_x+n} \Rightarrow t_x = \frac{S_x^{v_x+n} - p_x}{r_x}$$

$$y = S_y^{v_y+n} \Rightarrow t_y = \frac{S_y^{v_y+n} - p_y}{r_y}$$

$$z = S_z^{v_z+n} \Rightarrow t_z = \frac{S_z^{v_z+n} - p_z}{r_z}, \qquad (9)$$

The nearest intersection is defined by $t = \min(t_x, t_y, t_z)$.

Due to symmetry of the algorithm with respect to all three coordinate axes and due to the possibility given by the C language macro preprocessor to manipulate source code

```
#define CDstep( t_x, t_y, t_z, n )
    if( t_x ≤ t_y ∧ t_x ≤ t_z ){
        Step( x, y, z, n )
    else if(t_y ≤ t_z)
        Step( y, z, x, n )
    else
        Step( z, x, y, n )
```

```
#define Step( x, y, z, n )
    MasterStep( x, n )
    SlaveStep( x, y, n )
    SlaveStep( x, z, n )
```

Fig. 2. Traversal of rectilinear grids by cubic macro-regions: the algorithm kernel

symbols, the algorithm can be coded in a compact form, represented by two macros (Figures 2 and 3):

MasterStep updates the sample position and voxel coordinate for that axis ν, for which $t_\nu = \min(t_x, t_y, t_z)$. Versions **MasterStep_1** and **MasterStep_n** for single voxel and macro region traversal (Figure 3) differ only in the step size, which updates the coordinate value. The remaining two lines, which test if the voxel is within the scene bounds and update the point coordinate p_x, are the same.

SlaveStep updates the variables for the remaining two axes. Now, the macros differ significantly. In the single voxel step (**SlaveStep_1**) the new ray point is positioned on a wall of the same voxel as the previous point. Therefore it is sufficient to update only the point coordinate, while the voxel coordinate remains the same. The situation is different for the macro-region step (**SlaveStep_n**):

1. The ray may leave the scene in the y direction, therefore the new point coordinate should be compared with the scene bounding box, and
2. the voxel coordinate should be updated, since the ray may skip several voxels along the y direction. It is not possible to compute its value directly from the point coordinate p_y (as in the case of uniform or cartesian grid). Function **Locate** returns this coordinate by binary search in the array S_y of the grid point coordinates. Values v_y and $v_y + n$ define lower and upper bounds for this search.

The algorithm can be easily extended to arbitrary rays by mirroring the scene along the axes with negative projection vector coordinate:

```
if (r_ν < 0) then
```
$$p_\nu \leftarrow S_\nu^{N_\nu} - p_\nu$$
$$S_\nu^i \leftarrow S_\nu^{N_\nu} - S_\nu^i$$
```
endif
```

This inversion should also be taken into account when addressing the 3D attribute and data arrays.

A faster version of the algorithm can be obtained by replacing the sample coordinate p_ν by $\frac{p_\nu}{r_\nu}$, by which we remove the divisions in Eq. 9 and multiplications in **SlaveStep** macros (Figure 3). This change should be applied also to the S_ν arrays.

4 Results

We implemented the algorithm on a HP720 workstation equipped with 32 MB of main memory. The test data we used was the well known CT head from the VOLII data set provided by the University of North Carolina. Originally, the data is cubic. Therefore we converted it to rectilinear first, by summing several voxels in the top-bottom direction, to get a typical CT data set: the voxel was $1 \times 1 \times 2$ in the lower facial part of the skull and $1 \times 1 \times 4$ in the cranial part. The size of the data set thus reduced from $175 \times 235 \times 225$ to $175 \times 235 \times 94$. Figure 4(a) shows a distorted image when assuming cubic voxels. The distortion is removed in Figure 4(b), where proper voxel dimension were taken into account.

Figure 5 demonstrates the difference between the single voxel and macro-region versions of the grid traversal algorithm from the point of view of effectiveness. For each ray its cost was computed, given by the number of steps necessary to reach the first surface voxel. This cost is depicted by values of gray; dark pixels represent rays with smaller number of steps. We can see a significant difference between both cost maps, preferentially for rays missing the object. Table 1 summarizes results obtained by measuring rendering times for both cases. The *background traversal time* column represents time spent exclusively by traversal of the empty background, while the second *rendering time* column also includes time necessary for the surface point detection and shading. We see that the macro-region traversal introduces a more than three-fold speed up in the background traversal phase.

5 Conclusion

Direct processing of rectilinear data without resampling to cubic voxels can save much memory space and processing time. We proposed a ray generator defining a 6-connected ray in such rectilinear data grid. Traversal of rays in empty regions of the rectilinear grid can be speeded up by macro-regions, defined by chessboard distance transform in a secondary scene with cubic voxels. Experiment has shown, that the proposed technique can speed up the traversal more than 3 times.

```
                                       #define MasterStep_n( x, n )
                                           v_x ← v_x + n
#define MasterStep_1( x )                  if( v_x ≥ N_x )
    v_x ← v_x + 1                              return SceneExit
    if( v_x ≥ N_x )                        p_x ← S_x^{v_x}
        return SceneExit
    p_x ← S_x^{v_x}                    #define SlaveStep_n( x, y, n )
                                           p_y ← t_x * r_y
#define SlaveStep_1( x, y )                if( p_y ≥ S_y^{N_y} )
    p_y ← t_x * r_y                            return SceneExit
                                           v_y ← Locate( p_y, S_y, v_y, v_y + n )
```

Fig. 3. Traversal of rectilinear grids by cubic macro-regions: voxel and macro-region steps

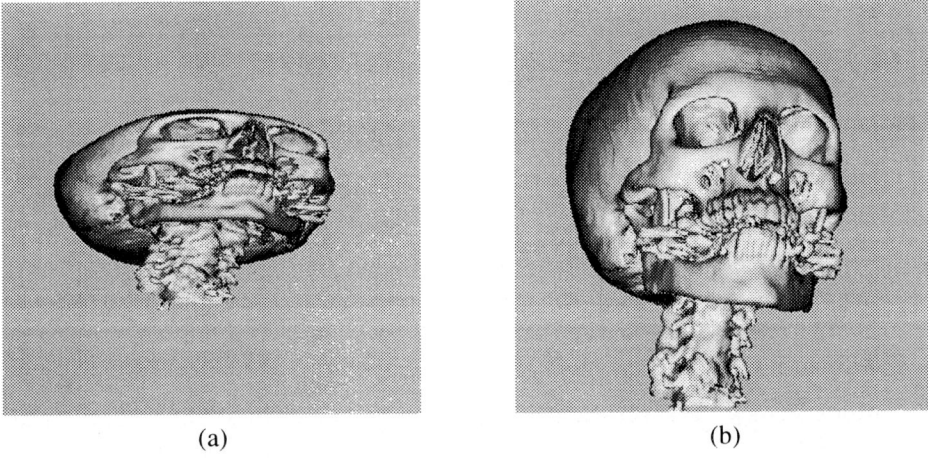

Fig. 4. Data set 1: (a) cubic voxel assumed, (b) voxel dimensions taken into account.

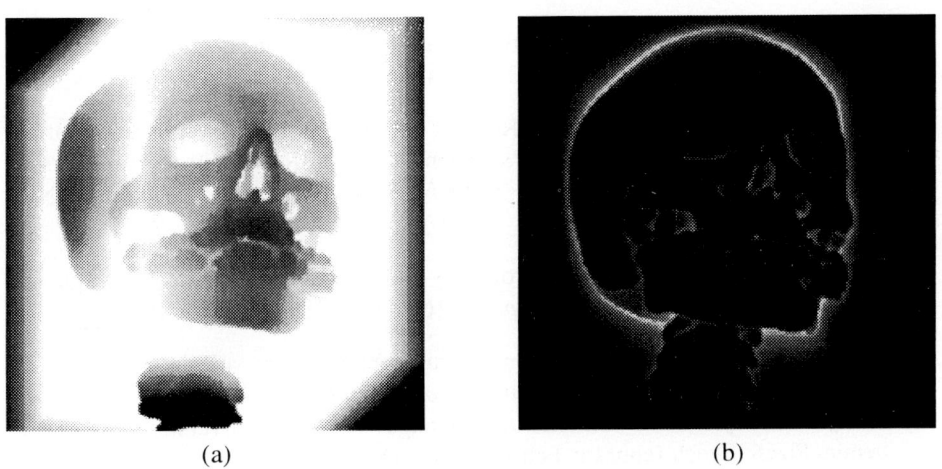

Fig. 5. Voxel traversal cost map: (a) single voxel traversal, (b) macro-region traversals

version	background traversal time [s]	rendering time [s]
single voxel	56.1	67.2
macro-region	18.5	29.1

Table 1. Comparison of background traversal and rendering times for the single voxel and macro-region versions of the algorithm (data set 1).

6 References

[1] Arie Kaufman and Eyal Shimony. 3D scan-conversion algorithms for voxel-based graphics. In Frank Crow and Stephen M. Pizer, editors, *Proceedings of 1986 Workshop on Interactive 3D Graphics*, pages 45–75, Chapel Hill, North Carolina, October 1986.

[2] Miloš Šrámek. Fast surface rendering from raster data by voxel traversal using chessboard distance. In R. Daniel Bergeron and Arie E. Kaufman, editors, *Visualization'94*, pages 188–195, Washington, D.C., October 17–21, 1994. IEEE Computer Society Press.

[3] John Amanatides and Andrew Woo. A fast voxel traversal algorithm for ray tracing. In G. Marechal, editor, *Proc. EUROGRAPHICS '87*, pages 3–10. North-Holland, 1987.

[4] Roni Yagel and Zhouhong Shi. Accelerating volume animation by space-leaping. In *Visualization '93*, pages 62–84, San Jose, CA, October 1993.

[5] Gunilla Borgefors. Distance transformations in digital images. *Computer Vision, Graphics, and Image Processing*, 34(3):344–371, 1986.

[6] Karel J. Zuiderveld, Anton H. J. Koning, and Max A. Viergever. Acceleration of ray-casting using 3D distance transforms. In R. A. Robb, editor, *Visualization in Biomedical Computing II, Proc. SPIE 1808*, pages 324–335, Chapel Hill, NC, 1992.

[7] Daniel Cohen and Zvi Sheffer. Proximity clouds - an acceleration technique for 3D grid traversal. *The Visual Computer*, 10(11):27–38, November 1994.

[8] Miloš Šrámek. A comparison of some ray generators for volume graphics. In Václav Skala, editor, *The Third International Conference in Central Europe on Computer Graphics and Visualization 95*, pages 466–475, University of West Bohemia, Plzeň, Czech republic, February 14 – 18, 1995.

Metric Volume Rendering

J. Smit[*], M. Bosma[*] and
J. Terwisscha van Scheltinga[**]

[*]University of Twente, Department of
Electrical Engineering, EF9250
POBox 217, 7500AE Enschede, The Netherlands
tel.: x–31–53 489 2838, fax: x–31–53 489 1060
e-mail: J.Smit@el.utwente.nl, Bosma@nt.el.utwente.nl
[**]ICS Advanced Development Philips Medical Systems B.V.,
Best, The Netherlands

Abstract

To what extent can the exact size and form of an object be reconstructed from volume data? Why can the rendering of a 3D dataset performed with a super-resolution volume rendering algorithm be magnified beyond the dimensions of the individual voxels without introduction of artefacts and/or unsharpness? These topics are covered with clear examples and new ways to present fundamental issues related to the reconstruction of 3D objects from grey-values on a 3D grid. Application areas are 3D rendering of medical, seismic and geometrical data, as well as the rendering of surface textures.

1 Introduction

The quality of volume rendered images is highly dependent on the method implemented. The extreme compute intensive nature of the volume rendering algorithm has lead to a wide variety of methods [1], [2], [3], [4], [5] as well as several (proposals) for architectures [6], [7], [8], [9], which can render a volume of substantial size in (near) real-time. The aspect of metric volume rendering introduced in this paper is a refinement of the super-resolution technique introduced earlier by the authors [10], [11], [12] as a technique to obtain renditions which are sharp *irrespective of the magnification used* to visualize the object. The concept of super-resolution deals with the exchange of amplitude resolution with spatial resolution, an effect which is closely related to the partial volume effect.

The concept of super-resolution has as effect that binary objects of arbitrary shape can, within certain limits, be reconstructed at a high spatial resolution which extends the spatial resolution of the dataset with the amplitude resolution at which the dataset has been acquired, c.q. is represented. In the limit it will not be possible to infer the actual shape of the smallest object. Instead an estimation of the volume involved may be given.

In Figure 1, an example is given of the image quality that can be obtained using the super-resolution approach.

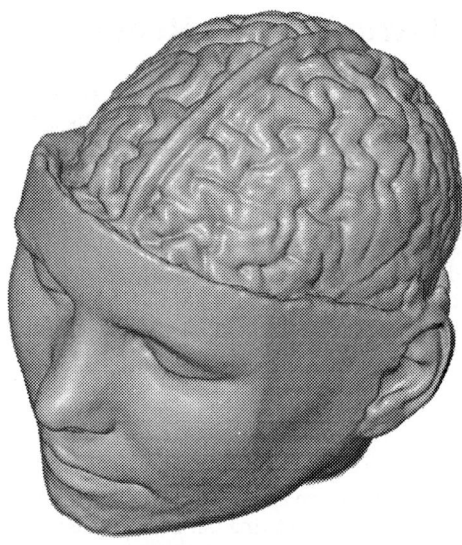

Fig. 1 Example of a visualization using the super-resolution algorithm

How dramatic image quality may differ when distinct visualization methods are used is shown in the Figures 2 and 3.

The sliced cone, represented by a 32^3 dataset, visualized in Figures 2 and 3, is an example of a synthetic 3D object which was sampled taking the partial volume effect into account, i.e. the grey-values are proportional with the proportion of the cone covered in the direct environment of the sample location. The three slits are of size 2, 1, and 1/2 voxel distance respectively.

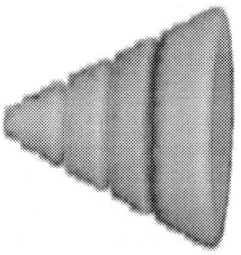 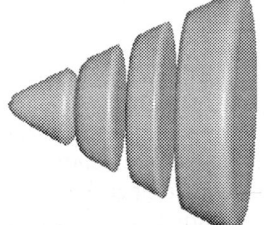 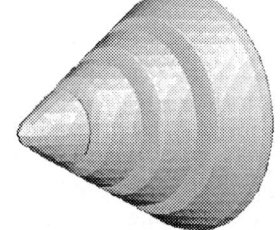

Fig. 2 Levoy's algorithm **Fig. 3** Intermediate gradients from the Super Resolution Algorithm **Fig. 4** Surface gradients of a tri-linearly interpolated volume

Figure 2 shows a rendition of the cone dataset from a given opacity dataset and a given color dataset. The algorithm, from which a flowchart is given in Figure 5, was originally developed by Levoy to render a grey-value dataset using an opacity and color dataset, precomputed for a given light and observer direction. The idea was to avoid the recomputation of gradients and colors.

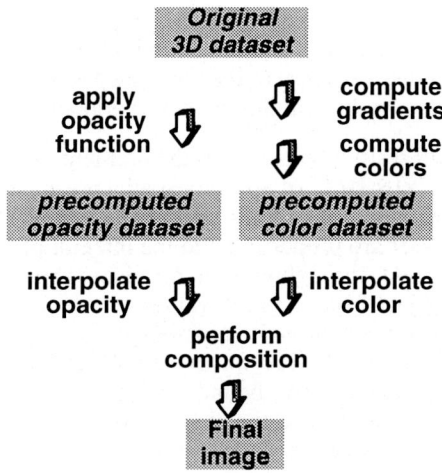

Fig. 5 Global flow within Levoy's algorithm

Figure 3 shows a rendition of the sliced cone dataset with the super-resolution rendering algorithm [10], [11]. This algorithm does not precompute color and opacity datasets, but calculates the color and opacity at the sample location, directly from the original 3D grey-value dataset. As a result of the more accurate opacity calculation, the slits are visualized as real slits, irrespective of the fact that they are smaller than one single voxel distance. The accurate gradient algorithm gives the additional realism. This approach results in high quality images. The efficiency of the color and opacity calculation, results in a marginal increase in the computational complexity. The method does not require any precomputing step, nor additional memory to store intermediate results. The visualization of the cone given in Figure 4 will be discussed later when the detailed form of the surface will be described.

2 Data acquisition

It is important to acquire data describing a binary 3D object, like the sliced cone, in such a way that the magnitude of the grey-value corresponds with the size of the volume in question. This is usually the case in equipment for data *acquisition* like CT, MRI, PET scanners and the like. I.e. the grey-value at the sample location will correspond to the integral of a continuous 3D grey-value function $g(x, y, z)$ over some local volume V_0, with the sample as center and an extent which depends on the width of the point spread function of the input device. The same procedure is natural for the *calculation* of the grey-value of an artificial object.

Although we are interested in the reconstruction of (binary) 3D objects from measured grey-values, it is considered to be of advantage to consider artificial objects, like the sliced cone, when it is important to understand the fundamental nature of the algorithms.

3 A norm for the reconstruction process

The Nyquist sampling theorem states that sampled (3D) data with a band limited frequency content can be reconstructed without error using an ideal low–pass filter.

The ideal lowpass filter has a sin (x) / x impulse response, with a cut-off frequency which equals the Nyquist frequency f = 1 / 2T, with T the sample distance. A small part of the sin (x) / x impulse response of the ideal lowpass is shown in Figure 6a. The adjective without error has to do with the frequency domain approximation used.

Within this paper we will restrict ourselves to the problem of the reconstruction of an original binary object B ($\overline{x}$) = {0,1} of arbitrary spatial resolution in three dimensions, which has been sampled on a grid of finite spatial resolution. The grey-values on the grid of the acquired dataset are proportional to the integral of B ($\overline{x}$) = {0,1} over the point-spread function used throughout the acquisition process. Our goal is to reconstruct the binary object from the grey-values on the grid using an interpolation filter to reconstruct the object through resampling and application of a threshold function at the sample locations. The reconstructed object R ($\overline{x}$) will be considered to be correct with respect to a given error bound when the set describing the disjunction between the original object B ($\overline{x}$) and the reconstructed binary object R ($\overline{x}$) ∈ {0,1} approaches a volume of zero size, i.e. the integral

$$M = \iiint (B(\overline{x}) - R(\overline{x})) \, d\overline{x}$$

will be used as norm for the quality of the reconstruction process. Note that this formulation assumes that the reconstruction is done at an arbitrarily fine resampling grid, and that the reconstructed object is either present or absent. Note that it is not necessary to assign an opacity to the reconstructed object.

4 Volumetric responses considered

We will now discuss the response of the reconstruction filters on a wide range of morphological objects, like for instance a single point, precisely located on the 3D grid, a collection of points on the 3D grid located on a line in the x, the y, or the z direction, as well as on an edge of a volume which has its border at an arbitrary x-location. Finally we will consider the ability of a linear interpolation filter to reconstruct exact location of the boundary of a binary object.

The emphasis in the discussion will be on the linear interpolation filter, other strong points of the other reconstruction filters will be indicated as well.

4.1 The response on a single voxel value

Figure 6 shows the response of some candidate 1D reconstruction filters on a unit impulse in the 1D case. The three dimensional reconstruction filters considered are derived from these 1D prototypes, through a sequence of applications of the filter in each of the three dimensions. This process involves the lookup of a set of filter coefficients in each of the dimensions followed by the application of Finite Impulse Response (FIR) filter operations with these position dependent parameters. In the case of a tri-linear interpolation, 7 multiplications are needed, whereas a 3D Spline uses 16 x 4 + 4 x 4 + 4 = 84 multiplications to resample the dataset. Figure 7 shows the general shape of the response on a single voxel value for the interpolation filters from Figures 6 b, c, and d, respectively.

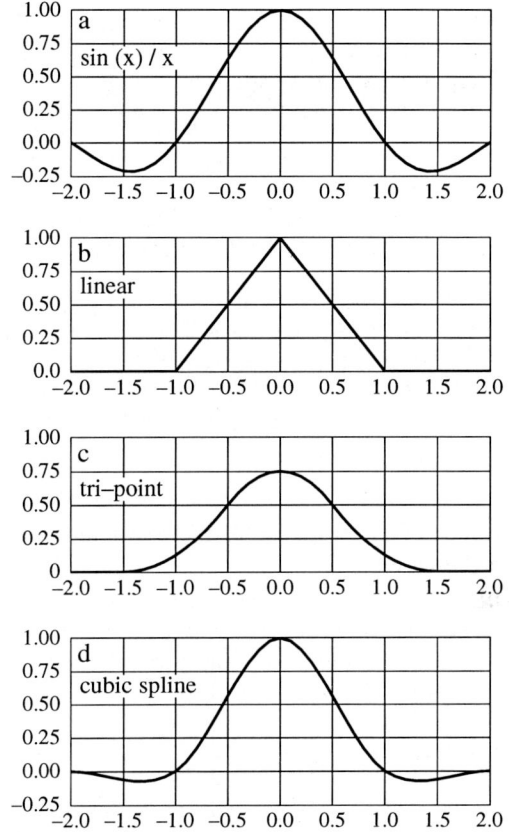

Fig. 6 Impulse response h (t) of some reconstruction filters.

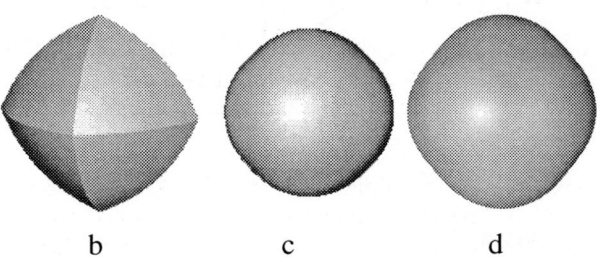

Fig. 7 The shape of the voxel response for distinct reconstruction filters.

The shape of the response on a single voxel value will vary as a function of the grey-value and the threshold which defines the set $R(\bar{x})$ describing the reconstructed object. This is shown in Figure 8 for a trilinear reconstruction filter with a unit grey-value applied and a threshold ranging from 0.75 to 0.125.

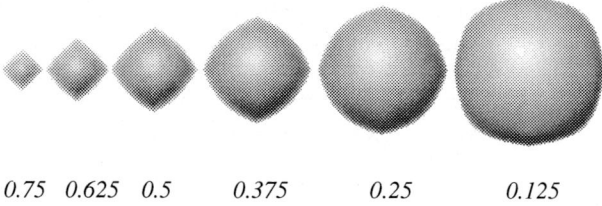

0.75 0.625 0.5   0.375   0.25   0.125

Fig 8 The voxel response for several threshold ratios.

Note that the responses in Figure 8 looks much smoother than the response in Figure 7 b. This is due to the use of intermediate difference gradients for the shading of the objects in Figure 8, whereas surface gradients were used in Figure 7b. It is easily seen from the response in the Figures 7b and 8 that the response of a *linear* reconstruction filter is *not* a volume bounded by a set of triangles, each described by a linear equation.

The equation:

$$iso\_val = (1 - |x|)(1 - |y|)(1 - |z|)$$

describes the iso-surface of the response of the linear interpolator on the unit grey value at a single voxel location.

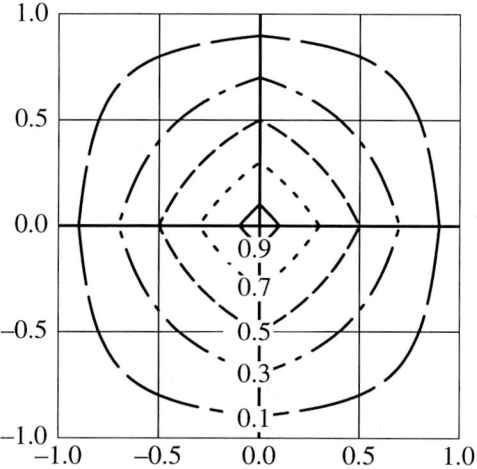

Fig. 9 Parametric description of the shape of the iso surface of the tri-linear interpolator at z=0

Figure 9 shows the shape of a cross section of the iso-surfaces of the voxel response of a tri-linear interpolator for z=0, for threshold values ranging from 0.1 on the outer contour, 0.3, 0.5, 0.7 to 0.9 on the inner contour.

There are two problems with the response shown. First of all, the reconstructed volume $R(\bar{x})$ is always centered at the voxel-grid position. Second, the volume V of the reconstructed object is of the order:

$$V(R(\bar{x})) = O(V(B(\bar{x}))^3)$$

with $V(B(\bar{x})) < 1$. I.e. the reconstructed object will cover just a fraction of the input volume. This is especially true for rather small input objects. This is considered not to be a big disadvantage for clinical applications as it avoids the visualization of artificial small objects due to noise in the dataset. The calculation of the response on a collection of voxels located on a grid line is similar in nature for very small values of the grey-values. A second order metric:

$$V(R(\bar{x})) = O(V(B(\bar{x}))^2)$$

can be observed for larger grey-values, i.e. when the boolean object given covers a larger fraction of the input space. In this case the 3D problem tends to a 2D problem derived from the 3D case using the quasi cylindrical extension of the problem along the grid line.

So far we have concentrated on the understanding of the metric for specific cases. The explicit calculation of the relation between the input volume and the output volume has not been performed for all cases discussed so far, as these calculations require long simulation runs. One of the most striking observations which can be made so far is that the observed volume is always located at the voxel-position(s). Hence a further investigation of the problem at hand will be needed. This can in general not be done without the characterization of the acquisition process. I.e. knowledge about the point-spread function of the input device, or the algorithms with which the voxels were calculated, will be needed to really understand the problem of the metric of the volume rendering problem. Before tackling this problem, we will analyze the 1D problem of the detection of the boundary of a semi infinite object bounded at some location x between two voxels. A linear interpolator is used to reconstruct the boundary of the binary object from the grey-values g0 and g1 at $x = 0$ and $x = 1$ respectively.

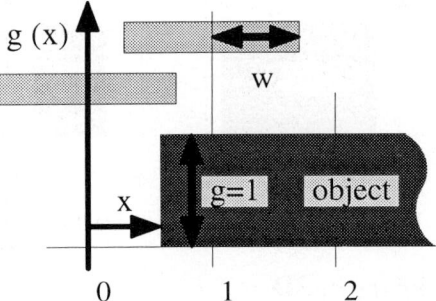

Fig. 10 A semi–infinite object bounded at x

Given a binary–pulse spread function with width 2w, as shown in Figure 10, one can calculate the grey–values as:

g0 = max (0, w − x)
g1 = min (2w, 1 − x + w)

Using a linear interpolation on g0 and g1 and application of a 50% threshold, one may calculate the reconstructed location x_r. Figure 11 shows the reconstruction error: $x - x_r$, as a function of the boundary location x, for w ranging from 0 to 1. Note that the reconstruction error is zero for w=1.

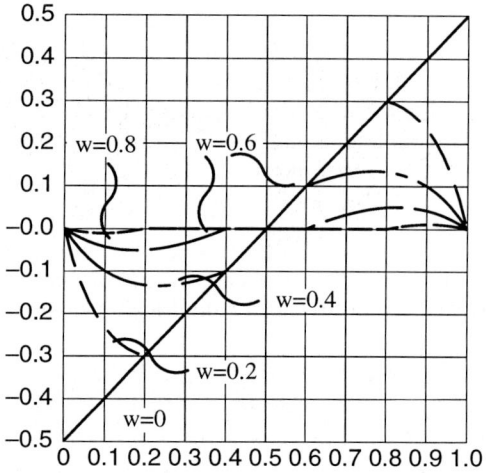

Fig. 11 Reconstruction error as a function of x and w

It follows from the derivation given that the 1D object does not have to be semi-infinite. Another edge, which makes the object finite, can be located somewhere in the interval $(1+w, \infty]$. The same calculation for the error-bound can be used in that case. This implies that both edges of a 1D binary object, can be ideally reconstructed, provided that the size of the object is equal or larger than twice the voxel interval, as shown in Figure 12.

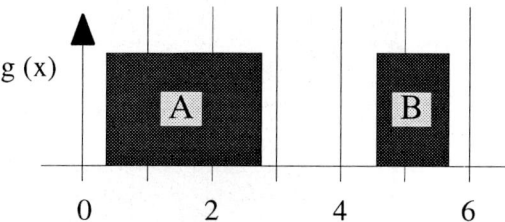

Fig. 12 The boundaries of object A can be ideally reconstructed

5 Reconstruction errors in 3D

A complete derivation of the reconstruction error in the general case, for multiple reconstruction filters, is outside the range of this paper. Instead we will discuss the 'observed' reconstruction error, using the results just derived for the 1D case as a basis for the discussion.

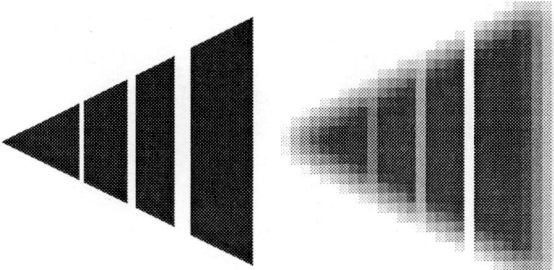

Fig. 13 Cross-section of the binary 'sliced-cone' object before and after acquisition

A cross-section of the binary 'sliced-cone' object is shown in Figure 13. The cone is aligned on the voxel grid with its top. The slits are located on voxel planes as well. The reconstruction of the slits is possible due to the fact that they are located on the grid. The situation is similar to Figure 12 A. The only difference is that the object is *absent* at the location of the slit, instead of *present*. Close examination of the circular edges at the end of the slits shows that these details get rounded as shown in Figure 14. This has as effect that the volume of the reconstructed object is slightly smaller than the volume of the original object.

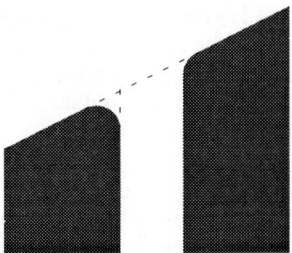

Fig. 14 Cross–section detail of the *reconstructed* 'sliced–cone' object

The top of the cone gets rounded as shown in Figure 15. Here again it is clear that the volume of the reconstructed object is less than the original volume.

Fig. 15 Cross–section detail of the *reconstructed* 'sliced–cone' object

Adaptation of the threshold value has as effect that the volume of the reconstructed cone object becomes either larger, for smaller threshold values, or smaller, for larger threshold values.

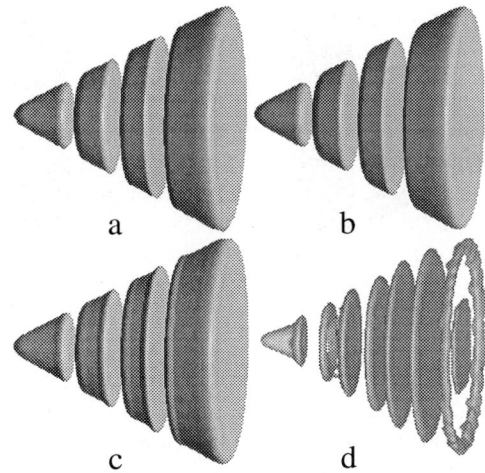

Fig. 16 Some visualizations of the sliced cone

Figure 16 shows the visualization of the sliced cone with: a) a tri-linear interpolator, b) a tri-point interpolator and c) a cubic-spline interpolator. Note that Figures 16a and 16b are almost identical, but that Figure 16b is slightly smoother due to the fact that the continuity of the derivative of the tri-point interpolator results in a continuous surface gradient. Figure 16c has strange additional rings directly adjacent to the slices, due to the overshoot of the cubic-spline interpolator. These rings, which in a sense, compensate for the loss of volume shown in Figure 14, become objects on their own for certain threshold settings, as shown in Figure 16d. The presence of objects which would be absent with other methods may be undesirable, as there is a nonzero metric which should actually be zero. The risk for ghost images is relatively high for a 15% overshoot in the step-response, as steps *in all three* dimensions can produce an aggregate overshoot in the order of 45%.

6 Additional reconstruction properties

The reconstruction of grey-values through interpolation involved the selection of appropriate filter coefficients at the positions of the sample grid. For instance, the resampling polynomial r (x) of the tri-point interpolation filter is defined as:

$$r(x) = \begin{array}{ll} -x^2 + 3/4 & 0 \leq |x| \leq 1/2 \\ 1/2\, x^2 - 3/2 x + 9/8 & 1/2 < |x| \leq 3/2 \end{array}$$

The reconstructed grey-value is:

$$g_r(x_j - m) = g_s(x_j-1)\, r(1-m) + g_s(x_j)\, r(m) + g_s(x_j+1)\, r(m+1)$$

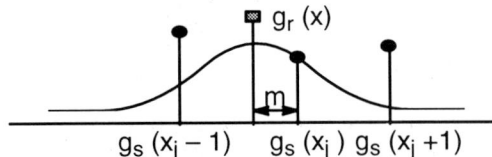

Fig. 17 Calculation scheme for the reconstructed grey-value $g_r(x)$

The tri-point interpolation function, shown in Figure 17, has as main properties that the sum of the filter coefficients $g_r(x_j-1)$, $g_r(x_j)$ and $g_r(x_j+1)$ equals one. This has as effect that the reconstruction is position invariant when a constant volume has to be resampled. The tri-point function is continuous in its first derivative as well. It is however not a true interpolation function, as its value is 0.75 in the origin and 0.125 at $x = -1$ and $x = 1$. The spline interpolation filter is better in this respect as it is a true interpolation function with $r(-2) = 0$, $r(-1) = 0$, $r(0) = 1$, $r(1) = 0$ and $r(1) = 0$. It has in addition many other desirable properties, which give it an excellent frequency response [13]. The overshoot in the spline-interpolation function is however highly unwanted, as this results in non-monotonicity in the metric of the reconstruction process.

7 Non binary problems

It is not necessary that the problem at hand is of a fully binary nature. The simplest extension concerns the case that the given object has two grey-values, g0 and g1, which are not necessarily elements of the set {0,1}. A simple scaling may be applied on the voxel values to create a binary problem. Medical datasets can be processed by taking the grey-value in a given (local) background into consideration. In some cases it may be desirable to select a low threshold value with respect to the background in order to visualize line-structures, like blood vessels, or bone fractures. Some of the reconstruction filters, like the linear and the tri-point filter, have the ability to suppress the visual effect of noise in the input data. The selection of a proper threshold depends on the desired metric fidelity for volume-objects and/or the extent to which fine details, like line and point structures should be visualized.

8 Related problems

Algorithms for the construction of iso-surfaces in the form of a triangulation of a 3D dataset are described in [15] and in [16]. The latter publication goes into the details of the ambiguity of the marching cubes algorithm in general. It has been shown in this paper that a tri-linear interpolator reconstructs the iso-surface as a collection of third order patches, whereas the marching cubes approach tries to find multiple linear patches. The identification of the 'correct' patches in the marching cubes approach is of a much more complicated nature than the application of a threshold after interpolation. The marching cubes approach has the ability of super resolution. It is so far not clear how the metric of this approach can be evaluated.

9 Conclusions

Various aspects of the reconstruction of a properly sampled binary object were discussed. It was shown that the boundary of a binary 1D object can be reconstructed without error, at an arbitrary high resolution, using a simple linear interpolator, provided that certain restrictions about the presence of multiple boundaries are met. The methods introduced are inherently unambiguous, when the interpolation filters are free of overshoot.

10 References

[1] M. S. Levoy, "Display of Surfaces from Volume data", *IEEE Computer Graphics and Applications*, 8(3):29–37, May 1988.

[2] R. W. Parrot, N.S. Systz, P. Amburn, and D. Robinson, "Towards Statistically Optimal Interpolation for 3–D Medical Imaging", *IEEE Engineering in Medicine and Biology*, 12(3):49–59, September 1993.

[3] A. Pommert, U. Tiede, G. Wiebecke, and K.H. Hohne, "Surface Shading in Tomographic Volume Visualization", *Proceedings of the First Conference on Visualization in Biomedical Computing*, 1:19-26, IEEE comp society press.

[4] S.P. Raya and J.K. Udupa, "Shape-Based Interpolation of Multidimensional objects", *IEEE Transactions on Medical Imaging*, 9(1):32-44, 1990.

[5] K.J. Zuiderveld, *Visualization of Multimodality Medical Volume Data using Object Oriented Methods*, PhD thesis, University of Utrecht, March 1995.

[6] H. Pfister, A. Kaufman and F. Wessels, "Towards a Scalable Architecture for Real-Time Volume Rendering", *Proceedings of the 10th Eurographics Workshop on Graphics Hardware*, volume EG95HW, pp 123-130, 1995.

[7] G. Knittel, "A Scalable Architecture for Volume Rendering", *Proceedings of the 9th Eurographics Workshop on Graphics Hardware*, volume EG94HW, pp 58-69, 1994.

[8] S.E. Molnar, J. Eyles, and J. Poulton, "Pixelflow: High-Speed Rendering Using Image Composition", *Computer Graphics*, 26(2): 231-240, July 1992.

[9] J. Lichterman, "Design of a Fast Voxel Processor for Parallel Volume Visualization", *Proceedings of the 10th Eurographics Workshop on Graphics Hardware*, volume EG95HW, pp 83-92, 1995.

[10] M. Bosma, and J. Terwisscha van Scheltinga, *Efficient Super Resolution Volume Rendering*, Masters thesis, University of Twente, August 1995.

[11] M. Bosma, J.Smit, and J. Terwisscha van Scheltinga, "Super Resolution Volume Rendering Hardware", *Proceedings of the 10th Eurographics Workshop on Graphics Hardware*, volume EG95HW, pp 117-122, 1995.

[12] J. Terwisscha van Scheltinga, J. Smit, and M. Bosma, "Design of an On-Chip Reflectance Map", *Proceedings of the 10th Eurographics Workshop on Graphics Hardware*, volume EG95HW, pp. 51-55, 1995.

[13] M. Bentum, *Interactive Visualization of Volume Data*, PhD thesis, University of Twente, ISBN 90-9008788-5.

[14] M. Bentum, B. Lichtenbelt, M. Boer, A Nijmeijer, M. Bosma and J. Smit, "Improving image quality of volume rendered three dimensional data", *Proceedings of the SPIE Medical Imaging 1996 Conference*, volume 2707, February 1996.

[15] A. van Gelder and J. Wilhelms, "Topological considerations in isosurface generation", *ACM Transactions on graphics*, 13(4):337-375, 1994, ISSN 0730-0301.

[16] J. Wilhelms and A. van Gelder, "Topological considerations in isosurface generation", *Computer Graphics*, 24(5):79-86, November 1990.

Scientific Visualization and Virtual Prototyping in the Product Development Process

Thomas Frühauf, Fan Dai

Fraunhofer Institute for Computer Graphics (Fraunhofer-IGD)
email: {thfrueha, dai}@igd.fhg.de
URL: http://www.igd.fhg.de/igd-a4

Abstract: In this paper we introduce our work within the DMU (Digital Mock-Up) project. The focus of this project is the development of technology for replacing physical prototypes with virtual prototypes. In particular, we discuss the integration of scientific visualization into virtual prototyping. Fraunhofer-IGD has implemented the DMU demonstrator - we describe those parts of the demonstrator where scientific visualization functionality was incorporated. Furthermore, IGD has carried out separate 'virtual prototyping' projects with two german car manufacturers where we realized 'immersive data visualization'. We describe those projects and discuss the various approaches to implementing immersive data visualization. From our experience with different approaches and applications we discuss the use and usefulness of virtual reality technology for scientific visualization.

Keywords: virtual prototyping, digital mock-up, functional simulation, information visualization, immersive data visualization, product presentation.

1 Introduction

Prototyping is an essential step in the product development process. Prototypes represent important product features, which are to be investigated, evaluated and improved. They are used to prove design alternatives, to do engineering analysis, manufacturing planning and often just to show a product to the customer. The actual demand on international markets is primarily determined by higher product quality, a shorter time to market philosophy and, due to customer oriented marketing, a growth in the number of variants and increasing product complexity.

Generating physical prototypes is very time-consuming and expensive. To shorten product development time, design evaluations have to be performed more rapidly, the results must be directly incorporated into the design process. As CAD software and CAE tools such as Finite Element programs are widely used in the manufacturing industry, a lot of product data is already digitally available. This provides a good basis for design evaluations, manufacturing planning, and product presentation electronically. However, there is usually no close link between the different databases which hinders the presentation of available product data as a *virtual prototype*. This demands for the further development of complete product data description standards [13]. Furthermore, a visualization environment has to be established which is able to integrate geometrical and other product information together with simulation data from multiple sources.

Another reason why physical prototypes are still used in most cases arises from their spatial presence. Especially for conceptual design and for product presentation, one can touch it, take them into the hand, and manipulate it to see whether it works properly. Therefore virtual prototyping asks for superiour man-machine interface. *Virtual Reality* (VR) is the enabling technology providing realistic presentation and intuitive direct manipulation of digital models. Within the last few years enormous progress was achieved in the field of VR technology. Tools and systems were realized with which the practical use of VR technology has been demonstrated for different application domains. First examples were walk-through presentations for architectural design, interior design and urban planning. Recently, the automotive and aeronautical industry began to investigate this technology.

IGD started its VR research and development in 1993 with the VR Demonstration Centre initiative [10] of the Fraunhofer Gesellschaft, one of the biggest research organizations carrying out applied research with the industry. Subsequently, a lot of VR research was performed and the *Virtual Design* [2] system was developed. First ideas and concepts of virtual prototyping have been developed and demonstrated [5]. Besides, several applications were realized for industrial partners where scientific simulation data was presented in a virtual environment [1, 7].

The idea of virtual prototyping is under investigation in the ESPRIT project *AIT - Advanced Information Technologies in Design and Manufacturing*[1]. The AIT consortium has identified a project called Digital Mock-Up (DMU) with the objective to develop the technology that allows designers, manufacturing planners, and even management to work on Virtual Products / Digital Mock-Ups. Within the DMU cluster a number of sub-programs have been established in which Fraunhofer-IGD is a partner. In this paper we describe our ideas and aims in these projects in the context of scientific visualization. Visualization requirements and possible solutions are presented. Furthermore, results from the AIT-DMU demonstrator which was developed by Fraunhofer-IGD and from direct cooperations between IGD and two german car manufacturers are described. From our experience with different approaches and applications we discuss the use and usefulness of virtual reality technology for scientific visualization.

1.1 The DMU process

The life-cycle of a sophisticated product like a car or an aircraft can be broken into several major steps: Product Definition starting with Market Requirements Analysis, Design of Product, Production Process, Production System and Distribution System, Design Validation, Production, Distribution, and Operational Use. About 80% of the total product costs are incurred during the early design stages and therefore major efforts are spent in improving the effectiveness of the design process.

The Digital Mock-up (DMU) comprises of a methodology (company or product specific) detailing how to manage and visualize structured data sets of product geometry and information coming from the design/engineering, manufacturing and product service environment and how to release these digital product data. Prerequisites for an

---

1. (ESPRIT Project 7704). The project partners are: Aerospatiale, BMW, Saab, BMW Rolls-Royce, Audi, Alenia, Dassault Aviation, British Aerospace, Renault, Reydel, Mercedes-Benz, CASA, PSA, VW, Magneti Marelli, Fiat, Rover

operative DMU are software tools to manage the high amount of different data, to navigate inside the digital model, to analyze and simulate product functionality, to visualize the large amount of geometric and engineering data and to support the communication and decision process in the concurrent engineering workflow, since DMU will be the only binding digital product description, the digital master (see Fig. 1).

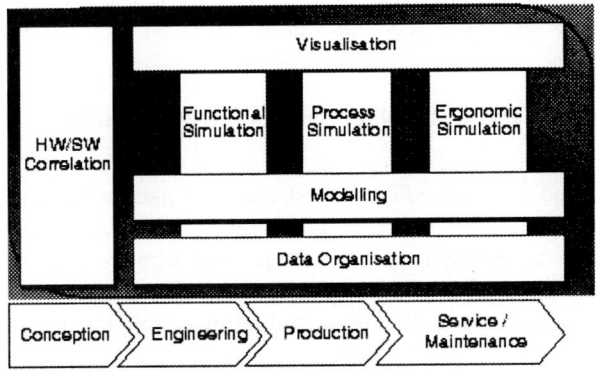

Fig. 1: Digital Mock-up building blocks. (copyright AIT)

The strategic goal is represented by the DMU definition: Digital mock-up is a realistic computer simulation of a product with the capability of all required functionality from design/engineering, manufacturing and product service environment which is used as a platform for product and process development, for communication and decision from a first conceptual layout up to maintenance and product recycling. The idea behind DMU is to evaluate the product design - from function and process view - within software (without building real physical mock-ups) and to have only one final verification in hardware.

By an innovative use of appropriate DMU visualization methodologies and tools - as one building element of DMU, a dramatic reduction of costs in the areas of product development, production, service and aerospace groundfloor support will be expected. Time to market will be shortened.

2 The AIT demonstrator

On behalf of the AIT consortium Fraunhofer-IGD has implemented a visualization demonstrator and presented it in June 1995. The scenario was defined by the consortium to show the DMU approach. The goal was to show how virtual reality can be applied to digital mock-up to support a rapid product development. Using the example of alternator exchange in a car, the story illustrated the use of VR techniques for the evaluation of design alternatives, for clash and clearance analysis, and for simulation of operation conditions. Since the focus of this demonstrator was mostly on VR techniques we will not describe these aspects here in detail, an in-depth description will be published soon [6]. But we identify those parts of the demonstrator where scientific visualization or functional analysis was incorporated.

2.1 Information visualization

As mentioned above, the demonstrator featured the alternator exchange of a car: In order to select a region of interest the user can draw a box which results in the display of all parts of the machine contained in that box (Fig. 2, left, see appendix). After the selection the car body disappears and all selected parts appear as 3D models. The user takes the alternator and puts it into a container. Before choosing a different alternator, on a virtual menu, a list of regulation rules is displayed. The user selects the rule for temperature change tests, and gets some information on the new alternator (Fig. 2, right, see appendix).

2.2 Functional simulation - simulation of operation conditions

The volume occupied by the engine block is of special interest for the assembly task which was addressed with the AIT demonstrator. The user has to decide whether the new alternator fits in, not only in the static assembly, but also if it fits under operation conditions. Therefore, the results of a vibration simulation are displayed in two ways: As an animation of the motion of the engine block, and as a transparent envelope indicating the volume which is occupied by the vibrating engine block.

3 Virtual prototypes featuring CFD results

Here, we describe work done in 1995 for two german car manufacturers, VW and BMW, where we incorporated specific visualization functions into a powerful VR system. The aim in both projects was to create a dedicated virtual environment for a specific application. In both applications CFD (computational fluid dynamics) data played a role.

We have developed a flow-visualization module for our VR system *Virtual Design II* in order to integrate product simulation data with geometrical design studies. Before we go into the description of the work, it has to be pointed out, that the focus of the projects was product presentation and not engineering analysis. Thus, flow visualization was one of several tools in the demonstration of certain product functions to a special audience. In one case - the BMW Virtual Seating-Buck - the audience were designers and managers who discussed car compartment design. In the other case - the VW fair presentations - the addressee of the visualization was the technically interested lay-audience at car fairs. The following visualization tools have been implemented (or are currently being implemented).

Vector field visualization. Most impressive in flow visualization is the interactive *particle tracing* in the velocity field. Unfortunately, most flow simulations are carried out on unstructured Finite Element grids [8]. Visualization algorithms for such grids require much more computational effort than those for regular or curvilinear computational grids. Our investigations have shown that real-time particle tracing at VR-frame rates is only feasible on regular grids or (in the computational space of) curvilinear grids when movements of hundreds of particles have to be computed simultaneously. Therefore, we resample unstructured CFD grids to a regular grid of adjustable spatial extension and density - *being aware that we trade visualization speed against accuracy.*

Our particle tracing module allows the release of particles at sources which are either coupled to the user's hand(-echo) or which can be positioned freely in the 3D scene by the user. The later alternative allows to position a fixed particle source and walk around in the scene in order to watch the advected particles from different points of view. The particles, which are rendered usually as flat squares, may be rotated by the rotational component of the velocity field (rot v) and/or may be connected to form *streaklines*. For transient flow data we provide *streamribbons* as an alternative visualization technique. Furthermore, particles or ribbons can be *colourcoded* according to the local speed or according to any other scalar data of the simulation results.

Scalar field visualization. Other SciVis techniques that also fit well into the concept of immersive and intuitive exploration of virtual prototypes are those techniques that require spatial interaction by the user. Beside particle tracing, this is *slicing* and *point probing*. We are currently integrating these techniques as modules in a our VR system.

The use of *isosurfacing* is to slice through the parameter range or to animate a fixed-value isosurface over time. It is already possible to animate isosurfaces which have been created within another system and have been loaded as polygonal objects into *Virtual Design II*. The porting of an isosurface extraction module to *Virtual Design II* has now been started. Isosurfacing in VR can be realized by pointing at a 3D position and computing the isosurface which is defined by a scalar value at the finger's position (as reported in [15]). But, usually, the user is interested in the spatial extension of a critical data value. Therefore, isosurfacing requires, in our view, a parameter selection in the data range and not in the geometrical space. In general, isosurfacing in an immersive VR system forces the user to scale down the geometry (or to move away from the isosurfaces) to get insight in the spatial data distribution.

The following describes the goal, the hardware used, and the features of the implementations for our customers from the automotive industry.

3.1 The BMW Virtual Seating-Buck

IGD developed a *Virtual Seating-Buck* for BMW. This project focussed on the challenge of using VR and SciVis to create a tighter integration between design and engineering analysis functions in the development process of automotive interiors. It was necessary to address graphic display quality as well as functionality, and interaction techniques in order to provide the user with a convincing feeling of immersion into the virtual environment. To further increase this effect, a physical mock-up consisting of seat, steering wheel and foot pedals was built. Other hardware components included a tracking system, data glove and Fakespace's BOOM 3C (Fig. 3, left, see appendix).

One important aspect in order to intensify the user's feeling of immersion was the precise coupling between real objects and virtual objects. This was achieved by calibrating the virtual steering wheel with its physical counterpart (held by the user) and implementing a virtual feedback, such that the virtual steering wheel rotates simultaneously with the physical one. An accurate collision detection algorithm allows us to realize this functionality without additional hardware, just using software to detect collision between hand and steering wheel and resolve the rotational constraints coupling the two.

Another point of interest was the embedding of CAE simulation results into the virtual environment. This was demonstrated through flow visualization with interactive particle tracing of a passenger compartment air conditioning simulation (Fig. 3, right, see appendix). Finally we addressed the use of VR for maintenance access verification and configuration studies. Again, using real-time collision detection on a large scale, conditions such as system location, space allocation and stayout envelopes could be interactively evaluated taking the air condition/heating unit as an example.

The system has been in prototypical use at BMW's R&D facility since November 1995 running on an SGI RE2 computer with two independent graphics subsystems. The results as well as user responses are promising.

3.2 The VW fair presentations in 1995

While we demonstrated the interactive analysis of the flow around a *Volkswagen Polo* at the *Hannover Messe '95*, we realized the immersive investigation of the *Volkswagen TDI* (Turbo Direct Injection) Diesel engine for two car fairs[1], the *IAA '95* in Frankfurt and the *Detroit Motor Show '95/'96*.

The characteristic features of the innovative motor concept of Diesel direct injection were to be demonstrated on the basis of numerical flow simulations which generated 3D transient data sets. Together with Volkswagen a demonstration scenario was worked out, which was aimed at the technically interested lay audience at the automobile fair. The scenario featured a cybernaut who navigates through different parts of the TDI motor introducing them to the audience. The audience watches through the eyes of the cybernaut (looking at a stereo projection) while the cybernaut navigates through the scene with a dataglove and a head-mounted display.

The geometry of the Diesel cylinder with inlet valve and piston was extracted from Finite Element grids which served for numerical simulations of the Volkswagen engineers. Other parts of the motor, such as air inlet channel and waste-gas tubes were reconstructed with a CAD system. IGD's virtual reality system Virtual Design II was extended with a module for steering of time-dependent scenes. Herein triggering of single events as well as controlling direction and speed of the presentation time were realized.

Flow processes around the valves and inside the cylinder as well as combustion were visualized on the basis of numerical simulations. This Finite Element data (local velocity, temperature and pressure) had been pre-computed at about 100 time-steps. In order to visualize the data in real-time, i.e. at 15 double-frames per seconds, we resampled the data from an unstructured grid to a grid regular in space and non-regular in time. The algorithms for stream- and streakline computation as well as for particle advection allowed for a interactive analysis of the flowfields by the cybernaut (Fig. 4, left, see appendix). The injection of Diesel fuel as well as the expansion of the combustion inside the cylinder were pre-computed and animated together with suitable sound effects.

---

1. The visualization was also shown at SIGGRAPH '96

Another visualization technique which is of great use for structural analysis as well as for CFD data - and which is already available in the VR system - is object deformation. We animate the piston as well as the valves of the TDI engine during the flow visualization. The diesel particles whose movements and momentary masses were precomputed in a Lagrangian form by the CFD program are animated as well. Isosurfaces of the temperature serve as an indicator of the momentary location of the flames when the air/diesel mixture is burning (Fig. 4, right, see appendix).

Volkswagen has purchased our VR system and uses it in the company's research center. Beside what was described here, the engineers investigate Finite Element crash test simulation data in virtual environments with the system

4 Immersive data visualization - a discussion

In the previous chapters we have reported on projects where immersive data visualization was used for product presentation. Beside the described software design approach, there are a number of other possible approaches. We discuss these approaches here - their pros and cons - together with some examples.

With the introduction of new interaction and display devices, known as VR technology, investigations were made to see whether this technology might be useful for data visualization. In our group the hardware approach for virtual environments was mostly fairly conventional, namely to use multidimensional input devices, like the *dataglove*, the *space mouse* or the *flying joystick*. For display we used head mounted displays plus stereo projection walls for passive users. Only for our *Arthroscopy Training Simulator* [18] were dedicated interaction devices built. Special VR hardware systems have been developed in other groups, e.g., the *CAVE* [4], the *Nanomanipulator* [17], and the *Responsive Workbench* [14]. On the software side several different approaches can be taken. A classification of these approaches is given in [7]. Here, we use this classification and present examples together with a discussion of the 'pros' and 'cons' of the different approaches. Experiences related to immersive visualization in general are discussed in chapter five.

4.1 Software design strategies for immersive data visualization

Five different software design strategies are distinguished for immersive data visualization:

i. *Rendered objects are precomputed by some existing, SciVis system, stored as files, and are then imported into an existing, VR system for investigation.*

An approach for a quick realization of immersive data visualization. In fact, several examples were realized within the CAVE system at Siggraph '94. Of course, no modifications regarding mapping parameters are possible if there are no SciVis capabilities implemented. In our group this approach was used in several cases to demonstrate off-line simulation results together with interior design. Results of a radiosity-based lighting simulation as well as from a particle-based acoustics simulation have been mapped to polygonal visualization objects and were incorporated into VR scenes [11].

ii. Some VR capabilities are added to an existing, powerful SciVis system.

An example for this approach is reported in [16] where VR devices have been combined with a dataflow visualization system / application builder. The main problem of this approach is that data communication between the modules slows down the visualization performance. Besides, user interaction with data is not easy in such a system because it requires upstream communication between modules. However, the 'must' of a VR system, in order to create the illusion of immersion, is real-time rendering and interaction without latency.

Coupling our monolithic visualization system *ISVAS*[1] [10] with the dataglove and stereo rendering was described in [1]. Here we experienced problems in the navigation via the dataglove because of the 'grab and rotate' paradigm of *ISVAS* (instead of using 'point and fly' as in most VR systems). Furthermore, *ISVAS* has a conventional 2D 'point and click' GUI for configuration. Working with the glove *and* the mouse was not comfortable at all.

iii. Some SciVis capabilities are added to an existing powerful VR system.

In chapter three we described examples of this approach in detail. It might be seen as a drawback that visualization algorithms and data structures have to be re-implemented that are already working in a different system. However, experience shows that VR based visualization demands, in some cases, special data structures and/or algorithm design, anyhow.

iv. A new system is designed from scratch offering some SciVis and some VR capabilities.

The classical example is the *Virtual Windtunnel* [3]. The benefits are tailored algorithms, data structures and interface design for a specific application. The drawback: A lot of implementation work for a dedicated system which can only be used for one kind of data, e.g., blockstructured CFD data.

v. An existing powerful SciVis system is coupled closely to an existing, powerful VR system; both systems exchange data at run time.

This approach has been realized by our group by connecting our visualization system *ISVAS* with our VR system *Virtual Design* [2]. Details of this work are described in [12]. Communication is realized via shared memory or via sockets in the case that both systems do not run on the same machine. The later can be useful since the VR system requires fast rendering processors while visualization algorithms of *ISVAS* need fast numerical processors. In contrast to the work with *ISVAS* described above (see *i).*), navigation is now realized in the VR system through 'point and fly' and parametrization of visualization modules is done via virtual buttons and sliders which are provided by the VR system, too. The parameters are translated to the *ISVAS* command language so that no 2D GUI is needed.

The benefits of this approach are: All visualization algorithms of the SciVis sys-

---

1. *ISVAS* is registered trademark of Fraunhofer-IGD

tems are available for the immersive data visualization. Also, the complete functionality of the VR system including collision detection, level-of-detail rendering, etc. can be utilized. Furthermore, having separate processes for both systems prevents the undesirable effect that rendering is slowed down by a computationally intensive visualization algorithm. However, this software approach does not take into account that the visualization performance of the existing visualization system may not be fast enough for a truly real-time investigation of the data. Another critical point is that simulation data and CAD data are usually not in the same coordinate system which requires careful translation, rotation and scaling in the data communication.

5 Conclusions

So far we have described virtual prototyping projects carried out by IGD for the AIT consortium and for two german car manufacturers. In the following we draw some conclusions regarding immersive data visualization.

5.1 Experiences with immersive data visualization

Discussing the use of virtual environments for SciVis is not easy and is naturally dominated by subjective experiences. Therefore, the following statements should be seen as our preliminary experiences. Further investigation of this subject has to be (and will be) undertaken. However, we have realized four of the five software design strategies as described in chapter 4.1 during the last years. With this background we identify the following aspects of immersive data visualization for discussion.

Hardware Environment. Today's supergraphic workstations allow virtual environments of remarkable complexity. But still, the installation of VR hardware suitable for industrial applications is quite expensive. A major drawback of immersive systems is that they do not fit into the normal engineering environment which is dominated by desktop workstations. The reliability and accuracy of trackers has been much improved in the last few years so that accurate positioning is more a software than a hardware problem. Display quality of head mounted displays - even of the best (non-military) HMDs - is still far from acceptable for routine work. Stereo projection walls seem to be more useful. Regarding input devices, the glove is still the only device which allows intuitive interaction strategies. But the hand is obstructed by sensors and cables, which makes it difficult to handle mouse and keyboard, to make a note on a piece of paper or even to answer the phone. You cannot rotate and move the hand arbitrarily and you get tired from moving around in the air.

Software Approach. We have described the possible software design strategies in chapter four together with pros and cons. If data from different sources - CAD geometry and simulation results - is processed, one data set has to be transformed into the other's coordinate system. If a VR system is coupled with a SciVis system these transformations have to be done on the fly. Furthermore, as long as visualization algorithms run as separate (shared memory) processes the frame rate is not affected by SciVis computations. In comparison with the more sophisticated coupling-approach a very stable system results.

Implementing single visualization modules into an existing VR system, as described in chapter three, has several benefits: The algorithms and data structures can be tailored to the special needs of the application with respect to the required speed and accuracy. Our experience is that visualization algorithms that require a notable amount of time are experienced more negatively in an immersive environment than within a desktop system. For example, if a particle tracing algorithm is slow because it is performed on unstructured Finite Element data, the non-smooth motion of the particles is disturbing. Thus, the aim and the addressee of the visualization have to been analyzed very carefully to decide what is more important, speed or accuracy.

Navigation and Interaction. The intuitive *point and fly* and *grab* metaphors are not suitable for all visualization tasks. Often, the user wants to restrict the effect of some input to a certain degree of freedom. E.g., a slicing plane shall be translated in the direction of the x-axis or an object shall rotate exactly around the y-axis. It may be even necessary to type-in a certain 3D position. This leads to one big problem of immersive data visualization: How to configure the many parameters of visualization modules. There are many tasks in configuration that can be realized more efficiently in 2D GUI's than in 3D, e.g., file selection or definition of a mapping transfer function. Further research is required in order to make immersive systems more user friendly. One focus of this research will be voice input.

Application Data. The use of VR is certainly not equal for all applications. Reviewing the successful VR applications helps identify those simulation data where immersive visualization might provide more inside than desktop systems. From our experience and from the reaction of our customers VR is regarded to be an efficient tool in a) *interior design and architecture*, b) *training* and c) *product presentation*. In all cases, users deal with geometrical data of great complexity to which they are not accustomed to. Thus, a CAE engineer who works with the same part for many days will not discover much new if he is immersed within the simulation data. However, if the simulation results are of complex spatial distribution or shape and cannot be foreseen, immersion is definitely of use. Examples are crash simulations and CFD studies of complex real-life products, like whole airplanes or passenger compartments of cars.

Visualization Task and Addressee. The answer to the question of whether immersive visualization may be useful is influenced greatly by the visualization task and the addressed audience. We have to be aware that explaining a complex technical process or machine to a lay-audience requires different media than if the addressed person is a simulation expert. Designers, manager, and politicians too, rely more on naturalistic visualizations than engineers who prefer and who are used to abstract presentations. On the other hand, some classical SciVis operations are, as explained above, hard to realize within an immersive system. Thus, if the visualization task is pure technical analysis, VR is certainly not the best fitting medium. We are convinced that here the new man-machine interface VR will accomplish the desktop analysis rather than replacing it. In the context of virtual prototyping immersive visualization is certainly necessary.

References

[1] Astheimer, P.; Frühauf, T.; Göbel, M.; Haase, H.; Karlsson, K.; Schröder, F.; Ziegler, R.: *How Scientific Visualization Can Benefit From Interactive Environments.* CWI Quarterly 7(2):159-174, 1994.

[2] Astheimer, P.; Göbel, M.: *Virtual Design II - An Advanced VR Development Environment.* In Göbel, M. (Ed.) *Virtual Environments.* Springer Verlag, 1995

[3] Bryson, S.; Levit, C.: *The Virtual Windtunnel.* IEEE Computer Graphics and Applications, 12(4):25-34, 1992.

[4] Cruz-Neira, C.; Leight, J.; Papka, M.; Barnes, C.; Cohen, S.; Engelmann, R.; Hudson, R.; Roy, T.; Siegel, L.; Vasilakis, C.; Defanti, T.; Sandin, D.: *Scientists in Wonderland: A Report on Visualization Applications in the CAVE Virtual Reality Environment.* Proc. IEEE Symposium on Research Frontiers in VR, San Jose (USA), Oct. 1993.

[5] Dai, F.; Göbel, M.: *Virtual Prototyping - an Approach using VR techniques.* Proc. 14th ASME Int. Computers in Engineering Conference, Minneapolis (USA), Sept. 1994.

[6] Dai, F.; Reindl, P.: *Enabling Digital Mock-Up with Virtual Reality Techniques - Vision, Concept, Demonstrator.* Submitted to 16th ASME Int. Computers in Engineering Conference.

[7] Dai, F.; Felger, W.; Frühauf, T.; Göbel, M.; Reiners, D.; Zachmann, G.: *Virtual Prototyping Examples for Automotive Industries.* Proc. Virtual Reality World '96, Stuttgart (Germany), Febr. 1996.

[8] Frühauf, T.: *Interactive Visualization of Vector Data in Unstructured Volumes.* Computers & Graphics, 18(1):73-80, 1994.

[9] Frühauf, T.: *Efficient 3D Interaction With Scientific Data Using 2D Input and Display Devices.* In: Göbel, M.; Müller, H.; Urban, B. (Eds.): *Visualization in Scientific Computing*, Springer Verlag, Wien, 1995.

[10] Frühauf, T.; Göbel, M.; Haase, H.; Karlsson, K.: *Design of a Flexible Monolithic Visualization System.* In: Rosenblum, L.; Earnshaw, R.; Encarnacao, J.; Hagen, H.; Kaufman, A.; Klimenko, S.; Nielson, G.; Post, F.; Thalman, D. (Eds.): *Scientific Visualization: Advances and Challenges.* Academic Press Ltd., 1994.

[11] Göbel, M.: *The Virtual Reality Demonstration Centre.* Computers & Graphics, Special Issue on Virtual Reality, 17(6), Nov. 1993.

[12] Haase, H.: *Symbiosis of Virtual Reality and Scientific Visualization System.* Accepted at Eurographics '96, Sept. 1996, Poitiers, France.

[13] ISO/IS 10303-1: *Industrial Automation Systems and Integration - Product Representation and Exchange- Part 1: Overview and Fundamental Principles.* International Organisation for Standardisation; Geneve (Switzerland), 1994.

[14] Krüger, W.; Bohn, C.; Fröhlich, B.; Schüth, H.; Strauss, W.; Wesche, G.: *The Responsive Workbench: A Virtual Work Environment.* IEEE Computer, 28(7):42-48, July 1995.

[15] Meyer, T.; Globus, A.: *Direct Manipulation of Isosurfaces and Cutting Planes in Virtual Environments.* Brown University Computer Science Technical Report 93-54, Dec. 1993.

[16] Sherman, W.: *Integrating Virtual Environments into the Dataflow Paradigm.* Proc. 4th Eurographics Workshop on Visualization in Scientific Computing, Abingdon, UK, April 1993.

[17] Taylor, R.; Robinett, W.; Chi, V.; Brooks, F.; Wright, W.; Williams, R.; Snyder, S.: *The nanomanipulator: A virtual reality interface for a scanning tunneling microscope.* Computer Graphics 27(2):127-134 (Siggraph '93).

[18] Ziegler, R.; Fischer, G.; Müller, W.; Göbel: *Virtual Reality Arthroscopy Training Simulator.* Computers in Biology and Medicine, 25(2):193-203, 1995.

Editors' Note: See Appendix, p. 319 for coloured figures of this paper

Characterizing global features of simulation data by selected local icons

R.-T. Happe, M. Rumpf

Institut für Angewandte Mathematik
Universität Freiburg, Germany

Abstract. Large data sets that represent complex physical phenomena require advanced tools that help to recognize and to study the essential features. The local behaviour of the numerical data in significant areas can provide insight in its global character. We present several types of icons, geometric objects, that symbolize selected local properties of the data, notably of flow fields and of deformation fields. Furthermore we discuss the choice of points where such icons should be placed.

1 Introduction

Complex physical phenomena can be simulated and resolved with large scale computations based on recent numerical methods, in particular adaptive, time–dependent, two and three dimensional finite element or finite volume algorithms based on unstructured grids. Characteristics of the solution, which are topologically invariant and globally describe the physical phenomena, are in general hidden in enormous masses of information. Standard methods like isosurface extraction, rendering scalar or vector fields on intersection planes and particle tracing in most cases are not sufficient to understand the peculiarities of the process. Instead of an "overall" visualization concepts to display selected important aspects are required. We are forced to carefully depict certain features of interest, which characterize the global solution. Various selection techniques have recently been studied. Globus et al. [5] propose to extract critical points from flow data sets. At these locations they graphically represent the eigenspaces. On boundary shapes, Helman and Hesselink [6] construct topological skeletons for vector fields. In [4] Demarcelle and Hesselink give a complete analysis of second order tensor field topology on two dimensional domains. Post et al. [9] apply methods based on mathematical morphology to locate interesting regions in large data sets. Finally the identification and extraction of structures, i. e. vortex filaments, is studied by several authors [3, 11]. To represent the local solution in regions of interest graphically icons have been investigated. An icon is a geometric object which acts as a symbolic representation for specific data quantities and features of the solution. DeLeeuw and van Wijk [7] have developed an iconic flow probe. Post et. al. [9] give several glyphs for various simulation features.

In this paper we contribute new icons and criteria for point selection suitable for different steady and time–dependent applications with the emphasis on flow fields and deformations. In section 2 a classification of solution types will lead to appropriate iconic representations for the solution gradients and a corresponding interpretation. Several methods to identify seed points at different levels of resolution of the local representation are discussed and compared in section 3. In particular we emphasize peculiarities of time–dependent flow and propose subsets with vanishing material derivative as a generalization of critical point sets in steady fields. Some important algorithmical aspects are examined in section 4 and conclusions are drawn in 5.

2 Local Behaviour of PDE solutions

Following the guidelines for the extraction of global features of numerical solutions to PDEs (partial differential equations) we will, in a first step, study how to analyze and visually represent the local behaviour of the solution at certain points of interest. Theoretically this is based on linearization and the calculus of ordinary differential equations (ODEs for short) [1]. Then, in a second step, these graphical representations, the proposed icons, will be placed at well chosen locations significant for global characteristics of the – typically physical – phenomena under consideration.

To start with, we first review some of the basic concepts well known in continuum mechanics. Partial differential equations in this field are derived from conservation laws, such as conservation of mass or energy and constitutive laws describing the material properties. The conservation laws can be formulated in two different coordinate systems. On the one hand, solutions can be interpreted as functions over some reference domain, for instance the initial state of the material. The underlying coordinates are denoted *Lagrangian* coordinates. An elastic deformation is a typical example. On the other hand, especially flow problems are in general represented in *Eulerian* coordinates. Here the unknowns are functions in some fixed spatial coordinate system, which can be regarded as the observer frame. They are not linked to material points. To be more specific, let X be a fixed material point at time t_0 and $x = \varphi(X, t)$ its location at time t where φ describes the deformation or the flow of the material in Lagrangian coordinates X, whereas $v(x, t)$, the velocity of a particle passing by some fixed point x at time t, is said to be described in Eulerian coordinates.

In the following, we will mainly focus on the two types of unknowns: deformations and velocities. They will be regarded as two significant representatives for a larger class of different applications.

The local behaviour of a differentiable PDE solution can be described in terms of its first order expansions. For velocity fields and deformations, we will now study the local expansions and their graphical description separately.

2.1 First order motion

There is a well known one–to–one relation between a velocity field and the induced flow φ defined by the ordinary differential equation (or ODE for short)

$$\dot\varphi(X,t) = v(\varphi(X,t),t)$$

where $\varphi(X,t) = x$ describes the motion of particles initially located at positions X driven by the velocity v in Eulerian coordinates. Therefore the above equation can be rewritten as $\dot x = v(x,t)$. Now we ask for the acceleration $\ddot x$ of a particle. By applying the chain rule we obtain the material derivative Dv/dt ($D/dt = v \cdot \nabla + \partial_t$ by definition) of the velocity v:

$$\ddot x = (v \cdot \nabla)v + \frac{\partial}{\partial t}v = \frac{D}{dt}v$$

If this derivative vanishes on a particle path, the corresponding particle is up to first order in a constant motion. The path $x = x(t)$ of a particle which passes the point x_0 at time t_0 can be expanded in terms of v and $\frac{D}{dt}v$

$$x_0(t) = x_0 + v(x_0,t_0)(t-t_0) + \frac{1}{2}\frac{D}{dt}v(x_0,t_0)(t-t_0)^2 + O\left((t-t_0)^3\right)$$

We will study the motion of particles moving along nearby paths y more closely and expand the offset

$$\begin{aligned}(y-x)(t) &= y_0 - x_0 + (v(y_0,t_0) - v(x_0,t_0))(t-t_0) + O((t-t_0)^2)\\ &= y_0 - x_0 + \nabla v(x_0,t_0)(y_0-x_0)(t-t_0)\\ &\quad + O(|y_0-x_0|^2 + (t-t_0)^2)\end{aligned}$$

Linearizing this equation we obtain

$$\dot\delta = \nabla v(x_0,t_0)\delta \qquad \delta(0) = \delta_0$$

In summary, the first order relative motion in a neighbourhood of a specific particle x_0 at time t_0 is described by the velocity $v(x_0,t_0)$ and the velocity gradient $\nabla v(x_0,t_0)$.

Now we ask for a graphical representation of this motion. Therefore let us look more closely at the induced linear field. ∇v has at least one real eigenvalue, which we will suppose to be the third. The others might be real as well or conjugate complex. If the real parts of all three eigenvalues are positive (negative) then x is a moving source (sink). But the flow of an incompressible medium in a closed system is source and sink free. Let us focus on this case. For differentiable velocities incompressibility is equivalent to vanishing divergence which equals the sum of the eigenvalues λ_i. Then one eigenvalue is real, say λ_3, and the real part of λ_1, λ_2 has the opposite sign. In the nondegenerate case, the eigenvectors e_1, e_2 corresponding to λ_1, λ_2 span a plane. The induced flow is hyperbolic, particles stream in along this plane and they stream away from x in the direction of e_3 or vice versa. Graphically the eigenspace spanned by e_3

is represented by a pair of arrows placed at x and pointing in or out depending on the sign of λ_3. The plane is shown by a disk centered at x and deformed according to e_1, e_2. If λ_1, λ_2 are real, the flow along the plane is of sink or source type. We characterize this flow by drawing a pair of arrows on the disk both for e_1 and e_2, the arrows being scaled by the respective eigenvalues (see Appendix). In the complex case the flow is swirling in or out along the plane. In a coordinate system with axes aligned to the real and imaginary part of e_1, the real part of the eigenvalue $\lambda_1 = \alpha + i\beta$ drives the particles into the center or away from it proportionally to $e^{\alpha t}$. That determines the period of time τ the particles need to traverse the disk. Afterwards, they'll have been swirled around the angle $\beta\tau$. We partition the above disk into 4 segments with alternating colour. The rim of the disk is twisted according to that angle, and the (initially circular) disk is deformed linearly as indicated by the real and imaginary parts of e_1. This leads to spiral shaped segments. The separation lines between these segments are integral curves of the linearized field (see Fig. 2).

2.2 First order deformation or growth

We have discussed the local behaviour of solutions, in particular flow fields, given in Eulerian coordinates. Elastic deformation and growth fields are typical examples for solutions of partial differential equations given in Lagrangian coordinates X. The local behaviour of a deformation $\varphi(X,t)$ is described by the deformation gradient $\nabla\varphi(X,t)$. At first, in three dimensions these are 9 degrees of freedom, which we have to represent graphically. The complexity can be reduced significantly by taking into account the polar decomposition. Any linear mapping A can be decomposed into a rotation $Q(A)$, possibly including a reflection, and a symmetric mapping $H(A)$. Applying this to deformation gradients we obtain

$$\nabla\varphi(X,t) = H(\nabla\varphi(X,t))\, Q(\nabla\varphi(X,t)).$$

If the material orientation is preserved under the deformation, which is true in most cases, $Q(\nabla\varphi(X,t))$ is a rotation without reflection. The polar decomposition comes along with a physical interpretation. Up to first order a test volume placed at X is first undergoing a rotation given by $Q(\nabla\varphi(X,t))$ and then a stretching described by $H(\nabla\varphi(X,t))$. Q can uniquely be described by an axis of rotation and a rotation angle, whereas H has three real eigenvalues, the stretching factors, corresponding to three orthogonal eigenvectors, the stretching directions. We obtain a graphical representation for arbitrary local deformations by displaying the symmetric and the rotational part separately (see Appendix). The rotation is symbolized by a disk in the plane of rotation which is perpendicular to the axis. The disc is segmented into regions of different colour and twisted by the angle of rotation similarly to the disc representing conjugate complex eigenvalues of velocity gradients. The symmetric mapping can be illustrated by a three dimensional cross pointing in the orthogonal stretching directions and scaled by the stretching factors. Considering the stretching of a sphere induced by H we find another possible icon for the symmetric part, where we display

$$\{X + H(\nabla\varphi(X,t))(Y - X) \mid Y \in \partial B^\delta(X)\}.$$

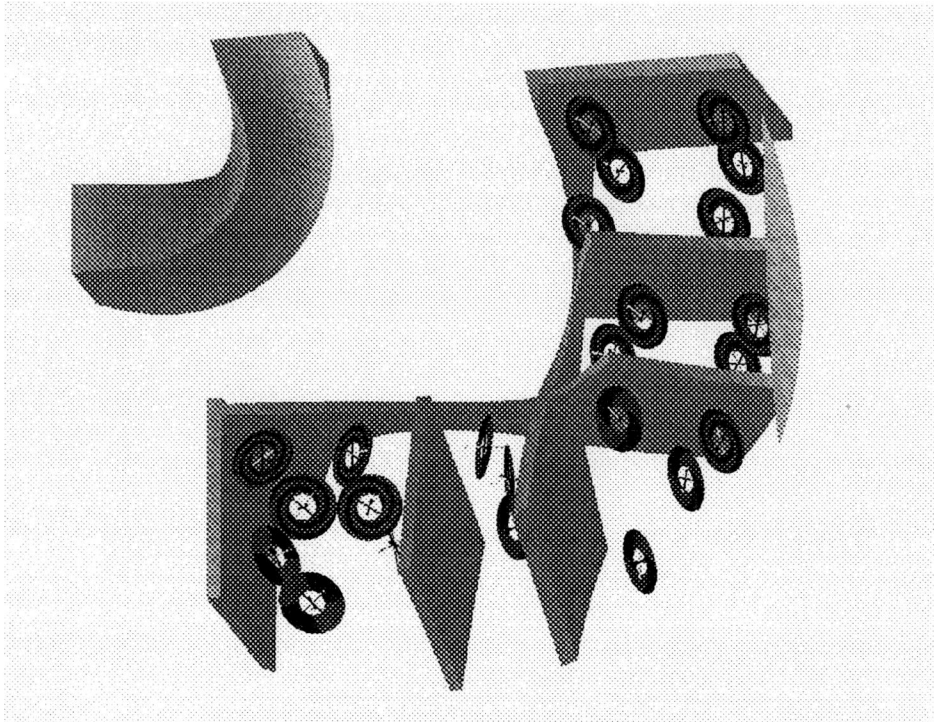

Fig. 1. Icons show the local deformation of an elastic bar factorized in gyration and stretching.

Physically this depicts what happens to the sphere under the deformation.

Instead of displaying the icons in reference coordinates X we can place them in the deformed configuration as well. Let us finally mention that growth fields $\sigma(X,t) = \dot{\varphi}(X,t)$. can be decomposed analogously. Then because of its interpretation the proposed second icon seems to be particularly useful (for details see [8]). If there are directions of positive and negative growth the sphere gets partly turned inside out (see Appendix).

2.3 Further interesting tensor fields

Up to now we have classified the local flow relative to a particular particle and local deformation or growth at a certain position in the reference domain. Graphically we have represented the corresponding gradients of the solution by finding appropriate icons for these second order tensors. But there are other important second order fields, most of them expressed as functions of the gradients, such as the rotation tensor of a flow or the stress tensors. The rotational part of the velocity gradient reduces to the vector quantity curl v, which can be displayed using the twisted disk icon already introduced above. Stress tensors are symmetric due to the conservation of angular momentum [13]. Therefore the icons

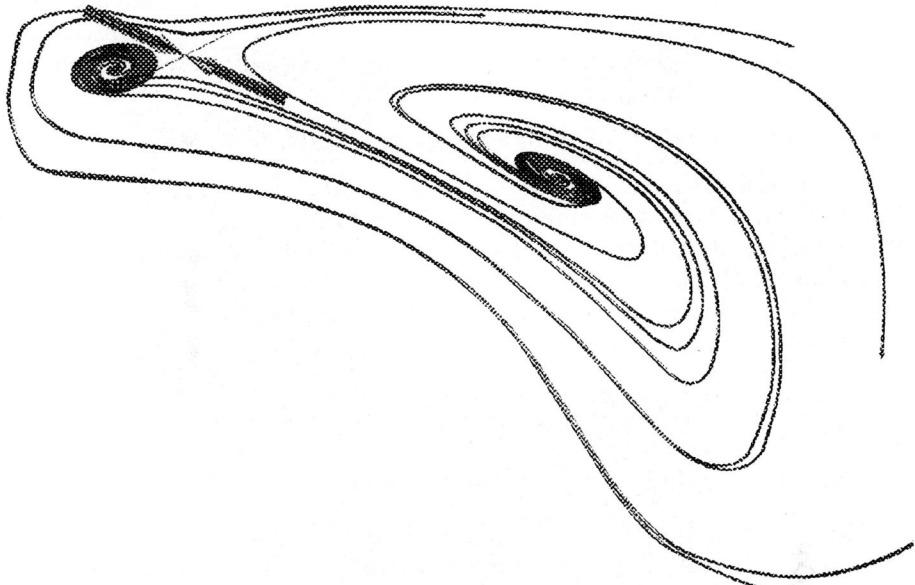

Fig. 2. Icons placed at critical points and streamlines in incompressible 3d flow. The streamlines that move into or out of a critical point form a surface separating the flow locally. The icon disks are tangential to these surfaces.

for symmetric linear mappings seem to be appropriate.

3 Spotlighting the global solution

In the preceding section, we have discussed the local behaviour of PDE solutions, in particular velocity fields in Eulerian coordinates and deformations in Lagrangian coordinates, and we have introduced graphical representations, the icons described above, which allow an intuitive physical understanding. Up to now, the question is still open where to position these icons.

At first hand, icons can be released at positions related to the domain geometry. Or icons may be aligned to appropriate particle lines of a flow field [7].

3.1 Critical points in flow fields

Critical points (roots) are of specific interest in velocity fields, in particular in the steady case. They are topological invariants of the underlying flow [2] and can be taken as seed points to reconstruct a topological skeleton (in two dimensions) [4]. We have used the icons of 2.1 to describe the local flow at critical points in a 3d volume (see Appendix). Since the reference particle in the critical point is unmoved, the icons show the absolute field (up to first order).

In unsteady flow, patterns emerge, e.g. drifting vortices, that are not present as such in the momentaneous field at any time. But nevertheless, critical points are still topologically invariant and give insight in qualitative aspects of the flow.

3.2 Points of constant motion in time–dependent fields

In this paragraph we will remark upon a generalization of critical points in the time–dependent case. In general points of constant motion are the appropriate objects we should ask for. Their physical meaning is that the underlying particle is not undergoing any acceleration. They are identified as the roots of the material derivative. To rule out points in laminar regions we demand a nonvanishing velocity gradient. Let us call a point (x, t) *center point* iff

$$\frac{D}{dt}v(x,t) = 0 \quad , \quad \nabla v \neq 0$$

To motivate our definition we note the following:

- In a moving observer frame centered at such a point, this point will, of course, appear as a critical point. Furthermore center points are invariant under any observer transformation in constant motion. Therefore the definition is not in conflict with respect to reasonable frame indifference requirements.

- In the steady case center points are either critical or $(v \cdot \nabla)v = 0$, which implies locally a constant motion in the direction of v and first order terms only in planes perpendicular to this direction. But this slight generalization seems to make sense as well, in particular if one thinks of a vortex filament lying in the axis of the principal motion.

- Vortices and vortex filaments are of specific interest, in particular for viscous flow at high Reynolds numbers. They are typically characterized as pressure extrema with nonvanishing curl [3, 11]. If we neglect the viscous term in the underlying Navier–Stokes equations we obtain the Euler equation $\frac{D}{dt}v = -\nabla p$, which clearly indicates a strong relation between pressure extrema and center points. Respectively, if particles are swirling around a point x of an inertial frame they are perpetually accelerated towards x (e.g. by the pressure gradient), so that the acceleration Dv/dt, if continuous, has to vanish in x, i.e. x is a center point.

Although sets of center points seem to be reasonable candidates for topologically interesting quantities it is hard to extract them from numerical data sets mainly because both time and space discretization errors play an important role and lead to non uniquely definable center points. Nevertheless, in our 2d example, a Karman vortex street, the fast line integral convolution method of Stalling and Hege [12] proves the vortices to be regions containing a center point (see Appendix).

4 Algorithmical Aspects

Solutions to PDE may exhibit features at various scales. The numerics, though, have to comply with resource limits and should provide a decent error control. Adaptive methods are well suited to resolve different scales in simulation processes. They resolve local phenomena by local refinement of the original grid. The data produced by such methods is typically based on unstructured grids, e.g. tetrahedral grids with cells of varying size and shape. In time–dependent problems, the discretization may change as the process goes on since local phenomena like vortices, reaction zones, shock fronts etc. may move – accompanied by the refinement zones. Our visualization concepts are based on this type of numerical data.

4.1 Reliability

The reliability of iconic visualization methods is closely related to error estimates given for the numerical results. Typically these estimates are known only in some energy norm, defined as integrals over the domain. For realistic simulations in general no pointwise estimates are known. But pointwise estimates for the solution and its gradient are necessary to reliably localize seed points and evaluate the icon parameters. For instance, the divergence free property in the data sets we have studied is not fulfilled pointwise. Therefore one should in general be very careful in interpreting the results based on pointwise evaluation. A promising alternative would be to replace point evaluation by integral averaging or in advance mollification.

Another serious problem is the stable calculation of eigenvalues and eigenvectors: eigenvectors do not depend continuously on the matrix.

4.2 Integrating an ODE near a critical point

Integral curves that start or end in a critical point x_0 of an ODE $\dot{x} = v(x)$ cannot be integrated beginning right in x_0 since the velocity in such a point is $v(x_0) = 0$ and we wouldn't ever get away from it. If we start near the point we need an adaptive "time" step control that gets on with a very low speed of propagation. In addition, it should correctly integrate a field that is not continuously differentiable or not even continuous on cell boundary faces.

5 Conclusions

We have discussed the use of icons to characterize global aspects of simulation data. Several kinds of icons have been proposed. The icons can be released by hand or at points extracted automatically. These may be critical or the above 'center points' for flow problems, and extremal or degenerate positions in deformation or growth fields. A stable algorithm computing center points in time–dependent flow fields on unstructured grids is subject of ongoing work.

The presented approach has been realized in the programming environment GRAPE [10]. This would not have been possible without the support of many people at the Institut für Angewandte Mathematik at Freiburg University and the SFB 256 at Bonn University among them R. Kleinrensing, M. Metscher, M. Wierse, and A. Schmidt. The numerical data have been kindly provided by E. Bänsch, A. Schmidt and M. Wierse.

References

[1] Arnol'd, V.I.: Ordinary Differential Equations. Berlin, New York 1992

[2] Asimov, D.: Notes on the topology of vector fields and flows, Tutorial Notes, IEEE Visualization '95, 1995

[3] Banks, D. C.: Singer, B. A.: Vortex Tubes in Turbulent Flows: Identification, Representation, Reconstruction, IEEE Visualization '94, 132–139, 1994

[4] Delmarcelle, T.; Hesselink, L.: The Topology of Symmetric, Second–Order Tensor Fields, IEEE Visualization '94, 140–147, 1994

[5] Globus, A.; Levit, C; Lasinski, T.: A Tool for Visualizing the Topology of Three–Dimensional Vector Fields, IEEE Visualization '91, 33–40, 1991

[6] Helman, J. L.; Hesselink, L.: Visualizing Vector Field Topology in Fluid Flows, IEEE CG&A 11, No. 3, 36–46, May 1991

[7] Leeuw, W. C. de; Wijk, J. J. van: A Probe for Local Flow Field Visualization, IEEE Visualization '93, 39–45, 1993

[8] Nakielski, J.; Rumpf M.: Growth in Apical Meristems of Plants, Visualization Tools and Growth Tensor Methods, Report 11, SFB 256, Bonn, 1992

[9] Post, F. J.; Walsum, T. van; Post, F. H.; Silver D.: Iconic Techniques for Feature Visualization, IEEE Visualization '95, 288–295, 1995

[10] SFB 256, University of Bonn: GRAPE manual, http://www.iam.uni-bonn.de/main.html, Bonn 1995

[11] Silver, D.; Zabusky, N. J.: Quantifying Visualizations for Reduced Modeling in Nonlinear Science: Extracting Structures from Data Sets, Journal of Visual Communication and Image Representation, Vol. 4, No. 1,, 46–61, 1993

[12] Stalling, D.; Hege C.: Fast and Resolution Independent Line Integral Convolution, Proceedings SIGGRAPH '95, 1995

[13] Truesdell, C. : A First Course in Rational Continuum Mechanics, Vol. 1, London 1977

Editors' Note: See Appendix, p. 320 for coloured figures of this paper

Doing It Right: Psychological Tests to Ensure the Quality of Scientific Visualization

Helmut Haase, Christoph Dohrmann

Fraunhofer Institute for Computer Graphics (Fraunhofer IGD),
Wilhelminenstr. 7, D-64283 Darmstadt, Germany
email:haase@igd.fhg.de – http://www.igd.fhg.de/~haase

Abstract

This paper discusses a general scheme for determining the quality of scientific visualization systems. It presents psychological tests which have been performed in order to find quantitative relationships for this scheme, and discusses why simple numerical relationships may be hard to find.

Our work is motivated by research into interactive and immersive scientific visualization which pose two opposing demands: maximum image quality at sufficient frame rates. We believe that these two factors are also crucial for many other applications, e.g., virtual reality. For this scheme, special focus is on the user's perception of the system. Three components of Visualization System Quality are identified: Data quality, image quality, and interaction quality. In order to migrate from a merely qualitative to a more quantitative model, psychological tests were performed to measure the influence of frame rate and rendering mode on the perception of visualized three dimensional vector data. Results of the tests are presented and general suggestions for good perceptual tests are made.

We believe that the experience we gained will be of benefit to many who are interested in questions of visualization system quality.

Keywords: Scientific Visualization, Realtime Interaction, Psychological Tests, Visualization System Quality

1 Visualization System Quality for interactive and immersive scientific visualization

Many different techniques for scientific visualization are known, and each technique can be parameterized in various ways. But what is the "best" visualization for a given problem, i.e., for a dataset and a user with a degree of experience and certain goals using hardware with specific features?

This is a tough question. To do visualizations well is a difficult task. Lately, some people have pointed out the importance of this question ([10], [18]). In [21], a case study is reported which addresses the question of visualization quality. In [16], a tool is presented which recommends visualization techniques for a given set of data.

We will address this topic by means of psychological tests. In the following, a general scheme for Visualization System Quality (VSQ) will be presented. By the term *visualization system* we mean a combination of hardware and software. Visualization systems can be classified according to various criteria, e.g., price, CPU speed, screen size, etc. We are mainly interested in user performance as a criterion for system quality. This approach is motivated by our previous work on Scientific Visualization, e.g., [7].

Increasingly, scientific data now is being visualized using Virtual Environment or Virtual Reality (VR)[1] techniques. This is due to easy availablitiy of hardware and software suitable for VR techniques as well as to the observable benefits of merging these two techniques to become Immersive Scientific Visualization.

Some applications which already utilize this synergy are reported in [2] (Virtual Windtunnel), [5] (several visualizations using the CAVE system), [20] (VR in dataflow systems), [15] (Responsive Workbench), and work by us: [12] (medical training, material testing, visualization of room accoustics, and 3D weather visualization), [13] (investigation of molecule datain VR), and [14] (coupling of general purpose VR and scientific visualization system). In all these examples, the opposing demands of image quality and rendering speed have been met in a certain way (see also [3]). Even though CPU performance and memory size increase drastically, the tension between image quality and frame rate will remain to be a crucial issue for all kinds of graphics systems. This is due to demands for an ever increasing level of detail in the data, no matter if it is finite element meshes, realistic landscapes, or medical data.

The solution to this problem lies in dynamic adaption of data and image complexity as well as of the degree of interaction to the current situation. This situation consists, among other factors, of system load, of the type and amount of data which is used by the system, as well as of the knowledge, strategy, and goals of the current user. It seems that there is need to measure quality of graphics systems which enables adjustment of system parameters depending on the situation in order to maximize the benefit of the system to each individual user. The perfect solution would be a quantitative measure for system quality allowing us to optimize system parameters according to the individual constraints of each possible user/data/system combination.

Starting from this observation, we developed a general scheme for determining the quality of a (3D) graphical system. It is presented in more detail in [13]. Visualization System Quality as described in the following is a special kind of Graphics System Quality since visualization systems are a special kind of graphics systems. Thus, VSQ describes the underlying system in terms of hardware and general performance but not the visualization technique used or the didactics of a visualization. This scheme still is only qualitative. We tried to determine some numerical input for this scheme by performing perceptual studies with test persons. Unfortunately, we discovered that valid, representative numerical results are not easy to obtain. Here we will report on the preliminary, qualitative scheme, on the tests that we performed, and on the implications of these tests.

The scheme does not explicitely comprise "hidden" features like memory size or processor speed, even though they may influence factors which we consider important for Graphics System Quality (GSQ), e.g., rendering speed. Rather, the scheme comprises features which are visible to the user directly.

The scheme consists of three main components: Data quality, image quality, and interaction quality. The details of these main components are summarized in Table 1.

Data Quality	Image Quality	Interaction Quality
• Data Semantics:	• Image space resol.	• Rendering speed
1. Only geometric or image data	• Color space resol.	(static,sequence,realtime)
2. Static semantics	• Rendering/shading (wireframe, flat, gouraud, phong)	• Degree of interaction (none, interactive, VR)
3. Dynamic semantics		• Number of users
• Object space resol.		(none, one, multiple)

Table 1: Components of Visualization/Graphics System Quality.

The following components of the GSQ scheme are explained in further detail.

Data quality stands for the semantics of graphic objects and resolution in object (data) space.

Image quality is a term which may be used with different meanings. Firstly, its definition may depend on the application area, e.g., text, technical drawings, or video. For the sake of this paper, we are mainly interested in (sequences of) raster images of scientific 3D data. Furthermore, image quality can be investigated on a very basic level (spatial resolution of pixels, dynamic range, etc.), on higher levels (geometric distortion, feature distortion, etc.), or even on a very high conceptual level (style, redundancy, etc.). For an overview of the state-of-the-art of definition and measurement of image quality, see [8].

Image quality is an assembly of several factors, all influencing the amount of information which is accessible from a single image. For our purposes, the following characteristics seem most important for the definition of image quality: Resolution in image space, resolution in color space, and rendering/shading method.

Finally, *interaction quality* is an important component of the GSQ scheme. It comprises: Rendering speed, degree of interaction, and number of users.

In order to further elaborate this scheme and to develop a quantitative measure for Visualization/Graphics System Quality, we performed some psychological tests. These tests made clear that users have very different visualization and perception strategies depending on their knowledge and goals. The data to

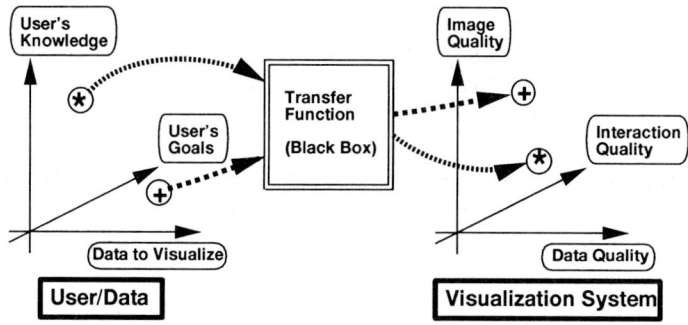

Figure 1: Main factors influencing Graphics System Quality.

visualize as well as knowledge and goals of the user constrain the best choice of data quality, image quality, and interaction quality. This can be seen as a kind of mapping or transfer function from 3D to 3D (see figure 1). Unfortunately, this transfer function is unknown to us. Investigation to determine this transfer function is worth-while in order to achieve better visualizations. Therefore, further perceptual tests need to be performed.

2 Testing the influence of rendering speed and rendering mode on perception of 3D vector fields

The previous chapter outlined our view on Visualization/Graphics System Quality. GSQ is obviously motivated by a great interest in the performance of a user of a graphics system. In general, a user of a graphics system may want a visualization of great complexity at the highest possible frame rate. Due to limitations in rendering speed and increasing amounts of data to be visualized, this demand cannot be fulfilled entirely. On the other hand, since human visual perception is limited in respect to spatial and temporal resolution [11], it could be assumed that parameters can be found which allow optimum human performance without exceeding the capabilities of a given graphics system. Exact numerical models of visual 3D perception are not available ([4] presents such a model for the limited task of text processing). Thus, rules or formulas for the optimal configuration of a visualization system are hard to specify. Psychological tests are one possibility to obtain a crude, simple model of the "visualization user".

Therefore, we investigated the possibility of perceptual tests. We are interested in mathematical relationships of parameters for visualization and their influence on human performance in perceptual tasks. Thus, a large number of parameter combinations must be tested. This implies that, in order to gain results that can be trusted with a certain confidence, a large number of test subjects must be involved which makes the test very expensive. Normally, only industry can afford to carry out tests with hundreds of subjects.

But even if we could perform such tests, the quantitative results by themselves may not be sufficient. We want to generalize from the specific test conditions to more general phenomena and therefore observations of the bahaviour and personal comments from subjects must be recorded and analyzed. It may be that the numerical results were strongly influenced by factors that are unexpected and unknown to the test designer, for example different strategies in solving a perceptual task.

It is also easier to look for new possible phenomena than to design a test which tries to verify a theory. To verify a theory with sufficient confidence, a large number of subjects is needed, maybe all with a similar background. To discover new phenomena, a smaller group with very different subjects can be sufficient. It should also be noted that there are different statistical methods that can only be used either to detect new phenomena or to verify expected phenomena. For example, analysis of variances should only be used to verify or falsify expected phenomena while cluster analysis should only be used to search for new phenomena.

2.1 Our tests

Since we have been concerned with Scientific Visualization for a couple of years, we chose perception of individual vectors as well as of vector fields as the task for the tests. Our main goal was to classify the influence of frame rate and of rendering mode of the vectors on the perception of the angles of individual 3D vectors ('detail' test) as well as on the holistic perception of a complex 3D vector field ('overview' test).

We started by doing some research into literature on visual perception. Gibson's ecological approach to visual perception [9] is the most fruitful for the explanation of perception of 3D structures. Unfortunately, it does not contain numerical models. This approach identifies "gradients" and "invariants" as the most important factors for spatial relations and object recognition. Cue-theory[11], which is based on feature extraction for the "cues" stereo, shading, texturing, movement, and focus, should be considered as a subset of the bigger concept of the ecological approach. It clarifies the different aspects of an animated image which all should be seen as building blocks of an overall image quality. Most of the cues have already been tested separately, but the effect of combinations of several parameters, which is essential in visualization systems, has not been examined in detail. The effect of combinations of different parameters on 2D data analysis currently is under investigation[19], especially in the case of dynamic presentations[17].

Our tests investigated four different frame rates and three different vector rendering modes (line, pyramid, and complex arrow). The pyramid consists of 5 polygons while the complex arrow has 34 polygons (see plate 1, appendix). Thus, complex arrows take considerabely longer to draw than pyramids while lines are the fastest mode. The intention was to obtain an overview of possible interactions between these two parameters, i.e., how to choose the best rendering mode for a given rendering speed and vice versa. Twelve subjects were used for these tests; they were computer science students with basic knowledge of computer graphics but no experience in visualization of vector data. All tests were performed using the ISVAS[1] 3.2 visualization system running on SGI hardware. The analysis of variances (ANOVA) was performed using the SAS/STAT software.

Two pilot tests were designed and performed on a few subjects; the results of these tests led to two more elaborated tests which were performed on all twelve subjects. For example, in the pilot test the users interacted with the system in order to select a point of view. We soon realized that this leads to test results which are mainly influenced by the strategy of each user instead of the parameters which were of original interest to us (e.g., rendering speed and rendering mode).

For the sake of brevity we will only report on one of the two final tests, the so-called 'detail' test.

2.2 'Detail' Test

In the 'detail' test, four vectors (all of them rendered in the same of the three possible rendering modes) were shown on a flat surface (see plate 2, appendix). The scene was rotating about the vertical axis at one of the four possible speeds (2, 6, 12, or 18 frames per second) at one degree per frame.

The subject's task was to find which vector out of the four was the most orthogonal to the surface as well as to estimate the exact angle between this vector and the surface. This experiment was motivated by the need to determine the correctness of boundary conditions in finite element simulations.

After a number of training cases to make the subject acquainted with the task, the test itself started. It consisted of 12 test cases. The whole session took approx. 60 minutes. For each test case we recorded

1. the 'most orthogonal' arrow as perceived by the subject,

2. the subject's confidence in this decission,

3. the estimated angle of the most orthogonal arrow to the plane,

4. the number of frames that were viewed until the correct arrow had been selected, and

5. misc. comments of the subjects.

We say that items 1 and 3 measured 'objective' entities since we have no reason to assume that these answers were biased by expectations. On the other hand, we say that items 2 and 4 measured 'subjective' entities since we believe that these results are influenced by the subjects' expectations. For example, if the subject expects that at a given frame rate it is more difficult to estimate an

---

[1]ISVAS is registered trade mark of Fraunhofer IGD, Darmstadt, Germany

angle, the subject will take longer to decide on this angle and the number of viewed frames (4) will be increased.

Now, let us discuss the test results. First, the resulting number of frames (4) are shown in figure 2.

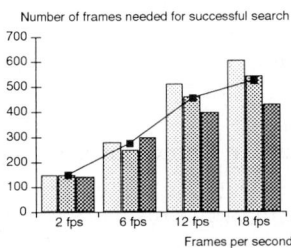

Figure 2: Number of viewed frames for the frame rates (2, 6, 12, 18 fps) and the three rendering modes (left to right in each block: line, pyramid, arrow).

It may be seen that for higher frame rates, more frames are viewed. This is due to the fact that the whole scene needs to be viewed for at least 20 seconds which is equivalent to 40 frames at 2 fps or to 400 frames at 20 fps (increasing number of frames with increasing frame rate).

By the way: If we use 'viewing time in seconds' instead of 'frames per second' in figure 2, the mean values of each block are decreasing from 2 to 18 fps. In this case, we get approx. 70 seconds for 2 fps, followed by 45, 37.5, and 30 seconds viewing time for 6, 12, and 18 fps. So the overall viewing time is decreasing and thus performance of a user is increasing with higher frame rates.

But we can observe something much more interesting: at 2 and 6 fps, all three rendering modes seem to be more or less identical, but at 12 and 18 fps, there is an advantage of arrows over pyramids over lines.

Source	DF	F-Value	p
FPS	3	29.14	0.0001
REND	2	0.81	0.4458
FPS*REND	6	0.49	0.8121

Table 2: ANOVA for number of frames.

The overall ANOVA for the number of frames leads to the numbers given in table 2. We can see that frame rate (FPS) has a strong (F=29.14) and significant (p=0.0001) influence on the number of frames. So the first observation from the graph is confirmed: with increasing frame rate, the number of frames increases significantly. On the other hand, rendering mode (REND) is not very strong and not significant. To be significant, p should be < 0.05 or at least < 0.1. So our second observation about arrows being better than pyramids and lines is only a trend but not a significant result. Finally, the interaction of these two variables is even less significant.

Source	DF	F-Value	p
REND (FPS= 2)	2	0.11	0.8995
REND (FPS= 6)	2	0.55	0.5837
REND (FPS=12)	2	1.22	0.3068
REND (FPS=18)	2	1.13	0.3342

Table 3: ANOVA for number of frames for each individual rendering speed.

We were looking for some influence of the rendering mode on user behaviour, so we were not satisfied with these results. Next, we investigated if the influence of rendering mode would be approximately the same with respect to rendering speed. Table 3 shows the results of this ANOVA.

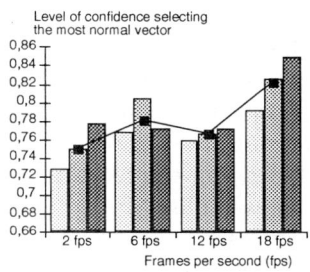

Figure 3: Level of confidence for the frame rates (2, 6, 12, 18 fps) and the three rendering modes (left to right in each block: line, pyramid, arrow).

We can see that for increasing frame rates, the rendering mode has increasing influence on the time subjects are examining the scene. At 2 fps, the three rendering modes are more or less identical in terms of user performance, but at 18 fps, arrows seem to be clearly superior to pyramids or to lines, even though this influence is still not signficant in our test (p=0.3342 is still too large).

The second subjective result (level of confidence, 2) is shown in figure 3. It can be seen that generally, confidence is higher with arrows than with pyramids or lines and that confidence is higher at high frame rates. ANOVA is not given here but again, the results are not significant.

Next, let's have a look at the 'objective' results of selection error: figure 4 shows the error in selecting the most orthogonal vector (1).

We can see that for these 'objective' results, lines are not well suited. Pyramids are slightly better than arrows. Also, high frame rates (dark bars) are better for test results than low frame rates (white bars) for the given task. ANOVA confirms that these results are not by chance (see table 4), and that

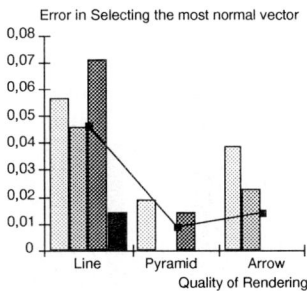

Figure 4: Error in selecting the most orthogonal vector: the rendering modes and four frame rates each (left to right in each block: 2, 6, 12, 18 fps).

the influence of rendering mode is much more significant than the one of frame rate.

Source	DF	F-Value	p
FPS	3	1.54	0.2067
REND	2	4.66	0.0111
FPS*REND	6	0.48	0.8193

Table 4: ANOVA for selection error.

Finally, figure 5 shows the 'objective' results of errors on estimation of angle. We can see that pyramids perform better than lines or arrows but it's hard to tell what frame rates are best: for lines, low frame rates (white) are better than high frame rates (dark), but for arrows, the highest frame rate (18 fps, dark) is best.

Concluding the discussion of this test, it can be seen that for feature extraction (error in selection, figure 4) high frame rates are better than low frame rates while for exact measurements, this is not so clear. In fact, if lines are used as drawing primitives, low frame rates are superior to high frame rates.

Another interesting result is that for both cases, pyramids seem to be the best choice for drawing primitives. This is an important finding: the most complex rendering objects need not necessarily be best suited for a given task. Since pyramids are faster to draw than detailed arrows, there seems to be no need for detailed arrows in a visualization system if tasks similar to our tests only need to be solved. But please note that we do not claim that pyramids are superior to detailed arrows in all or even in most cases; to make such a provocative statement, much more test cases would be needed.

From our observations during the tests as well as from comments of test subjects we learned something that we did not expect in the beginning: even in a quite homogenious group of subjects as in our test (all 20 to 30 years old,

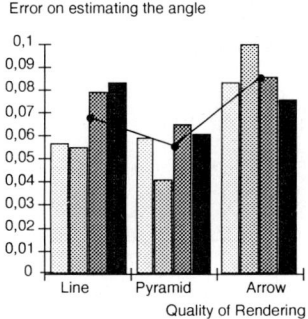

Figure 5: Error in estimating the angle: the rendering modes and four frame rates each (left to right in each block: 2, 6, 12, 18 fps).

computer scientists with computer graphics backgroud, all from Darmstadt, etc.) there were different strategies in solving the tasks of the test. For example, in order to find the most orthogonal vector, some subjects would try to perceive the whole scene at once and see which vector would 'jitter' fewest while others would try to determine each angle sequentially and then calculate which one is most normal to the surface.

In the second test ('overview'), a regular grid of vectors was given (6 x 6 x 6). Plate 3 (see appendix) shows a screen shot with test environment and the vector field in the middle. For the tests, a 21 inch monitor was used. As shown in the plate, vectors were not identical but changed slowly in lengthand direction from one corner of the cube to the other. Test subjects had to find a discontinuity of this function. Here, we made a similar observation: Some subjects would try to perceive the whole scene at once in a holistic manner while others would try to use certain orientations of the dataset to 'take a bearing of' rows of vectors. These different strategies also lead to different preferences: The holistic group needed a certain frame rate to get a good 3D impression of the scene while the second group prefered lower frame rates where there is more time to investigate the data set in a 'stable' orientation.

In conclusion, some interesting things that we learned from the test are:

- Personal preferences and objective performance need not be correlated.

- Personal strategies for interaction and investigation of a scene influence the effects of visualization parameters (e.g., of frame rate and of rendering mode).

- Humans are pretty good in detecting a feature and much worse in estimating a numerical value.

- The formulation of a task and the goal of the viewer determine his perception by making him select alternative strategies.

- Kind and amount of data influence the suitability of different graphical primitives for scientific visualization.

2.3 Some things we learned about tests in general

Testing the effect that different parameters of a graphics system might have on a user's performance involves detailed preparation of the psychological test. This includes precise ideas about parameters to be tested, the kinds of subjects (e.g., experts or laypersons), test data, perceptual tasks, and performance indicators. These items are not independent of each other.

The number of parameters (e.g., rendering mode and rendering speed) and the number of values of each parameter (e.g., 8, 12, 16 frames per second for rendering speed) that will be tested have a great influence on the number of tests that must be conducted to gain significant results. Experienced psychologists claim that significant test results require the number of subjects to be in the order of 10 times the number of all possible combinations of parameters. This means that for our "detail" test where we tested 3 x 4 = 12 parameter combinations, approx. 120 test subjects would be needed.

Statistical significance also is influenced by the homogeneousness of the subjects. If all subjects have very similar backgrounds, there will be a higher confidence level for the test results, but the results will only be valid for a smaller subset of possible users. If the subjects vary greatly from each other, results will be less significant but will apply over a wider range of persons.

Also, to avoid learning effects, there should be as many datasets as the number of trials for each subject. There need to be some additional training data sets for each subject to make it familiar with the task before the actual test starts. All datasets should be of similar difficulty. Since it may be impossible to get enough sets of real world data which fulfill all these criteria, it can be better to generate synthetic data. This also allows a precise variation of the parameters under investigation.

The task must be apropriate for the test subjects. E.g., the task "determine if there is a tumor visible in a medical data set" can be suitable for an experienced physician but not for a layperson.

The solution of a task should be easy to verify for the test personnel. Errors introduced by verbalization should be minimized. An example for this is the perception of angles. If test subjects are asked to sketch a perceived angle onto a piece of paper, this result generally is much better than a verbal estimation of the angle.

Some general recommendations concerning psychological tests with graphics systems:

1. Make a hypothesis and select a task which will be suitable to evaluate this hypothesis.

2. Select a simple task which is not influenced by too many variables; try to eliminate any side effects which may influence the perfromance of your subjects.

3. Use a large number of subjects in order to minimize personal differences.

4. Use a homogenious group of subjects with similar backgrounds.

5. Design and carry out preliminary tests in order to improve your test setup, take plenty of time for this.

6. Try to get the help of someone who has experince in psychological tests unless you have have this experince yourself.

7. Know your statistical methods and your software packages for analyzing test results well.

3   Conclusion and Future Work

In this paper we have presented a qualitative scheme for Visualization Sytem Quality, we have reported on perceptual tests that were performed in order to gain more quantitative input for such a scheme, we have discussed the results of these tests, and we have given hints to test design in general. Especially the strong influence of user goals and user knowledge on the best settings for Visualization System Quality in each case has been demonstrated.

There is need for further investigation and classification of rendering methods and other factors influencing Visualization System Quality. Only a quantitative metrics of Visualization System Quality will allow us to build systems which can automatically select the best combination of image quality and interaction quality on a given hardware configuration for each specific set of data and for each individual user.

If we want to do it right, if we want to ensure the quality of scientific visualizations, the role of human perception in scientific visualization must be further investigated.

4   Acknowledgements

We wish to thank all our subjects for participation in the tests, all those who contributed to the ISVAS visualization system (Kennet Karlsson, Peter Fritzen, etc.), and Prof. Dr.-Ing. J. Encarnação for providing the environment which made this work possible.

References

[1] Astheimer, P., Dai, F., Göbel, M., Kruse, R., Müller, S., Zachmann, G.: *Realism in Virtual Reality*, In: Thalmann, N., Thalmann, D. (Eds.): Artificial Life and Virtual Reality, John Wiley & Sons, 1994, pp. 189-210

[2] Bryson, S., Levit, C.: *The Virtual Windtunnel*, IEEE Computer Graphics and Applications, 12, 4, pp. 25-34, 1992

[3] Bryson, S., Levit, C.: *Lessons learned while implementing the virtual wind-tunnel project*, Visualization '92, Tutorial # 2, 4.1–4.7, 1992

[4] Card, S.K., Moran, T.P., Newell, A.: *The psychology of computer human interaction*, Lawrence Erlbaum Associates, Inc. Publishers, Hilldale, 1983

[5] Cruz-Neira, C., Leight, J., Papka, M., Barnes, C., Cohen, S.M., Das, S., Engelmann, R., Hudson, R., Roy, T., Siegel, L., Vasilakis, C., DeFanti, T.A., Sandin, D.J.: *Scientists in Wonderland: A Report on Visualization Applications in the CAVE Virtual Reality Environment*, Proc. IEEE Symposium on Research Frontiers in VR, San Jose, pp. 59–66, October 1993

[6] Encarnação, J.L., Astheimer, P., Felger, W., Frühauf, Th., Göbel, M., Müller, S.: *Graphics & Visualization: The Essential Features for the Classification of Systems.*, In: Proc. International Conference on Computer Graphics ICCG'93, Bombay, India, February 1993

[7] Frühauf, T., Göbel, M., Haase, H., Karlsson, K.: *Design of a Flexible Monolithic Visualization System*, in: Rosenblum, L., Earnshaw, R., et al. (eds.): Scientific Visualization - Advances and Challenges, Academic Press, London, 1994, pp. 265-286

[8] Gerfelder, N., Müller, W.: *Quality Aspects of Computer Based Video Services*, in: Proc. of the 1994 European SMPTE Conference, Cologne, Germany, pp. 44–67, Sept. 1994

[9] Gibson, J.J.: *The ecological approach to visual perception*, Houghton Mifflin, Boston, 1979

[10] Globus, A., Uselton, S.: *Evaluation of Visualization Software*, Computer Graphics, pp. 41-44, May 1995

[11] Groß, M.: *Visual Computing - The Integration of Computer Graphics, Visual Perception and Imaging*, Springer, 1994

[12] Haase, H., Göbel, M., Astheimer, P., Karlsson, K., Schröder, F., Frühauf, Th., Ziegler, R.: *How Scientific Visualization can benefit from Virtual Environments*, CWI Quarterly, The Netherlands, 1994

[13] Haase, H., Strassner, J., Dai, F.: *Virtual Molecules, Rendering Speed, and Image Quality*, in: Göbel, M. (ed): Virtual Environments '95, Springer Verlag, Wien, pp. 70-86, 1995

[14] Haase, H.: *Symbiosis of Virtual Reality and Scientific Visualization System*, Computer Graphics Forum, Vol. 15, No. 3, Proceedings Eurographics '96, Poitiers, France, August 1996

[15] Krüger, W., Bohn, C.-A., Fröhlich, B., Schüth, H., Strauss, W., Wesche, G.: *The Responsive Workbench: A Virtual Work Environment*, Computer, Vol. 28, No. 7, pp. 42-48, July 1995

[16] Lange, S., Schumann, H., Müller, W., Krömker, D.: *Problem-oriented visualization of multi-dimensional data sets*, Proc. International Symposium on Scientific Visualization '95, Chia, Italy, World Scientific Pub., Singapore/London, pp. 1-15, 1995

[17] Rheingans, P.: *Dynamic Exploration of Multiple Variables in a 2D Space*, Ph.D. Thesis at the Department of Computer Science, University of North Carolina at Chapel Hill, 1993

[18] Robertson, P.K., Silver, D.: *Visualization Case Studies: Completing the Loop*, IEEE Gomputer Graphics and Applications, pp. 18-19, July 1995

[19] Rogowitz, B.E., Treinish, L.A.: *Using perceptual rules in interactive visualization*, Proceedings of the IS&T/SPIE Symposium of Electronic Imaging Science and Technology, San Jose, Feb. 1994

[20] Sherman, W.R.: *Integrating Virtual Environments into the Dataflow Paradigm*, Fourth Eurographics Workshop on Visualization in Scientific Computing, Abingdon, UK, April 1993

[21] Treinish, L., Silver, D.: *After the Storm: Considerations for Information Visualization*, IEEE Gomputer Graphics and Applications, pp. 12-15, May 1995

Editors' Note: See Appendix, p. 322 for coloured figures of this paper

CSE
A Modular Architecture for Computational Steering

Robert van Liere

Center for Mathematics and Computer Science
P.O. Box 4097, 1009 AB Amsterdam, The Netherlands

Jarke J. van Wijk

Netherlands Energy Research Foundation ECN
P.O. Box 1, 1755 ZG Petten, The Netherlands

Abstract Computational steering is the ultimate goal of interactive simulation. Steering enables users to supervise and dynamically control the computation of an ongoing simulation. We describe CSE: a modular architecture for a computational steering environment. The kernel of the architecture is designed to be very simple, flexible and minimalistic. All higher level system functionality is pushed into modular components outside of the kernel, resulting in a rich and powerful environment. For these modular components (called satellites) a uniform user interface metaphor for users, based on a tray of cards, has been used. The card tray metaphor is very simple to understand and provides users with a simple mechanism to organize and retrieve the tools. Several applications of the environment are shown.

1 Introduction

Computational steering is the ultimate goal of interactive simulation in which users have direct control over the parameters of a simulation and are able to supervise and dynamically control the computational process. The benefits of computational steering are well known. For example, according to Marshell et al. [1] : "Interaction with the computational model and the resulting graphics display is fundamental in scientific visualization. Steering enhances productivity by greatly reducing the time between changes to model parameters and the viewing of the results".

There are three reasons why software tools for computational steering are more demanding than those found in traditional scientific visualization environments. First, in traditional visualization systems, a visualization expert can first prepare a visualization, which then is analyzed by the scientific user. Inherent to computational steering is that the user will be an active participant in the visualization loop. Furthermore, due to the exploratory nature of steering, these tools will be used iteratively. Hence, tools must be programmable and modifiable during the analysis cycle, preferably by the end users. Second, end users are usually non-professional programmers who have neither the time nor the training to create a new interface. Therefore, the specification and usage of tools must be very simple and hide the underlying complexity of the system. Third, because of the inherent complexity of large scale simulations, effective usage of distributed computing resources must be guaranteed.

In [2] we introduced CSE, an Computational Steering Environment that encourages exploratory investigation by the researcher of an ongoing simulation. The CSE kernel is designed to be very simple, flexible and minimalistic. Although we were able to demonstrate a number of applications, the CSE required substantial knowledge and expertise to use. In particular, it was tedious to develop individual tools and use these tools in concert. In this paper we focus on how original design principles of the CSE are used to overcome these difficulties. The governing concept is the modularity of tools. Instead of extending the CSE kernel, we extend the environment by defining new tools that build upon the basic CSE primitives. These tools provide functionality that is usually hard wired in the kernel of other environments.

In section 2 we summarize the kernel and the underlying concepts of the CSE. In section 3 we present the underlying principles of the visualization tools – called satellites – and discuss the life cycle of a satellite. In section 4, a standard user interface metaphor based on a card tray is introduced. In section 5 the trigger manager satellite is introduced. Trigger management allows users to define the control of satellites. In section 6 we give an example of how all pieces of the CSE fit together. Finally, in section 7 we compare the CSE with other extensible visualization environments.

2 Architecture

An overview of the architecture of the environment is shown in figure 1. The architecture

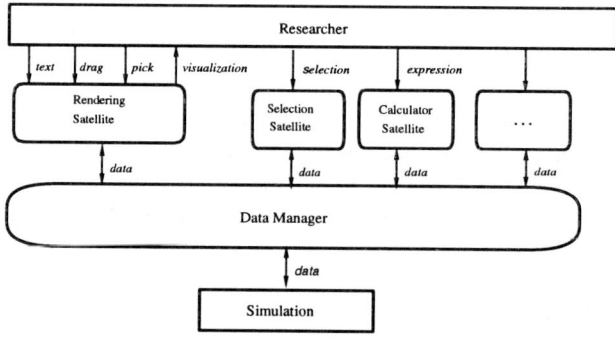

Fig. 1. The CSE architecture

of the environment is centered around a data manager that acts as a blackboard for communicating values, and satellites that produce and visualize data. The purpose of the data manager is twofold. First, it manages a database of variables. Satellites can create, open, close, read, and write variables. For each variable the data manager stores a name, type, and value. Variables can be scalars or arrays. Second, the data manager acts as an event notification manager. Satellites can subscribe to events that represent state changes in the data manager. Whenever such an event occurs the satellite will receive an event from the data manager. For example, if a satellite subscribes to mutation events on a particular variable, the data manager will send a notification to that satellite whenever the value of the variable is mutated.

The foremost satellite is the PGO editor, an interactive graphics editing tool, [3]. The central concept for the graphics editor is the Parametrized Graphics Object (PGO) : an interface is built up from graphics objects whose properties are functions of data in the data manager. Users sketch an interface and bind the graphics objects to variables by parameterizing geometry and attributes with data in the data manager. Simulations may drive the interface by mutating the data bound to the graphics objects. Similarly, users may drive the simulation by interacting with graphics objects. Hence, a two-way communication between graphics and data in the simulation is supported.

The design of the CSE kernel was driven by a number of underlying concepts. First, low-level primitives were used exclusively. The CSE kernel uses a simple data model and graphics objects. The interfaces to these are familiar to the satellite developer and user : a UNIX-like I/O library is the API to the data manager and a MacDraw-like editor for the graphics. Second, no higher level semantics are defined for data and graphics. For example, the data manager provides no support for defining and maintaining data dependencies between variables. As a result, the environment is general and flexible. Third, all operations in both the data manager and the graphics editor are based entirely on data. Dragging, picking and text input are translated into mutations of data. Finally, satellites rely on late binding of variable names. Name matching is used to bind names in a satellite specification to named variables in the data manager. As a result of late binding, it is possible to incrementally define new visualizations of the data output by the simulation, while the simulation continues to run.

We were able to demonstrate a number of applications using the CSE kernel. However, developing satellites was a tedious task. Developers needed to implement all aspects of the interface to the satellite, including the interoperability and user interface, from the low level primitives. Moreover, satellite usage was not straightforward. For example, there was no support for combining satellites into a network of cooperating tools, and each satellite had a different style of interface. In the next section we describe a standard satellite framework that was defined to overcome these problems. The framework defines the behavior of an individual satellite and how it interfaces with its environment. In section 4 we describe the standard user interface for the satellites.

3 Satellite framework

An abstract satellite is shown in figure 2. Basically, it consists of an operator that transforms input data into output data. Control determines when this operation has to be carried out, or, in other words, when a satellite is triggered. By defining control externally, instead of using a fixed, built-in control-strategy, a wide variety of cooperation styles between satellites can be realized. The actual definition of the operation is defined by an additional set of parameters. Parameters are manipulated through the satellites user interface: via predefined widgets or by interactions with geometry within the PGO editor.

Three phases in the life cycle of a satellite are distinguished: *satellite development, edit*

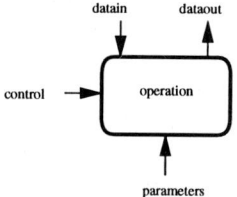

Fig. 2. Interfaces to an abstract satellite.

mode, run mode. During satellite development, a developer will design and implement an operator which may or may not be parameterized. The operator is packaged into a satellite. Examples of operators are a slicer (selection of data), a calculator (calculation of derived data), and the PGO editor (the visualization and user input of data).

In edit mode the user specifies a parameterization of the operator. This is done by entering names for each parameter of the operator. Examples of parameterizations are for the slicer the name of the input variable, the name of the output variable, and the names or values of the slice bounds; for the calculator a mathematical expression; and for the PGO editor a set of graphics objects, parametrized to names of variables.

In run mode the satellite will bind parameter names to values in the data manager. Name matching is used to bind parameter names to named variables in the data manager. Each triggering of the satellite will result in the re-evaluation of the operator with new input data and the effected output values will be written to the data manager. In run mode, the slice operator will be re-evaluated and the output wil be written whenever the input variable or a slice bound is mutated. For the calculator, if a name in the right hand side of the expression is mutated the left hand side is re-evaluated and written. Finally, when a name in the drawing of the PGO editor is mutated, either by changes in the data manager or by interaction on a graphics object, the drawing will be re-rendered. Users will typically iterate a number of times between edit and run mode.

Development and usage of the satellite is simplified through standardization. A satellite development environment is offered, that includes high level libraries and tools that hide the underlying complexities of the satellite's interface. In addition to the development environment, a standard user interface metaphor to a satellite is provided. Standardization on the user interface of the satellite reduces the learning time to operate a satellite.

4 The card tray as a user interface metaphor

All satellites in the CSE adhere to a simple user interface metaphor. The metaphor is a tray of cards, with a browsing mechanism to iterate through the cards. Each tray implements a class of operations and each card represents a particular parameterization of the operation. On the left side of figure 3 the user interface for the slicing satellite is shown. It consists of three panels, of which the top and bottom panel are the same for all satellites. The top panel is responsible for the connection administration with the data manager. Every satellite contains a variable browser and trigger editor. The right side of figure 3 shows the popup panels for the variable browser and trigger editor. The variable browser can be used to define or inspect properties of variables that belong to the satellite. The trigger editor is used to specify variable names that will control the satellite. By default a unique variable name will be generated, but users can change this to any name. The details of triggering and trigger names will be explained in section 5. The bottom panel of the card tray is responsible for the card administration. In edit mode, users can add or delete operators by creating or destroying cards. In run mode, users can browse through the tray and pull cards out of the tray.

The middle panel contains the operator specific user interface. In figure 3 the user interface consists of specifying an input and output variable and a slice name. The slice name itself is parameterized with four variable names and two constants. There are a

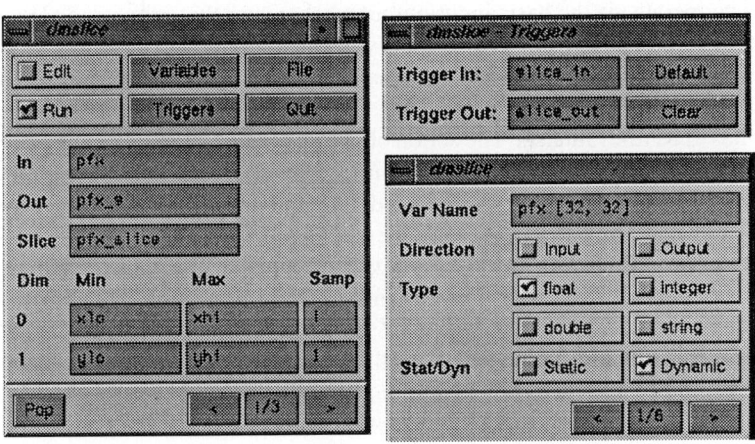

Fig. 3. The slicer card tray with variable and trigger browser.

number of advantages in choosing a simple user interface metaphor :

- Since the interface of the satellite is standardized, the user interface to this functionality is the same for all satellites. Uniform variable and trigger editors are generated giving powerful browsing facilities for names local to each satellite. These editors provide the functionality needed to interface the satellite to the rest of environment. Satellite developers need only to supply the functionality of the operator itself.

- The card tray administration is also standardized. The user interface to this functionality is the same for all satellites and is generated automatically.

- Users have a standardized way of interacting with the functionality provided by the card tray. Only the user interface to the operator must be learned. This facilitates the user's task of learning to use new satellites.

- The use of card trays reduces clutter of the screen. Push and pop functions allow for selective control on the number of simultaneously visible cards. The card tray metaphor is scalable in the number of cards in the tray. Efficient card browsing facilities can help locate individual cards within the tray.

The CSE contains a large collection of general purpose satellites. For example, *dmpgo2D* and *dmpgo3D* are the general purpose graphics editors, *dmslice* allows data selections, *dmannot* is a generalized annotation satellite, *dmcalc* is a calculator for scalar and array values, *dmtrans* is a fourier transformation satellite, *dmtimer* provides a general purpose clock, *dmscheme* is a satellite that interprets Scheme scripts, and *dmlog* logs a history of values. The development time of these satellites was greatly reduced by the standard framework.

5 Trigger manager satellite

Satellites cooperate via the basic input/output mechanisms that are provided by the data manager for variables. Writing to a variable will cause an event to be sent to all satellites subscribed to that variable. This mechanism is used in two ways. First, the user can specify that only if one particular variable, the *input trigger variable* is changed, the operator has to be re-evaluated. The action of operator re-evaluation is called *triggering*. Second, if no such trigger variable is specified, then upon each mutation of any input variable the output variables are re-evaluated. The satellite will subscribe to all its input variables, and every mutation will cause the satellite to re-evaluate the operator.

The user can also specify an *output trigger variable*. This variable is written to each time the operator has been re-evaluated, and can be used to link the control flow for satellites.

Using mutations on data to trigger satellites provides tremendous flexibility. However, this flexibility also introduces additional complexity. Users must provide distinct output trigger names of the producing satellite which, in turn, must match the input name of the consuming satellite. This is not a problem when using a few satellites, but becomes unmanageable when many satellites are involved.

A trigger manager satellite, *dmTM*, has been developed to simplify the definition of trigger variables. The *dmTM* satellite allows users to define triggers by linking two named variables from independent satellites together. When one variable is written, the trigger manager will copy its value to the second variable. The effect is that the satellites owning the second variable will get a mutation event from the data manager. Notice that copying can be potentially inefficient when applied to large data values. In practice, however, only scalar variables will be used as triggers.

Linking two variables defines a data dependency between these two variables. Linking a number of variables results in an undirected graph, which we call the *trigger graph*. Users may build and edit the trigger graph whenever satellites are connected to the data manager. The task of *dmTM* is to manage the trigger graph.

In addition to managing triggers, *dmTM* is used to monitor the flow of data between satellites. This is done by recording the satellite that has written to a variable, resulting in a directed flow dependency graph of write operations on a variable.

The user interface of the trigger manager satellite can be implemented in many ways. However, since the CSE already provides a general purpose graphics editor, the user interface of *dmTM* is implemented as a card in the PGO satellite. A snapshot of the satellite configuration of the smog prediction model discussed in section 6 is shown in the appendix. The nodes of the graph represent the satellites connected to the data manager. The blue edges indicate data flow dependency. A blue arrow indicates a directed data dependency. Green edges indicate the trigger graph. The trigger graph can be edited at any time. The panel on the top right provides additional variable information of a selected satellite. The panel on the bottom is the interface to the trigger graph editor.

The most important advantage in having a satellite, rather than the kernel, manage the trigger and dependency graphs is that synchronization is not intrinsically defined within the kernel of the CSE. Alternative synchronization schemes can be realized by replacing the trigger manager satellite. An additional advantage is that the visual representation and interactions with the underlying data dependency and trigger graph is a card in the PGO editor. The user interface to the graph can be modified at any time.

As an illustration of the functionality provided by *dmTM*, consider the three cases illustrated in figure 4. This typical satellite configuration consists of a simulation satellite, a data mapper satellite and the PGO editor. The time dependent simulation dumps its output to the data manager after every time step. In the configuration on the left, the simulation will run asynchronously with the PGO editor. Data may not be visualized, as the simulation may be dumping data at a higher rate than the mapper or PGO can consume. In the configuration in the middle, the simulation will run synchronously with the PGO editor. The PGO editor will trigger the simulation after it renders one frame. In the configuration on the right, the satellite *dmbutton* will trigger the simulation. *dmbutton* is triggered manually. By editing trigger graph, the user

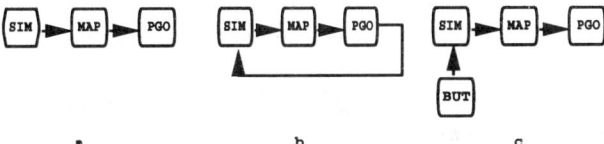

Fig. 4. Three different synchronization configurations.

can switch between the three configurations while the simulation is running. When the simulation is in a non-interesting state, the user may wish to run the simulation asynchronously. When the simulation is in a semi-interesting state, the user may wish to run synchronously. Finally, when the simulation is in a critical state and each time step requires careful study, the user may wish to trigger the simulation manually.

6 Application

The CSE was applied to the simulation of a model for smog prediction over Europe. The full blown model forecasts the levels of air pollution, which is characterized by approximately 104 reactions between ca. 70 species. For example, the concentrations of ozone (O_3), sulphur dioxide (SO_2) and sulphate aerosol (SO_4) are calculated. The vertical stratification is modeled by four layers; the surface layer, the mixing layer, the reservoir layer, and the upper layer. The physical and chemical model is described by a set of partial differential equations that describe advection, diffusion, emission, wet and dry deposition, fumigation, and chemical reactions.

An important numerical utility to solve these equations is local grid refinement. This technique is used to improve the quality of the model calculations in areas with large spatial gradients (for example in regions with strong emissions). The tradeoff to be made in local grid refinement is calculation accuracy versus computation speed.

We have used the CSE to steer various aspects of the smog prediction simulation. We name a few of these aspects: control of the tolerance value that determines where refinement is necessary; editing of the emission data; control over simulation time; and the use of a bounding box as a concentration probe. The coordinates of the bounding box steer the slicing satellite, which in turn triggers the calculator and logging satellites. The result of the logging satellite triggers the PGO editor.

In the appendix a snapshot of a step in the simulation is shown. Satellites can easily be configured to address this question. The graph on the lower left shows a log of the number of cells that were refined and the maximum Courant number. The *dmlog* satellite records the data for display. Hence, the effects of changes on the tolerance or the simulation time will be displayed immediately.

Similarly, average concentration probes of a region of interest can be defined through the combination of the *dmslice*, *dmcalculator* and *dmlog* satellites. The user specifies the region of interest is specified by dragging the red bounding box. *dmslice* slices the region of interest, *dmcalculator* calculates the average of the sliced area, and *dmlog* maintains the log. The log of these variables is plotted in the lower right. Notice that values output from *dmslice*, *dmcalculator*, and *dmlog* are derived variables and are not variables in the simulation. A different operation on the area of interest, for example the maximum concentration, can be plotted by simply changing the expression in *dmcalculator*.

This particular configuration runs at approximately three frames a second on a modern workstation. The amount of data involved is substantial. Depending on tolerance level, the amount of data may vary between one and four megabytes per time step. The simulation has 447 time steps. Approximately 90 percent of the CPU time was taken by the simulation satellite. The remaining 10 percent was used by the other satellites.

7 Comparison with other systems

Many research and development teams have designed and implemented interactive visualization environments. Giving an in depth analysis of other visualization environments is outside the scope of this paper. Instead, we discuss only some issues that resemble those in the CSE. Many of the concepts in this paper have their counterparts in other systems. However, their combination and application to steering is novel.

In data flow environments operators are combined by linking output and input ports. Operators are executed upon availability of data on the input port. Operators are packaged as modules, and most environments provide high level tools for building modules. IRIS Explorer [4] is an example of an advanced data flow visualization environment. However, there are many fundamental differences between IRIS Explorer and CSE. First, direct manipulation is very difficult to achieve in data flow environments.

In IRIS Explorer there is no one-to-one relation between geometry and the corresponding Lattice object in an upstream module. This makes direct manipulation of objects in the simulation very tedious. In contrast, with CSE's binding mechanism direct manipulation is ensured. Second, IRIS Explorer's mechanism to manage data transport differs from CSE's. Global and local controllers are configured as a result of the topology of the data flow map. Finally, in contrast to IRIS Explorer's rigid and hard-wired firing algorithm, CSE's control rules are very flexible and are managed by a satellite. Many other IRIS Explorer functions are built in the run-time system.

VIEW [5] is a system that is based on a tight coupling of on-screen geometry with a database. A data drawing tool allows users to define composite geometric objects by selecting primitive graphical components from the database. In addition, an event-definition mechanism allows the user to customize interaction sequences. A tool scripting language is used to specify these interaction sequences, and simple selection functions are offered to bind names in the scripts to geometry in the database. Event monitors are used to execute scripts. A principle difference between VIEW and CSE is event handling. VIEW provides event monitors to customize interaction sequences. Events in VIEW include changes in input device state and picking of geometry. CSE notion of events is based exclusively on state changes within the data manager. Satellites may receive events by subscribing on the state change.

Spreadsheet Images [6] is a data visualization system based on spreadsheets. Cells may contain graphical objects, widgets, or formulas written in a scripting language. The output of a cell can be referenced by other cells, resulting in a number of dependency relationships between cells. These dependency relationships are represented by a directed acyclic graph which, when a cell is modified, is updated through a predefined firing algorithm. A similar aspect with Spreadsheet images is the strong emphasis of a common user interface metaphor. Spreadsheets are conceptually easy to learn, and the screen space is used very effectively. In contrast, however, CSE groups operators with similar functional behavior in one card tray instead of scattering them throughout the spreadsheet.

GRASPARC [7] has defined a model of a problem solving environment. It defines an architecture in which tools for computation and visualization are embedded in a framework which assists in the management of the problem solving process. A key component in this framework is based on the History Tree concept, which reflects the search process used be a scientist in reaching an optimal solution to a simulation. GRASPARC includes an integral data management facility which allows an audit trail to be recorded. Although both GRASPARC and CSE share the common goal of providing tools for interactive simulation, the approaches and focus are quite different. For example, both environments are modular and open, allowing new tools to be added without much effort. However, GRASPARC has chosen to place substantial emphasis on support of a History Tree concept, allowing a end useer to explore parameter spaces. CSE does not provide such support, although such functionality would be added by developing an additional satellite.

8 Conclusion

CSE is a modular computational steering environment that provides an interface between a researcher and an ongoing simulation. The interface consists a wide range of cooperating satellites that implement various visualization functions. The kernel of the CSE architecture is designed to be very simple, flexible and minimalistic. All higher level functionality is pushed into the satellites, thus ensuring that a rich environment can be developed yet maintaining the simplicity and flexibility of the underlying architecture.

The notion of modular satellites is certainly not new, and has been applied to many visualization environments. However, CSE takes this modularity one step further by defining systems functions in satellites. These system functions, which are usually hard-wired in the runtime systems of other visualization environments, can be tailored to meet the specific needs of the simulation environment. We presented *dmTM* as an example of a systems satellite.

We have presented a standard user interface metaphor for all satellites. The card tray can be viewed as a generic operator and individual cards are viewed as parameterizations of the operator. The card tray is easy to understand since it provides an intuitive metaphor for organizing and retrieving cards.

References

[1] R.E. Marshall, J.L. Kempf, D. Scott Dyer, and C-C Yen. Visualization Methods and Simulation Steering a 3D Turbulence Model of Lake Erie. *1990 Symp. on Interactive 3D Graphics, Computer Graphics*, 24(2):89–97, 1990.

[2] J.J. van Wijk and R. van Liere. An Environment for Computational Steering. Technical Report CS-R9448, Centre for Mathematics and Computer Science (CWI), 1994. Presented at the Dagstuhl Seminar on Scientific Visualization, 23-27 May 1994, Germany, proceedings to be published.

[3] J. Mulder and J.J. van Wijk. 3D Computational Steering with Parameterized Graphics Objects. In *Proceedings Visualization '95*. IEEE Computer Society Press, Los Alamitos, CA, 1995.

[4] Explorer Development Team. Iris Explorer 2.0 Module Writer's Guide. Technical Report 007-1369-020, Silicon Graphics Inc, 1993.

[5] L. Bergman, J. Richardson, D. Richardson, and F. Brooks Jr. VIEW – An Exploratory Molecular Visualization System with User-Definable Interaction Sequences. *Computer Graphics*, 27(6 (SIGGRAPH '93)):117–126, 1993.

[6] M. Levoy. Spreadsheets for Images. *Computer Graphics*, 28(6 (SIGGRAPH '94)):139–146, 1994.

[7] K. Brodlie, A. Poon, H. Wright, L. Brankin, G. Banecki, and A. Gay. Grasparc - A Problem Solving Environment Integrating Computation and Visualization. In *Proceedings Visualization '93*, pages 102–109. IEEE Computer Society Press, Los Alamitos, CA, 1993.

Editors' Note: See Appendix, p. 323 for coloured figures of this paper

The Dataflow Visualization Pipeline as a Problem Solving Environment

Helen Wright[†], Ken Brodlie[†] and Martin Brown[‡]

[†]School of Computer Studies, University of Leeds, Leeds LS2 9JT, UK
Email: helenw, kwb@scs.leeds.ac.uk
[‡]British Gas plc, Gas Research Centre, Ashby Road, Loughborough LE11 3QU, UK
Email: martin.brown@bggrc.co.uk

Abstract. Visualization systems based on the dataflow paradigm are enjoying increasing popularity in the field of scientific computation. Not only do they permit rapid construction of a display application, but they also allow the simulation to be incorporated, giving the scientist the opportunity to interact with the calculation as well. However, if these systems are to realise their full potential for problem solving, additional support must be given for the iterative investigation which characterises this activity. This paper will review these systems, identify some of their shortcomings as problem solving environments and describe current work which addresses these deficiencies. An implementation of our ideas for the IRIS Explorer system will demonstrate their effectiveness in a study of gas turbine exhaust emissions.

1 Introduction

Visualization has been a tool of the computational scientist from the time of the first mainframes, through the rise and fall of the minicomputer and nowadays in conjunction with powerful desktop workstations. In the early days programs would run overnight, outputting a file of results which in turn was processed by a specially-written graphics program. But with the change in computing environment has also come a change in our way of working; the trend has been to move away from application-specific visualization in favour of re-usable software packages and, most recently, towards the so-called Modular Visualization Environments (MVEs).

This paper will give an overview of these systems – what they offer in visualization and, moreover, as Problem Solving Environments (PSEs). We then identify some of their shortcomings in this respect and describe current work to extend one such system. The tools developed will be demonstrated in a case study taken from reaction chemistry and the paper concludes with some possibilities for future work.

1.1 Modular visualization environments

Cameron [1] gives a useful summary of what constitutes an MVE – all tend to consist of building blocks, or modules, performing separate functions. Blocks are connected by links, typically within a visual programming environment, so that together they describe the series of transformations the data will undergo. These systems allow visualization program development without programming knowledge, though there is still a learning curve involved in their use. Four visualization systems in common usage can be classed as MVEs; these are AVS [2], IRIS Explorer [3], IBM Data Explorer [4] and Khoros [5].

A key feature of MVEs which contributes to their growing popularity in scientific computing is their extensibility, allowing the simulation process to be incorporated into the environment and the results delivered directly into the visualization pipeline. Mathematical parameters can be implemented as widgets on the simulation module, giving the opportunity to steer [6, 7] the calculation and perhaps halt part-way if the visualized results so indicate.

MVEs make use of the dataflow paradigm [8, 9], where processes are categorised as performing filter, map or render functions. Input data can be read in or generated within the environment if steering a calculation. The original dataflow model is an excellent paradigm for visualization but has limitations as an environment for problem solving. One is the inherently uni-directional flow which makes it difficult to query data held at, say, the filter stage, by interacting with a render process. Another is the difficulty in preserving previous states of the pipeline during the iterative solution of a problem – for example, when comparing results with those from an earlier run employing different parameters.

As MVEs develop there have been improvements made which can be seen as an extension of the dataflow model. For example, envisioning data flowing upstream as well as downstream is the basis of current systems' image probing capabilities; that is, display functions which return a geometric position to an earlier visualization process in order to retrieve data values. Likewise, facilities to perform animations by varying process parameters in sequence can be thought of as adding loop constructs to the dataflow model.

Both of these extensions go some way towards supporting the iterative process which is inherent in problem solving, but even modern MVEs fall short of the comprehensive facilities which are needed for this activity. Steering applications of the type described remain a rarity and MVEs tend not to be used as PSEs – hence the motivation for our current work.

1.2 GRASPARC

GRASPARC (GRAphical Support for PARallel Computing [10]) looked at the way an investigation progressed and put forward the history tree as a model for computational problem solving. The objective was to record information (input parameters and output results) as the simulation progressed, so that the calculation could be stopped at any stage and rolled-back to some previous point. Here a modified set of parameters could be specified based on the recorded set, and the simulaton restarted. This created a branch point in the tree. An important feature was that the *tree as well as the data* was recorded, providing an audit of how the problem had been tackled.

GRASPARC treated the simulation and visualization processes as external to a central, invariant core of software which provided the tree-oriented database and user interface. Interaction by the scientist was by means of the tree – for example, "start a new branch here", "halt this branch", "start a new tree" and so on (Figure 1). Given the chosen architecture, it followed that GRASPARC

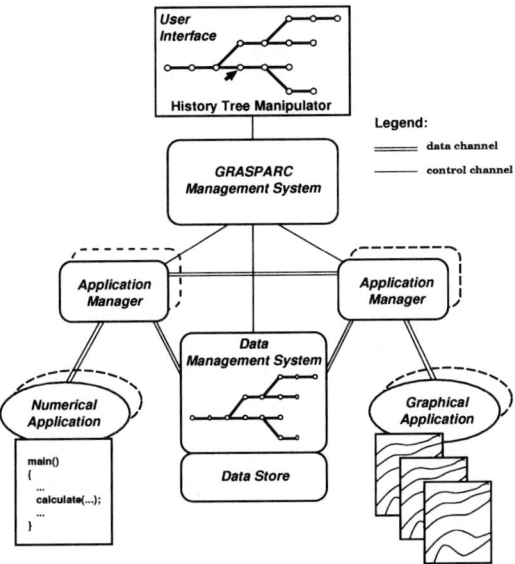

Fig. 1. The GRASPARC Architecture

adopted its own data model, so Application Managers were needed to convert the external numerical and visualization formats into GRASPARC format.

A number of demonstrators were constructed during the GRASPARC project to demonstrate the validity of the approach and some of these used MVEs as their visualization component. The problems tackled ranged from computational physics, computational fluid dynamics and planetary motion [10], to reaction chemistry [11]. Whilst successful in terms of their problem solving approach, a considerable development effort was needed to construct the Application Managers and configure these demonstrators. The thrust of our current work, therefore, has been to find a more accessible means of delivering this type of support to potential users.

2 HyperScribe - problem solving support for dataflow

Brodlie and Wright [12] describe a number of ways of delivering this support. One suggestion is to turn the GRASPARC architecture 'inside out', that is, instead of having an MVE attached to the GRASPARC framework, we could put GRASPARC functionality inside the MVE. We have investigated what this entails within the dataflow paradigm and have implemented a first version for IRIS Explorer in the form of the HyperScribe module. Wright and Walton [13] furnish a detailed description of the implementation – here we give just a brief overview in order to present our case study.

2.1 Architecture

GRASPARC functioned by passing messages between the various components so that the central management system could direct the attached applications

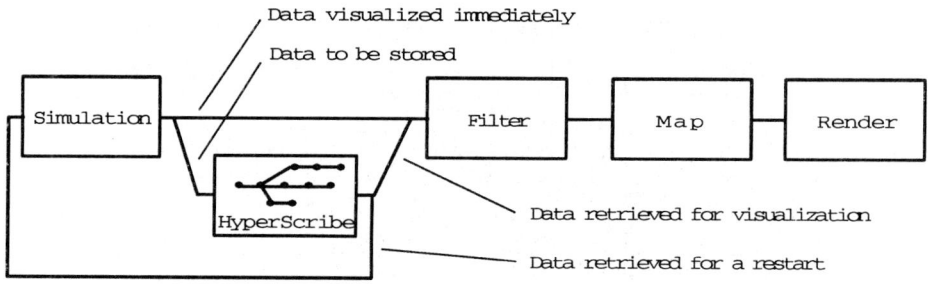

Fig. 2. The HyperScribe architecture

to perform tree-building operations. For example, if the user wanted to compute a new branch, the data store would be requested to provide the restart data and pass it to the computational part, which in turn would generate new data to be passed back to the data store. The processes in a dataflow system, however, are activated only when new data arrives; the potential for directing the flow of data is thus very limited by comparison with a GRASPARC system.

As we might expect in a dataflow environment, the key to resolving this difficulty is to concentrate on the data rather than the tree operations. HyperScribe has therefore been designed around the concept of data inputs and data outputs, as the architecture in Figure 2 shows.

The price paid for this simplification is that the user must decide which data sets to store and how to place them to form the tree – functions that were formerly carried out by the GRASPARC management system. Similarly the user must decide which data sets to retrieve and how to route them to other modules in order to effect a computation restart, or to perform visualization of previously computed data.

2.2 Implementation

The IRIS Explorer implementation of this architecture consists of two parts: the first part is the HyperScribe module itself which deals with the storage of the data and the physical representation of the tree. The second part is a dedicated Render module which draws the tree and handles the user's interaction with it when they specify which data to store or retrieve. Communication between the two is by means of the Geometry and Pick datatypes. Data inputs to the HyperScribe part are implemented as text slots on the left of the user interface panel, whilst the corresponding data outputs appear as text slots on the right hand side. The two modules can be grouped together if desired, as shown in Figure 3.

Data and problem independence. Using text slots within HyperScribe rather than integers, floats or doubles ensures that *any* type of scalar parameter can be stored since all are first converted to a character string. A slot may also be used to record some comment typed in directly by the scientist to describe the current state of the experiment. For non-scalars such as lattices, pyramids, images or geometry the data must first be passed through a WriteLat, WritePyr, WriteImg or WriteGeom module to generate a file – only the file name need then be stored by HyperScribe. Furthermore, when HyperScribe is first launched in

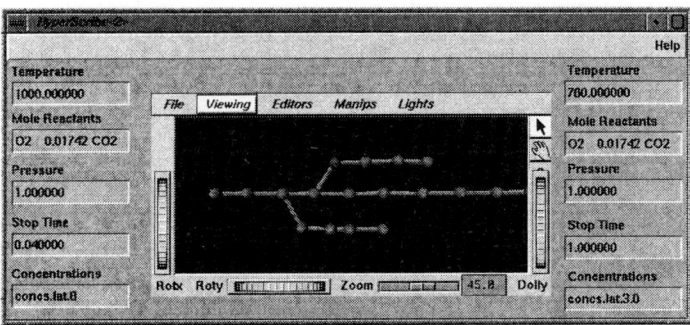

Fig. 3. The HyperScribe/Render module combination

the map the user is given the opportunity to re-label the text slots however they wish, so the module is completely problem-independent.

Data capture and retrieval. HyperScribe's set of input text slots capture parameter values and the file names of any associated data sets delivered from the upstream simulation. The dataflow model ensures that each new occurrence upstream is delivered to HyperScribe immediately it is generated, but the final decision on whether to record the information rests with the experimenter. If it is to be recorded, an *add* event is signalled at an appropriate point on the tree. This is received by HyperScribe, which enters the input information into its database and generates a sphere as the physical representation of this stored data set. The location of the sphere is determined by the coordinates of the mouse cursor when the event was generated. Pairs of spheres can be linked together by cylinders in order to develop the tree structure.

Subsequent retrieval of the information is by interaction with its representative sphere. When a *retrieve* event is specified for a sphere, the stored information is found in the database and delivered to the set of output text slots, from where it can either flow down the map for visualization, or upstream to restart some computation process. Since retrieved data flows immediately from the text slots as soon as it is delivered, we have also found it useful to implement an *inform* event. This behaves just like *retrieve* but delivers values to the input side of HyperScribe's interface. Thus it is possible to browse the tree to find a particular data set before committing the information to flow into the map.

The database exists in shared memory whilst the module is running but HyperScribe also allows for it to be written to file between sessions. When the module is restarted the user is given the option to continue with a previous experiment, or to start afresh.

3 Case Study

Our case study is taken from the field of chemical kinetics, where the computational task is to determine the time-varying concentrations of a number of chemical species taking part in a reaction. The system is modelled as a set of ordinary differential equations, one for each species plus possibly temperature and pressure.

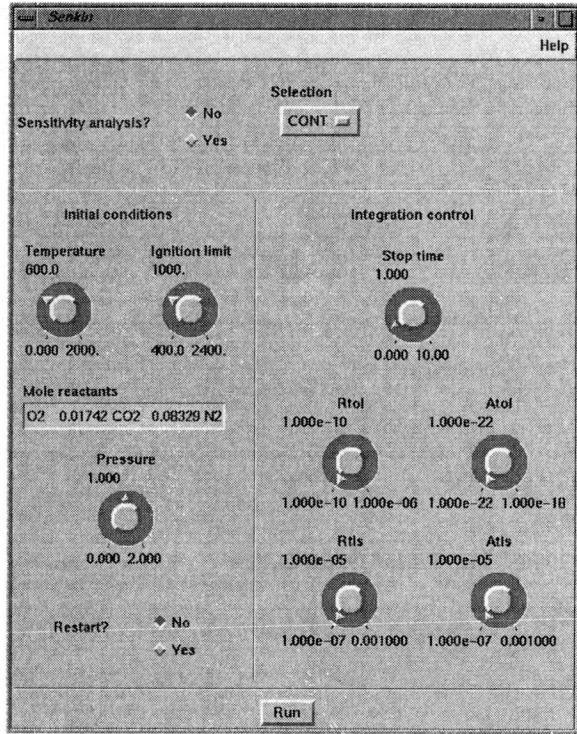

Fig. 4. The SENKIN module user interface panel

3.1 Computation component

The physical process being modelled is the combustion of fuel in gas turbine based Combined Heat and Power systems, with particular reference to the impact on different exhaust gas concentrations of changes in operating conditions [14]. In this paper we will pay particular attention to the conversion of NO to NO_2 at different initial temperatures of the gas mixture, since the relative concentrations of these are significant when considering emission limits for such systems.

The computation component has been developed from the SENKIN program distributed as part of the CHEMKIN system [15] by Sandia National Laboratories, California. For this study we have implemented SENKIN as an IRIS Explorer module which can be used in the Map Editor along with any of the system-provided modules. SENKIN's original keyword input file has been replaced by a user interface panel with interactive widgets (Figure 4), whilst the output results comprising species concentrations and sensitivities are generated in the form of the IRIS Explorer lattice datatype. The user specifies their problem by altering widget values and starts the computation by pressing the *Run* button. Once the integration is completed the results flow down the map and are visualized immediately. Experimentation with the input parameters is very easy – for instance, a sequence of time traces (plots of species concentrations *vs.* time) at various temperatures can be created and visualized within just a few minutes.

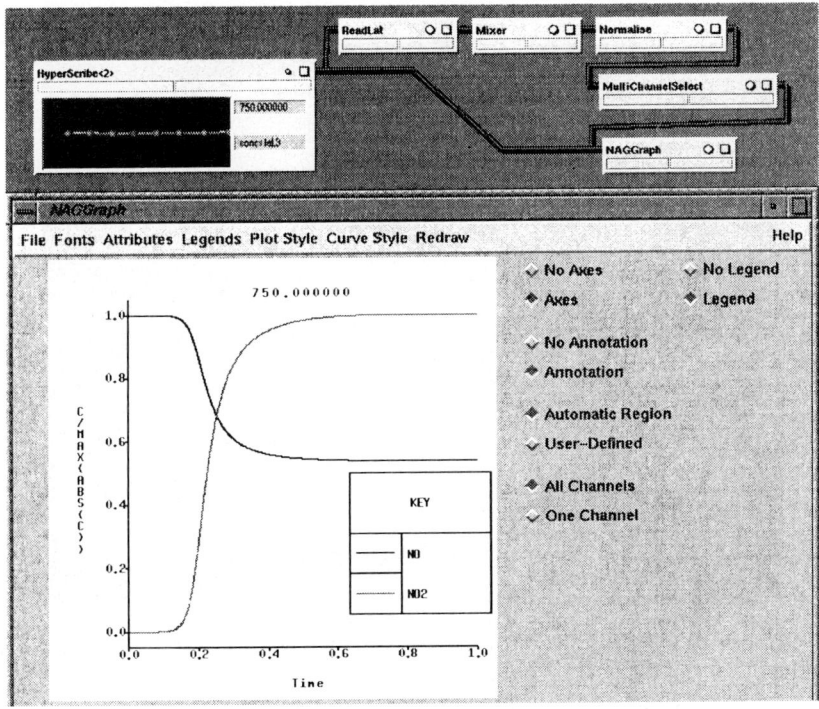

Fig. 5. Offline visualization of time series plots

3.2 Problem solving support

Having made a quick pass through the time traces for a number of temperature values, the experiments are re-run in a systematic way using HyperScribe to record the initial gas composition, temperature increasing by 50K intervals, pressure and the file name in which the corresponding lattice of results is recorded.

In figure 5 HyperScribe has been combined with its Render module to give a simplified composite interface, where only the retrieved temperature and file name parameters are exported to the map. The upper connection carries the file name to the standard ReadLat module, whose lattice output then flows into the visualization pipeline. The lower connection carries the corresponding temperature value used to title the plot. Using HyperScribe's data retrieval facility we can thus traverse the tree to bring back the results and view them offline in *flipbook* style.

Individual SENKIN outputs represent species concentrations as a function of time, whilst the axis of the tree in Figure 5 can be thought of as denoting the changing temperature parameter. It follows that if we now combine a number of datasets from the tree, the composite result will represent concentrations as a function of time *and* temperature. We achieve this using a module called DaisyChain, which has been written to concatenate recalled lattices. The user moves along the tree specifying *retrieve* events for the required datasets, and once the traverse is completed a Switch is opened to pass the data into a contour module (Figure 6).

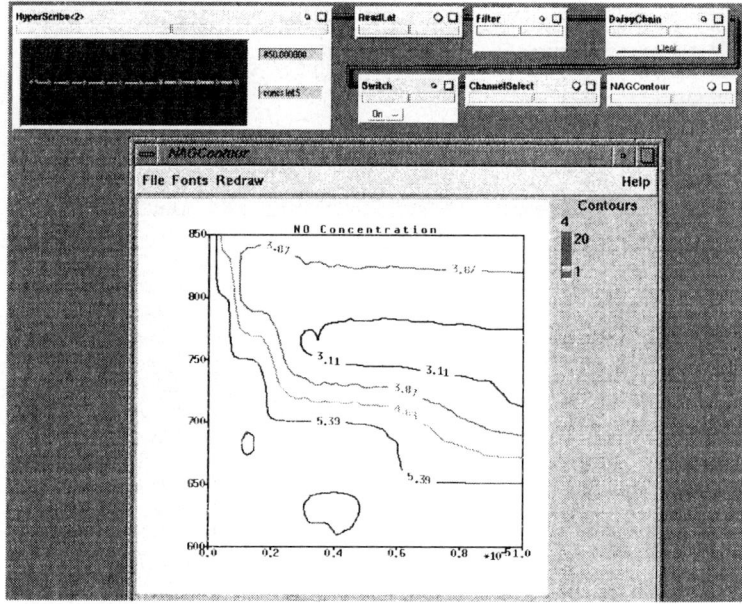

Fig. 6. Concatenating data sets to make a 2D plot (NB. the 'Filter' module in this map is just a collection of three standard modules grouped together for greater clarity)

3.3 Results

Figure 6 shows the contour plot of NO concentration resulting from the original experiment specifying temperatures at 50K intervals. The area of greatest interest is a region of low NO concentration (and correspondingly high NO_2 concentration) lying between 700 and 800K, which is worthy of investigation at a greater resolution of the temperature parameter. However, no data is available so HyperScribe is used to reset the SENKIN module parameters for the 700K experiment. The temperature is increased to 710K, new data is generated at 10K intervals and is recorded by HyperScribe alongside the original data. To reinforce the idea of having re-run the simulation in order to insert data, the new data sets are recorded as a branch rooted at the original 700K set. The process is repeated from 800K and once the requisite area of data has been 'filled in', the tree is traversed again to create the composite data for NAGContour, but this time including the branched data. Figure 7 shows the new tree and set of contours, with the minimum of NO concentration now clearly pinpointed.

4 Conclusions and further work

An architecture for problem solving support within a dataflow environment has been proposed and an implementation demonstrated in the IRIS Explorer MVE. Results from the case study show that the resulting module is readily incorporated into the visualization pipeline and that complex sequences of parameters and results can be managed using it.

Future work will include developments to HyperScribe, such as a facility to

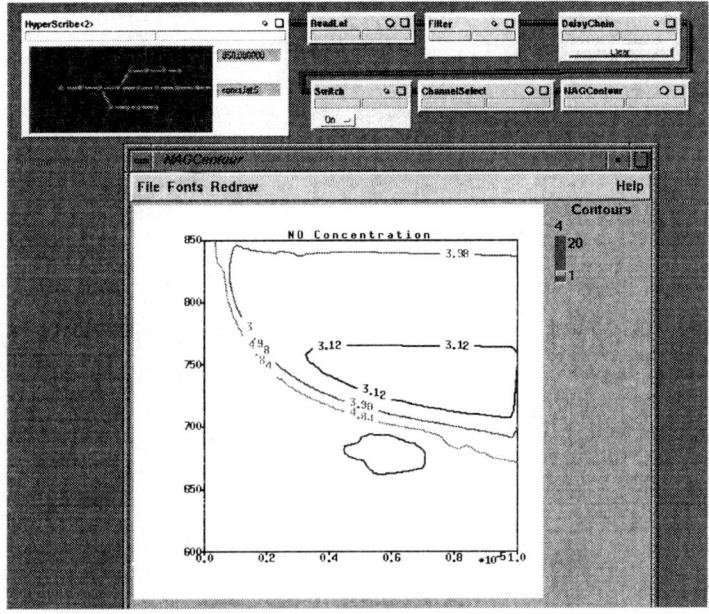

Fig. 7. A 2D plot with new data between 700 and 800K

delete stored information, and the addition of further tools like the DaisyChain module to collate data sets retrieved from the tree. We are also working with the COVISA project [16] at the University of Leeds, which is developing collaborative visualization facilities, and are investigating the potential of paradigms other than the history tree for problem solving.

Acknowledgements

Helen Wright gratefully acknowledges the support of NAG Ltd in carrying out this work. We are also indebted to colleagues in the School of Chemistry at the University of Leeds, in particular Professor Mike Pilling for his interest and encouragement; to the IRIS Explorer team at NAG Ltd, especially Jeremy Walton for assistance with technical aspects; and to British Gas plc for permission to use the case study. Finally, many people contributed to the GRASPARC project, without which the present work would have had no proper foundation.

References

1. Gordon Cameron. Modular visualization environments: Past, present and future. *Computer Graphics*, 29(2):3–4, 1995.
2. Hambleton D. Lord. Improving the application development process with modular visualization environments. *Computer Graphics*, 29(2):10–12, 1995.
3. David Foulser. IRIS explorer: A framework for investigation. *Computer Graphics*, 29(2):13–16, 1995.

4. Greg Abram and Lloyd Treinish. An extended data-flow architecture for data analysis and visualization. *Computer Graphics*, 29(2):17–21, 1995.

5. Mark Young, Danielle Argiro, and Steven Kubica. Cantata: Visual programming environment for the Khoros system. *Computer Graphics*, 29(2):22–24, 1995.

6. R. Marshall, J. Kempf, S. Dyer, and C. Yen. Visualization methods and simulation steering for a 3D turbulence model for Lake Erie. *ACM SIGGRAPH Computer Graphics*, 24(2):89–97, 1990.

7. G.D. Kerlick and E. Kirby. Towards interactive steering, visualization and animation of unsteady finite element simulations. In G.M. Nielson and D. Bergeron, editors, *Proceedings of IEEE Visualization 1993 Conference*, pages 374–377, Los Alamitos, CA, 1993. IEEE Computer Society Press.

8. C. Upson, T. Faulhaber, D. Kamins, D. Laidlaw, D. Schlegel, J. Vroom, R. Gurwitz, and A. van Dam. The Application Visualization System : A computational environment for scientific visualization. *IEEE Computer Graphics and Applications*, 9(4):30–42, 1989.

9. R.B. Haber and D.A. McNabb. Visualization idioms : A conceptual model for scientific visualization systems. In B. Shriver G.M. Nielson and L.J. Rosenblum, editors, *Visualization in Scientific Computing*, pages 74–93. IEEE, 1990.

10. Ken Brodlie, Lesley Brankin, Greg Banecki, Alan Gay, Andrew Poon, and Helen Wright. GRASPARC: A problem solving environment integrating computation and visualization. In G.M. Nielson and D. Bergeron, editors, *Proceedings of IEEE Visualization 1993 Conference*, pages 102–109, Los Alamitos, CA, 1993. IEEE Computer Society Press.

11. H. Wright, G.A. Stead, and K. W. Brodlie. Interactive exploration of chemical reaction mechanisms using novel visualization and integration techniques. In M. Göbel, H. Müller, and B. Urban, editors, *Visualization in Scientific Computing*, Eurographics, pages 166–173. Springer-Verlag, 1995.

12. Ken Brodlie and Helen Wright. From a Modular Visualization Environment to an environment for computational problem solving. *Computer Graphics*, 29(2):29–32, 1995.

13. H. Wright and J.P.R.B. Walton. HyperScribe: A data management facility for the dataflow visualization pipeline. IRIS Explorer Technical Report IETR/4, NAG Ltd, 1996.

14. M.J. Brown, D.P. Graham, B. Strugnell, and R.M. Davies. Environmental impact of gas turbine CHP systems. In *Proceedings of 1995 International Gas Research Conference*, pages 491–500. Vol. V Industrial Utilisation, 1995.

15. R.J. Kee and J.A. Miller. A structured approach to the computational modelling of chemical kinetics and molecular transport in flowing sustems. Technical Report SAND86-8841, Sandia National Laboratories, Livermore, California, Reprinted 1993.

16. Jason Wood, Helen Wright, and Ken Brodlie. CSCV - Computer Supported Collaborative Visualization. In *Proceedings of BCS Displays Group International Conference on Visualization and Modelling*, 1995.

Unhiding Hidden Markov Models by Their Visualization (Application in Speech Processing)

Daniel Hajek, Jan Nouza

Department of Electronics and Signal Processing, Technical University of Liberec
Halkova 6, 461 17 Liberec 1, Czech republic

Abstract: The hidden Markov model (HMM) technique has become very popular in the signal and data processing areas during the last 10 years. It is not easy, however, to understand its complex nature that is 'hidden' behind a 'veil' of two probability functions, one associated with the given space of data parameters and the other with the temporal data flow. Our system, named Visual Markov, aims at removing the veil by visualizing the continuous density HMM and displaying its individual states. Moreover, it is able to show the iterative process of HMM training, step after step. In a similar way, also the HMM based classification can be presented. The system is a highly illustrative tool that is well suited both for research and teaching purposes. In the article, we demostrate its application in the speech recognition domain.

1. Introduction

The hidden Markov model (HMM) technique [1,2] has been used in data and signal processing since 1970s. Nowadays, its largest application domain seems to be speech recognition, where its introduction in mid 1980s meant a breakthrough toward more accurate and more reliable voice-input systems.

Most of the recent speech recognition systems are based on continuous density hidden Markov models (CDHMM). The CDHMM relies on continuous probability functions rather than on discrete distributions as it was in the older, discrete, version of the HMMs. A practical implementation of this technique, however, is not an easy job. That is why several development kits for building and investigating CDHMM systems have been designed. Some of them are commercially available, e.g. the HTK software by Entropic [3]. These kits are widely used, particularly, at universities for teaching and research purposes.

The development kits offer their users many advantages; allowing them an easy design of an experimental recognition system and providing them by testing data as well as by scoring tools. A student or a researcher can start first experiments shortly after reading a manual. What most of the users really miss, however, is a deeper knowledge of the modelling technique itself and better understanding of what actually happens when a model is being trained or used in classification. Thus the substance of the HMM and the events inside the models remain 'hidden' for many people who employ this popular technique in a black-box manner.

Learning more about the CDHMMs is not just a matter of understanding the theoretical foundations of the HMMs but also the only way to make any improvements in HMM recognition systems. On the other side, it is quite difficult to investigate the model internal structure, mainly because of its non-trivial formal description, many parameters and complex evaluation algorithms. Up to the authors' knowledge, neither an educational tool nor an HMM study system offering an insight into the heart of the models has been presented yet.

In order to cover this gap we have developed a system called Visual Markov. It is primarily aimed at graphic presentation of the CDHMMs. The system enables its user a detailed investigation of individual states in a so called *left-to-right model*, i.e. in the form that is standardly used in word modelling. The graphically oriented software displays both the multi-dimensional state ouput functions as well as the state-to-state transitions. Animated time snaps offer a highly illustrative picture of dynamic processes that take place inside the model during its training or matching with an unknown word. A wide range of system options allows to conduct various comparative experiments, which gives the user answers on many frequently asked questions about the CDHMM nature. The system may also serve as a helpful research tool for analysing and improving the performance of a practical recogniser.

The article is laid out in the following way: The next section gives a brief overview of the hidden Markov model technique and its application in speech recognition. In sections 3 and 4, essential basic tasks of the Visual Markov software are presented; namely the training of a model and testing the model. Some implementation issues are briefly dealt in section 5. In the concluding part we mention the system evaluation that has been done both in our lab as well as at several other institutions abroad.

2. HMM and speech recognition

The main problem in speech recognition is a very high level of variability in speech signals, both in the time and frequency domain. This is caused by the large speaking-style variability among people as well as by many other factors, like different microphone and input-device transfer characteristics, environment noise, etc. This variability must be handled by a sophisticated statistical approach. This is just the case of the hidden Markov model technique.

2.1 Models for discrete-utterance recognition

Let us introduce the HMM approach on a discrete-utterance recognition (DUR) task, a simplified subtask of the general speech recognition problem. Within the DUR, an utterance (either a single word or a word sequence) is spoken separately, i.e. it is preceded and followed by short pauses. Each vocabulary utterance has got its model in the recognition system. The system classifies an unknown utterance by matching its parametric representation with all the models. The goal is to find the most likely match.

transition and output probabilities. From outside we may but guess the process inside the model and have to rely on a maximum likelihood estimation.

2.2 Recognition with the HMMs

Within the recognition process, a measure of similarity between the classified utterance and each of the models is evaluated. The measure has a meaning of the likelihood that the utterance, represented by the vector **X**, is generated by the given Markov model. The log likelihood of model Ψ is evaluated for the most probable state sequence Q^* that is determined using the Viterbi algorithm [2]:

$$\ln P(\mathbf{X}|\Psi) = \sum_{f=1}^{F} (\ln a_{q_{f-1}q_f} + \ln b_{q_f})], \quad \text{where } q_f \in Q^* \text{ and } a_{q_0 q_1} = 1 \quad (3)$$

The likelihood measure is calculated for each of the N models representing the complete vocabulary. Finally, the utterance is classified as belonging to model n^*, when:

$$n^* = \arg\max_{n=1...N} P(\mathbf{X}|\Psi_n) \quad (4)$$

i.e. if the match between the **X** and model Ψ_{n^*} yields the maximum likelihood score.

2.3 Training the HMMs

While the classification itself is not so difficult problem, creating the models is a much more complex task. If we want the model to represent all the variabilities of the given utterance, we must train the model on a large material. Usually some tens of samples of the same utterance spoken by different speakers are needed to produce a good model.

The goal of the training is to estimate the parameters **A**, **w**, **X̄** a **C** by applying the maximum likelihood estimation (MLE) principle. It consists in the search for the parameter values that maximize the sum of likelihoods computed (by eq. (3)) for all the training data. Generally, the search is performed in two phases: 1) initial estimation and 2) reestimation. In each of the phases several iterative steps are necessary until the parameters reach a stable state. For the reestimation, the well known Baum-Welch algorithm [2] is used.

3. Visualization of the training process

A researcher or a student involved in training a continuous density hidden Markov model usually asks several essential questions:

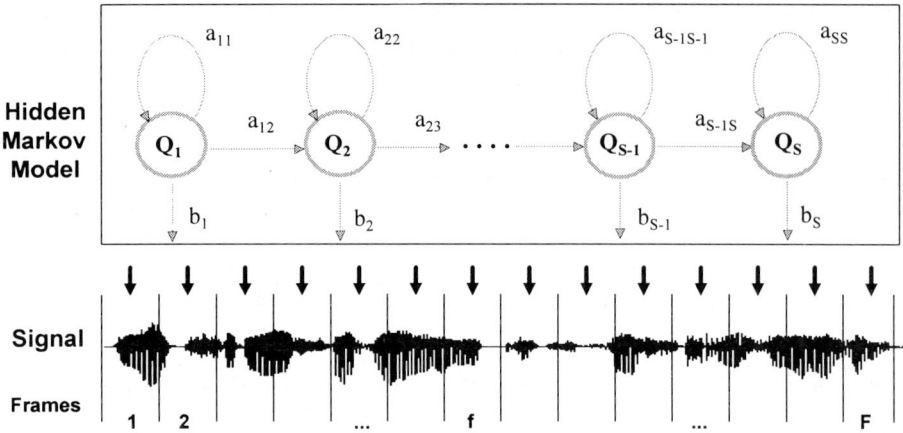

Fig. 1. A speech signal assumed as being generated by a left-to-right HMM

In a standard speech processing system, the utterance to be classified is represented by multi-dimensional vector $\mathbf{X} = (\mathbf{x}_1, \ldots \mathbf{x}_f, \ldots \mathbf{x}_F)$ consisting of F frame vectors $\mathbf{x}$, each being composed of P signal features $\mathbf{x} = (x_1, \ldots x_p, \ldots x_P)$. Using the hidden Markov model approach we suppose that vector $\mathbf{X}$ has been generated by a model with the simple left-to-right structure shown in Fig.1. Such a model has S states interconnected by transition paths that are either self-loops or moves to the adjacent state. The transitions are described by their probabilities a_{ij}:

$$a_{ij} = \text{Prob}(q_t = Q_j | q_{t-1} = Q_i) \qquad (1)$$

Each state generates an output that is characterised by state output function b_s. In the case of the CDHMM, the output is a continuous probability density function defined as a mixture of M normal distributions:

$$b_s(\mathbf{x}) = \sum_{m=1}^{M} \frac{w_{sm}}{\sqrt{(2\pi)^P \det \mathbf{C}_{sm}}} \cdot \exp[-\tfrac{1}{2}(\mathbf{x} - \bar{\mathbf{x}}_{sm})^T \mathbf{C}_{sm}^{-1}(\mathbf{x} - \bar{\mathbf{x}}_{sm})] \qquad (2)$$

In most of the practical DUR systems, the models belonging to individual utterances have the same number of states. The utterance-specific characteristics are stored in the matrix of transition probabilities $\mathbf{A} = \{a_{ij}\}$ and in the output function parameters $\bar{\mathbf{x}}_{sm}$ (the mean), $\mathbf{C}_{sm}$ (the covariance matrix) and w_{sm} (the mixture-weighting factor). All these parameters must be estimated during a model training procedure.

Let us explain the attribute 'hidden' in the method's name. As indicated in Fig. 1, there is no straightforward correspondence between the speech signal frames and the model states. In general, each state can generate any of the frame vectors. The model itself is hidden behind a double 'veil' made of two uncertainities represented by the

- How do the output probability functions in each state look like?
- What happens to the output and transition probabilities during the training procedure?
- How much does the model likelihood change during the training phases?
- How much do the models with different numbers of states and mixtures differ each from other?
- How much do the models trained on different amount of speech material differ?
- How much do the models of different utterances differ each from other?, etc.

All these questions can be easily answered when the model is visualized. In our system this is accomplished by the Visual Markov I program. It performs and displays the CDHMM training procedure. An example of its graphic output is in Fig. 2.

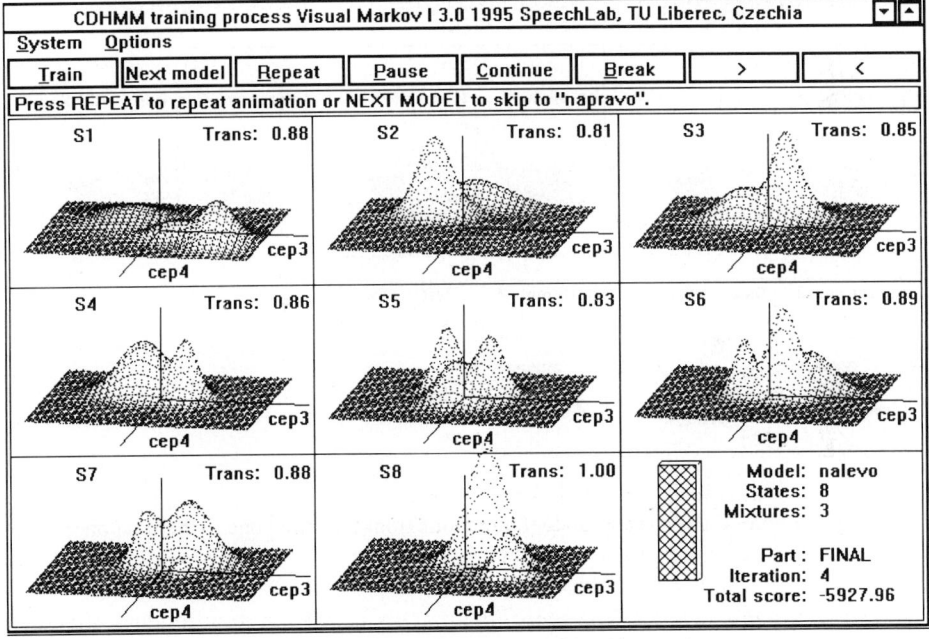

Fig. 2. Visualization of a model that is being trained

In the figure we can see an 8-state 3-mixture model trained for Czech word „nalevo" („left"). Each state has its own window where the output pdf is displayed as a function of two optionally selected signal features. In Fig. 2, the pdf values (z-axis) are plotted for two of the 8 cepstral coefficients ($cep3$ along the x-axis and $cep4$ along the y-axis). In the upper right corner of each of the windows, the probability of staying in the state is shown. The last window gives an overview of the running training process by displaying the current process status, the iteration counter and the total likelihood score.

The user can choose from a wide range of options. The system options, like the choice of the database and the vocabulary, the amount of the training data, the number of features representing the speech signal, the features to be displayed, the 3D plot parameters, as well as the complete choice of model parameters, are available. Additional facilities, like the run, pause, step, backstep buttons allow the user to control the training and the animation. An example of the time evolution of the model state parameters is shown in Fig. 3.

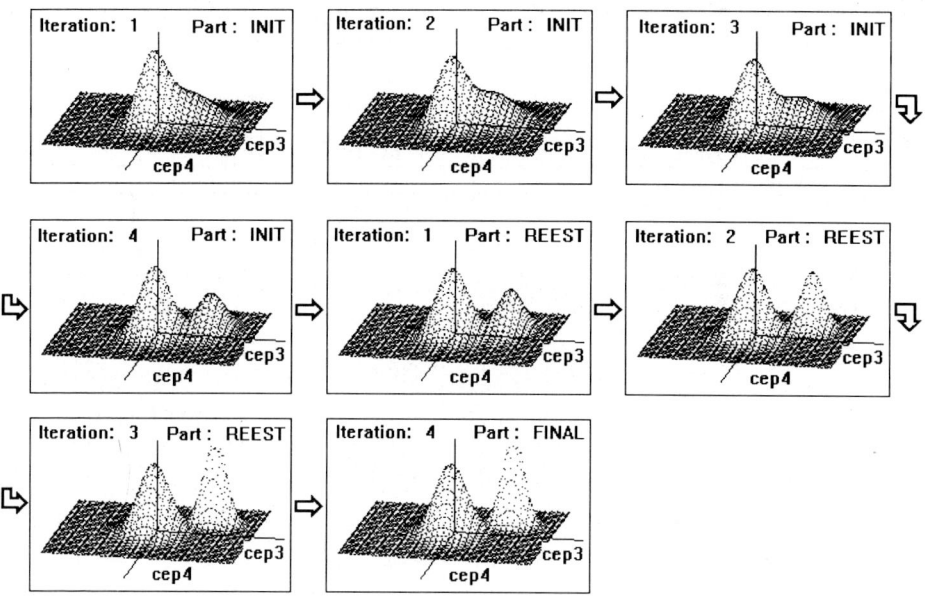

Fig. 3. Evolution of a model state (8 iterations from the initial one to the final one)

4. Visualization of the HMM matching process

As mentioned in section 2, the recognition of an unknown utterance consists in a series of matches between the parametric representation of the utterance and the models. Again, one involved in the HMM investigation may ask several essential questions, like:

- Which states are assigned to the utterance frames by the Viterbi decoder?
- What is the difference between matching the correct and a wrong model?

- How does the matching score evolve during the Viterbi procedure?
- What is the difference between matching models with different model parameters?, etc.

The second of the Visual Markov package programs, the Visual Markov II, has been designed to assist in answering the above stated questions. Its screen, very similar to that described in the previous section, is shown in Fig. 4.

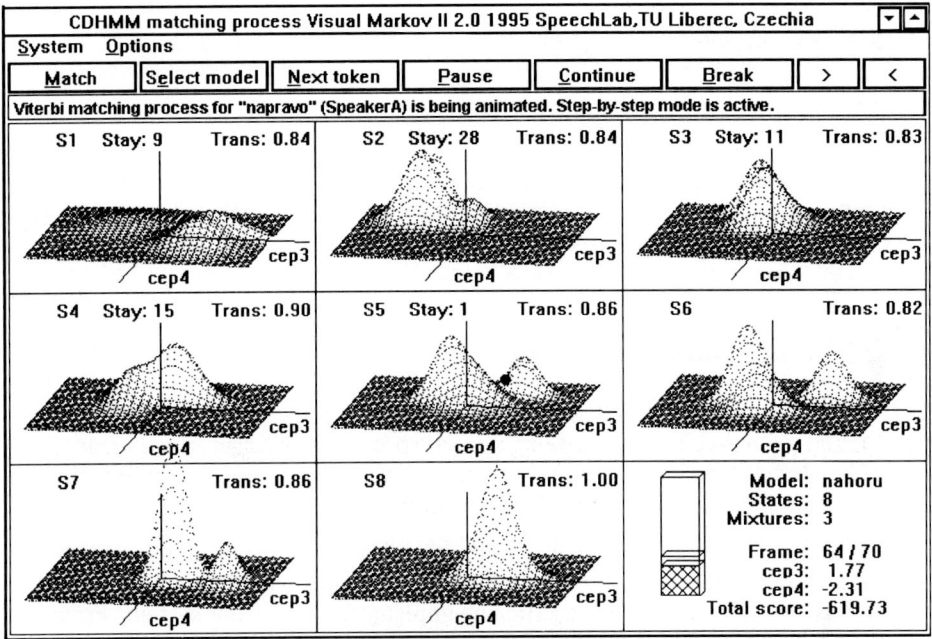

Fig. 4. Matching word „napravo" with a model of word „nahoru"
(Currently, the word's 64th frame is assigned to model state 5.)

The program displays the selected model and performs the match frame by frame. The matching process is demonstrated by a green ball travelling through the model. Each of its travel stops corresponds to one speech frame. The actual position of the ball is determined by the currently processed frame vector (on the screen represented again by two arbitrary chosen features) and by the Viterbi decoder that had estimated the most likely state sequence. The evolution of the log likelihood score can be watched and compared with the score achieved by the best model. This gives the user an excellent opportunity to see how much the model fits the utterance, both on the local, state, level as well as on the global level. Again, the user can choose from several options, like the choice of the utterance and the model, the two displayed features, the plot parameters and some others. A set of buttons is available to control the flow of the animation. Fig.5 on the next page is an attempt to present the animation in a single picture.

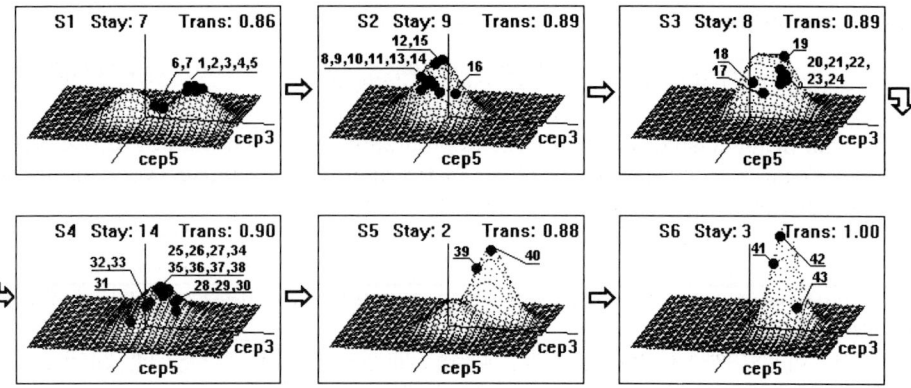

Fig. 5. An example of matching word „nahoru" with a 6-state 2-mixture model of that word. (Positions of each of the 43 frame vectors of the matched word with regard to the model states assigned by the Viterbi decoder are depicted by small numbered circles.)

5. System implementation issues

The first version of the Visual Markov system [4], that was originally written for DOS, found a positive response among speech specialists and proved a usefulness of such a graphic system. Therefore, in this second version, we aimed at developing a tool that would meet a wide range of practical demands.

The system runs under the Windows environment, now. This makes its usage much easier and allows simple copy, store and display operations with the graphic output. A lot of effort has been put into the efficient implementation of the system. From the computation load point of view, the two most critical implementation issues were the training procedure and the animation of the 3D plots of the state output functions. The former problem was solved by adopting a set of optimized routines [5]. The 3D plots are drawn with the use of the floating horizon method combined with a view transformation to solve the invisibility problem. In order to make the animation smoother, we adopted a screen swapping technique. As a result, the complete software operates fast enough even on a PC machine with a 486/50 processor.

The system allows to perform investigations on an arbitrary speech database. The analysed objects can be either single words, subword units or short utterances with maximum duration of 2 s (for 8 kHz sampling rate). The constraints for the Markov models are: 20 features, 12 states and 3 mixtures per state. Up to 8 model states can be displayed at one moment. The system parameters are set either manually using the menus inside the program or they can be prepared in an external file before an experiment starts. Though the Visual Markov package has been developed primarily for the speech recognition, its application domain is not restricted just to the speech processing. It can be utilized in any area where data series are modelled by the CDHMM technique.

6. Conclusions

In the article we have presented a graphic system, named Visual Markov, that was designed for practical and theoretical investigation of continuous density hidden Markov models with a special focus on the application in the speech processing domain. The system enables a user to study the complex dynamic processes that take place inside the models during their training and recognition. It is a highly illustrative tool for studying the behaviour of the CDHMM as well as a useful piece of software supporting the design of a speech recognition system. In our lab, it assisted us in several studies and projects dealing with the CDHMM (e.g. [6]). Recently, we have offered the system to the other colleagues in the speech research community. Up to now, its copies have been registered at some tens of universities and institutes in Europe and Japan.

References:

1. Huang, X.D., Ariki, Y, Jack, M.A: *Hidden Markov Models for Speech Recognition.* Edinburgh University Press, Edinburgh, 1990.
2. Rabiner, L.R.: *A Tutorial on Hidden Markov Models and selected applications in speech recognition.* IEEE Trans. on ASSP, February 1989, pp.257-286.
3. - :*HTK Hidden Markov Model Toolkit Manual.* Entropic Research Laboratories, 1993
4. Hájek, D., Nouza, J: *Software for Graphic Presentation and Investigation of Continuous HMM Used in Speech Processing.* In Abstracts of 5th Czech-German Workshop on Speech Processing, Prague, Sept. 1995.
5. Hájek, D.: *Optimized Implementation of Transcendental Functions for Real Time Tasks.* In Proceedings of 2nd ECMS'95 Workshop, Liberec, June 1995, pp. 31-34.
6. Nouza, J.: *On the Speech Feature Selection Problem: Are Dynamic Features More Important Than the Static Ones?* In Proceedings of EUROSPEECH'95 Conference, Spain, Madrid, September 1995, pp. 919-922.

Visualization of Turbulent Flow by Spot Noise

Willem C. de Leeuw   Frits H. Post   Remko W. Vaatstra

Delft University of Technology, Faculty of Technical Mathematics and Informatics,
P.O.Box 356, 2600AJ Delft, The Netherlands. E-mail: w.deleeuw@twi.tudelft.nl

Abstract: Turbulent flow is often modelled using statistical models. In these models the flow is described using average velocity at a certain level of scale, and velocity variations at smaller scale are described by some quantity indicating turbulence intensity. In this paper several methods are described which utilize spot noise texture to visualize turbulent flow modelled in this way. With spot noise the separate fields are combined in one visualization which shows both data fields and how they are related in an intuitively clear way. Different aspects of turbulent flow can be shown using different mappings. The utility of this approach will be shown in two hydrodynamical case studies.

1 Introduction

In contemporary scientific research a large amount of computational power is devoted to flow simulations. Although computers become more powerful by the day, it is still not possible to simulate fully developed three dimensional turbulence at realistic scale using the Navier-Stokes equations in reasonable time. Therefore, turbulent flow is often modelled using statistical turbulence models. In these models the large scale flow is represented using an average velocity and on a small scale the flow is described statistically. Thus, at different levels of scale a single flow is described by different quantities.

Several techniques have been developed for the visualization of turbulent flow. Briscolini and Santangelo visualized the vortex structures of two dimensional turbulence using animation [1]. They show the vortices of various sizes due to turbulence, but they need a complete description of the flow field (as generated by direct numerical simulations of turbulent flows) to make such pictures. The method cannot handle separate fields for turbulence intensity and average velocity. Sakas and Westermann [2] presented a method for modelling turbulent phenomena using fractal functions, which are visualized using volume rendering.

Spot noise [3] is a texture synthesis technique which has been successfully used for the visualization of flow fields. In de Leeuw and van Wijk [4] the technique was extended to handle a larger variety of flow data. By utilizing graphics hardware, the spot noise textures can be rendered fast and inspected interactively. In de Leeuw et al. [5] spot noise was used for the visual simulation of skin friction images taken from wind tunnel experiments. The pictures generated showed several effects, such as the skin friction field on a surface, the convergence and material distribution over the surface, using several parameters to control texture generation. In this paper we will show that spot noise can also be used to visualize turbulent flow field data. Different aspects of turbulence such as dispersion and velocity variation can be mapped onto parameters of spot noise so that intuitively clear pictures are produced.

The paper has the following structure. In section 2 we will discuss turbulence and related work on the visualization of turbulence. Section 3 will describe spot noise. The techniques used to visualize turbulence using spot noise will be covered in section 4. In section 5 some examples will be presented, and in section 6 we will draw conclusions.

2 Turbulence

Turbulent flow is a hot topic in flow research. Although a direct simulation of turbulent flow using Navier-Stokes equations is possible in theory, in practice statistical models of turbulent flow are often used to reduce of computation time. Statistical models are based on Reynolds decomposition, in which a turbulent flow is described by mean velocity and turbulence intensity components. A Reynolds-averaged turbulent flow simulation uses a statistical model, such as the k-ϵ model, where turbulence is characterized by kinetic energy k and dissipation rate ϵ. The resulting data from a Reynolds-averaged simulation are mean velocity and eddy-diffusivity E. In general, E is a tensor quantity, but it is usually represented by a vector if the main directions align with the coordinate axes. For isotropic turbulence, E reduces to a scalar quantity.

Turbulent flow has many characteristics and effects, such as randomness and rotational motion. The detailed motion patterns, such as the rotational pattern of eddies, cannot be fully reconstructed from data generated by a statistical model, but the random nature of the motion can be visualized in a generic way. For example, the amount of fluctuation can be shown as a perturbation of particle motion.

In Hin and Post [6], particle motion is used to visualize both convective and turbulent motion by combining particle path integration of mean velocity data and random fluctuations derived from eddy-diffusivity data. This technique effectively shows local turbulence in 3D flow fields, but is limited by the number of particles in the flow. Ma and Smith [7] have visualized turbulent dispersion using conical surfaces. The core of the conical surface is determined by a stream line of a particle advected by the average velocity while the radius of the cone increases downstream depending on turbulent dispersion. This increase of the radius is proportional to the local turbulence along the stream line. Hin [8] also visualized turbulent dispersion by animation of concentration fields, derived from particle motion. Both methods do not show turbulent motion itself, but only the dispersion of material caused by this motion. The particles [6] show this motion in a generalized way, but this technique is local by nature. We will use texture generation to give a global view of fluid motion, including turbulent effects.

3 Spot noise

Spot noise was introduced by van Wijk [3]. A texture can be characterized by a scalar function f of position $\mathbf{x}$. A spot noise texture [3] is defined as

$$f(\mathbf{x}) = \sum a_i h(\mathbf{x} - \mathbf{x}_i), \qquad (1)$$

in which $h(\mathbf{x})$ is called the spot function. It is a function everywhere zero except for an area that is small compared to the texture size. a_i is a random scaling factor with a zero mean, $\mathbf{x}_i$ is a random position. In non-mathematical terms: spots of random intensity are drawn and blended together at random positions in a plane (Fig. 1).

The use of a spot as a basis for a texture has two nice consequences. First the shape of the spot determines the characteristics of the texture; the global appearance of the texture can be controlled by the shape of the spot. Different textures result from different spot shapes. Second, local control of the texture is possible. Vector fields can be effectively visualized, if the shape of the spot is adapted to the data at the position of the spot. The visualization of vector fields is achieved by scaling the spot in the direction of the vector field, proportional to the vector magnitude. To keep the other properties of the texture constant the spot is also scaled perpendicular to the flow, such that the area of a spot is preserved (Fig. 1c). The advantages of spot noise over other techniques for the visualization of vector fields are a global visualization of the field and possibilities to generate pictures similar to pictures obtained from experimental techniques [5].

The anisotropic scaling used for the visualization of vector fields is just one choice out of a wide range of possibilities to control the texture. Other choices are the shape, size and intensity distribution of the spots. All these parameters have a different effect on the texture generated. To

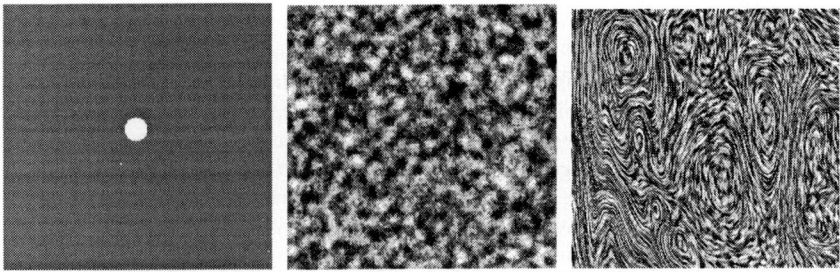

Fig. 1. Principle of spot noise: single spot (a) spot noise texture (b) and spot noise used to visualize a vector field (c).

predict the effect of the different spot shapes on the final texture we can use the fact that the spot and the resulting texture have the same energy distribution in the Fourier transform.

Spot noise is also very suitable for visualization of turbulent flows. It produces a global view of a flow over a surface, which is a useful addition to the particle advection technique [6, 8]. We will show in the next sections that spot noise offers a suitable set of control parameters for texture generation that can be mapped to the mean velocity and turbulence intensity data.

4 Visualization of turbulent flow

If we want to visualize turbulent flow, several mappings can be considered. The final goal is a clear representation of the average velocity and turbulence intensity data. In this section we will consider a number of ways to achieve this. In this section we will use an artificial data set of a jet in an almost still fluid, as described in detail by Hin [8]. It was generated using profile functions for mean velocity and eddy-diffusivity on a regular grid, and we have used one central vertical slice of 40×20 cells for the spot noise visualizations.

4.1 Colour

Separate visualization of mean velocity and eddy-diffusivity is possible using for example spot noise for the mean velocity and colour for eddy-diffusivity (Fig. 2). This separate visualization gives a good view of the spatial distribution of turbulence intensity, but it does not show any turbulent motion, nor any effects of it, such as dispersion.

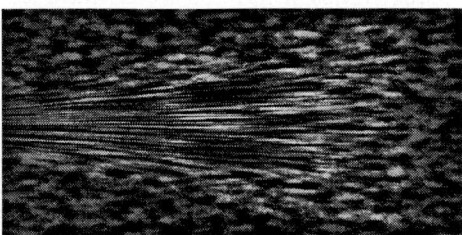

Fig. 2. The plume data set visualized using spot noise for the average velocity and colour for the eddy-diffusivity (see Appendix).

4.2 Intensity range scaling

One parameter of spot noise that can be used to visualize an additional scalar value of a field is the intensity range of the spots. The intensity of a single spot is random, but changing the range from which the intensity of a spot is chosen affect the appearance of the texture. Here we scaled the intensity range by the turbulence intensity.

In images generated by this method the range of random spot intensity increases with turbulence intensity, and thus the high-turbulence regions are highlighted by a higher contrast. Attention is focussed on these regions. Low-turbulence regions with low contrast tend to recede into the background. In practice it appeared to be better to use a minimum intensity range: even where eddy-diffusivity is zero the spots still have some variation in intensity, to ensure that in regions without turbulence the flow is still visible.

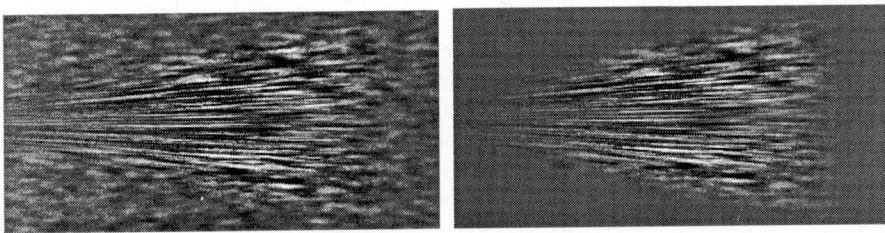

Fig. 3. The plume data set visualized using spot noise with eddy-diffusivity mapped to the intensity of the spots. Left with, and right without a minimum intensity range for zero eddy-diffusivity.

4.3 Velocity perturbation

One effect of turbulence is fluctuation of velocity. The simulation has a mean velocity as a result, but the actual velocity at a point is unknown. However, by combining the *Fokker-Planck equation* and the *advection-diffusion equation* (eq. 3) a velocity distribution function of possible velocities can be constructed [6]. Particle paths can be calculated with the following differential equation:

$$dX_\alpha = (\overline{u}_\alpha + \frac{\partial E_\alpha}{\partial \alpha} + \sqrt{2E_\alpha} N_\alpha)dt \qquad (2)$$

where X is the position of a particle, α is the coordinate direction (x, y or z), $\overline{u}$ is the mean velocity, E is the eddy-diffusivity and N is a sample from a trivariate normal distribution with zero mean and unit standard deviation. This equation can be used to generate velocity values with a realistic distribution. These values can be used as input to the transformation and advection of spots in the spot noise generation process.

In this way the velocity directions will vary strongly in areas of high turbulence intensity, giving an appearance of randomness. In low turbulence areas, the appearance of smooth motion is achieved by mean velocity with little directional perturbation.

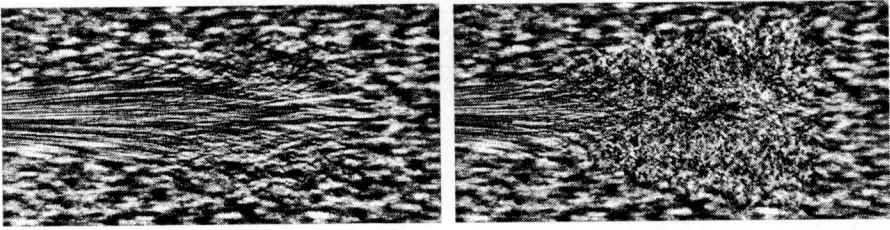

Fig. 4. The plume data set visualized using velocity perturbation spot noise for average velocity and eddy-diffusivity data. In the picture on the right the maximum eddy-diffusivity is 4 times as high as on the left side.

Figure 4 shows two images of the plume data set with different mappings of eddy-diffusivity to velocity magnitude. The highly turbulent regions can be easily detected in both images. The higher frequency of the texture in regions with high turbulence is caused by the fact that the spot orientation becomes almost random, so the width of the spot determines the texture frequency in all directions. This effect is in accordance with the intuitive idea of chaos increasing with the amount of turbulence.

4.4 Texture blurring

Another effect of turbulence is dispersion. The idea we used for this mapping is to regard the spots in the textures as the concentration of material inserted in the flow. The spot initially is disc-shaped with sharp edges, but due to turbulence the material is diffused and therefore the sharp edges become blurred proportional to the turbulence. This will show an effect of blurred texture in turbulent regions. This blurring effect is also an intuitive representation of the uncertainty of the velocity information presented. We will now describe the physical foundation and implementation of this idea in more detail.

In fluid mechanics the dispersion process is modelled by the *advection-diffusion equation* given by:

$$\frac{\partial c}{\partial t} = -\nabla \cdot \overline{\mathbf{u}} c + \nabla (\mathbf{E} \nabla c) \qquad (3)$$

In this equation c denotes concentration of inserted material, $\overline{\mathbf{u}}$ is the average velocity and $\mathbf{E}$ is the eddy-diffusivity. If we view the spot function as a local concentration function of the inserted material, then we can use the above equation to modify the shape of the spot over time. A full solution of equation 3 would give the local dispersion pattern of the spot, but would be very time consuming. To limit the calculation time we make some simplifying assumptions: $\overline{\mathbf{u}}$ and E are assumed constant over the surface of a spot. The justification of this is that spots are small with respect to the whole texture. If we apply these simplifications to equation 3 it reduces to:

$$\frac{\partial c}{\partial t} = \mathbf{E} \nabla^2 c \qquad (4)$$

in discrete form for a 2D position (x, y) and a time step Δt this equation can be written as:

$$C_{x,y,t+\Delta t} = C_{x,y,t} + (E_x \frac{\Delta^2 C_x}{\Delta x^2} + E_y \frac{\Delta^2 C_y}{\Delta y^2}) \Delta t \qquad (5)$$

If we assume that $E_x = E_y$ (isotropic eddy-diffusivity) and $\Delta y = \Delta x$ then $C_{x,y,t+\Delta t}$ becomes:

$$C_{x,y,t} + E \Delta t (\frac{C_{x+\Delta x,y,t} + C_{x-\Delta x,y,t} + C_{x,y+\Delta y,t} + C_{x,y-\Delta y,t} - 4C_{x,y,t}}{\Delta x^2}) \qquad (6)$$

This equation can be implemented as the addition of the original spot image with an image of the spot processed using the digital filter:

0	1	0
1	-4	1
0	1	0

scaled by the local value of $E \Delta t$.

We have to take care with numerical stability of this integration process. If we choose the time step Δt too large, i.e. the value of $E \Delta t$ has a dynamic range which is too large, numerical instability will occur. Figure 6 shows the result of using a too large time step for the integration. If filtering with a large time step is desired the same effect can be achieved by filtering n times, with a time step equal to $\Delta t/n$. In the pictures presented in this paper using this technique, 20 filtering steps were applied using a time step just within the bounds in which the numerical process is still stable. It can be proved using Von Neumann analysis [9] that $E\Delta t$ should not exceed 0.25 in order to keep the process stable.

Figure 5 shows the result of applying this technique to the plume data set. The difference between the images is a result of using a different time step used for the filtering operation.

Because a spot noise texture is the accumulation of intensities of individual spots, this equation can be applied to each spot individually as well as to the whole texture. Because each pixel in the texture is covered by multiple spots it is obvious that the latter is cheaper.

Visualization in a single image is possible by choosing a time interval to determine how long the spots are influenced by the turbulence. Another possibility is to use animation. Here all spots initially have the same size, and they are influenced by the flow (by advection) as well as the turbulence over time.

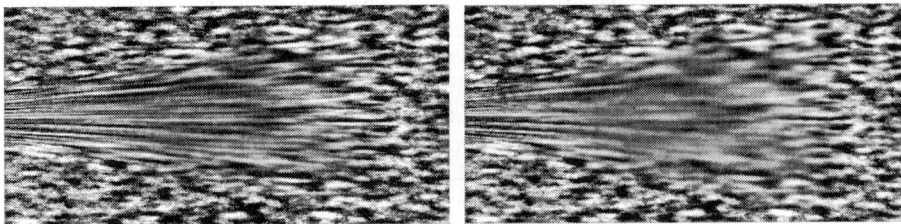

Fig. 5. The plume data set visualized using spot noise with texture blurring.

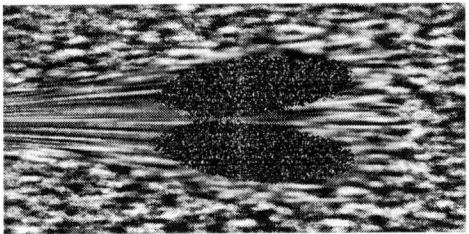

Fig. 6. Texture filtering to visualize eddy-diffusivity: this image results from choosing a too large value of $E\Delta t$.

5 Examples

In this section we will describe two cases in which the techniques presented are applied to real-life data sets. Both data sets are slices from 3D layered hydrodynamic simulations [10].

In the process of mapping velocity to spot noise we can adjust many parameters. In the following cases the parameters showing the velocity are equal for each image and chosen such that mean velocity direction and magnitude is clearly visualized over the entire field. Bent spots and rectilinear texture space [4] are used for better texture and image quality. The size of the textures is 512×512.

All pictures were made using the graphics hardware accelerated implementation described in de Leeuw and van Wijk [4]. Each of the data sets is visualized using the four methods described in section 4. The results are shown in figures 7 and 8.

The *Lith harbour* (Fig. 7) is a 3D simulation of a flow in a river passing a harbour entrance [10]. The river is shown at right in the figure, and the main flow direction is upward in the images. The harbour is at the top left, and is partly separated from the river by a narrow dam. No texture was mapped onto the land regions at the lower left. The middle horizontal grid slice was used here, with a size of 79×38 cells. The goal of the simulation was to study the material transport from the river to the harbour, and to design the harbour entrance geometry to minimize the deposition of river sediment in the harbour.

All images clearly show the large difference in flow speed between the river and the harbour. Turbulence intensity is highest at the transition, with two peaks at each side of the harbour entrance. The speed difference complicates the perception of turbulence levels for all methods except the colour mapping. Discrimination between velocity variations and turbulence (both occurring at the harbour entrance) is difficult, because both turbulence and velocity variations affect material transport, and thus can be visualized in the same way.

The *bay of Gdansk* (Fig. 8) is a simulation of the flow in a coastal region in the North of Poland driven by wind and the inflow of the river Vistula. This results in a complicated flow pattern with a few small regions of high turbulence. The set size is 42×27 cells.

Because of the small size of the turbulent area, intensity range scaling of the spots to visualize turbulence (Fig. 8 top right) gives a poor result. The larger part of the flow is not turbulent and in that case rendered with low intensity. The resulting image lacks contrast in a large part of the image. The velocity perturbation technique and texture filtering technique give better results because the turbulent regions are clearly visible without affecting the visibility of the flow pattern in the rest of the data set.

6 Conclusion

In this paper four techniques for the visualization of flow fields with statistical turbulence data using spot noise were described. The textures give a good global impression of turbulent velocity in a 2D vector field. The velocity perturbation and filtering techniques are based on physical processes occurring in the turbulent flow. These methods show actual processes taking place in the flow: variation of flow velocity and dispersion. The intensity scaling has no physical basis but is a visual technique to highlight turbulent regions in the flow. We think there is no single *best* technique in all cases, as each one has its own merits and drawbacks. Which technique to use depends on the application and the personal preference of the user.

Spot noise gives an integrated view of a turbulent flow, in which the separate mean velocity and turbulence data are re-united in the same visual effects. This corresponds to the physical reality of the flow, where the different variables are affecting the same phenomenon. Turbulent spot noise shows this very clearly, but the individual fields may not be visually distinct. If orthogonal visualization of velocity and turbulence data is required, then the use of spot noise for velocity and colour for turbulence gives a good result. This technique can be easily combined with any of the others.

An obvious advantage of spot noise based visualization techniques over techniques using colour is ease of reproduction. Data visualized using spot noise can usually be reproduced on grey scale output devices, which are still cheaper and more common than colour devices.

The spot noise images look very similar to pictures of turbulent flow made by experimental techniques [11], such as injection of smoke or dye into the flow. Comparative visualization [12] is a promising application of the techniques presented. However, some care must be taken in the comparison of results from statistical simulations to observations of physical experiments. The former shows instances of a set of abstract statistical distribution functions, while the latter show a sample of the actual flow. A fair comparison would require both to be represented by statistical distributions. Further research into generating images for comparing the results of physical experiments and numerical simulations is needed before conclusions can be drawn from a comparison.

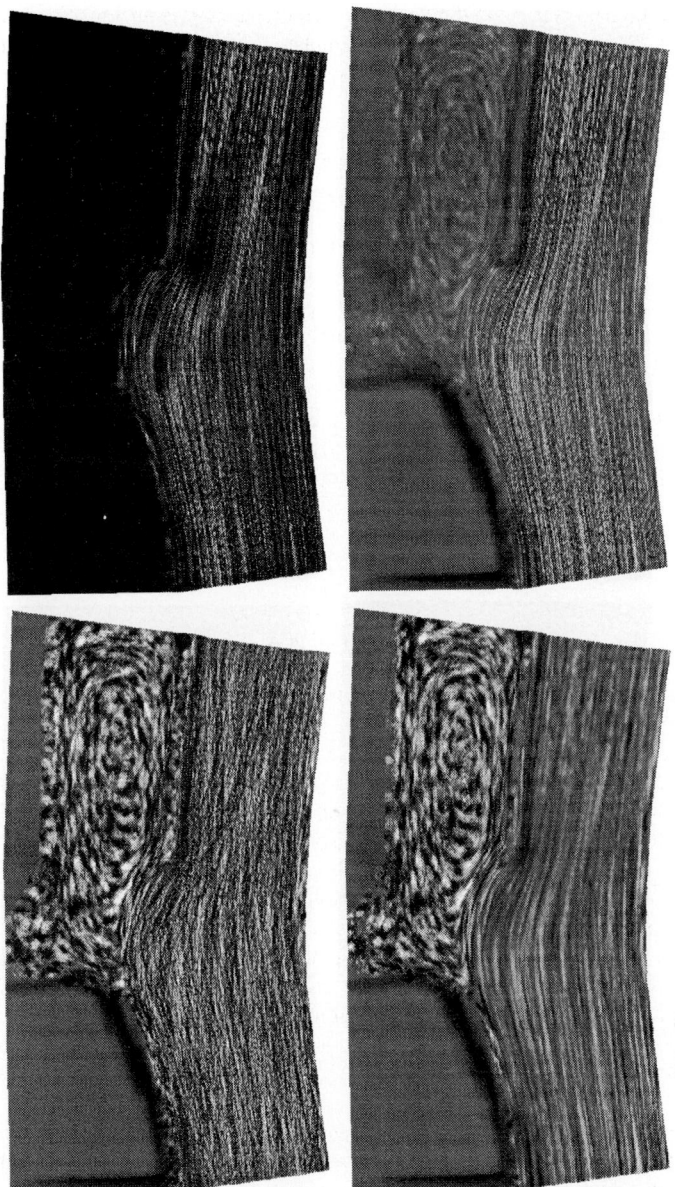

Fig. 7. Slice from the Lith harbor data set visualized with different methods: colour (see also Appendix), spot intensity scaling, velocity perturbation and texture blurring.

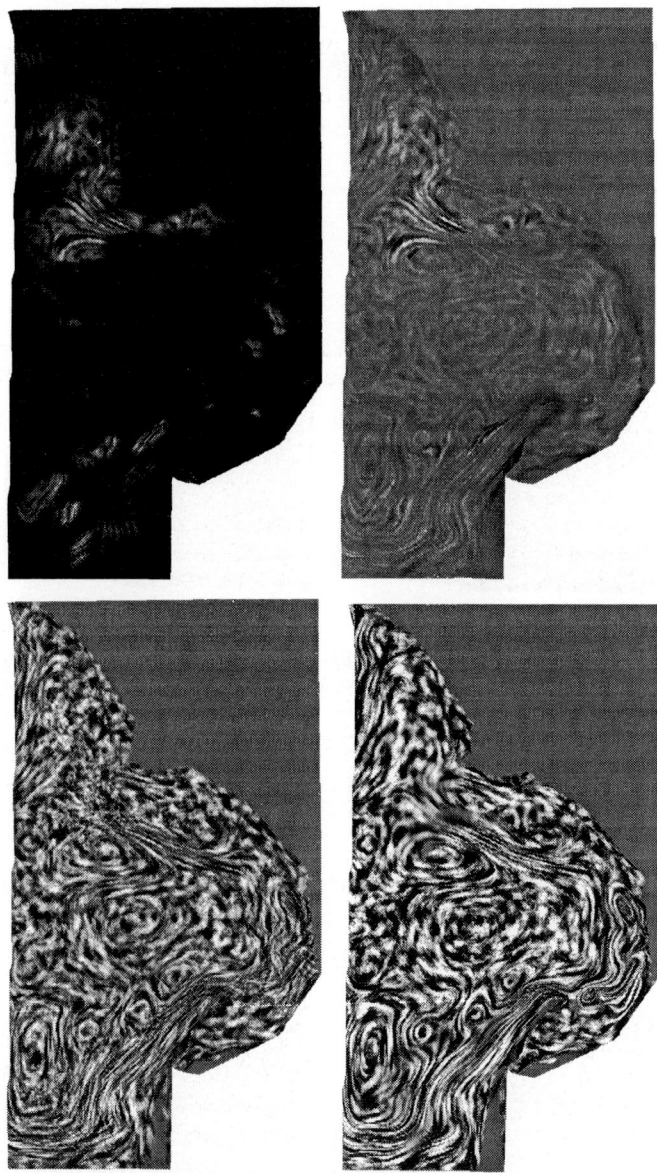

Fig. 8. Slice from the bay of Gdansk data set visualized with different methods: colour (see also Appendix), spot intensity scaling, velocity perturbation and texture blurring.

Acknowledgements

The authors are grateful to Delft Hydraulics for providing the data sets of Lith (Fig. 7) and Gdansk (Fig. 8) and to Andrea Hin who provided the plume data set. We thank Jack van Wijk for his valuable comments and suggestions on this work. This work is supported by the Netherlands Computer Science Research Foundation with the financial support from the Netherlands Organization for Scientific Research(NWO).

References

1. M. Briscolini and P. Santangelo. Animation of computer simulations of two-dimensional turbulence and three-dimensional flows. *IBM Journal of Research and Development*, 35(1/2):119–138, january/march 1991.

2. G. Sakas and R. Westermann. A functional approach to the visual simulation of gaseous turbulence. *Computer Graphics Forum (proc EUROGRAPHICS'92)*, II(3):107–117, 1992.

3. J.J. van Wijk. Spot noise – texture synthesis for data visualization. In Thomas W. Sederberg, editor, *Computer Graphics (SIGGRAPH '91 Proceedings)*, volume 25, pages 263–272, July 1991.

4. W.C. de Leeuw and J.J. van Wijk. Enhanced spot noise for vector field visualization. In G.M. Nielson and D. Silver, editors, *Proceedings Visualization '95*, pages 233–239. IEEE Computer Society Press, 1995.

5. W.C. de Leeuw, H.-G. Pagendarm, F.H. Post, and B. Walter. Visual simulation of experimental oil-flow visualization by spot noise images from numerical flow simulation. In R. Scateni, J.J. van Wijk, and P. Zanarini, editors, *Visualization in Scientific Computing '95*, pages 135–148. Springer Verlag, 1995.

6. A.J.S. Hin and F.H. Post. Visualization of turbulent flow with particles. In G.M. Nielson and R.D. Bergeron, editors, *Proceedings Visualization '93*, pages 46–52. IEEE Computer Society Press, 1993.

7. K.-L. Ma and P. Smith. Cloud tracing in convection-diffusion systems. In G.M. Nielson and R.D. Bergeron, editors, *Proceedings Visualization '93*, pages 253–260. IEEE Computer Science Press, 1993.

8. A.J.S. Hin. *Visualization of Turbulent Flow*. PhD thesis, Delft University of Technology, 1994.

9. P.J. Roache. *Computational Fluid Dynamics, Revised Edition*. Hermosa publishers, 1985.

10. A.E. Mynett, I.A. Sadarjoen, and A.J.S. Hin. Turbulent flow visualization in computational and experimental hydraulics. In G.M. Nielson and D. Silver, editors, *Proceedings Visualization '95*, pages 388–391. IEEE Computer Society Press, 1995.

11. M. van Dyke. *An Album of Fluid Motion*. The Parabolic Press, 1982.

12. H.-G. Pagendarm and F.H. Post. Comparative visualization – approaches and examples. In M. Göbel, H. Müller, and B. Urban, editors, *Visualization in Scientific Computing*, pages 95–108. Springer Wien, 1995.

Editors' Note: See Appendix, p. 324 for coloured figures of this paper

Flow Visualization for Multiblock Multigrid Simulations

Roberto Grosso, Martin Schulz, Jan Kraheberger, Thomas Ertl

Lehrstuhl für Graphische Datenverarbeitung (IMMD 9)
Universität Erlangen-Nürnberg
Am Weichselgarten 9, 91058 Erlangen
{grosso,mnschulz,jnkraheb,ertl}@informatik.uni-erlangen.de

Abstract.
Multiblock multigrid finite volume methods based on hexahedral control volumes are computationally efficient and widely used for solving the Navier-Stokes equations. Due to the enormous amount of data generated during an instationary 3D simulation visualization plays an important role for problem analysis and development. Two different approaches for the interactive steering of multigrid computations in combination with the IRIS Explorer visualization package are investigated. The strategies for the visualization of complex multiblock grids which are presented are based on a new visualization data type, on a concept for the reusability of available visualization modules for curvilinear grids, and on a special algorithm for particle tracing, which does not depend on the connectivity information between blocks.

1. Introduction

Due to the advances in computing hardware and software, computational fluid dynamics becomes a more and more complex field. Very efficient numerical methods for solving the Navier-Stokes equations are based on multiblock multigrid finite volume methods. Many implementations of these methods use hexahedral control volumes, so that blocks can be described as a curvilinear grid. An important property of multiblock grids is their capability for describing complex geometries. In practical applications, multiblock grids have very often more than one hundred blocks.

For such complex numerical simulations, efficient visualization tools play a key role. Tracking and steering are desirable techniques, that allow the scientists to control the evolution of their numerical simulation by means of parameter and data exchange. These techniques are especially important for very large simulations of time dependent problems, where it becomes impossible to save enough time steps for detailed post-processing. Flow visualization tools based on particle methods are an important topic of research [4, 7, 1, 6]. Special attention has to be paid to multiblock particle tracers since they have to be able to follow the particles through the various blocks.

In this paper we are concerned with the interactive steering and visualization of fluid flow simulations based on the multiblock multigrid method for finite volumes with hexahedral control volumes. In section 2 we briefly analyze multigrid methods and propose different models for interactive steering. In section 3 we investigate aspects of visualization algorithms for multiblock grids and propose strategies for extending the

IRIS Explorer visualization environment to handle such data structures. The problem of implementing a particle tracer will be considered in more detail in section 4. Finally, we present some results and draw conclusions.

2. Multiblock Multigrid Flow Simulations

One important topic of research in computational fluid dynamics is the numerical solution of the Navier-Stokes equations for the case of three dimensional, steady and unsteady, incompressible and compressible flows. Very efficient methods for solving these partial differential equations are based on collocated multigrid methods and grid partitioning techniques. Block-structured or multiblock grids are very common data structures within efficient numerical software due to their adaptability to complex geometries and due to the possibility of local refinement in different blocks. In spite of these elaborated algorithms the processing time demands still require the Navier-Stokes solver to be run on a high-performance computers generating very large data sets. Especially in the case of time dependent simulations, the storage demand is on the order of some GBytes when saving a few time steps. A solution to this problem and an important aspect during the development of numerical codes is the interactive steering of the simulation and its integration within the visualization.

2.1. The Multigrid Method

In order to couple the numerical simulation and the visualization and to facilitate the interaction and steering of the simulation process, we revise the multigrid method in more detail. The multigrid method is among the fastest methods for solving systems of equations with a large number of unknowns. Fedorenko [3] was the first that formulated a two- and multigrid algorithm and showed that the complexity grows as $O(n)$ with the number of unknowns (see also [5]). The key point is to note that standard iteration algorithms are smoothing, that means they eliminate the oscillating (high frequency) component of the error function very fast. The long wave (low frequency) components of the function, however, should be computed on a coarser grid. The building blocks of a multigrid method are the iterative repetition of the relaxation steps at the fine grid in order to reduce the oscillating terms in the error and the approximate computation of the smooth components at the coarse grid. A multigrid method is defined recursively and the principal steps are the apriori-smoothing iterations, the coarse grid corrections, and the posteriori-smoothing iterations. Depending on the sequence of smoothing iterations and coarse grid corrections one usually speaks of *V-cycles* or *W-cycles*.

In this paper we restrict ourselves to the case of V-cycles and consider two different techniques depending on whether steady or unsteady problems are solved. The ideas presented can easily be extended to other techniques and to W-cycles. For unsteady cases, a Full Approximation Scheme (FAS) starts from the finest grid level and iterates some V-cycles to compute a time step. For steady cases, the Full MultiGrid (FMG) method obtains good initial values for the computation on the next finer grid starting from coarser grid levels (see figure 1). In this case, the additional effort on the coarser grids is over-compensated by the better convergence on the finest grids, since iterations on coarse grid levels are much cheaper with respect to computational costs than fine grid iterations.

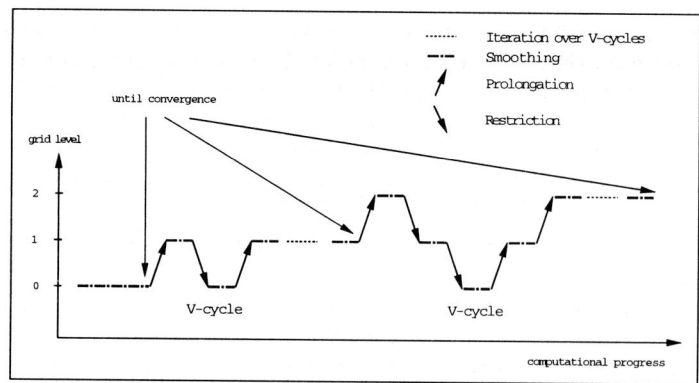

Figure 1: *Full Multi Grid technique on 3 grid levels*

2.2. Coupling the Numerical Simulation and the Visualization

In order to observe and to control the development of the numerical simulation, one has to be able to visualize the flow and the scalar fields and their evolution during the iterative process. There are quite some post-processing programs and libraries available for flow visualization, however, the support for multigrid and multiblock data types and the means for integrating the visualization with the computation are usually very limited. Therefore, we decided to base our work on a modular visualization environment like IRIS Explorer, which is easily extendible with respect to new functionality, new data types, and distributed computing. The modular nature of these visualization packages make them ideal for rapid prototyping and for exchanging applications with users in form of *maps*.

Concerning the visualization of data derived from a multigrid solver it is important to be aware of the fact that only the data on the currently finest grid level corresponds to an approximate solution of the physical problem. The fields that are computed at coarse grids within a V-cycle are solutions of the correction equations and do not have an explicit relation to the physical variables. Actually, the so called defect equations of the non-linear problem which corresponds to the Navier-Stokes equations are solved. In figure 1 this corresponds to the *smoothing* iterations. After the completion of a V-cycle convergence will be checked on the finest grid level. The iteration over the V-cycles at a given level is simply carried out by a loop. Our model of interaction between the simulation and the visualization consists of the exchange of control parameters and data after the completion of a certain number of V-cycles which has to be determined by the user. A finer granularity for data exchange is possible, but this would require a deeper intervention in the original code in order to isolate the smoothing iterations at the finest grid within a V-cycle. On the other hand, no significant changes in the physical variables can be observed at this level. Thus, such finer granularity for interaction does not seem to be necessary.

This interaction model can be realized in many different ways. The first one we propose is made up of two completely independent applications, where one is the numerical simulation and the other one is the visualization package. Within the numerical code only some slight modifications in the read and write routines have to be implemented replacing the file I/O with socket communication to a well known port. On the side of the visualization package we have written a module which opens and accepts a connection to a socket with that known port number. This module can also read and write data in the format specified by the application. Thus, the simulation can be run independently of the visualization. After each iteration it will try a connection to the socket, and as long as a socket with that port number was not opened, this connection will fail and the simulation will continue with its iterations. When the visualization is started, the socket port is opened and both processes will couple and synchronize by means of the `accept` system call, where blocking sockets are used. When the visualization is stopped, the simulation will continue with its iterations.

A second approach we realized is based on the complete integration of the numerical simulation code as a computation module into the visualization environment. Here, the specific distribution mechanism of the visualization package has to be taken into account. In IRIS Explorer each computation module is a separate Unix process which is waiting for messages from a master process. When a message arrives, the process responds to the required actions by executing the module's functions. On the other hand, the V-cycle iteration at each grid level, the convergence check and the change between cycles of different level are usually realized by nested `DO` loops and `GOTO` statements. Thus, within the computation module, this structure has to be replaced by equivalent function calls and global variables used as loop counters, and by the encapsulation of program parts of the Fortran main routine into C functions. In our implementation we have introduced a C++ class hierarchy to encapsulate a complete V-cycle and all the necessary administrative operations to change from a level to the next. The methods of theses classes perform operations such as initialization, V-cycle iterations, setting of physical parameters, writing and reading data, and setting control parameters which are related to the numerical method like under-relaxation factors or the number of iterations within the various steps of the nonlinear multigrid technique.

3. Multiblock Flow Visualization

After having considered the problem of coupling a multigrid simulation with the visualization we have to investigate how to visualize the data structures they exchange, i.e. a complete multiblock grid with all the associated solution fields. In this paper we only deal with multiblock data structures with blocks of curvilinear grids, neglecting multiblock unstructured grids or even hybrid variants. This is not a real restriction since most of the widely used finite volume methods are based on multiblock grids with hexahedral volume elements. In this section we consider the problem of extending visualization algorithms and software packages in order to support multiblock data structures. In practical applications, where the geometry of the domain is very complex, a large number of blocks is needed. Examples of multiblock grids with more than one hundred blocks are quite common. Due to the fact that standard IRIS Explorer modules do not support multiblock data structures, we have decided to introduce them as a new data type allowing us to manage such complex situations. Design considerations and some implementations details will be given at the end of this section.

3.1. Visualization Algorithms

Most of all flow visualization techniques are based on two fundamental classes of algorithms, the ones which correspond to an Eulerian formulation of the flow fields, such as arrow plots, isosurfaces or cutting planes, where the complete field under consideration is visualized at a certain instant of time, and particle methods which correspond to a Lagrangian formulation. In the later case, where particles are placed into arbitrary positions which are then traced through the blocks of the grid according to the local vector field, it is obvious that information from neighboring blocks is required for the accurate integration of the path. These multiblock particle tracing algorithms will be analyzed in more detail in section 4. For Eulerian algorithms it seems that an independent handling of all blocks could be sufficient. In order to analyze the details we first need to review some aspects of finite volume methods on multiblock data structures.

Typical multiblock grids can be classified into matching grids, grids with local refinement and the most general case of non-matching grids with local refinement, where no relation exists between the control volumes at the boundary of one block and the corresponding ones at the neighboring block The common surface between two blocks will be called block interface or internal boundary. In matching grids, which is the most simple case, the computed physical fields have the same values at the common nodes of neighboring blocks, i.e. the physical fields are continuous at the block interfaces. Numerical algorithms for multiblock grids with local refinement are very complex and an important topic of research in computational fluid dynamics with the first commercial software packages using general grids with local refinement just appearing on the market. For visualization purposes, we are interested to know how the physical fields behave at the internal boundaries. For general grids with local refinement it is very difficult to estimate the continuity of the fields in those regions. The solution might be discontinuous and the strength of the discontinuity will in some sense be proportional to the gradient of the fields across those regions and to the *jump* in the discretization. This jump is given by the discretization size and the relation between the number of control volumes of the neighboring blocks. A typical example is a shock wave traveling between two blocks where at the block interfaces the wave will stretch into the block with the coarser discretization.

In the case of matching grids, physical fields are continuous at block transitions. The marching cubes isosurface algorithm for example computes the intersection of the surface with the cell edges using linear interpolation. Since the values of the scalar fields on common nodes of neighboring blocks coincide, the computed intersection of the surfaces at the block interfaces will also coincide and the surfaces will be continuous, i.e. there will be no steps or holes. Discontinuities might, however, appear in the gradient of the field on the isosurface if for the computation forward or backward differences are used independently in the neighboring blocks. Since the gradient is used for illumination purposes this might result in visual artifacts along the block interfaces (see figure 2). The marching cubes algorithm can be slightly modified in order to produce correct results. If common nodes of the corresponding neighboring blocks are searched at the block boundary, central differences can be used for the computation of the gradient on the isosurface. A more simple solution would be to compute the normals at those points independently using forward or backward differences and then take the mean value for the normal at those boundary points. Similarly, if a cutting plane through a multiblock grid is computed running a standard algorithm for a curvilinear grid on each of the blocks independently, the resulting slice will be continuous, if short range interpolation filters like nearest neighbor or trilinear interpolation are used for the computation of the field values on the cutting plane. We remember that these algorithms will use some suitable boundary conditions, such as symmetric or periodic, at the block borders.

In the most general case of non-matching grids with local refinement where the numerical solution might be discontinuous at the internal boundaries one would expect to see these discontinuities also in the visualization. In this case or if interpolation of

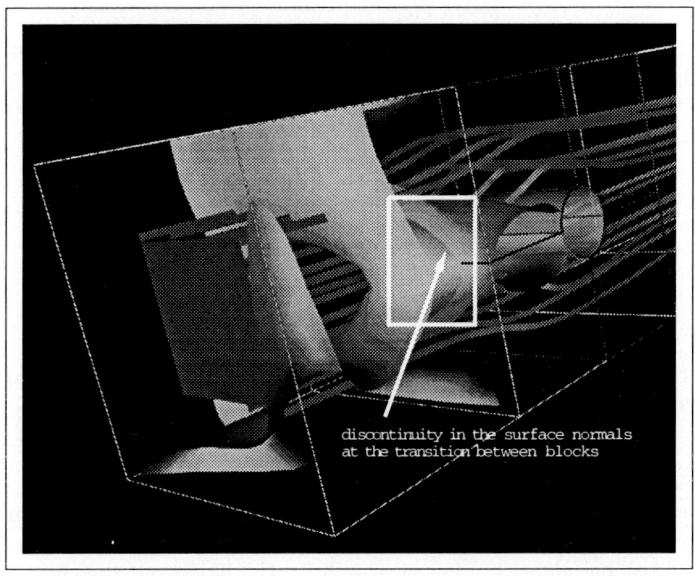

Figure 2: *Isosurface computed using marching cubes independently at each block of matching grids.*

order higher than one is used, the marching cubes and the cutting plane will correctly produce results which are discontinuous at the block interfaces (see figure 3). If the numerical solution for non-matching grids is continuous at the block interfaces, then these visualization algorithms will generate correct results with the exception of the computation of the normals.

3.2. A Multiblock Data Type

From the last section it seems that at least for the broad class of Eulerian visualization algorithms matching multiblock grids could be treated by applying the standard curvilinear algorithm to each of the blocks successively. As shown for isosurfaces and cutting planes those algorithms would generate the correct result with the exception of the behavior of the normal at the block interfaces. In the context of IRIS Explorer this means that if a read module would deliver the various blocks as a set of separate lattices, which is the Explorer data type for curvilinear grids, then a replication of the isosurface module for each of the lattices would generate a geometry stream which could be combined to be feed into the render module. Obviously, this approach is feasible only for a few different blocks (for example for 100 blocks one has to start 100 isosurfaces modules and make the connections between them). For real applications with hundreds of blocks a special multiblock data type has to be introduced in order to handle all the blocks in a unified and simple manner. While the integration of new data types is possible in IRIS Explorer, the disadvantage of this approach is, that the new data type is completely unknown to the existing modules, which means that all relevant modules have to be re-implemented in order to support the new data type.

When designing a new data type, two aspects have to be considered: efficiency and

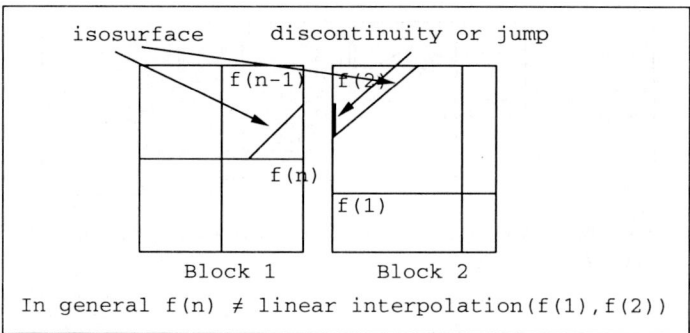

Figure 3: *For grids with local refinement the marching cube algorithm might produce discontinuous surfaces.*

practical issues. We first investigate the efficiency requirements of algorithms like a particle tracer which heavily depend on the data structures used. When a particle leaves one block, the tracing algorithm has to search for the block and the corresponding cell which contains the new particle position. In order to achieve this a naive method based on the stencil walk algorithm can be implemented. This can be costly if the multiple evaluations of higher order integration schemes again require information from the previous block, but its implementation will be very simple. In general, numerical methods for multiblock data which have to interpolate field values at the block interfaces or between points of neighboring blocks impose complex problems. For an efficient search of neighboring blocks and corresponding cell indices these algorithms use the *logical connection* information which describes the topological structure of the grid.

While from a point of view of realizing a multiblock particle tracer efficiency would require the implementation of the logical connection information within the new data type, this information is usually not available. There are two file formats for multiblock grids, which are widely used. The PLOT3D format from the Ames Research Center and the Tecplot file format from Amtec Engineering Inc. Both of them store the number of blocks constituting the multiblock grid, the values of the fields in the different blocks and the corresponding coordinates. However, no topology information concerning the neighborhood relations or boundary conditions between blocks is known, if a multiblock grid is read from these data sets.

Due to the fact that for many applications, where the data comes from a file in PLOT3D or Tecplot format, and because many algorithms such as marching cubes or cutting plane for a single curvilinear grid can be run as if they were within a loop over all blocks, we have decided to introduce a simple data type in IRIS Explorer. This data type consists of an integer indicating the number of blocks in the grid, and an array of Explorer lattices containing the blocks. The declaration of these new data type has the form:

```
shared root typedef struct {
        long       NBlocks;           /* Number of Blocks */
        cxLattice  Lat[NBlocks];      /* Array of Lattices */
} mBlock;
```

This new data type can easily be generalized to include the logical connection infor-

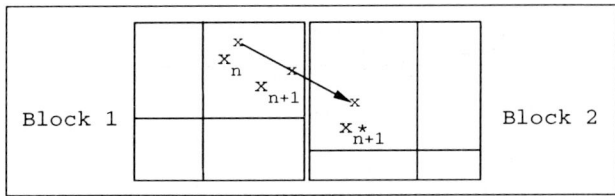

Figure 4: *A case where the search for the block containing the final position of the integration step has to be started twice*

mation, which is saved in form of integer arrays. But this will be a topic for a future work.

In order to process multiblock data with IRIS Explorer we have implemented some key modules. A channel selector module `MBSwitch` to select a special block to be visualized with the standard tools. A lattice to multiblock module `LatToMB` in order to process standard single curvilinear grid data with our multiblock visualization modules. The most important implementation work is a pair of modules conceived to reuse such Explorer modules as the isosurface, cutting plane or wire frame modules. The first module `MBLoop` realizes an internal loop over the blocks which have to be processed. It reads a multiblock data type and writes lattices. By means of the input parameters it can be decided which block will be processed. The output lattices are sent to the standard Explorer modules for curvilinear grids. The resulting geometry objects are sent to the second module `MBMagic` which collects all incoming geometry information into a new single geometry stream. This module is synchronized with the loop-module in order to know, how many objects it has to collect. When it is done it sends the result to the renderer. In this way we can reuse many Explorer modules without any extra implementation work.

4. Particle Tracing

In this section we discuss particle tracing algorithms for multiblock data structures in more detail. By particle tracing we mean the numerical solution of the differential equation:

$$\frac{d\mathbf{x}}{dt} = \mathbf{v}(t, \mathbf{x}) ,$$

where $\mathbf{x}$ is the position of the particle and $\mathbf{v}$ the velocity. The pseudo-code for a multigrid particle tracing algorithm is of the same form as for a single curvilinear grid:

```
find cell containing initial position              (point location)
while (particle within grid and not too many iterations)
     interpolate velocity                          (interpolation)
     compute new particle position                 (integration)
     find cell containing new position             (point location)
endwhile
```

The only difference is the way the `point location` works. For multiblock grids, the cell containing the new particle position may be in a neighboring block which introduces the new class of problems mentioned in section 3.

According to the data type we have introduced in Explorer we do not have any logical connection information, thus no knowledge of neighborhood relations and boundary conditions between blocks is available. In this article we analyze a naive algorithm, where point location is based on the stencil walk method. This method has to be slightly modified in order to *walk* through all the blocks. The new position of a particle leaving a block is determined by a linear search of the lattice array. If the particle is not within the block with the next higher block number, the search is continued until a block is found which contains the particle. If no block is found, the particle has left the computational domain. This generalization seems to be natural and it works fairly well. But for performance reasons the situation has to be analyzed more carefully, if the integration method is of second or higher order. When considering the second order Runge-Heun-Kutta scheme the new position $\mathbf{x}_{n+1}$ at the time t_{n+1} is derived from the old position $\mathbf{x}_n$ at a time t_n by:

$$\mathbf{x}_{n+1} = \mathbf{x}_n + \frac{\Delta t}{2}\left(\mathbf{v}(\mathbf{x}_n) + \mathbf{v}(\mathbf{x}_{n+1}^*)\right) \quad \text{where} \quad \Delta t = t_{n+1} - t_n, \quad \mathbf{x}_{n+1}^* = \Delta t\, \mathbf{v}(\mathbf{x}_n)$$

From this formula it is obvious that at block interfaces it might happen that the intermediate position $\mathbf{x}_{n+1}^*$ is in a neighboring block, and that the final position $\mathbf{x}_{n+1}$ is in the previous block (see figure 4). That means, that the linear search algorithm will probably cycle two times through all the blocks for computing only one integration step. Taking this into account, the performance of the algorithm can be improved very easily. At the block interface, when the particle leaves a block, the cell indices and the block `id` are kept and reused for the point location of $\mathbf{x}_{n+1}$, if this position is not in the same block as the intermediate position $\mathbf{x}_{n+1}^*$.

We have implemented an IRIS Explorer module, which due to historical reasons is called `Streakband`, which computes path lines and streak lines, and corresponding generalizations such as stream ribbons, and stream balls on arbitrary curvilinear multiblock grids. The particle traces are computed in the physical space domain (P-space-algorithm) [7].

5. Results and Conclusions

Interactive Steering. In this paper we have proposed two different models for the integration of a multiblock multigrid finite volume code into a distributed simulation and visualization environment. For our tests we have used the Navier-Stokes solver FASTEST-3D of the CFD department of the University of Erlangen [2, 8]. Our first approach is characterized by a completely asynchronous run of the parallel simulation program and the visualization package. While the computation is running, the visualization can be started and stopped at various time steps. Interactive setting of control parameters or reading and writing of data is possible only at these times. In this case, only minor changes in the structure of the numerical code had to be done. This is important if the software is still under continuous development in order to include new features, such as different physical or chemical models.

A different strategy is the complete integration of the numerical software into the visualization package in the form of a computational module. In this case, one takes advantage of the tools that already exist in the visualization environment, such as a comfortable user interface, which assists in defining the parameters that will be exchanged and in controlling the simulation process by simple buttons, dial or slider manipulation.

grid	size of block 1	size of block 2	size of Block 3	CPU time sec.
1	5x64	5x10x4	5x6x4	0.26
2	8x10x6	8x18x6	8x10x6	1.94
3	14x18x10	14x3410	14x18x10	13.16
4	26x34x18	26x66x18	26x34x18	108.40

Table 1: *CPU-time of V-cycles on different grid levels*

The rate of interaction, i.e. the number of data sets that one can obtain from the simulation per time unit, strongly depends on the physical problem being considered and on the performance of the hardware being used. Table 1 shows the computing time needed between V-cycles for different levels for a three block configuration. The number of control volumes for the different grid levels is also given. The measurements were carried out on a SGI Indigo[2] HighImpact with a MIPS R4400 processor running at 250 MHz. This example shows, that an acceptable rate of interaction is only possible for the first three grid levels. However, this presents a realistic preproduction application and offers a comfortable environment providing rapid insight into the physics of the problem being modeled. Of course, in order to achieve better interaction in more complex problems, they have to be simulated using high performance computers.

Multiblock Flow Visualization. We have shown, that the visualization of data defined on multiblock grids may become a cumbersome task. In this paper we have proposed a strategy for the visualization of multiblock fields which is based on the following three aspects: a new data type in order to be able to handle large and complex multiblock grids, a concept for the reusability of many available visualization tools for single curvilinear grids and, finally, a special visualization module for particle methods, i.e. streak lines and path lines, as well as stream ribbons and stream balls.

Figure 5 show stream ribbons of a benchmarking data set of a flow around a cylinder where the multiblock grid consists of 8 blocks and has a size of 13 MBytes. As we have already seen in section 3, isosurfaces may exhibit artifacts at block interfaces, if a standard marching cubes algorithm for curvilinear grids is applied to each of the blocks successively (see also figure 2). Thus, in order to interpret the visualization results correctly, one has to be conscious of the limitations of the method.

A second data set containing a helical flow spiraling through 120 blocks of size 21x21x11 was artificially generated in order to test the efficiency of the position location method of our particle tracer. We generated two extreme cases where in the first data set the numbering of the blocks increases in the direction of the flow, and a second one where the block numbering decreases in the direction of the flow. For the latter case, the point location algorithm will always search for the new particle position in the wrong direction. We have repeated the measurements for the naive and for the optimized version of the algorithm presented in section 4. Each time we have counted the number of block transitions, i.e. how often the algorithm has to search for the new particle position in a different block. Table 2 clearly shows, that when the enumeration of the blocks runs in the opposite direction of the flow, the particle tracer not only needs a larger computing time, but also performs about a factor of 3 more block transitions. For all measurements we had a maximum number of 30,000 integration steps. The

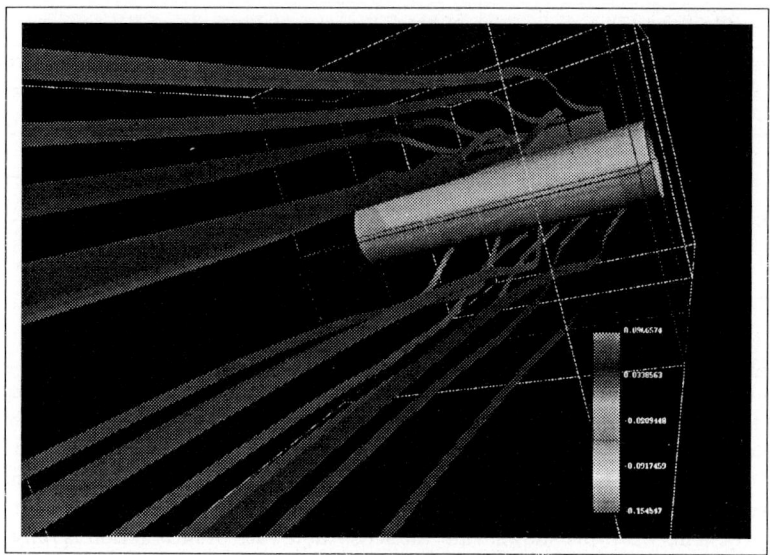

Figure 5: *Visualization of a flow around a cylinder. Pressure values are used for coding the colors on the stream ribbons.*

version	numbering direction	CPU time sec.	block transitions
optimized	downwards	9.59	13211
optimized	upwards	17.68	37694
non optimized	downwards	17.30	33582
non optimized	upwards	26.69	54341

Table 2: *CPU-time and number of block transitions for computing a streak line using a maximum of 30,000 integration steps*

performance improvement between the non-optimized and the optimized version is a about factor of 2 which approximately corresponds to the expected results.

The new data type introduced in the visualization package Explorer does not include any logical connection information concerning the neighborhood relations or the boundary conditions between blocks. We have justified our decision based on the fact that widely used file formats for multiblock data do not include this information. However the data type can easily be extended to include this information for modules which can make use of it. Standard algorithms like marching cubes will still see lattices only, thus running unmodified. We are planning to investigate this extension in the future.

References

1. B. Becker, D. A. Lane, and N. L. Max. Unsteady Flow Volumes. In G.M. Nielson and Silver D., editors, *Visualization '95*, pages 329–335, Los Alamitos, CA, 1995.

IEEE, IEEE Computer Society Press.

2. F. Durst, H.J. Leister, M. Schäfer, and E. Schreck. Efficient 3-D Flow Prediction on Parallel High-Performance Computers. In *Computational Fluid Dynamics on Parallel Systems*, volume 50 of *Notes on Numerical Fluid Mechanics*, pages 59–65. Vieweg Verlag, 1995.

3. R. P. Fedorenko. A Relaxation Method for Solving Elliptic Difference Equations. *USSR Comput. Math. math. Phys.*, 1(5):1092–1096, 1961.

4. T. Frühauf. Interactive Visualization of Vector Data in Unstructured Volumes. *Comput. & Graphics*, 18(1):73–80, 1994.

5. W Hackbusch. *Multigrid Methods and Applications*. Springer Verlag, Berlin - Heidelberg - New York, 1985.

6. D. N. Kenwright and D. A. Lane. Optimization of Time-Dependent Particle Tracing Using Tetrahedral decomposition. In G.M. Nielson and Silver D., editors, *Visualization '95*, pages 321–328, Los Alamitos, CA, 1995. IEEE, IEEE Computer Society Press.

7. A. Sadarjoen, T. van Walsum, A. J. S. Hin, and F.H. Post. Particle Tracing Algorithms for 3D Curvilinear Grids. In *Fifth Eurographics Workshop on Visualization in Scientific Computing*, 1994.

8. M. Schäfer, E. Schreck, and K. Wechsler. An Efficient Parallel Solution Technique for the Incompressible Navier-Stokes Equations. In F.-K. Hebeker, R. Rannacher, and G. Wittum, editors, *Numerical Methods for the Navier-Stokes Equations*, volume 47 of *Notes on Numerical Fluid Mechanics*, pages 228–238. Vieweg Verlag, 1994.

Appendix: Colour Figures

Example process plant (Hubbold et al., Fig. 3)　　Example radiosity solutions (Hubbold et al., Fig. 4)

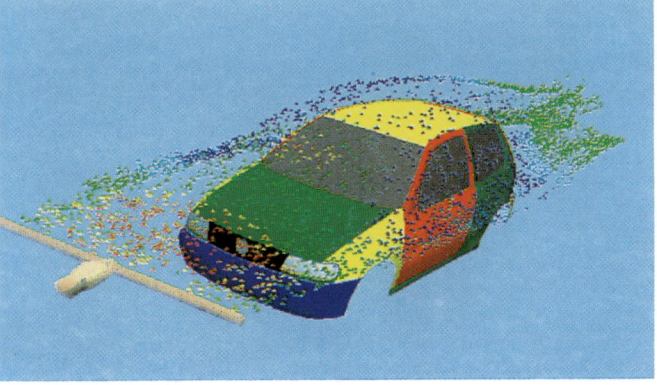

(del Pino)

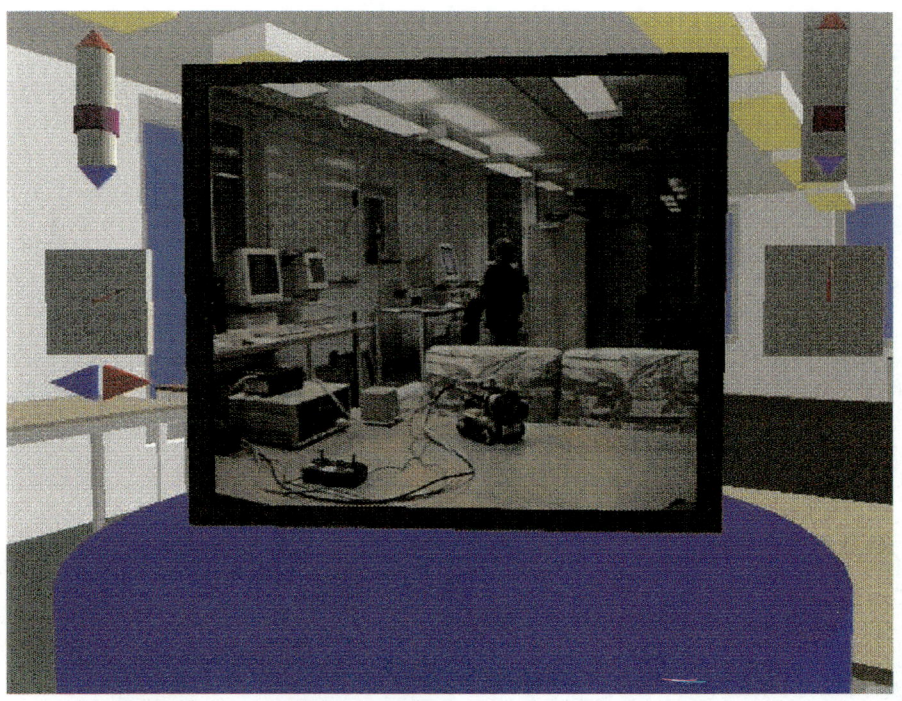

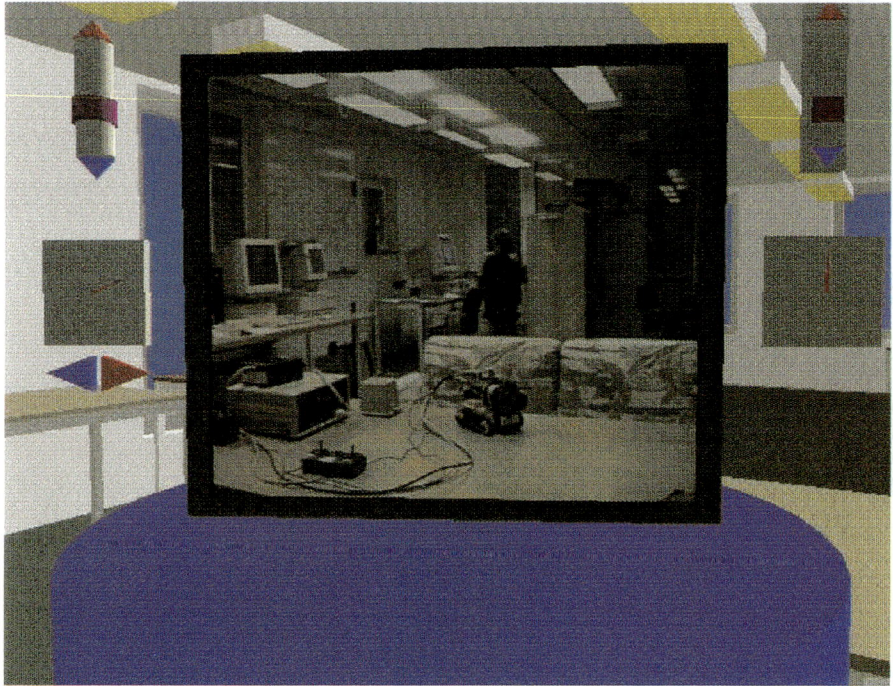

(Simsarian et al.)

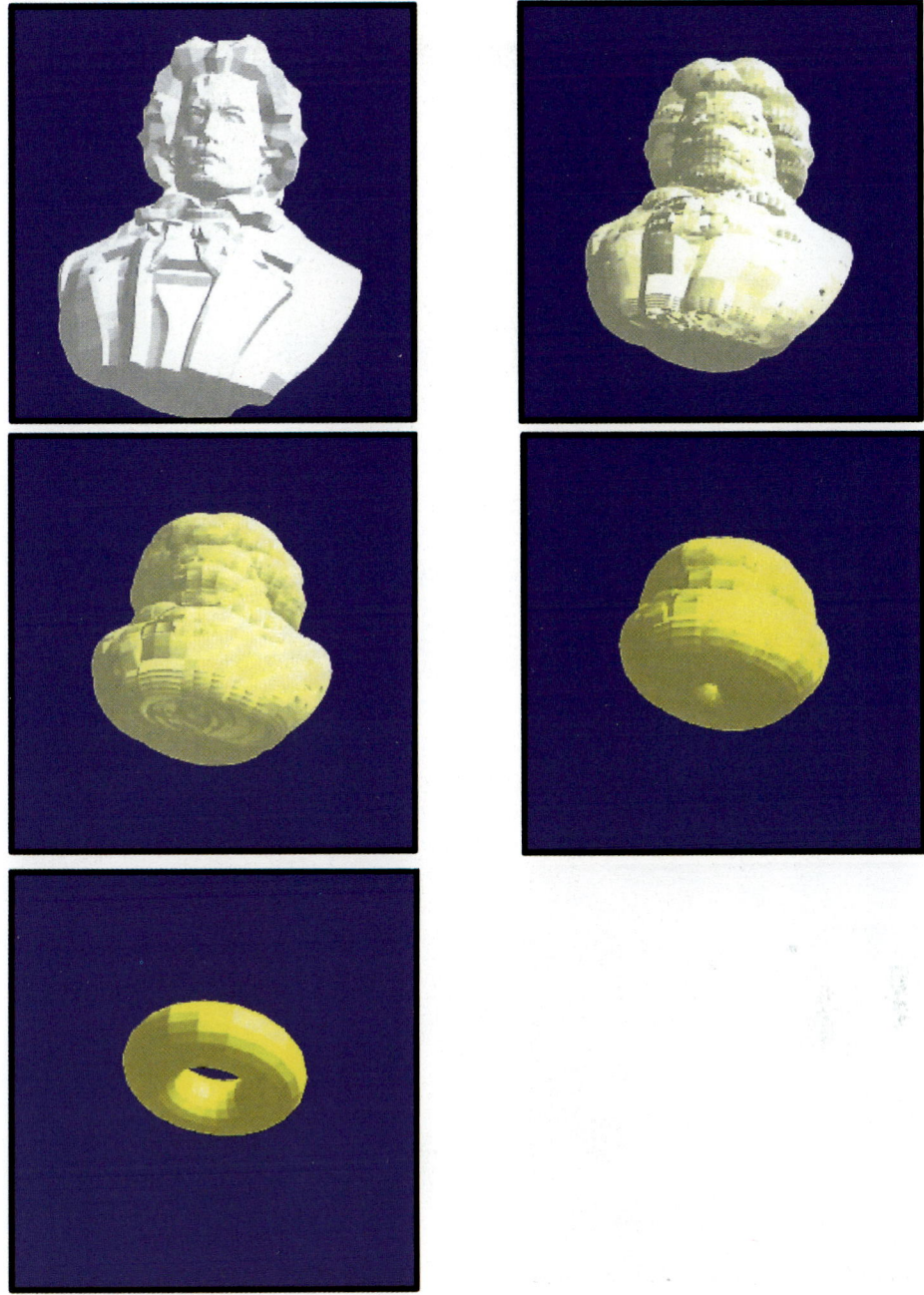

Morph between a Beethoven-bust and a torus. The PIP-algorithm is used for this example. The morph-object consists of 34,000 faces (Astheimer and Knöpfle)

Morph between a tree and a Beethoven-bust using the NoTop-algorithm (Astheimer and Knöpfle)

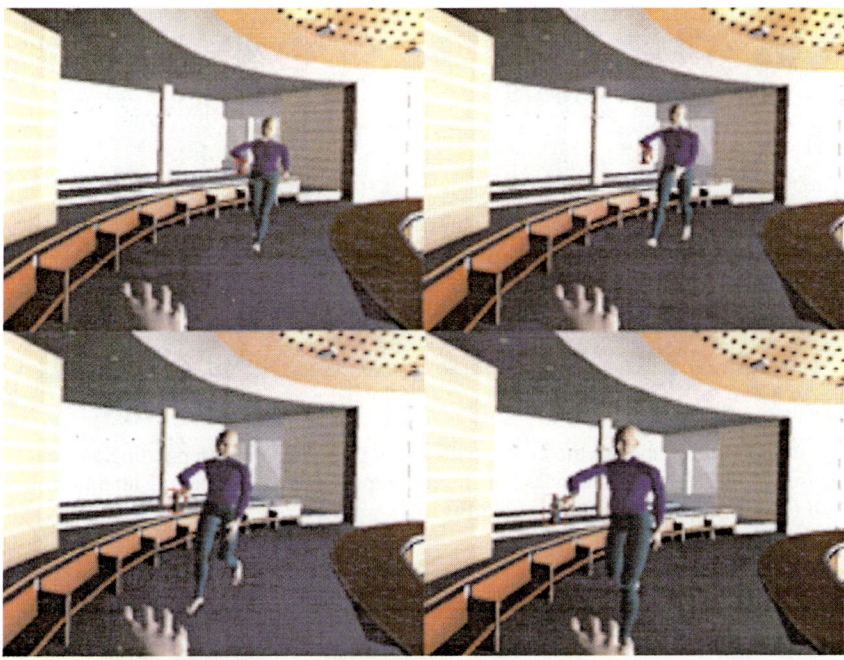

An example of real-time walking sequence (Pandzic et al., Fig. 1)

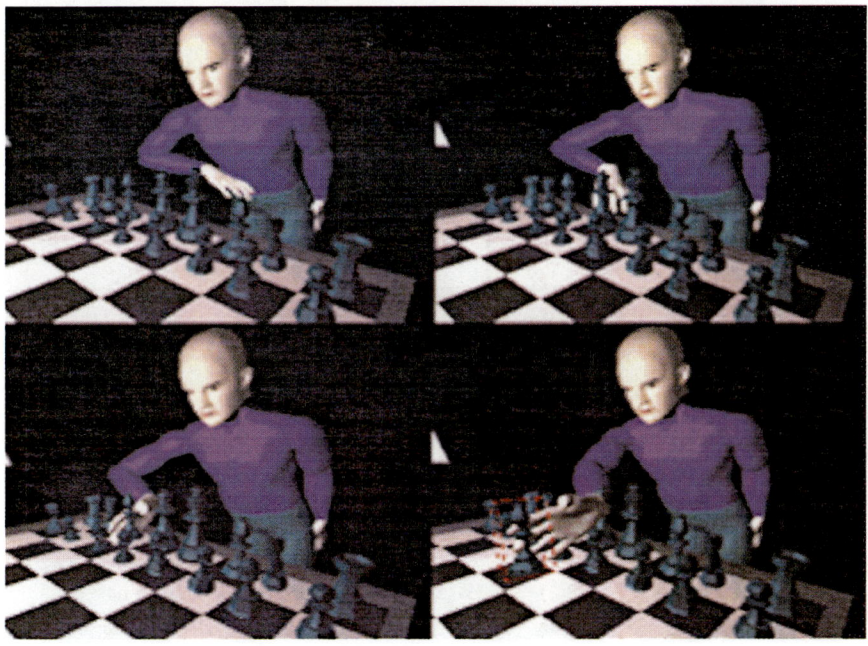

An example of real-time grasping sequence (Pandzic et al., Fig. 3)

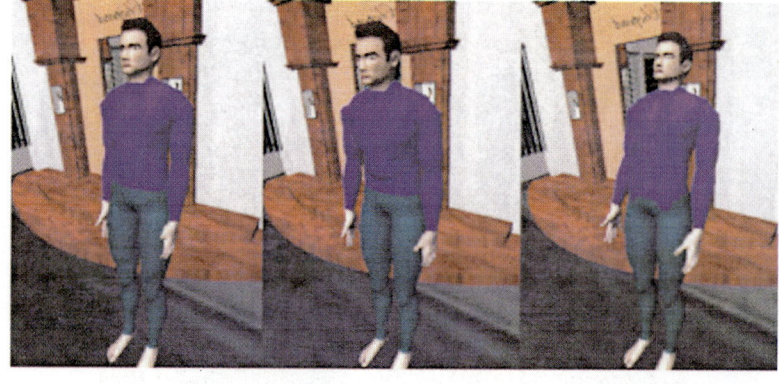

a b c

Emotion Motor updates the joints on the upper part of the body depending on the user's input. Some of the possible emotion representations: **a** paying attention, **b** tired, **c** surprised (Pandzic et al., Fig. 4)

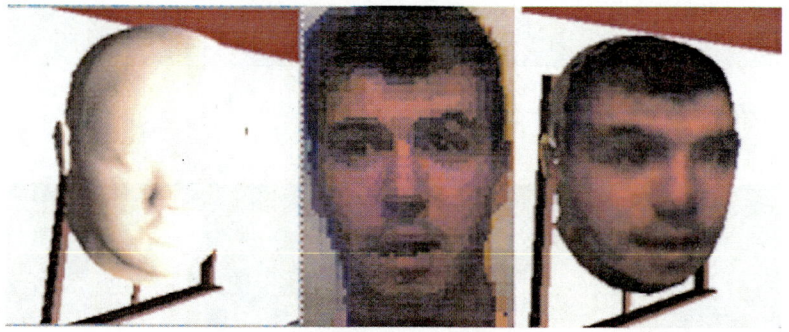

Mapping of the face to the 3D virtual actor. Usage of simple head provides a compromise between 3D geometry and texture quality (Pandzic et al., Fig. 5)

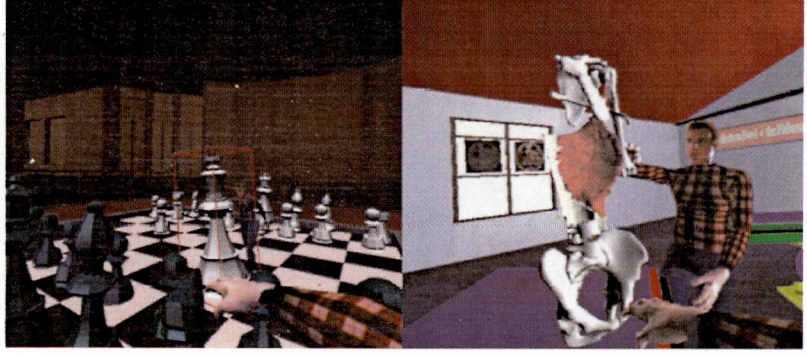

Some application examples (entertainment, medical) (Pandzic et al., Fig. 7)

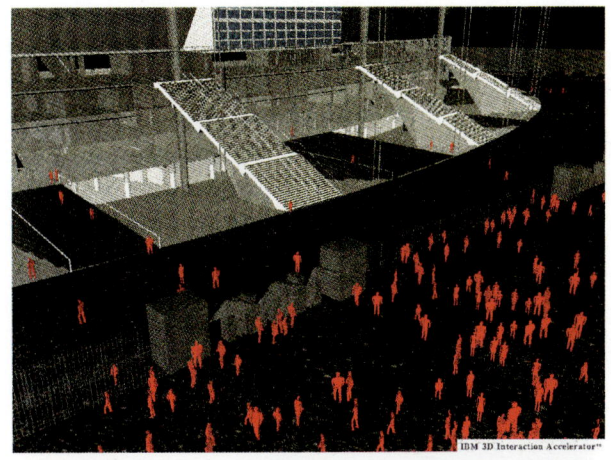

(Bouvier and Guilloteau)

After initially deforming the sweeping tool the designer uses it to sweep out a curved surface above her head. This surface can be further reshaped by applying appropriate forces to it (Usoh et al., Plate 1)

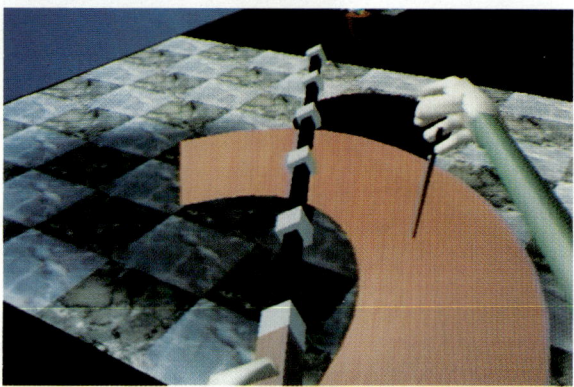

The designer sweeps out a flat curved surface and applies a single force to it (Usoh et al., Plate 2a)

The result of applying the upward force to the surface (Usoh et al., Plate 2b)

Virtual cancer hospital (Oyama, Fig. 1)

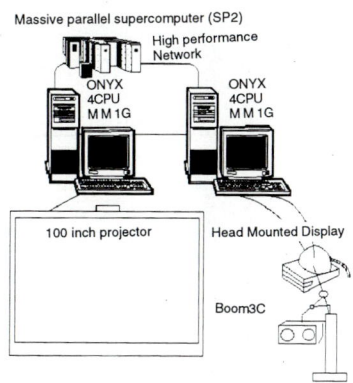

System configuration of medical virtual reality (Oyama, Fig. 2)

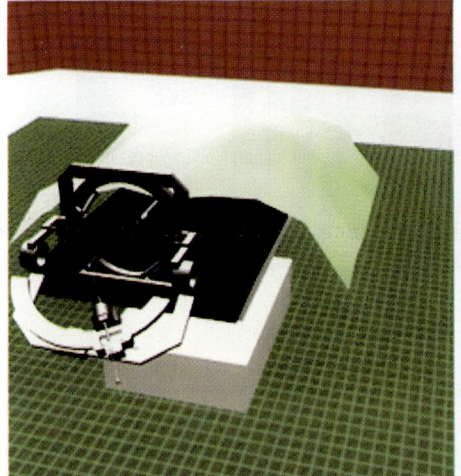

Virtual operation room (Oyama, Fig. 3)

Liver cancer in virtual environment (Oyama, Fig. 5)

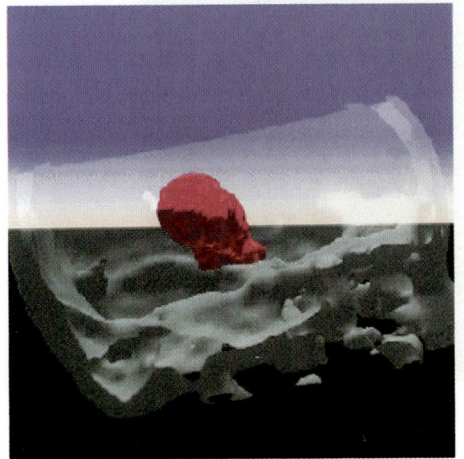

Brain tumor in virtual environment (Oyama, Fig. 4)

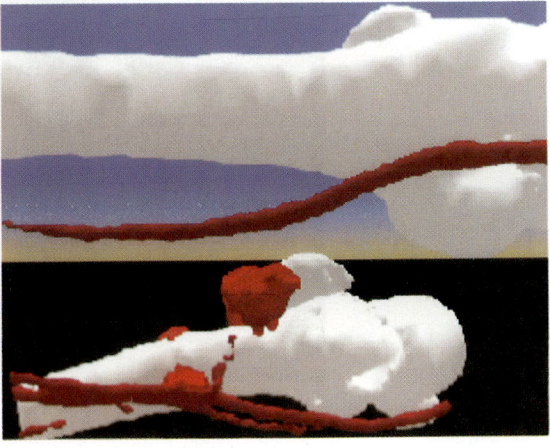

Metastatic renal cell carcinoma invaded in bone shaft (Oyama, Fig. 6)

Main, info, view and graphics output windows (Criscione et al., Fig. 6)

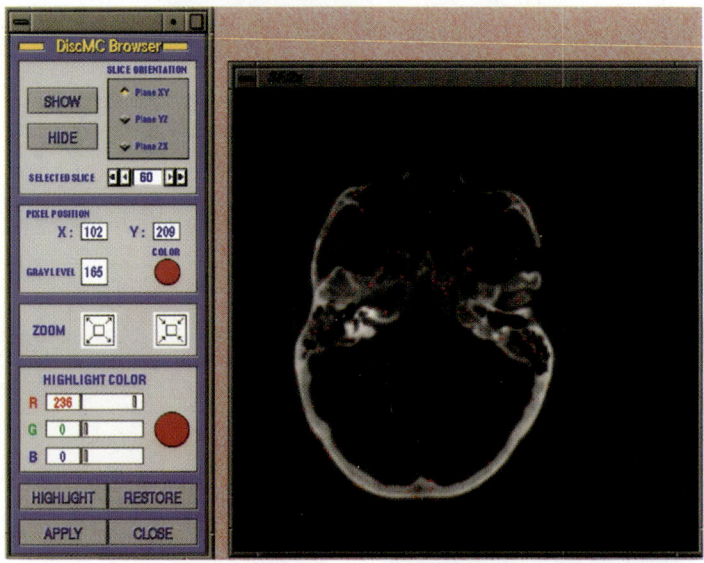

Image browser windows (Criscione et al., Fig. 7)

 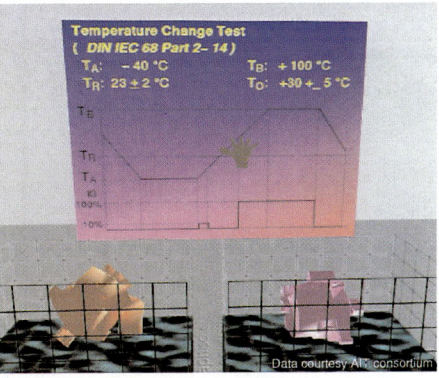

Showing selected part list (left). Acquiring technical data (right). Data courtesy of AIT consortium (Frühauf and Dai, Fig. 2)

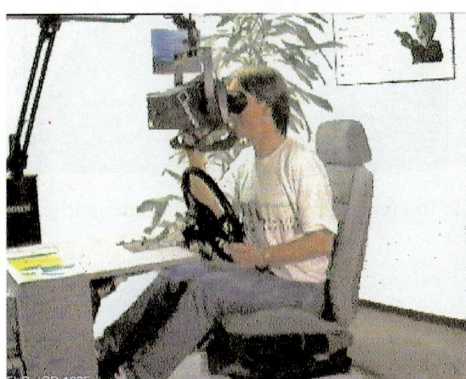 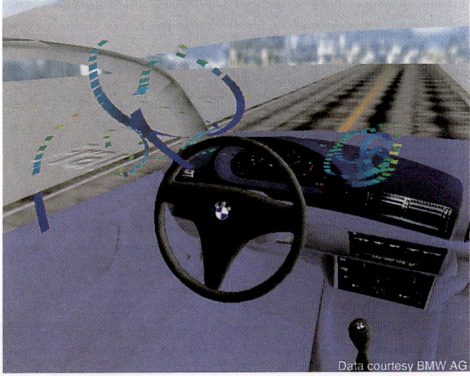

The physical equipment of the BMW virtual seating-buck (left). Air conditioning visualization with particle tracing (right). Data courtesy of BMW AG (Frühauf and Dai, Fig. 3)

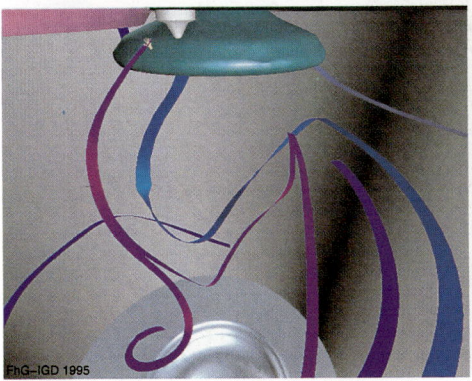 

Streamribbons visualize the transient flow field inside the cylinder (left). Temperature-Isosurfaces symbolize the advancing combustion front (right). Data courtesy of VW AG (Frühauf and Dai, Fig. 4)

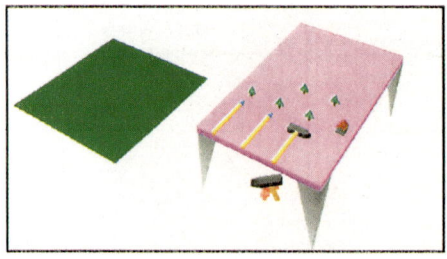 

A countryside modelling application: using deformation tools users can build mountains and dig lakes (Torguet et al., Plate 1)

Another modelling session: two users co-operate to create a complete countryside landscape (Torguet et al., Plate 2)

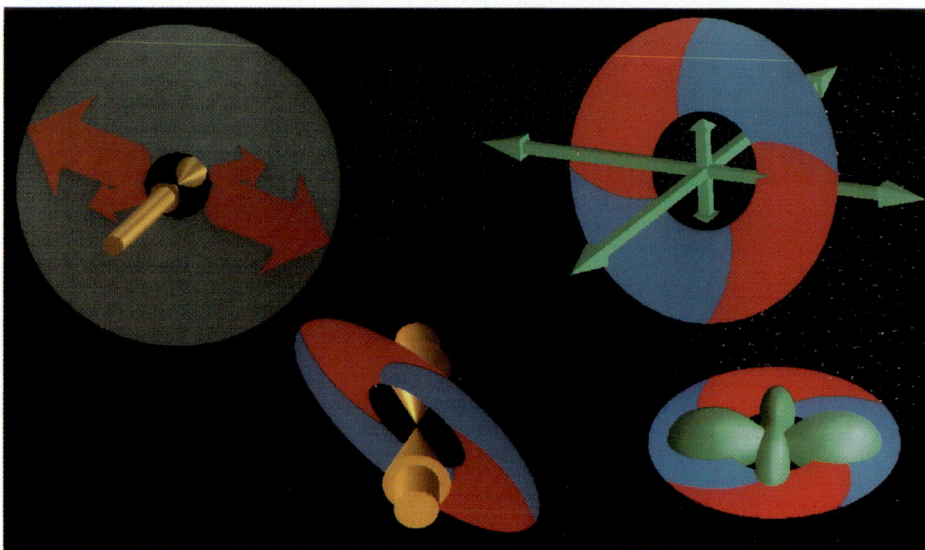

On the left icons representing the motion of nearby particles in an incompressible flow field relative to a specific particle, on the right icons representing the deformation and growth in Lagrangian coordinates (Happe and Rumpf, Fig. 1)

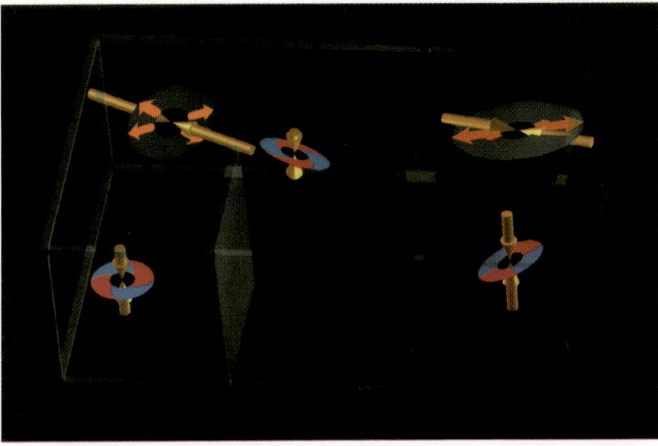

A view of incompressible flow in three dimensions. Icons placed at critical points indicate the flow induced by the velocity field (Happe and Rumpf, Fig. 2)

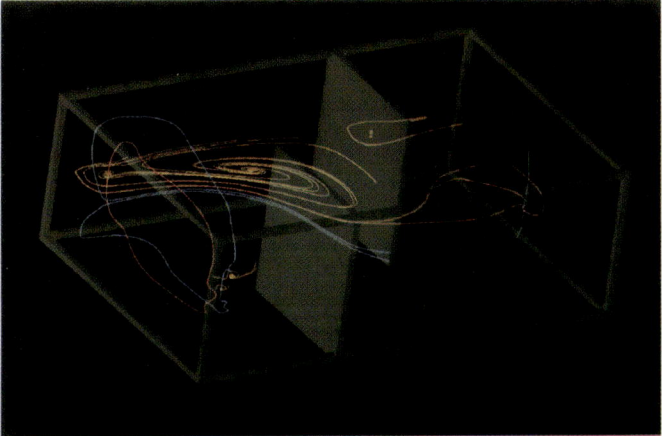

Some streamlines that start or end critical points of incompressible flow (same as in Fig. 2) (Happe and Rumpf, Fig. 3)

Fast LIC image of the material derivative in a two dimensional karman vortex street combined with a traced and adaptively refined line. Blue/red colour indicates low/high pressure (Happe and Rumpf, Fig. 4)

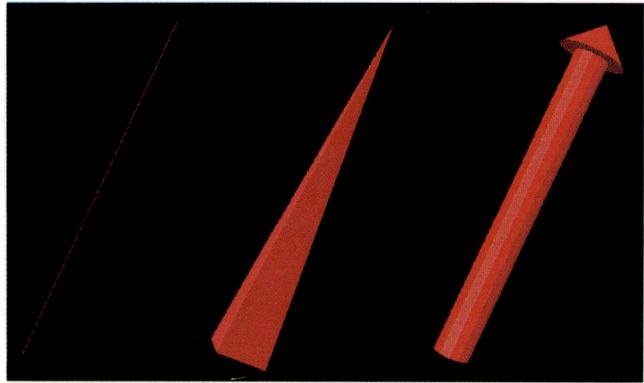

The three investigated rendering modes: line, pyramid, detailed arrow (Haase et al., Plate 1)

Detail test: which of the four vectors is most orthogonal to the surface? (Haase et al., Plate 2)

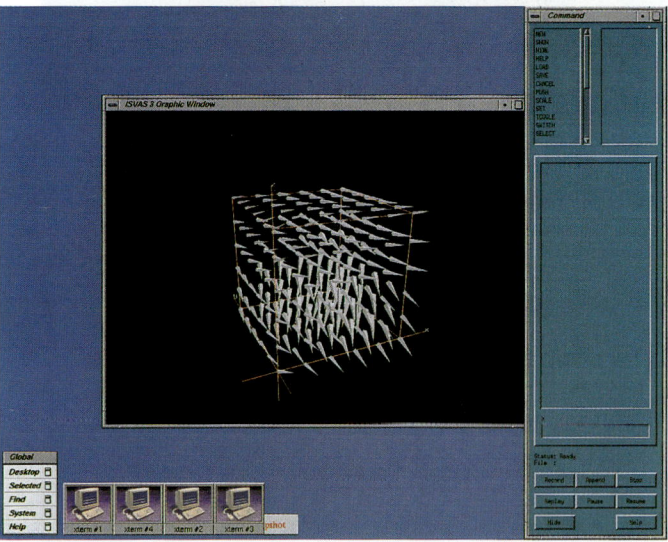

Test environment and one view of the second test ("overview") (Haase et al., Plate 3)

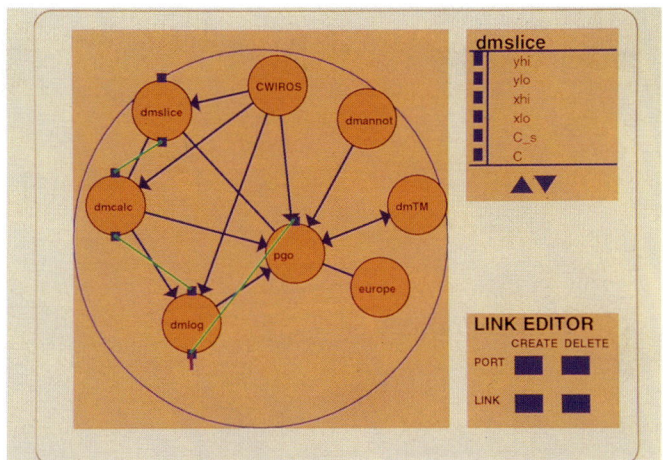

PGO interface to the trigger manager satellite
(van Liere and van Wijk, Fig. 5)

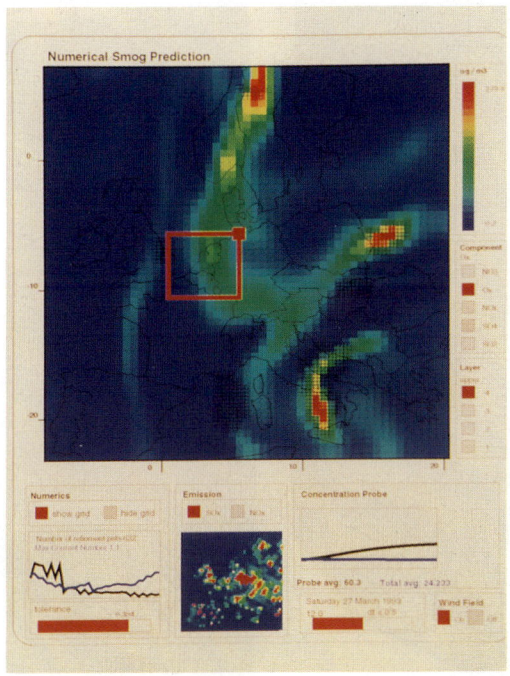

Smog prediction (van Liere and van Wijk, Fig. 6)

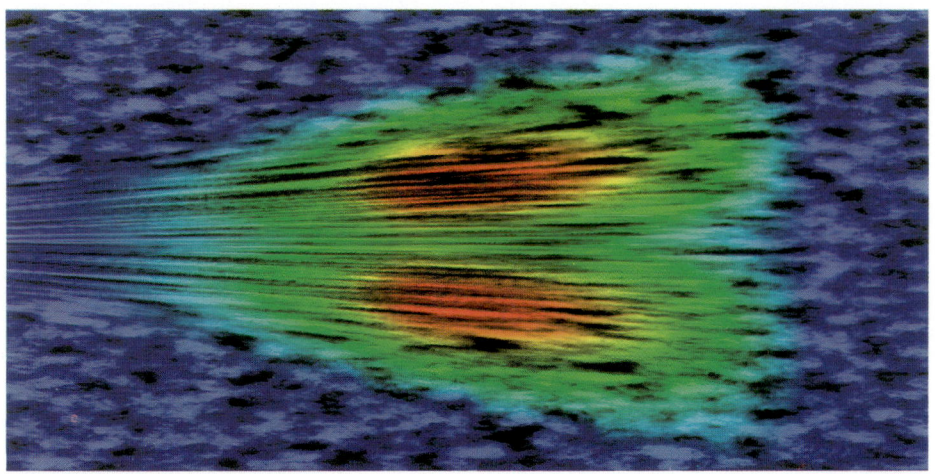

(de Leeuw et al., Fig. 2)

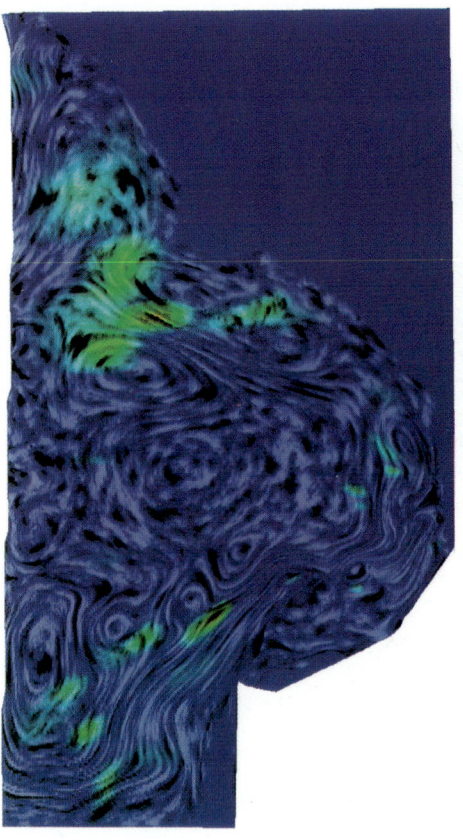

(de Leeuw et al., Fig. 7a)

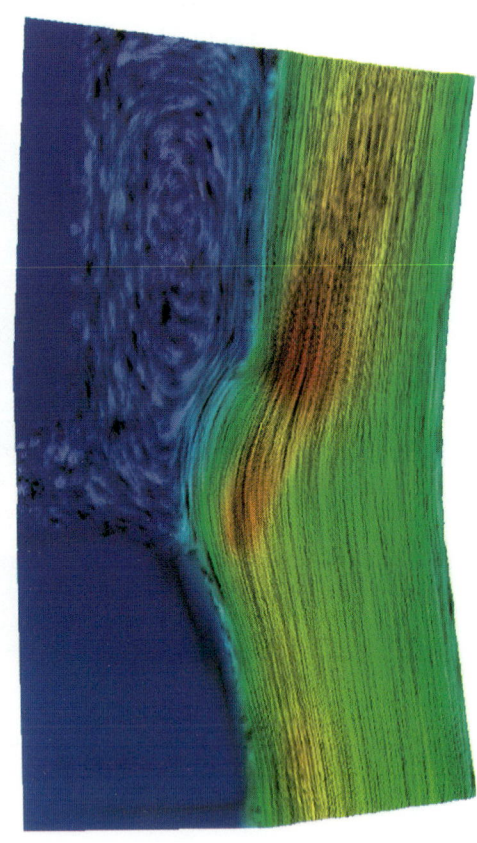

(de Leeuw et al., Fig. 8a)

SpringerEurographics

Ronan Boulic, Gerard Hegron (eds.)
Computer Animation and Simulation '96

Proceedings of the Eurographics Workshop in Poitiers, France, August 31 – September 1, 1996
1996. Approx. 240 pages.
Soft cover approx. DM 89,–, öS 625,–
ISBN 3-211-82885-0

The 14 papers in this volume vividly demonstrate the current state of research in real-time animation. Half of the papers are dedicated to algorithm allowing the real-time animation of complex articulated structure in particular (humans, legged robots, plants) and of dynamic scenes in general. The proposed approaches cover from motion capture to motion reusability which are essential issues for high-end applications as 3D games, virtual reality, etc.
Other topics treated are motion management for fast design of realistic movements, 2D and 3D deformations, and various optimization techniques for simulation (adaptive mass-spring refinement, huge particle systems).

Xavier Pueyo, Peter Schröder (eds.)
Rendering Techniques '96

Proceedings of the Eurographics Workshop in Porto, Portugal, June 17–19, 1996
1996. 197 figures. X, 294 pages.
Soft cover approx. DM 120,–, öS 840,–
ISBN 3-211-82883-4

27 contributions treat the state of the art in Monte Carlo and Finite Element methods for radiosity and radiance. Further special topics dealt with are the use of image maps to capture light throughout space, complexity, volumetric stochastic descriptions, innovative approaches to sampling and approximation, and system architecture.
The Rendering Workshop proceedings are an obligatory piece of literature for all scientists working in the rendering field, but they are also very valuable for the practitioner involved in the implementation of state of the art rendering system certainly influencing the scientific progress in this field.

P.O.Box 89, A-1201 Wien • New York, NY 10010, 175 Fifth Avenue
Heidelberger Platz 3, D-14197 Berlin • Tokyo 113, 3-13, Hongo 3-chome, Bunkyo-ku

SpringerEurographics

Demetri Terzopoulos, Daniel Thalmann (eds.)
Computer Animation and Simulation '95
  Proceedings of the Eurographics Workshop in Maastricht, The Netherlands, September 2–3, 1995
  1995. 156 partly coloured figures. VIII, 235 pages.
  Soft cover DM 89,–, öS 625,–, US $ 69.00
  ISBN 3-211-82738-2

Riccardo Scateni, Jarke J. van Wijk, Pietro Zanarini (eds.)
Visualization in Scientific Computing '95
  Proceedings of the Eurographics Workshop in Chia, Italy, May 3–5, 1995
  1995. 110 partly coloured figures. VII, 161 pages.
  Soft cover DM 85,–, öS 595,–, US $ 69.00
  ISBN 3-211-82729-3

Patrick M. Hanrahan, Werner Purgathofer (eds.)
Rendering Techniques '95
  Proceedings of the Eurographics Workshop in Dublin, Ireland, June 12–14, 1995
  1995. 198 partly coloured figures. XI, 372 pages.
  Soft cover DM 118,–, öS 826,–, US $ 98.00
  ISBN 3-211-82733-1

Martin Göbel, Heinrich Müller, Bodo Urban (eds.)
Visualization in Scientific Computing
  1995. 150 figures. VIII, 238 pages.
  Soft cover DM 118,–, öS 826,–, US $ 85.00
  ISBN 3-211-82633-5

Wolfgang Herzner, Frank Kappe (eds.)
Multimedia/Hypermedia in Open Distributed Environments
  Proceedings of the Eurographics Symposium in Graz, Austria, June 6–9, 1994
  1994. 105 figures. VIII, 330 pages.
  Soft cover DM 118,–, öS 826,–, US $ 79.00
  ISBN 3-211-82587-8

SpringerWienNewYork

SpringerEurographics

Bodo Urban (ed.)
Multimedia '96
  Proceedings of the Eurographics Workshop in Rostock, Federal Republic of Germany,
  May 28–30, 1996
  1996. 71 figures. VII, 178 pages.
  Soft cover DM 85,–, öS 595,–, US $ 67.00
  ISBN 3-211-82876-1

Theoretical concepts and specific applications for handling multimedia data, still and motion pictures on the net, WWW and multimedia, collaborative multimedia, and multimedia and education are dealt with in this volume. The reader will profit in getting up-to-date information about current trends in multimedia/hypermedia services and applications in open distributed environments.

Remco C. Veltkamp, Edwin H. Blake (eds.)
Programming Paradigms in Graphics '95
  Proceedings of the Eurographics Workshop in Maastricht, The Netherlands, September 2–3, 1995
  1995. 41 partly coloured figures. VIII, 172 pages.
  Soft cover DM 85,–, öS 595,–, US $ 59.00
  ISBN 3-211-82788-9

Philippe Palanque, Rémi Bastide (eds.)
Design, Specification and Verification of Interactive Systems '95
  Proceedings of the Eurographics Workshop in Toulouse, France, June 7–9, 1995
  1995. 153 figures. X, 370 pages.
  Soft cover DM 118,–, öS 826,–, US $ 95.00
  ISBN 3-211-82739-0

Martin Göbel (ed.)
Virtual Environments '95
  Selected papers of the Eurographics Workshops in Barcelona, Spain, 1993,
  and Monte Carlo, Monaco, 1995
  1995. 134 partly coloured figures. VII, 307 pages.
  Soft cover DM 108,–, öS 756,–, US $ 85.00
  ISBN 3-211-82737-4

SpringerWienNewYork

P.O.Box 89, A-1201 Wien • New York, NY 10010, 175 Fifth Avenue
Heidelberger Platz 3, D-14197 Berlin • Tokyo 113, Hongo 3-chome, Bunkyo-ku

*Springer-Verlag
and the Environment*

WE AT SPRINGER-VERLAG FIRMLY BELIEVE THAT AN international science publisher has a special obligation to the environment, and our corporate policies consistently reflect this conviction.

WE ALSO EXPECT OUR BUSINESS PARTNERS – PRINTERS, paper mills, packaging manufacturers, etc. – to commit themselves to using environmentally friendly materials and production processes.

THE PAPER IN THIS BOOK IS MADE FROM NO-CHLORINE pulp and is acid free, in conformance with international standards for paper permanency.